RADICAL
TRADITIONS

THEOLOGY IN A POSTCRITICAL KEY

SERIES EDITORS

Stanley M. Hauerwas, Duke University,
and Peter Ochs, University of Virginia

RADICAL TRADITIONS cuts new lines of inquiry across a confused array of debates concerning the place of theology in modernity and, more generally, the status and role of scriptural faith in contemporary life. Charged with a rejuvenated confidence, spawned in part by the rediscovery of reason as inescapably tradition constituted, a new generation of theologians and religious scholars is returning to scriptural traditions with the hope of retrieving resources long ignored, depreciated, and in many cases ideologically suppressed by modern habits of thought. RADICAL TRADITIONS assembles a promising matrix of strategies, disciplines, and lines of thought that invites Jewish, Christian, and Islamic theologians back to the word, recovering and articulating modes of scriptural reasoning as that which always underlies modernist reasoning and therefore has the capacity — and authority — to correct it.

Far from despairing over modernity's failings, postcritical theologies rediscover resources for renewal and self-correction within the disciplines of academic study themselves. Postcritical theologies open up the possibility of participating once again in the living relationship that binds together God, text, and community of interpretation. RADICAL TRADITIONS thus advocates a 'return to the text,' which means a commitment to displaying the richness and wisdom of traditions that are at once text based, hermeneutical, and oriented to communal practice.

Books in this series offer the opportunity to speak openly with practitioners of other faiths or even with those who profess no (or limited) faith, both academics and nonacademics, about the ways religious traditions address pivotal issues of the day. Unfettered by foundationalist preoccupations, these books represent a call for new paradigms of reason — a thinking and rationality that are more responsive than originative. By embracing a postcritical posture, they are able to speak unapologetically out of scriptural traditions manifest in the practices of believing communities (Jewish, Christian, and others); articulate those practices through disciplines of philosophic, textual, and cultural criticism; and engage intellectual, social, and political practices that for too long have been insulated from theological evaluation. RADICAL TRADITIONS is radical not only in its confidence in non-apologetic theological speech but also in how the practice of such speech challenges the current social and political arrangements of modernity.

The Jewish–Christian Schism Revisited

John Howard Yoder

Edited by Michael G. Cartwright
and Peter Ochs

WILLIAM B. EERDMANS PUBLISHING COMPANY
GRAND RAPIDS, MICHIGAN / CAMBRIDGE, U.K.

Originally published 2003 in Great Britain by
SCM Press, London

This edition published 2003
in the United States of America by
Wm. B. Eerdmans Publishing Company
255 Jefferson Ave. S.E., Grand Rapids, Michigan 49503 /
P.O. Box 163 Cambridge CB3 9PU U.K.
www.eerdmans.com

Manufactured in the U.K.

07 06 05 04 03   5 4 3 2 1

ISBN 0-8028-1362-3

Contents

Part IV: Christians and Jews Seeking the *Shalom* of the City

Acknowledgements

Stanley Hauerwas recommended that this volume be published in the *Radical Traditions* series published by Eerdmans and SCM Press. We join him in expressing the hope that this volume will contribute to the emerging 'third stage' conversation between Jews and Christians that has emerged in the past decade through such ventures as the *Christianity in Jewish Terms* project and the related publication of the *Dabru Emet* statement in September 2000.

Stanley Hauerwas also suggested that we collaborate on this project, and we are grateful for his remarkable instincts in this and other matters. Michael Cartwright is Dean of Ecumenical and Interfaith Programs at the University of Indianapolis. He edited a major collection of John Howard Yoder's essays *The Royal Priesthood: Essays Ecclesiological and Ecumenical* (Eerdmans, 1994; Herald, 1998), and has interpreted Yoder's work in several essays and articles over the past decade. In addition to being Bronfman Professor of Modern Judaic Studies at the University of Virginia, Peter Ochs is the co-editor of the Radical Traditions Series. As a series editor, Ochs has joined with Cartwright to represent the interest of the Radical Traditions series in Yoder's work and to offer a Jewish as well as Christian reception to Yoder's work.

We are grateful to the family of John Howard Yoder for their receptivity to the proposal to publish these essays posthumously. Martha Yoder Maust, one of John Howard's daughters, had an active interest in this project from beginning to end. We are especially grateful for her making available to us Yoder's files on this project, including his correspondence with Steven Schwarzchild. Ms Maust also proofread an early draft of the document and offered several perceptive observations about how the manuscript could be edited for the purpose of communicating Yoder's views to a broader audience. (We are also grateful to Shalom Communications, Inc. for defraying some travel costs related to the editors gathering to complete work on this project.)

Several people assisted in the preparation of manuscripts of these essays for publication. Mrs Susan Downard was very helpful in re-formatting several of the documents and transcribing two of the essays. Two student research assistants at the University of Indianapolis were involved with the early stages of this project. Ms Shalimar Holderly proofread several documents and assisted with the first stages of editing Yoder's essays. Mr Jared Tucher read the manuscript and assembled an initial list of words to be included in the glossary.

Cartwright's appointment as Scholar-in-Residence at the Tantur Ecumenical Institute for Advanced Theological Study in Jerusalem during the summer of 2001 provided the occasion for him to begin exploring the problem of Christian supresessionism as well as to research the ways in which Mennonite missions and peacemaking provide living contexts for understanding the implications of Yoder's approach to interreligious dialogue. The hospitality offered by Rector Michael McGarry and his staff during that time was gracious and the staff of the Tantur Library were unfailingly helpful. Michael Cartwright counts it a great honour to have been able to live and work at the same place where in 1976 John Howard Yoder wrote two of the essays included in this collection.

Michael is also grateful to the University of Indianapolis for a one-semester sabbatical during the spring of 2002 during which the manuscript was prepared for submission to the publisher. During that time he was blessed to receive the hospitality of the staff of the Benedict Inn Conference and Retreat Center where he enjoyed the solitude as well as participated in the Liturgy of the Hours with the community of Our Lady of Grace Monastery, Beech Grove, Indiana.

We are also grateful to our families who made it possible for us to work together at various points over the past two years. Michael is grateful for the hospitality he received during the time that he stayed with the Ochs family for several days in December 2000. He is also grateful to his wife, Mary Wilder Cartwright, and children, Hannah, Erin, James, and Bethany for their patience and understanding during the months that he worked on this project.

Michael G. Cartwright and Peter Ochs

Editors' Introduction

MICHAEL G. CARTWRIGHT and PETER OCHS

We are proud to publish on these pages the posthumous writings of John Howard Yoder, of Blessed Memory: *The Jewish–Christian Schism Revisited*. Students and colleagues of Yoder's have, for some years now, had the privilege of reading many of these essays in the form of a website of his unpublished writings made available courtesy of his colleagues on the faculty of the Department of Theology at University of Notre Dame. We present here the complete set of essays as Yoder envisioned them (in the 'Shalom Desktop Packet' that he put together in 1996): redacted, corrected and annotated by M. Cartwright; with explanatory and interpretive comments by P. Ochs (appended to each essay) and by Cartwright (as an *Afterword*).

The Jewish–Christian Schism Revisited appears here as part of the book series *Radical Traditions: Theology in a Postcritical Key*, edited by Stanley Hauerwas and Peter Ochs and co-published by SCM Press and Eerdmans. The Radical Traditions Series invites Jewish, Christian, and Muslim thinkers to retrieve their scriptural resources and give voice to their theological claims without having to submit or reduce them to strictly modern standards of meaning and truth. While each book in the Series celebrates the voice and integrity of a particular Abrahamic tradition, the Series as a whole also offers each book as a contribution to religious understanding within and among all the Abrahamic faiths.

Yoder's essays make a powerful contribution to all these goals of *Radical Traditions*. Nevertheless, we recognize that some readers of the Series would benefit from the commentaries we have attached to his essays: our efforts to explain how he understood various aspects of Biblical and Rabbinic Judaism and to interpret what he meant by criticisms (as well as affirmations) of some varieties of Christianity and Judaism. We want all readers of the Series to be able to enjoy and benefit from Yoder's extraordinary venture in Jewish–Christian understanding: the many readers who will treasure Yoder's words for their own sake, as well as those who may ask for some accompanying account of how others, Jewish practitioners in particular, might respond to his challenging claims.

I. Yoder's Witness to the People Israel

PETER OCHS

The work of John Howard Yoder is of great significance for contemporary Jewish theology beyond the fact that Yoder has left us, posthumously, with this remarkable collection of writings on the relations between Judaism and Christianity. Yoder's work is significant for Jews because our Judaism, like his Christianity, is a 'biblical religion after'. After, that is to say, the demise of the great modern paradigms of reasoning that have had such a profound influence on life in and outside of the Academy and also in and outside of the Church and Synagogue. It is also after the devastations of western civilizations in the twentieth century, the devastations of Shoah (or Holocaust), as well as the devastations of Soviet Communism and the persistent effects of the devastations of colonialism, western nationalism and imperialism, and unchecked or uncompassionate capitalism. For Yoder's Christianity, this also means after Christendom, meaning after the demise of Constantinian Christianity, when Christians begin to see themselves, like Jews have for 2000 years, as members of minority traditions, outposts for biblical piety, in a political world not of their own making. Yoder's Anabaptism provides a unique preparation for religious life 'after' in these several ways. It means he speaks already out of a religious tradition that affirms the authority of Scripture's communal, litur- gical, and ethico-political voice, but also its voice of protest against unwieldy accommodations between religious and political authority and against the tenden- cies of either Church or Synagogue to abuse even its appropriately extra-political mandate. Yoder's Anabaptism displays a Christianity that neither fears nor condemns life apart.

Contemporary Jews inherit millennia of Jewish experience in living 'after'. The Israelite religion of the written Torah itself was a religion 'after' the first Exile in Babylonia. The religion of Rabbinic Judaism was 'after' the destruction of the Second Temple and the diaspora after it. The texture of Rabbinic Judaism is, through and through, the texture of a faith that knows how to affirm the life of a biblical people away from home, deep in exile, and deeply wounded by loss and dislocation. It is also the texture of a life lived apart: apart from other traditions, other communities, as well as apart from dimensions of human life that threaten rather than serve as a vehicle for a life lived in imitation of God. For Rabbinic Judaism, God's 'holiness' and Israel's holiness displays the root meaning of the Hebrew word for holy, *kadosh*, as 'separate', or 'other than', or 'apart'. But, for Rabbinic Jews as for Yoder, this separateness is not necessarily literal or visible, as if it is meant only 'out of all social contact with', or 'in a segregated bit of geography', or 'out of touch with the immediate sufferings of the rest of the world'. At times it may mean these things, but the general rule is that Israel's holiness is a separateness *in* life, while in society, while dispersed through the world, while filled with responsibility for the agonies of life in the world. It is holiness in living – *hitbodedut* or 'inner-separation'– and therefore living always in the presence of God while living in the presence of God's creation and God's creatures. Always Here but always bound up There, therefore always political but always not, always material but always not.

These are some features of Rabbinic Judaism. But Rabbinic Judaism is part of the challenge of contemporary Judaism. There is, in one sense, no other Judaism for Jews than that which comes by way of Rabbinic Judaism, or the Judaism of *Mishnah*, Talmud, synagogue, prayer book, and Torah study that emerged after, in spite of, and in response to the loss of the Second Temple. All of the new Judaisms that have appeared since have appeared from out of and in terms of this Rabbinic Judaism. But each new Judaism appears as the reformation and renewal of Rabbinic Judaism that follows some subsequent destruction, and each reformation and renewal is lived only as refuge from some period of terrible loss and doubt. Our own Judaisms emerge today after Shoah, after the demise of the great secularisms of modernity, and also after the Orthodoxies who defined themselves over against modernity have lost their strength and constructive voice. Our Judaisms must therefore forge a new pattern of life 'after', and they will leave behind many features of the kind of Rabbinic Judaism that preceded them. The Sadducees who rejected Pharisaism and the Rabbinic Judaism that followed it judged this Judaism to be anti-biblical. Similarly, Jews accustomed strictly to the Rabbinic Judaisms of modernity – both Orthodox and humanistic – may judge the Judaisms now emerging to be 'anti-Rabbinic'. The Sadducees were wrong however; Rabbinic Judaism gave new life to the Bible. Similarly, both Orthodox and secular-leaning, or humanistic critics of the new Judaisms would be wrong if they do not see in these Judaisms a new life for Rabbinic Judaism. But this leaves open the question of which aspects of the previous Rabbinic Judaism will live on in the present and how. It means that Judaism is now in the process of profound transformation and rebirth. And it is in this context that contemporary Jewish thinkers may gain much from their dialogue with Yoder's Anabaptism.

Theologians and scholars of today's emergent Judaisms will be energized, first, by Yoder's own interest in Judaism itself. For Jews suffering their own crises of faith, it may be encouraging to learn that others, in this case Christian theologians, have renewed interest in and respect for the very Jewish sources that may be troubling for contemporary Jews. The interest that Yoder shows in Judaism may appear to such Jews as an unexpected sign of divine comfort. 'Comfort ye, comfort ye.' The sign may seem to say: 'You have suffered dearly, your cities lie in ruin; if you still know Me at all, you may think of Me only as one who has cast you off, divorced you, or who has moved you to divorce Me; so I now say "comfort ye my people"; I remain your God, please receive me back.' When the Gentile, albeit Gentile Christian, reaffirms Israel's covenant with God, how can the Jew, broken as she is, not listen and take hope? That is one reason why Jews after the Shoah will be moved to hear Yoder's voice.

A second reason is that Yoder is interested in Judaism as a way of responding to some of the same failings of western civilization that move Jews today to seek new forms of Judaism. One of these failings is what we might call cultural colonialism: the tendency of western thinkers, secular or religious, to interpret the scriptural traditions only according to the conceptual categories and standards set by a few non-scriptural traditions of philosophy and science. Another failing is a tendency of Western 'universalisms' to breed totalitarianism or at least 'totalism' – the effort, that is, to adopt some finite set of humanly constructed beliefs as the basis for judging the nature and worth of all human institutions and societies. For Yoder, these failings are deeply associated with the specifically Christian failing of 'Constantinianism', or the tendency, after the third century, to redefine Christianity as the religion of the Roman Empire and, later, to redefine it as the religion of a variety of world dominating empires and nation states. In Yoder's view, Constantinianism has, more recently, also bred comparable tendencies to identify Christianity with any of a variety of universalizing political, economic, and social institutions: from the market economy to various military, industrial, economic, and political vehicles for controlling human behaviour on a mass scale. Many Jewish thinkers who share in efforts to renew Judaism after the Shoah criticize these same failings in the West and in Christianity, as well as in the dimensions and movements of Judaism that have been shaped by the West. These Jewish thinkers have much to gain from engagement with Yoder's work.

Of course, Yoder's radical reformation of modern and of western Christianity remains a Christian reformation, and not all of it will speak to or on behalf of Jewish reformers. This is how it should be. The post-western Christian reformer retains his otherness as a dialogue partner to Jewish reformers, sharing an area of overlapping belief and commitment but also serving as a challenge or stimulant. The areas of challenge are as important as the areas of overlap. For example, Yoder speaks on behalf of a model of first-century Judaism that is *not* the proto-Rabbinic Judaism that will be displayed in the *Mishnah* of the second century and the more hegemonic Talmudic Judaism of the third century and after. In Yoder's vision, this is a Judaism that would be as genuinely fulfilled in Nazarene Judaism (what will become Christianity) as in any of the other myriad forms of first-century Judaism. Theologians of today's emergent Judaisms may value Yoder's understanding of first-century pluralism but may also find his pluralism tendentiously egalitarian: as if the tendencies of late Second Temple Judaism that led to the Rabbinic movement also led with as much hermeneutical and theological consistency to Paul's version of Nazarene or Christian Judaism. There is a contemporary polemic implicit in Yoder's reading of first-century Judaism that should stimulate a competing polemic by Yoder's Jewish dialogue partners. These are competing positions, but it is a good, healthy, and constructive competition. On his side, Yoder will argue that the 'pre-Schismatic Judaism' of both Paul and the Pharisees is marked by what he calls 'Jewish pacifism' and 'Jewish universalism'. Of course, these 'isms' anticipate two of the central features of Yoder's own Anabaptist Christianity and its radical reformation of the modern Church. The Rabbinic Judaism that remains the source for contemporary Judaisms is, however, neither anti- nor pro- pacifism and universalism. Contemporary Jewish thinkers should be troubled, in fact, by the conceptual purity of Yoder's 'isms' and by the way this conceptual purity leads him to divide his theological universe radically between what is purely pacifist and universalist and what is not. For theologians of post-Shoah Judaism, Yoder's purisms retain too much of the conceptualism that marked the colonialist philosophies of western civilization, even if they are offered beautifully and virtuously on behalf of God's gracious compassion for human suffering. We should therefore not expect Yoder's Jewish dialogue partners to agree with him on all counts, nor to see his Anabaptist Christianity as simply the Christian complement to their post-Shoah Judaisms. But this does not render the dialogue any less crucial, profound, and sustaining for the work of contemporary Jewish reformation.

Among the varieties of contemporary Jewish theologians, there is at least one movement of Jewish thought already predisposed to share in such a dialogue with

Yoder. This is the movement of theology associated with the Society of Textual Reasoning: a twelve-year-old society of now 300 members that seeks to articulate the patterns of Rabbinic and post-Rabbinic reasoning that could guide religious reformation after the Shoah.[1] For 'textual reasoners', contemporary Jewish theology should no longer be governed by first principles of reasoning imposed by the modern Academy *nor* by the efforts of anti-modern Rabbinic scholars to insulate an 'indigenous' Rabbinic tradition from any exposure to the 'alien' influences of modern thinking. For textual reasoners, Jewish theology emerges *from out of* traditional practices of reading Scripture and *Mishnah* and Talmud, but only as they eventuate in practices of interpretation that are refined by disciplines of academic reasoning. From the late Second Temple period on, Jewish interpretation has lived *through*, rather than in isolation from, the intellectual technologies of its day. What is 'indigenous' to Judaism is the Torah, and the Torah is irreducible to the plain sense of any text or to the finite interpretations promoted by any particular community of Jewish interpreters. To study Torah is always also to enter into direct relation to the living God, and it is only by way of that relation that Judaism has had the capacity to be resurrected and renewed after each of the Jewish people's major catastrophes. Each time Judaism is reborn, the body of all its inherited texts is given new life through the spirit of God that breathes through them once again and that animates the life of new movements of Jewish theology, Jewish law, and Jewish reasoning. The spirit that animates Yoder's work will not animate contemporary Jewish theology in the same way or for all of the same reasons, but its appearance will energize Yoder's dialogue partners to look for the signs of this spirit's movements in their own work and life.

Members of the Society for Textual Reasoning are already dialogue partners with 'post-liberal' or 'post-critical' Christian theologians. Among these are students and peers of the 'Yale' theologians Hans Frei, of blessed memory, George Lindbeck, Stanley Hauerwas, and others;[2] post-liberal Lutheran theologians like Robert Jenson; post-liberal Anglican theologians like Daniel Hardy, David Ford, Rowan Williams, and John Milbank; and many interpreters of Karl Barth, particularly in Germany and the USA.[3] In addition to scholarly conversations among post-liberal Jewish and Christian theologians, there are also projects of shared institution building. In 1995, for example, a group of these theologians formed the Society for Scriptural Reasoning, dedicated to the dialogic study of scriptural interpretation among Jewish, Christian, and Muslim scholars – a study performed in a spirit of both academic discipline and religious sanctity.[4] The book series, *Radical Traditions*, which hosts the present volume, is another example: an effort to promote works that liberate Jewish, Christian, and Muslim theologies from the 'cultural colonialism' of the modern West, reconnecting academically disciplined minds from various fields to the primordial witnesses of the scriptural traditions. A final example is the book project, *Christianity in Jewish Terms,* sponsored by the Institute for Christian and Jewish Studies: the first collective effort by Jewish theologians to offer a Jewish theological account of Christianity and, in the process, to engage Christian scholars in theological dialogue.[5]

The theological dialogue already in place among these theologians and in these projects and institutions provides a welcoming environment for Yoder's work: a place where Yoder's readers could promote, extend, and also evaluate his way of revisiting the Jewish–Christian schism. In fact, this broader dialogue will set the context for the running commentaries I will offer on each of Yoder's essays in this volume. I will offer a Jewish commentary on Yoder's vision of Judaism: a particular Jewish commentary, that is, originating in the post-liberal movement of Textual Reasoning, which means in a movement of Jewish philosophers and text scholars who work for a Jewish renewal and reformation after the Shoah and after modernity.

This commentary therefore represents an approach to Judaism that already parallels Yoder's efforts to renew and reform Christianity after modernity. It is in this sense a sympathetic and appreciative commentary in *dialogue* with Yoder's work. At the same time, dialogue presupposes difference, and this commentary will also attend to troubling aspects of Yoder's reading of Judaism. At times, I will suggest that Yoder depicts a Judaism that my Textual Reasoning colleagues and I would not recognize, either in the Biblical, Rabbinic, or contemporary Judaisms that we study. In this case, I will be asking him – through his students and peers today – to re-read the sources and evidences with us and see why he reads them a certain way and we, perhaps, another way. At other times, I will suggest that Yoder appears to reason or argue in a way that may still reflect some of the logic of modernity, in particular, the logic that divides the world of thought and of belief into radically opposing positions – one purely good and one not. In this case, I will be asking him if he would not, indeed, want to join my Christian – as well as my Jewish – colleagues, whose post-modernism and post-liberalism leads them to a somewhat different logic – a logic of threes, we might say, rather than twos, or of relationality rather than of a warring essences. In this case, my Christian model will often be the work of Stanley Hauerwas (even when I do not cite him explicitly), since he is, at once, already so close to Yoder and his work, but also equally close to the 'triadic' logics of these other post-liberal Christians and 'scriptural reasoners'.

Dialogue drives this volume, on many levels, and this means extending the hand to the one with whom one talks, and argues, in a spirit of reason, and of love and appreciation. Wanting his hand, I will address him at times through dimensions of Stanley's witness to him and also, of course, to Michael Cartwright's. My primary teacher on Yoder's work, Michael is also principal editor of this volume, gracing it with the results of his years of work advancing, extending and also challenging Yoder's reformation. My dialogic commentary with Yoder therefore emerges from dialogues with Michael, of which some remain in the background as sources of the commentary and others, as you will see, come to replace and complete the commentary.

II. Yoder's Witness to the One Who Came Preaching Peace

MICHAEL G. CARTWRIGHT

This collection of essays comprises Yoder's most ambitious – and some would argue, his most deeply flawed – scholarly project. Most ambitious because more than any other book-length project that Yoder ever initiated, the four sets of essays that comprise *The Jewish–Christian Schism Revisited* display the full range of his wide-ranging scholarship. These ten essays also display the extent of Yoder's dialogical practice which extends in several directions at once. In one sense, these essays can be located within the context of a particular Jewish–Christian friendship, namely Yoder's two-decade-long scholarly conversation with Rabbi Steven Schwarzschild (see Part III of the Editors' Introduction below) to whom this volume is dedicated. At the same time, as we will attempt to show (here and in Cartwright's *Afterword*), the argument of these essays has everything to do with Yoder's lifelong engagement with a host of Christian traditions, a set of conversations that ranged over the vast terrain of ecumenical contestatation, but never strayed from Yoder's commitment to Christian nonviolence. [6]

Therefore, readers of this volume should not ignore the possibility that the revisionist account that Yoder offers of the Jewish–Christian reality of the second to the fourth centuries of the Common Era not only has implications for how Jews should regard themselves in relation to Christianity (past and present) but also has significance for how various Christian traditions – Roman Catholic, Greek Orthodox, 'mainstream' Protestant, and the heirs of the 'radical reformation' – should *regard themselves in relation to one another* as well as in relation to contemporary Jews.[7]

A. Evangelical Revisionism: John Howard Yoder's Conception of Witness as Vocation and Practice

Just as it would be a serious mistake to ignore the integral character of John Howard Yoder's practice of ecumenical dialogue to his vision of the Church,[8] one cannot expect to clarify Yoder's understanding of the Jewish–Christian schism apart from his theological understanding of *what it means for Christians and Jews to share the God-given vocation* to be 'missionary' peoples *to* and *for* the nations. At the same time, I will argue that one cannot fully grasp the significance of the latter vocation apart from Yoder's own understanding of the significance of the 'witness' of Jesus Christ, to whom Yoder is bearing witness throughout the essays of *The Jewish–Christian Schism Revisited*. As this fourfold relationship suggests, the thesis being argued in the essays collected in this book lies at the heart of the wider set of published and unpublished writings that make up Yoder's theological *oeuvre*.

Further, the implications of such a claim are not merely to be registered theoretically, but also have practical applications – for Jews and Christians alike – for what it means to thinking about peacemaking, reconciliation, and the tension between proselytizing and interreligious dialogue. Unlike many other theologians whose orientation to Jewish–Christian dialogue could be analysed, Yoder's contributions were not limited to the contexts of classroom and writing. Yoder was very much involved in missionary activities and peacemaking efforts throughout his adult life. For that reason, the editors have included Appendix B to this volume for those readers who would like to trace the parallels between Yoder's reconstructed conception of Jewish–Christian 'dialogue' and the development of Mennonite missions and peacemaking activities to Christians and Jews in Israel and Palestine during Yoder's lifetime.

For the moment, however, it is enough to pay attention to Yoder's own stated objective(s) as a practitioner of 'evangelical revisionism' who bears witness to 'the capacity of the Christian *euangelion* to "unendingly meet new worlds"'.[9] Yoder offered very precise reasons why it is important that Christians dare to rewrite history in ways that call into question what the majority of people have thought about the possibilities and limits of human efforts to live peaceably with one another.

> The reason history needs to be reread is not merely that every generation must claim the right to begin writing world history over from scratch, nor that in particular the children of the bourgeois cannot get out of the nest without soiling it, but that *at certain points* there is specifiable good news about the human condition, the goodness or the newness of which those who hitherto have been controlling the storytelling had not yet appropriated.[10]

As this statement suggests, for Yoder, writing history from this perspective of 'evangelical revisionism' was profoundly important for how one regards oneself as a historian of pacifism as well as a Christian theologian. Yoder always saw himself as bearing witness to the reality of God's self-revelation in Jesus Christ.

Because Yoder believed *the historiographical task* cannot ultimately be separated from either interfaith dialogue or confrontation with the enemy, he warned that historians of Christian nonviolence must remember that 'love of enemy must include love of the intellectual adversary, including intellectual respect for the holders of the positions one must in conscience reject'.[11] In all of these ways, and more, those who would practise 'evangelical revisionism' must conduct themselves in their conversations and their historiography in ways that display that they are fundamentally 'for the nations' just as the good news of the gospel is for all peoples in all times and places. Although Yoder did not always describe his project as employing a 'hermeneutics of peace' others have claimed that description for the way he went about teaching in the context of University of Notre Dame's ROTC (Reserve Officer Training Corps) programme as well as his teaching of Roman Catholic students and those who advocated a just war ethic that ran contrary to his own pacifist convictions.

In sum, according to John Howard Yoder, interfaith dialogue is never to be treated one-dimensionally – as if it can be isolated from other forms of human inquiry and other disputations – but must be pursued in the awareness that any particular conversation has implications for other disciplines of learning and other dialogical partners. It is in this sense that Yoder believed that it is a mistake to think of interfaith dialogue and missionary endeavours as *segregated* activities. To that end, he liked to invoke the perspective of Jewish rabbi-theologian Shemaryahu Talmon to support his contention that 'mission and dialogue are not alternatives: each is valid only within the other, properly understood'.[12]

According to Yoder, then, the 'disavowal of Constantine' is required for one reason only: 'because all that we ultimately have to contribute in interfaith dialogue is our capacity to get out of the way so that instead of, or beyond, us or our ancestors, us or our language systems, us or our strengths or weaknesses, the people we converse with might see Jesus'. Thus, Yoder concludes: 'there is no alternative but painstakingly, feebly, repentantly, patiently, locally to disentangle that Jesus from the Christ of Byzantium and of Torquemada'.[13] In sum, Yoder's alternative vision of dialogue between Christians and Jews seeks to take into account the historical issues that have prevented the conversation from unfolding as fruitfully as might otherwise have transpired.

This set of statements also reveals Yoder's deep distrust of 'human traditions' to mediate truth of divine revelation. What may initially appear to some readers of this statement as an unequal pairing of two substantially different christologies – the Eastern christology of Greek Orthodoxy and the coercive regime of the Spanish Inquisition in the late medieval period which persecuted Jews who refused to convert to Christianity – are examples, for Yoder, of mutually implicated forms of theological error. These are not complexes that can be used, they can only be *disavowed* in the service of seeking truth beyond the traditional frameworks. Thus, both Christians and Jews are invited to embrace the freedom of inquiry and dialogue that opens up when the socio-historical frameworks that have constituted both sets of religious traditions are renounced in favour of the 'good news' of the yet-possible reality of Jewish–Christian community as a reconciled embodiment of God's intent for all of creation.

As this initial explication of Yoder's conception of interfaith dialogue makes clear, Yoder's way of proceeding is structured within a set of binary oppositions that in effect disallows any 'third term' between the possibilities of faithful and unfaithful witness. However, as the full argument unfolds, it is clear that Yoder also regards the option that he proffered as having been, in fact, a third way. In other words, when presented within the context of what Constantinian Christianity of Protestant and Catholic varieties have displayed with respect to Jewish communities in the West, Yoder is calling attention to *tertium datur* – the split between Christianity and Judaism 'did not have to be' (see Chapter 1) precisely because in the wake of the life, ministry and resurrection of Jesus of Nazareth a new kind of politics came into being in which former Jews and former Gentiles were 'reconciled' in Christ.

B. The Social Embodiment of the Christian Evangel

Prominent in virtually all of Yoder's depictions of this 'reconciled body' is his reading of the text of Ephesians 2–3, where Gentile and Jew are depicted in a 'new social reality' that is itself defined 'by the overcoming of the Jew/Gentile barrier'.[14] The passage from the New Testament writings that informs his argument most directly is Ephesians 2.11–21:

> So then, remember that at one time you Gentiles by birth . . . remember that you were at that time without Christ, being aliens from the commonwealth of Israel, and strangers to the covenants of promise, having no hope and without God in the world. But now in Christ Jesus you who once were far off have been brought near by the blood of Christ. For he is our peace, in his flesh he has made both groups into one and has broken down the dividing wall, that is the hostility between us. He has abolished the law with its commandments and ordinances, that he might create in himself one new humanity in place of the two, thus making peace and might reconcile both groups to God in one body through the cross, thus putting to death that hostility through it. So he came preaching peace to you who were far off and to those who were near; for through him both of us have access to one Spirit through the Father. So then you are no longer strangers or aliens, but you are citizens with the saints and all members of the household of God, built upon the foundation of the apostles and prophets, with Christ Jesus

himself as the cornerstone. In him the whole structure is joined together and grows into a holy temple in the Lord; in whom you also are built together spiritually into a dwelling place for God. [NRSV][15]

The significance of the Ephesian vision of the new humanity for Yoder's project is displayed in the title of Yoder's volume of 'Bible lectures' *He Came Preaching Peace*, which is taken from Ephesians 2.17.[16] In his Bible lecture on 'The Broken Wall', Yoder provided his most direct – and succinct – explication of this passage.[17]

The death of Jesus Christ is spoken of in the New Testament in many different ways. Sometimes it is spoken of as a sacrifice, sometimes as a ransom. This time it breaks down a wall. There was of course literally a wall of masonry in Jerusalem, separating the outer court where the Gentiles could come from the temple court proper. Is Paul referring to that wall itself as a symbol? Or is his meaning still more indirectly symbolic?

What Jesus did was to remove the barrier between the 'in' people and the 'out' people. Our ordinary picture is of the cross as reconciling me to God over the barrier of my sins, and reconciling you to God over the barrier of your sins, and reconciling her over the barrier of her sins so that as a result we find ourselves all (one by one) together in this new saved status. In this text the logic runs the other way. The barrier is not anyone's sin. The barrier is the historical fact of separate stories. It is the fact that 'we Jews have the law and you don't.' It is not a barrier of guilt, but of culture and communication. It is not a barrier between each person and God but between one group and another.

The causal line does not run where it does in many modern religious (and for that matter secular) views of the human predicament. It is not the case that inner or personal peace comes first, with the hope that once the inward condition is set right then the restored person will do some social good. In this text it is the other way around. Two estranged *histories* are made into one. Two hostile *communities* are reconciled. Two conflicting *lifestyles* flow together. [18]

Here, Yoder articulates a view of Jewish–Christian relations that clearly attempts to avoid the patterns of supersessionism that have defined Christian perspectives of Judaism for much of the history of Christianity. He is able to do so, in large part, because Yoder envisions another *telos*, for which the *social embodiment* of this Jewish–Christian reality is itself the necessary means of communication.

That purpose is nothing less than making known the good news of the gospels to the 'principalities and powers' or 'cosmic authorities. . . . They are not human persons. Yet they influence human events and structures. What we call the state, the economy, the media, ideology – these are their instruments. . . .'[19] Here again, Yoder turns to the letter to the Ephesians where 'Paul makes it clear that this wider cosmic realm is impacted by the cross and resurrection of Jesus Christ'.

These cosmic powers did not know that the goal of God from all eternity was to make one new humanity. They thought that the meaning of history was the prosperity of the free world, or the growth of the gross national product, or the spread of democracy across the globe (or of Nazism, or of Marxism, or whatever). Their vision of the meaning of history was divided and centered on domination.

Paul helps us understand that their idolatry will be smashed and their pride will be sobered. The cosmic powers will not be destroyed, but they will be tamed, as they too will find their place in the new humanity.

... Only when it is a fact that Jewry and paganism are set at one (are 'atoned'), only when Jew and Gentile are eating at the same table and lovingly adjusting their lifestyles this may happen without offense, only then can it be said to the powers that peace is God's purpose ... How does our life reenact the melding of two histories and two cultures? Where does our banqueting celebrate the new humanity created by the crosses of our time breaking down the walls of our time so that the cosmic powers of our time can see what God is about? [20]

For Yoder, then, 'dialogue' between Christians and Jews can take place within the horizon of the 'good news' that a new social and historical possibility has been disclosed that makes it possible for them to embrace a new reality. They, like the apostle Paul, no longer have to regard one another from a 'human point of view' as 'Jews' and 'Gentiles' but rather can operate out of the horizon described in 2 Cor. 5.17 – 'The old has passed away; behold the new has come.' Accordingly, 'Jew' and 'Gentile' are (unstable) sociological constructions to be overcome, not constitutive identities that have stability that inheres in traditioned practices, narratives, etc. [21]

At the risk of belabouring the obvious, this vision of human enactment of God's peace stands in an uneasy relationship with many aspects of the Jewish tradition. The 'dividing wall' that is destroyed is often said to represent the wall of the Temple in Jerusalem that separated the Court of the Gentiles from those 'inner' courts where Jewish women, men, and priests were permitted to gather in worshipping God. More scandalous still, from a Jewish perspective, is that the Temple in Jerusalem has been supplanted by a 'new temple' that comes about through the cross of Jesus Christ and incorporates the human society of the reconciled company of Christians and Jews. Moreover, the new 'dwelling place for God' has no space other than that of those who gather in reconciliation. Nor does it have a tradition given the abolition of the commandments, Torah, etc. In the process of such shifts, the covenantal basis of Jewish identity also is eclipsed in a way that breaks apart the trilateral unity of land, God and people.[22]

Given the effects of Yoder's reading on this rabbinical consensus, readers of this volume of essays may be surprised and perplexed to discover that John Howard Yoder did not believe that the theme being explored through these essays was 'novel' in any way.[23] What could he have meant by such an assertion? On the one hand, this assertion can be read as tactical appeal to readers. Namely, Yoder's own argumentative appeal is grounded in the contention that *in fact* at one point in human history, Jews and Christians *were* actually reconciled in a way that was socially transformative for themselves and others and Yoder is trying to report that historical datum as clearly as he possibly can. While some will find this contention rather disingenuous, there is no reason to think that Yoder was dissembling. In fact, at some levels, he really believed that he was simply 'passing on to the reader' an emergent consensus that grows out of the recognition that early Christianity and early Judaism were both far from monolithic.

On the other hand, it is also important to Yoder to claim that what he is doing here is not inconsistent with respect to the wider set of claims that he has made about what it means for Christians to live out their existence as a social embodiment of the 'politics' of Jesus. In this second sense, Yoder sees himself as merely 'follow-ing through' on the logical implications of a set of arguments that he has made *throughout* his life as a theologian, pacifist, churchman, ecumenist, and practitioner of dialogue with a variety of religious and secular persons, groups, and positions. In other words, putting this claim about the 'non-novelty' of his position into perspec-tive requires taking into account the varied sets of conversations in which Yoder had the privilege of participating from the 1950s until near the end of his life in 1997.[24] Only then will we be in a position to evaluate the nature of Yoder's contribution in relation to contemporary 'dialogue' between Christians and Jews.

III. Yoder's Conversations and Correspondence with Rabbi Steven S. Schwarzschild

From some angles of vision the audiences of these collected essays are extraordi-narily diverse, addressed as they are to a wide range of Christian and Jewish audi-ences. Yoder spoke before highly specialized gatherings of theologians and scholars as well as more informal gatherings of church leaders, before interfaith assemblies as well as before classes of Mennonite seminarians, and in diverse linguistic and international contexts. From another vantage point, however, while the occasions may have varied, Yoder's own perspective remained fairly constant – to the point that one is tempted to think that Yoder did not so much attempt to address the specific concerns of a given audience as it might be said that he used all such occa-sions to present his arguments and theses within a slightly varying set of exemplars, texts, and appeals. The truth of the matter may very well lie somewhere between these two perspectives.

Continuity of perspective can perhaps best be located in Yoder's decades-long conversation with Rabbi Steven S. Schwarzschild. In retrospect, it is fitting that a project that Yoder recalls as having originated in the context of a decades-long friendship between a Jewish rabbi and a Protestant theologian should evolve in the context of an emergent friendship between Yoder and an American Jewish rabbi.[25] In the late 1960s Yoder came into contact with Schwarzschild, a philosopher who served as Professor of Judaic Studies at Washington University in St Louis, Missouri. While Yoder had no apparent interest in Schwarzschild's work on Herman Cohen, Kant, and Marx (for which Schwarzschild was better known in philosophical circles), he was very interested in this Jewish rabbi's work on the Talmudic roots of Jewish pacifism. While not equally evident in every essay in this collection, Yoder's ongoing exchange with this Jewish rabbi-philosopher proved to be catalytic for the development of the project that ultimately became *The Jewish–Christian Schism Revisited*. Not surprisingly, Yoder dedicated the project in memory of this Jewish rabbi-philosopher with whom he enjoyed an extended dialogue that would span nearly three decades.

Archived correspondence between Schwarzschild and Yoder exists as early as 1972, but retrospective comments in their letters suggests that they must have been in conversation for several years prior to that time. However they may have met, Yoder notes that their correspondence unfolded with particular intensity in the wake of Scwarzschild's 1968 paper 'On the Theology of Jewish Survival'.[26] Shortly thereafter, Yoder begins to draw upon Schwarzschild's scholarship for his own purposes. For example, Yoder cites correspondence with Schwarzschild in a footnote discussing evidence from rabbinic sources for the practice of the jubilee year in his book *The Politics of Jesus* (1972).[27] The fact that Schwarzschild was one of the scholars who endorsed Yoder's work in response to a request from Eerdmans Publishing Company also can be taken as a salient indicator of the value that Yoder and Schwarzschild placed on one another as occasional conversation partners.[28]

Over the years, this on-again off-again conversation – conducted primarily through correspondence and occasionally when the two were together at academic conferences – evolved into a dialogue characterized by candour, personal warmth as well as intellectual acumen. Schwarzschild's letter of 25 September 1972 provides a good example of the kinds of exchange that Schwarzschild and Yoder had with one another. It begins with Schwarzschild's assessment of *The Politics of Jesus* (which at the time was in press at Eerdmans Publishing Company). After providing detailed feedback on the first two pages of the letter about where he judged Yoder to have *misread* texts of the Bible and the Talmud – as well as to have misread Schwarzschild's own work! – Schwarzschild concludes the letter on page three with this opinion: '. . . you are, I think, substantively and importantly right in identifying imitatio with ethical following (discipleship) and the Messiah with the Servant, but for neither is . . . Jesus needed . . .; in fact, all of Jewish literature is full of these identifications. In these matters, in other words, I think you are a good Jew and – though you do not like to hear this – a bad Christian.'[29]

Five weeks later, Yoder responded to Schwarzschild's letter by offering his own straightforward analysis of the latter's judgement: 'You suggest that I probably would not like to have you say that my position is that of a good Jew but a bad Christian. I hardly consider that description a bad one since what you would call a "good Christian" is something you would not be interested in being. I understand what you would call a "good Christian" would be using the adjective good as meaning "true to type"; and the definition of the type is discussing hellenistic ontology and persecuting the Jews. That is my definition of a bad Christian.'[30] As this set of remarks signalled, Yoder was not willing to have the traditional conceptions of Christian identity frame his own theological self-understanding. With puckish affection, Schwarzschild returned a copy of Yoder's letter with a note scribbled in the margin: 'OK . . . you're . . . a better Jew than I. Love, Steve.'[31]

This exchange from the fall of 1972 provides a window into the beginnings of a searching exploration of how issues that interested these scholars might be re-framed. In the wake of the Six Day War in Israel and America's participation in the war in Vietnam many Christians and Jews were seeking new possibilities for peacemaking. In this context, Yoder and Schwarzschild were searching for new ways to describe the struggles of their respective religious communities during an era of profound social upheaval. At a time when the apparent 'triumph' of Zionism constituted the majority opinion, Yoder was beginning to articulate his belief that the significance of the Jewish peace witness 'from Josiah to Ben Gurion' had been poorly understood by Christians and Jews alike. Twenty years later he would declare his belief that 'Jewry represents the longest and strongest experience of religious-cultural-moral continuity in known history, defended without the sword.'[32]

Yoder spent the 1975–76 academic year on sabbatical at the Ecumenical Institute for Advanced Theological Studies at Tantur/Jerusalem. During the first few months that Yoder was there, Schwarzschild corresponded with Yoder. Yoder initiated the exchange in a letter (30 September 1975) in which he informed Schwarzschild that he would be studying 'the earliest Talmudic roots (personages? ideas, debates?) underlying your kind of pacifism.'[33] Schwarzschild responded with an extended set of suggestions about which Jewish rabbinical scholars and Jewish historians Yoder could contact in Jerusalem who would be helpful for Yoder's research interests.[34] It remains unclear how much contact Yoder actually had with those Schwarzschild commended to him – or for that matter whether Yoder's argument actually took into account any of the objections that such scholars and historians would offer in response to his thesis – but Yoder certainly had the opportunity to benefit from the advice of this Jewish rabbi-philosopher.[35]

Yoder's correspondence with Schwarzschild continued and intensified during the five year period following Yoder's sabbatical at Tantur. Yoder and his colleague Charles Primus collaborated in an effort to make arrangements for Schwarzschild to be invited to be a Visiting Professor at Notre Dame – in part with the hope that they might engage Schwarzschild to write in a more focused way about the Talmudic roots of Jewish pacifism.[36] Ultimately they were successful. In the Spring of 1981, Schwarzschild spent a semester as Visiting Professor at the University of Notre Dame. Oddly enough, however, despite their close proximity Yoder and Schwarzschild had limited contact during the latter's residency in South Bend. They continued to exchange memoranda about the 'roots' of Jewish pacifism during this period and Yoder was also present for the last session of the graduate seminar that Schwarzschild offered on 'The History and Conceptuality of Jewish Pacifism'.[37]

A follow-up exchange of letters between Yoder and Schwarzschild indicate that enough substantive issues had unfolded in their one sustained encounter at Notre Dame to fund a continuing debate about hermeneutical criteria with respect to Jewish sources of pacifism and contemporary struggles against various forms of violence. In particular, Yoder pressed Schwarzschild to state what he used as the 'criteria' for interpretive judgements:

> If the course of interpretation is not dictated by the original text's having only one self-evident meaning, and if there is a variety of possible interpretations branching out from a given text in almost all directions, equally arguable if not equiprobable, then how would an outside historian respond to the question of whether there is meaning and direction in the course which the actual communities choose to follow? To stay with the course already chosen: although the holy wars that model [violence] and from the adventures of the Maccabees, Menachem and Bar Kochba to the nearly total nonviolence on the practical level, and from the many grounds for the death penalty in the Torah to its practical rejection, rather than the other way . . . it is significant if despite all this flexibility and subjection to arbitrariness and interest, the long range evolution is in a specific direction and specifically the one that you and I for various additional reasons should choose to prefer. Is that an utterly arbitrary manifestation of whimsy on the part of history or is there some rhyme to it after all?[38]

After posing this complex set of queries, Yoder proceeds to articulate two theses that correspond closely to the argument that lies at the heart of *The Jewish–*

Christian Schism Revisited and also reflect the reasoning that found its way into several essays from *The Priestly Kingdom*, a book that he completed between 1981 and 1982.

> One answer might be to claim that there is an intrinsic direction in the shape of the initial story, which, although it begins with talion and holy war, still plants the seed of a movement in the later nonviolent direction, through some organic necessity which the 'rules of debate' will enable us to watch unfolding. It could be argued that the 'rules of debate,' although developed in the medieval period and even before, have an effect analogous to the rules of grammar and historiography in modern times, and do a favor of objectivity in letting the text defend itself against its interpreters, so that even though the flexibility is great it is not (despite the iconoclastic initial impact of your aphorism) utterly a wax nose after all. If Abraham and Moses began taking steps of faith, the ultimate result of that pilgrimage could be spelled out after the fact.
>
> Another thesis equally applicable, so that I would not know how to disentangle the two and decide that one is more right than the other, would be to say that it is the filter of 2,000 years of life in galuth which gave to the Torah which had come from heaven a dominantly nonviolent interpretation. If there had been many experiences of successful independent kingdoms back in the heartland behind Russia, or if the experiences of privilege in Gentile courts had multiplied beyond those times of ephemeral prosperity like Spain in the late middle ages, or France before Dreyfus, or Germany two generations before Hitler, then the violent strand from the Torah would have been picked up again, and the nonviolent one forsaken, just as is now being done in the light of Hertzl, in the shadow of Auschwitz, and in the name of Masada and the Warsaw ghetto.
>
> The question is obviously circular and hopeless in short-range debate, if we were to ask what would count as arguments now between you and your Zionist confrerees. Obviously, the maintenance of debate with ultimate seriousness about the law is all that can be asked for. But I am asking for something more by way of explanation as to where the other line, which was dominant before Hertzl, had come from.[39]

This sequence, in turn, leads Yoder to remark on the related issue of what constitutes hermeneutical criteria for judgement within the Jewish tradition. In Schwarzschild's final seminar lecture at Notre Dame, Schwarzschild had referred to the Protestant parallel conception of 'the testimony to the Holy Spirit'. Yoder returns to this allusion, offering his own analysis of several possible meanings of this appeal. Here, in a way that I find quite telling, Yoder goes out of his way to offer objections to the 'Catholic' understanding that the witness of the Holy Spirit can be identified with the 'conviction that the course which the community has taken over generations must not be wrong: as for instance when today many Roman Catholics still grant that the early church did not baptize infants and that there is no biblical mandate for an interpretation of the sacrament of baptism which would make it proper that infants be baptized, but that the church evolved in that way over the centuries in so much good faith and for such a long time that it could not possibly have been wrong. If the appeal to the holy spirit can mean all of these things, then it is just one more label for our problem, rather than a pointer toward a better answer.'[40]

Schwarzschild's letter in reply offered a twofold response to Yoder's queries: Schwarzschild briefly explains the 'total hermeneutic freedom' that is 'Jewishly . . . conditioned [produced] by belief in "Torah from Heaven" and Torah-learning (i.e., one has to take the text with infinite seriousness and know more of and about it than any man ever really can). . . . unlike you, I don't see any 'wax-nose' in this, that one could shape any old way one wants to. Every question, therefore, remains in principle eternally open – until the Messiah, really Elijah, comes.' Second, he (re-)asserts his commitment to a neo-Kantian distinction between pure and practical reason. In this context, Schwarzschild specifies that his usage of 'the holy spirit' is oriented by Herman Cohen's (and Kant's) conception of 'holiness' as 'the morality as God practices it, i.e., perfectly'.[41]

As this exchange of views indicates, the dialogue between Yoder and Schwarzschild located several significant hermeneutical differences. At one level Schwarzschild can be said to be trying to help Yoder locate the 'never-ending conversation' with Torah that lies at the heart of Talmudic reflection and thereby the hermeneutical basis for moral judgements about *halakah*. At another level, Schwarzschild is going beyond the tradition of Talmudic reflection to venture his own hermeneutical sensibilities as a philosopher committed to pacifism. In the process Schwarzschild searches for analogies within the Christian tradition for the kinds of judgements that he as a neo-Kantian philosopher finds most intellectually satisfying. Finally, in this May 1981 exchange we also find the clearest instance of Yoder grappling with the interpretative issues that informed the argumentation in the series of lectures on 'The Jewish–Christian Schism Revisited' that he gave at Earlham College in 1982 and at Bethel College in 1985.

Given the disagreements that the preceding correspondence highlights, it is important to locate the background judgements that informed this exchange of correspondence. During this same time period Schwarzschild is beginning to publish a set of articles that constituted an extended commentary about pacifism in the Jewish tradition. In his introduction to a collection of essays on the *Roots of Jewish Nonviolence* (1981), Schwarzschild observed that 'the question of Jewish pacifism or conscientious objection'[42] initially surfaced for many American Jews during the Vietnam War, but that concern began to spread in the years following the Six Day War (1967) as Israelis and Jewish leaders throughout the world alike found themselves confronted with the spectre of what might transpire if Jewish leaders failed to restrain those Israelis who aspired to take over the Temple Mount in Jerusalem.[43] The difficulty that Schwarzschild and company faced, however, was that 'the vast classical resources of Judaism, extended over 4,000 years and the whole world, can be cited to any and all effects' in debates about war.[44]

In such a context, Schwarzschild was inclined to believe (as Yoder did) that 'the chief problem' facing Jewish advocates of nonviolence was one of 'the criteria of selection and interpretation'.[45] In ways that Yoder found to be congenial to his own anti-Constantinian modes of argument, Schwarzschild contended that the requisite criterion

will have to turn out to be the Messianic fulfillment, as in any rational system the end determines the means. The Messianic fulfillment, now, is, as all are bound to agree, the state of peace, justice and truth. Equipped with this criterion, it becomes relatively easy to demonstrate, indeed one is overwhelmed by the majesty of the evidence, that Jewish law (*halachah*) has effectively reduced the legitimacy of war to the zero-point and that Jewish doctrine (*aggadah*) is an uniquely powerful system of ethical peacefulness.[46]

Further, citing those persons of nonviolence who died 'for the sanctification of God's name', Schwarzschild was also inclined to read the 'actual history of the Jewish people' from Jeremiah through the Holocaust as a 'singular enterprise of moral peacefulness in the whole panorama of human history'.[47] Not surprisingly, Yoder found Schwarzschild's narrative assessment of the history of Jewish pacifism to be congenial to the argument that he was crafting in the body of work that evolved into *The Jewish–Christian Schism Revisited*.

In Steven Schwarzschild, Yoder found a Jewish pacifist-philosopher who in addition to sharing his disposition to offer alternative readings of Jewish history was inclined to agree with him about how *at least some* of the questions of contemporary Jewish–Christian dialogue might be reframed. While Schwarzschild clearly arrived at some of his own conclusions from a different context of argumentation, and often differed with Yoder even about the inferences to be drawn from the evidence, their personal dialogue appears to have been generative for both. Given Yoder's famous reticence about matters of hermeneutical method, it is interesting to consider the extended conversation the two had about Jewish patterns of interpretation and Schwarzschild's own willingness to discuss what he thought it meant to interpret 'within the rules' while also attending to the 'spirit's guidance'.

In reviewing the correspondence between these two men, one is struck by the sense in which their argumentation from time to time resembled a rabbinical debate. (Whether that is owing to Schwarzschild's own rabbinical training or to either or both of their dispositions does not have to be determined.) In a sense, Yoder's dialogue with Schwarzschild enabled him to participate in a limited way in the ongoing conversation of Judaism about Torah. Yoder's conception of his scholarly role was also analogous to some aspects of the roles rabbis serve in Jewish circles. One is tempted to speculate that Schwarzschild's friendship helped compensate for the kind of interpretive exchange about Scripture texts and peacemaking that Yoder longed for but rarely found elsewhere. Given the duration, intensity, and candour of Yoder's dialogue with Schwarzschild, it is not surprising to discover that Yoder dedicated this collection of essays to Schwarzschild.

Despite the obvious affection and respect that existed between these two scholars, one wonders whether Yoder really understood the degree to which Schwarzschild's own interpretive slant on the Talmudic roots of Jewish pacifism was mediated by his own neo-Kantian philosophy. If he did, Yoder appears to have disregarded it, although the principal essay that Schwarzschild wrote on these matters specifically states the ways in which he finds Herman Cohen's work to be very helpful for making sense of the sense in which 'authentic Judaism is and always has to be pacific if not pacifist' in relation to 'all the literary and historical evidence, both past and especially present, that contradict this thesis'.[48] Schwarzschild dealt with the 'gap between program and actuality' by invoking Herman Cohen's method of 'idealization'.

The process of 'idealization,' of self-purification, . . . is a literally infinite process in history. It has to continue to be carried out today and on every tomorrow by responsible people – in Judaism and in every other culture. Indeed, according to Jewish law, the so-called Noachic covenant, which is divinely binding on all mankind, begins morally with the prohibition of murder . . . and climaxes morally with the obligation to establish a judiciary, so that first and foremost the ultimate crime will be eliminated. . . . Under Jewish dispensation, the non-Jewish world is indisputably obligated to accept the imperatives of the Noachic covenant and Jewry is obligated to disseminate it.

This, too, is, of course, an infinite Messianic task. None of us is as yet, or will ever be even close to this goal – be it the goal of Jewish plenitude or that of universal plenitude. The task that, therefore, faces us in our respective societies, Jewish and non-Jewish, and in our respective cultures, is to engage in the untrammeled self-criticism and self-purification which will incrementally bring us nearer to one another and, in the process, nearer to the kingdom of God on earth.[49]

This distillation of Schwarzschild's understanding of the Jewish basis for pacifism is important for at least two reasons. First, this set of remarks makes clear the generative sense in which Schwarzschild thought about the Jewish tradition as authorizing pacifist commitment in relation to Yoder's own understanding of the way Christian tradition can and cannot authorize such convictions. For Schwarzschild, *it is possible* to discern directionality within the tradition that emerges in the context of ongoing rabbinical conversation about Torah (provided that the trajectory is oriented within the horizon of the messianic task or vocation of the Jewish people in human history). By contrast, Yoder tended to be suspicious of any notion of tradition as 'organic' or evolutionary with respect to pluralism. According to Yoder, human beings never get beyond the necessity of having to 'prune back the vine' of human traditions that tends to develop around 'the original traditions which enshrine the commandments of God'. In order to 'continue to have access to the sap that makes the fruit of the vine possible',[50] Yoder contends, Christians find themselves in 'a story of constant interruption of new growth in favor of pruning and a new chance for roots. This renewed appeal to origins is not primitivism, nor an effort to recapture some pristine purity. It is rather a "looping back," a glance over the shoulder to enable a midcourse correction, a rediscovery of something from the past whose pertinence was not seen before, because only a new question or challenge enables us to see it speaking to us.'[51]

Closely paralleling the words of his letter to Schwarzschild, Yoder summarizes his views about what it means for Christians to be engaged in a project of 'perpetual reform' this way:

What we find at the heart of our tradition is not some proposition, scriptural or promulgated or otherwise, which we hold to be authoritative and to be exempted from the relativity of hermeneutical debate by virtue of its inspiredness. What we find at the origin is already the process of reaching back to the origins, to the earliest memories of the event itself, confident that the testimony, however intimately integrated with the belief of the witnesses, is not a wax nose, and will serve to illuminate and to adjudicate our present path.[52]

Second, as a statement of Schwarzschild's own conception of peace, the preceding distillation reveals how deeply he is committed to the philosophical task as oriented by the neo-Kantian framework displayed in the work of Herman Cohen. Here too there is an important difference to be registered. From Yoder's point of view, Cohen has a different kind of significance in so far as he can be taken as one of several prominent examples of the way Jewish intellectuals have felt free to 'borrow' from Christianity. As he observes in the essay on 'Judaism as a Non-Non-Christian Religion',

> Jewish culture and philosophy have not only interacted with Christian and non-Christian models in the last centuries, but have borrowed extensively from them, and with no apology. The most adequate continuing advocacy of the moral philosophy of Immanuel Kant may very well be the Jew Herman Cohen. That involved no sense of betrayal or acculturation. It was like Philo or Maimonides believing that everything true that classical Greek thinkers taught they had received from Moses. Similarly, the best interpreter of the thought of Reinhold Niebuhr in mid- [twentieth] century America was Will Herberg.[53]

While Schwarzschild might very well have agreed with Yoder's general observations, he probably would not have consented to the sense in which Yoder would detach such instances of 'dialogue' from the ongoing rabbinical conversation with Torah.[54]

There is a sense in which Yoder and Schwarzschild came closer to agreeing about the embodiment of a common messianic vocation for Christians and Jews than they could ever come to agreeing about the content of the covenants involved. For Yoder, the gathered community around Torah (i.e., the synagogue) was sufficient for sustaining the Messianic identity. For Schwarzschild the mandate for carrying out the 'messianic task' is itself derived from – and ultimately ordered by – the process of Talmudic reflection that is oriented by the Mosaic and Noachic covenants. Whereas Yoder would eclipse the difference between Christians and Jews in the name of a common destiny, Schwarzschild would preserve the difference in the awareness of covenantal difference and a different set of hermeneutical criteria for judgement.

IV. Overview of Yoder's Argument in The Jewish–Christian Schism Revisited

A. The Free Church Vision

Yoder's 'free church' vision[55] marks this collection of essays in at least two ways. First, the sociological observations that he develops in his seminal essay 'The Otherness of the Church' are deployed here in much the same way that he deploys them elsewhere to oppose the Constantinianism of mainline Protestant and Catholic Christianity. From Yoder's point of view, a shift occurs that has consequences for the shape of Christianity: 'prior to Constantine, the church was visibly distinct from the world, even from the church's point of view, as the unity of the church and the world were presupposed under the lordship of Jesus Christ'. With Constantine's conversion, a transformation in the life of the church occurs in which 'the two visible realities, church and world, were fused.' Constantine is not so much the author of this shift (indeed Yoder believes it begins to happen prior to Constantine) as his reign as the 'Christian' emperor of Rome constitutes the social symbol of 'Constantinianism'.[56]

Yoder also described the pattern of 'anti-Constantinianism' as having a set of 'Jewish characteristics' that unfold from the Free Church 'concern for the particular, historical, and therefore Jewish quality and substance of New Testament faith in Jesus'. These include:

- the opposition of radical monotheism to superstition and idolatry,
- missionary vigour derived from the conviction that a new messianic age is dawning,
- courage to stand as a minority in a hostile environment, i.e., the destruction of the religious homogeneity of culture,
- rejection of violence, based upon trust in God's protection.[57]

In addition, Yoder would argue that the 'the relativizing of the hierarchical dimensions of the church in favor of maximum freedom and wholeness in the local congregational fellowship' had a specific set of parallels in Jewish life and culture. 'The juridical authority of the local synagogue is defined by the presence of a minyan or quorum of ten. No authorization or legitimation is needed from elsewhere.'[58]

Given Yoder's *decentralized conception* of religious authority, which he locates within a radically synchronic conception of the congregation/synagogue, the meaning of history itself has looming significance. Here is where the overarching significance of Yoder's 'evangelical revisionism' is most apparent as he reads human history from the perspective of the new set of social and political possibilities that comes into being as a consequence of God's self-revelation in the life, death, ministry, and resurrection of Jesus Christ.[59] Arguably, traces of this historiography can be discerned in virtually all of Yoder's books, but there is a sense in which it becomes even more prominent in his last book, *For the Nations: Essays Public and Evangelical* (1997). There Yoder once more explores the implications of what it means to embody 'good news' of the gospel in human history, but this time with attention to the power of the Christian witness to engage any cultural circumstance precisely because the witness is not any particular linguistic framework but is embodied in the people of God wherever they find themselves in their vocation of *galut*. Thus, Christians and Jews are 'for the nations' however much they may appear in given instances to stand over against the idolatrous practices of the peoples of the earth.

More generally, while not falling captive to overstated patterns such as Thorlief Boman's conception of the Hebraic and the Greek 'minds',[60] Yoder used phrases like 'the Christ of Byzantium' as a catchall designation for dismissing classical Catholic and Protestant conceptions of the life, ministry, death and resurrection of Jesus. Yoder rejected these conceptions because they constitute 'the abandonment of Jewish substance' substituting 'insight for obedience'.[61] Yoder also associated patterns of error in Judaism with the Constantinian legacy in so far as he believed that 'the Davidic Project' to constitute a monarchy in Jerusalem was prototypical of Christian forms of faithlessness. Thus, he argues that 'the error of the age of

Samuel'[62] is repeated in variant forms of Constantinianism that evolve over the course of the history of western Christianity. By contrast, Free Churches would bear witness to a different conception of divine rule, which Yoder found most aptly adumbrated in the prophecy of Jeremiah.

B. The Jeremianic Turn

Although not identical with the vision of the new humanity described in Ephesians 2.11–21 (see section II-B above), Yoder's account of the 'Jeremianic turn' does present a different context of reading history and discloses a new sense of Jewish self-understanding. Yoder's revisionist narrative of Jewish history is centred in the exile, where 'the synagogues and the rabbis of Babylon' entered 'creatively into the Jeremianic phase of creating something qualitatively new in the history of religions.'[63] According to Yoder's inductive reconstruction of the logic of this shift, 'living without a temple, while yet retaining the mythic memory of the temple and the hope of the return to the messianic age, enabled the creation of a faith community with a globally new gestalt' marked by five key characteristics:

1. The primary vehicle of identity formation is a text which can be copied, and can be read anywhere.
2. Reading and singing the texts constitutes the basis for worship.
3. Anywhere in the world a valid Jewish community can be constituted wherever ten households exist. Only the role of scribe is retained as the function of the rabbi.
4. The international unity of the people does not require a hierarchy of priests but can be sustained by such practices as intervisitation, intermarriage, commerce and rabbinic consultation.
5. Jewish identity is located in the common life itself: 'the walk, *halakah*, and the shared remembering of the story behind it'.[64]

In the context of this new sociological location, Yoder contended that 'the foundational narrative from the Davidic age and institutions is now placed in a wider frame where Abraham, then Joseph, then Shiprah and Puah, then Moses, then Daniel and his three friends, then Esther and Mordecai live among the nations, confounding the Gentile seers and emperors with the superior wisdom and power of the one authentic God'.[65]

The generative significance of this aspect of Yoder's historiographical conception should not be underestimated. Its application is not limited to his understanding of Judaism, but provides a paradigm that arguably *overshadows* his earlier thesis about the effects of Constantinianism on western Christianity.[66]

C. The Vocation of *Galut*

Yoder's reading of the Babel story of Genesis 11 (see Chapter 10) provides the context for disclosing his understanding of the 'real mission of the scattered Jews'[67] in the context of the Babylonian captivity where they are to settle down in an alien culture, make homes for themselves (e.g., marry their children, purchase land, eat its produce, buy houses) and seek the peace of the city to which they have been sent. In that context, they are free to exercise 'enormous flexibility and creativity' in their engagement with Babylon (and/or 'Babel'). What they cannot do is to succumb to the temptations of idolatry. Here, Yoder draws upon Jeremiah again to contend that beginning in 587 BC, Jews are called to 'seek the welfare of the city where I have sent you, and pray to the Lord on its behalf, for in its welfare you will find your welfare'. Yoder's reading of this text of Jeremiah 29.7 goes beyond grammatical exegesis. He attempts to find what he regards as 'a dynamic English equivalent' and ultimately puts forward 'seek the salvation of the culture to which God has sent you . . .'[68]

The significance of this set of claims about the vocation of *galut* (diaspora) is important for Yoder for another reason. He contends that the Jeremianic model 'prefigured the Christian attitude to the Gentile world'. This in turn enables him to link the pacifist ethos of early Christianity with the 'ethos of Jewry',[69] thereby placing the belief in Jesus as messiah within the same interpretive horizon as the 'call of Abraham'. From Yoder's perspective, then, the story of Babel in Genesis 11 arises out of the experience of those exiles who found themselves in Babylon. Rejecting what he regards as the 'palestinocentric reading' of Jewish history, Yoder contends that it is the Babylonian experience of captivity that has proved to be constitutive and in many respects generative for Jewish identity. Jewish people were scattered for mission in the sense in which seeds are broadcast 'to bloom where they were sown'.[70]

In sum, the vocation of *galut* is set within a counter-narrative that Yoder employs to link several otherwise disparate historical developments. The hermeneutical trajectory that Yoder ultimately discerns within the canons of Scripture in the Old and New Testaments links the call of Abraham in Genesis 12 to the prophecy of Jeremiah 29. It then reads the latter texts through the lens of Ephesians 2–3, which provides the vision of reconciled humanity that Yoder sees dramatically displayed in St John's visions in Revelation 5, 7, and 22. While Yoder does not always invoke all four sets of texts at the same time, the frequency with which he will invoke one or another pairing is sufficient to demonstrate the interpretive pattern I have described.

Conclusion: Implications of Yoder's Argument for Christian Understanding of Judaism

As the preceding discussion shows, Yoder's argument is directed at overthrowing the assumptions of Constantinian Christianity as they have shaped *virtually all* forms of religious practice in western civilization since the second century CE. From his perspective, this not only involves *disentangling* Christianity from its western instantiations but also delineating a *committed* Judaism that is 'voluntary' not ethnic. For Yoder, this makes even more sense once rabbinic Judaism is understood as having been constituted as a reaction to Christianity, which ultimately resulted in the 'abandonment of missionary perspective on the part of Judaism'. Yoder contends that the process of the 'Christianization of Judaism' ultimately extends to the rise of twentieth century Zionism. Indeed, from Yoder's perspective, the creation of the secular democratic nation-state of Israel actually replicates the sociological features of Christian existence in American context. As a result, 'Committed Judaism, i.e., people who visibly order their lives around the Torah, is a minority sect in Israel just as the Christians.'[71]

Using this sociological observation as a pivot, Yoder argues that 'the ideal typology that calls Christianity "voluntary" and Judaism "ethnic" dodges the issues . . . since the Christian faith of the first century was a Jewish stance that was voluntary'. He argues that if one reads 'real history inductively' a different pattern of Jewish existence can be discerned:

> to be Jewish after Jeremiah often included some element of freedom. Not only were Gentiles able to join the synagogue community; children of Jewish parents could also lose themselves in the crowd. Sometimes in fact the surrounding pressure exerted on Jews a positive pressure to abjure; thus Jewish identity persisted because it was voluntary. Persons who could have done otherwise took it on themselves wittingly and at some cost to reaffirm as adults the identity of their fathers. Such pressure to convert continued in the modern world until this generation. Thus the Judaism with which we are able to converse has faced the freedom to apostasize no less directly than has Catholicism, and more so than has the principal current of mainstream Protestantism which in the Western experience is still heir to centuries of establishment even though the formal enforcement has been loosening for generations.[72]

On this reading of the historical evidence, Yoder contends that it is *not possible* to ascribe a 'stable and autonomous identity to either Christianity or Judaism'.[73] At the same time, believing as he does that 'the reconciliation of people is essential in defining the nature of the Church and her reconciling message', Yoder contends that the truthfulness of Christian existence and/or witness must be linked to its sociological shape.[74]

In sum, Yoder wants to 're-shape the dialogue within the story' for a twofold purpose: (a) to help Christians to recognize the necessity of the voluntariness of their faith and (b) to enable Jews to realize that Judaism is more decentralized than the 'story of Western Civilization' suggests. From this vantage point, what it would mean for Judaism to be a 'non-non-Christian religion' would be *to remove* the historical obstacles that have resulted either in Christians bearing witness to Jews *in coercive ways* or in Christians *not bearing witness to Jews at all*. At the same time, on his reading, Judaism should resume its 'calling' as a missionary people and thereby re-engage the 'messianism' of its own heritage. This recognition, in turn, he believes would *re-situate* the conversation surrounding the messianic witness of Jesus of Nazareth, 'who came preaching peace to you who were far off and peace to those who were near' (Ephesians 2.17). As the *Afterword* to this volume explains, there are good reasons to believe that Yoder's attempt to re-situate that conversation in the context of the vision of the 'pacifism of the messianic community' not only does not aptly characterize the deviance of the 'pacifism of rabbinical nonviolence' but also displaces the necessity for contemporary Jewish–Christian dialogue.

Notes

1. The Society is presently co-chaired by Steven Kepnes and Peter Ochs, with an electronic conversation-line managed by Michael Zank (at mzank@bu.edu; tr@bu.edu) and an electronic *Journal of Textual Reasoning* edited by Steven Kepnes and Shaul Magid and published by the University of Virginia (http://etext.lib.virginia.edu/journals/tr/). Members of the Society meet for two annual meetings, integrating textual study and philosophic reflection.

2. Among the relatively younger dialogue partners are Greg Jones, James Buckley, Jim Fodor, Bruce Marshall, Eugene Rogers and of course Michael Cartwright.

3. The best-known voices in Germany are Friedrich Marquardt and Peter von der Osten-Sacken.

4. The Board of the Society for Scriptural Reasoning currently includes Kurt Richardson, Basit Koshul, David Ford, Daniel Hardy, Elliot Wolfson, Peter Ochs, Kris Lindbeck, Steven Kepnes, Shaul Magid, James Fodor, William Elkins, and William Young. The Society works to retrieve, correct, and restore the scriptural discourses of the Abrahamic traditions as first principles, not only of our community-specific theologies, but also of western academic inquiry. The Society's goals are further articulated in the Statement of Purpose of the Radical Traditions book series, as it appears in the frontispiece of this book.

5. Tivah Frymer-Kesnky, Steven Kepnes, David Novak, Peter Ochs, David Sandmel, and Michael Signer (eds.), *Christianity in Jewish Terms*, Boulder CO: Westview, 2000. The editors also authored *Dabru Emet: A Jewish Statement on Christians and Christianity,* which appeared as a full-page ad in the *New York Times*, signed by approximately two hundred rabbinic leaders (see http://www.icjs.org/what/njsp/dabruemet.html).

6. Here I note but one example, which can be taken as representative of Yoder's dialogical practice. Along with Douglas Gwyn, George Hunsinger, and Eugene F. Roop, Yoder co-authored *A Declaration on Peace: In God's People the World's Renewal Has Begun,* Scottdale, PA: Herald Press, 1991. This 'contribution to ecumenical dialogue' was sponsored by the Church of the Brethren, the Fellowship of Reconciliation, the Mennonite Central Committee, and the Friends General Conference, with each of the authors representing one of these 'historic peace churches'. One of the appended documents included in that volume was Yoder's chronology of the attempts over a forty-year period by these four groups to bring justice and peace issues before ecumenical theological dialogues sponsored by the World Council of Churches and other ecumenical conversations. Yoder himself figured prominently in such efforts to get the Christians of the world to agree 'not to kill other Christians'.

7. Indeed, one of the issues that must be assessed in evaluating the contribution of this book is whether the agenda of the book may not be more effective in addressing Christians than Jews, and if so whether the concerns of the latter have not in some measure been short-changed in the midst of the dialogue that Yoder seeks to enable to come into being (again). This point is not simply to reiterate the fact that the principal audiences of these essays were predominately Christian, but to raise the question from the outset whether the agenda has not already been constituted not only within the missiological problematic of Christian witness to the nations, but also within the ecclesiological conundrums of western Christianity, within which Judaism not infrequently has been

made to play a role that de-legitimizes one social configuration of Christian witness over against the other. Should this turn out to be the case with Yoder's collection of essays that would be tragic; it would mean that the effect of his project runs contrary to the intent of the 'evangelical revisionism' that constitutes his overall intent.

8. See Michael G. Cartwright, 'Radical Reform, Radical Catholicity: John Howard Yoder's Vision of the Faithful Church' [editorial introduction] in John Howard Yoder, *The Royal Priesthood: Essays Ecclesiological and Ecumenical*, Grand Rapids, MI: Eerdmans, 1994, 1–3.

9. For an overview of Yoder's lifework, see Michael G. Cartwright, 'Radical Catholicity: The witness of John Howard Yoder, 1927–1997' in *The Christian Century*, 21 Jan. 1998, 44–6. Cartwright's memorial article focuses on Yoder's reading of the Epistle to the Hebrews 2.8–9 as found in his article '"But We Do See Jesus": The Particularity of Incarnation and the Universality of Truth' found in *The Priestly Kingdom*, Notre Dame, IN: University of Notre Dame Press, 1984, 46–62.

> For our world it will be in his ordinariness as villager, as rabbi, as king on a donkey, and as liberator on a cross that we shall be able to express the claims which the apostolic proclaimers to Hellenism expressed in the language of pre-existence and condescension. This is not to lower our sights or to retract our proclamation. It is to renew the description of Jesus crucified as the wisdom and power of God. This is the low road of general validity. . . It thereby frees us to use any language, to enter any world in which people eat bread and pursue debtors, hope for power and execute subversives. The ordinariness of the human Jesus is the warrant for the generalizability of his reconciliation. The nonterritorial particularity of his Jewishness defends us against selling out to any wider world's claim to be really wider, or to be self-validating. . . . There is no road but the low road. The truth has come to our side of the ditch. . . . The real issue is not whether Jesus can make sense in a world far from Galilee, but whether – when he meets us in our world, as he does in fact – we want to follow him. We don't have to, and they didn't then. That we don't have to is the profoundest proof of his condescension and thereby of his glory. (*The Priestly Kingdom*, 62)

10. 'The Burden and Discipline of Evangelical Revisionism' in *Nonviolent America: History Through the Eyes of Peace*, ed., Louise Hawkley and James C. Juhnke, North Newton, KS: Bethel College, 1993, 22.

11. 'The Burden and Discipline', 22.

12. John Howard Yoder, 'The Disavowal of Constantine' in *The Royal Priesthood*, 255.

13. 'The Disavowal of Constantine', 261.

14. So prominent is Yoder's use of this imagery from Ephesians 2 that one of the principal commentators of John Howard Yoder's approach to ecumenism entitled an overview of Yoder's ecumenical efforts 'He Came Preaching Peace'. The article by Mark Theissen Nation published in *The Conrad Grebel Review*, Spring 1998, 65–81.

15. The significance of this passage for Yoder can be registered in other ways. For example, see the title of Yoder's collection of Bible lectures: *He Came Preaching Peace*, Scottdale, PA: Herald Press, 1985, see especially pp. 11–14.

16. Yoder, *He Came Preaching Peace*. This volume of essays was 'sponsored by the New Call to Peacemaking' and served as a resource for Historic Peace Church congregations.

17. *He Came Preaching Peace*, 108–15. In that same context, Yoder also provides his own translation of this New Testament text (111).

> He is the peace between us.
> He has made the two into one.
> He has broken down the barrier
>   which used to keep them apart.
> He destroyed in his person the hostility
>   caused by the rules of the Law.
> This was to create one single new humanity
>   in himself out of the two of them.
>
> Later he came to bring the good news of peace;
> Peace to you who were far away (you Gentiles);
> Peace to those who were near at hand (us Jews);
> Through him both of us have
>   in the one Spirit
> our way to come to the Father;
> So you Gentiles
>   are no longer aliens
>   or visitors;
> you are citizens like all the saints.

18. Yoder, *He Came Preaching Peace*, 111–12. Some scholars might question the use of this summary taken from a 'Bible lecture' for use in the context of explaining Yoder's more scholarly work.

19. *He Came Preaching Peace*, 114.

20. *He Came Preaching Peace*, 115.

21. Of course, this is already problematic from the point of view of most representatives of Jewish traditions except for those who would claim the identity of 'Messianic Jews'. In the latter case Yoder's argument would merely serve as 'preaching to the choir'.

22. It is easy to see how this imagery has been deployed within various species of supersessionism, but it is not immediately obvious how Yoder's own use of this passage – in the context of the practice of the nonviolent 'politics of Jesus' – can escape the errors of supersessionist ecclesiology.

23. As Yoder noted at the end of his 'second preface' (see the sermon in Appendix A), 'The theme of this set of essays is in no way novel; they seek to bring together in an accessible form the recently accumulated clarifications and corrections which a generation of dialogue and scholarship since the end of WWII have patiently been gathering' (typescript 17; 1996).

24. Based on the missionary and peacemaking activities that Yoder knew were taking place in Israel and Palestine (see Appendix B), he may have regarded himself as providing an explanation for the eschatological significance of messianic Jews and Palestinian Christians finding their way to reconciliation in the context of their 'fellowship' as 'believers'.

25. As Yoder noted in the preface to this collection, the 'core provocation' for the project that became *The Jewish–Christian Schism Revisited* was the invitation from José Míguez Bonino and Rabbi Marshall Meyer to come to Buenos Aires, Argentina to make a set of presentations about what perspective the radical reformation tradition might provide for the contemporary Christian–Jewish conversation.

26. Schwarzschild's paper 'On the Theology of Jewish Survival' was initially published in the *Central Conference of American Rabbis Journal*, Oct. 1968, 16ff. and

subsequently reprinted in *Judaism and Ethics*, ed., D. Silver, New York: Ktav Publishing House, 1970, 289–314.

27. John Howard Yoder, *The Politics of Jesus*, Grand Rapids, MI: Eerdmans, 1972, 37, n. 13.

28. See Schwarzschild's 25 September 1972 letter to Eerdmans Publishing Company which included his endorsement of *The Politics of Jesus*. The 'blurb' Schwarzschild wrote indicated broad sympathy with Yoder's way of interpreting the 'politics' of Jesus. A separate letter, also dated 25 September 1972 details specific objections (p. 1) Schwarzschild registered with Yoder about what he regarded as mistatements and misinterpretations of the relevant evidence. That letter closes (p. 2) with a very warm statement of Schwarzschild's love for Yoder and the observation that 'there are few people, of any faith, with whom I seem to be speaking a language so similar as yours'. Yoder's correspondence with Schwarzschild and related documents are available at the Archives of the Mennonite Church, 1700 S. Main St., Goshen IN 46526.

29. Schwarzschild's 25 September 1972 letter to John Howard Yoder, p. 2.

30. Yoder's 8 November 1972 letter to Schwarzschild, pp. 1–2.

31. Schwarzschild returns Yoder's letter with a note scribbled in the margins that had the date stamped 15 November, 1972.

32. Yoder, *Nevertheless: Varieties of Religious Pacifism*, Scottdale, PA: Herald Press, 1992, 125.

33. Letter from John H. Yoder to Stephen S. Schwarzschild (30 September 1975), p. 1.

34. In his letter of 22 October 1975, Schwarzschild (in response to Yoder's letter of 30 September 1975) discouraged Yoder from contacting Jacob Neusner but urged him to contact several Talmudists, e.g. Prof. Ephraim Urbach, at Hebrew University (Schwarzschild notes: '. . . he probably shares few of our views. His books and monographs are, however, very learned, oriented to the right kind of questions, and quite seminal.'), Isaiah Leibowitz, Nechamah Leibowitz, both of Hebrew University and the 'polymath' André Neher, who according to Schwarzschild 'knows where the problems lie'. Schwarzschild also encouraged Yoder to contact Ernst Akiba Simon, who would 'know a lot of sources that would be of importance to you in these matters'.

35. Yoder's response of 13 November 1975 reveals that he has been in contact with Neher and has had several exchanges of correspondence.

36. See Yoder's memoranda to the chair of the Theology Department and his 1979 letter to Schwarzschild reporting on what he and Charles Primus have in mind.

37. It appears that another outgrowth of the exchange between Schwarzschild and Yoder made possible a 1981 gathering of Mennonite and Jewish pacifists in Elkhart, IN. See Yoder's side reference to this gathering in Yoder's *Christian Attitudes to War, Peace and Revolution: A Companion to Bainton*, Co-Op bookstore at Goshen Biblical Seminary, Elkhart, IN, 1983, 129. Chapter eight of that volume focused on 'The Nonviolence of Rabbinic Judaism', 131–9.

38. See Yoder's 11 May 1981 letter to Schwarzschild, p. 2.

39. Yoder letter of 11 May 1981, pp. 2–3.

40. See Yoder's 11 May 1981 letter to Schwarzschild, p. 3.

41. See Yoder's 11 May 1981 letter to Schwarzschild, p. 3.

42. Stephen S. Schwarzschild (ed.), *Roots of Jewish Nonviolence*, Nyack, NY: Jewish Peace Fellowship,1981, 4.

43. For a very helpful account of the dangers that emerged in the wake of Israel's capture of the Temple Mount at the end of the Six Day War in 1967, see Amos Elon, *Jerusalem: City of Mirrors*, Boston, MA: Little, Brown Company, 1989, 88–97.

44. Schwarzschild, 'Introduction' to *Roots of Jewish Nonviolence*, 5.

45. *Roots of Jewish Nonviolence*, 5.

46. *Roots of Jewish Nonviolence*, 5.

47. *Roots of Jewish Nonviolence*, 5.

48. Rabbi Steven S. Schwarzschild, 'Shalom' in *The Challenge of Shalom: The Jewish Tradition of Peace and Justice*, ed., Murray Polner and Naomi Goodman, Philadelphia, PA: New Society Publishers, 1994, 22.

49. *The Challenge of Shalom*, 23.

50. See Yoder's essay on 'The Authority of Tradition' in *The Priestly Kingdom: Social Ethics as Gospel*, Notre Dame, IN: University of Notre Dame Press, 1985, 69–70.

51. *The Priestly Kingdom*, 69.

52. *The Priestly Kingdom*, 70.

53. See below Ch. 7, p. 154.

54. In the revised and expanded edition of *Nevertheless: Varieties of Religious Pacifism* (1992), Yoder added a chapter on 'Nonviolence of Rabbinic Pacifism'. In one of the footnotes to that chapter, Yoder stated 'Since 1948 the pacifist subculture within Jewry has been shouted down, but its strongest thinkers have not had their minds changed' (176, n. 3). Not surprisingly, Yoder cites Schwarzschild as a case in point.

55. It should be noted that Schwarzschild appears to have had an active curiosity about matters Anabaptist and often included titbits of what he was learning in his correspondence with Yoder.

56. For an overview of Yoder's ecclesiology and its implications for Christian ecumenism, see Michael G. Cartwright's introductory essay 'Radical Reform, Radical Catholicity: John Howard Yoder's Vision of the Faithful Church' in Yoder, *The Royal Priesthood*, 1–49. For the most comprehensive account of Yoder's ecclesiology offered to date, see Craig Carter, *The Politics of the Cross: The Theology and Social Ethics of John Howard Yoder*, Grand Rapids, MI: Brazos Press, 2001, see especially pp. 179–223.

57. Yoder, *The Royal Priesthood*, 247.

58. *The Royal Priesthood*, 247, n.14.

59. Yoder offers his clearest statement of what it means to write history from the perspective of the gospel of Jesus Christ in 'The Burden and Discipline of Evangelical Revisionism' (see n. 10 above). Yoder provides the following succinct statement about why such historiography is needed: 'The reason history needs to be reread is not merely that every generation must claim the right to begin writing world history over from scratch, nor that in particular the children of the bourgeois cannot get out of the nest without soiling it, but that at certain points there is specifiable Good News about the human condition, the goodness or the newness of which those who hitherto have been controlling the story telling have not yet appropriated' (24).

60. In Chapter 6, n. 9, Yoder clarifies the difference between his own position and that of Boman. 'I am not espousing a permanent ethnocentrism, in the style of Thorlief Boman, with Hebraic thought forms always sacred and safe and Greek always pagan. My objection is not to entering the Hellenistic world as a cultural arena. Jews had been doing that long before Jesus and Paul. Paul did it again, with no sacrifice of his Jewishness or his faithfulness to Jesus. What is to reject is the subsequent abandon of Jewish substance, as the "apologetes" succeeded the apostles and the goal of insight displaced that of obedience.' Yoder's shorthand reference to Thorlief Boman is a gesture toward the latter's study *Hebrew Thought Compared With Greek* (Philadelphia: Westminster, 1960). Yoder provides a fairly nuanced discussion of the difference between his version of 'biblical realism' and Boman's position in *To Hear the Word*, 136–9.

61. See below Ch. 6, p. 143, n. 9.
62. See below Ch. 8, p. 162.
63. See below Ch. 10, pp. 186–7.
64. See below Ch. 10, p. 187.
65. See below Ch. 10, p. 187.
66. Indeed as Gerald Schlabach has argued, much of what Yoder wants to contend for could be argued based on this rather than the thesis about Constantinianism. See Gerald Schlabach's article in *The Wisdom of the Cross: Essays in Honor of John Howard Yoder* ed. Stanley Hauerwas, Harry Huebner and Mark Theissen Nation, Grand Rapids, MI: Eerdmans, 1999, 449–71.
67. See below Ch. 10, p. 190.
68. See below Ch. 10, p. 202, n. 60. This reading can be questioned at several levels of exegetical and hermeneutical inquiry. While it serves Yoder's desire to clarify the missiological vocation of the exilic community, it does so by collapsing into a monologic what can arguably be said to be a much more complex set of concepts beginning with but not limited to the meanings ascribed to the Hebrew word 'shalom'.
69. See below Ch. 10, p. 191.
70. See below Ch.10, p. 197, n. 9.
71. See below Ch. 7, p. 154.
72. See below Ch. 7, p. 155.
73. See below Ch. 7, p. 150.
74. See below, Ch. 7, pp. 150–1.

Preface:

What Needs to Change
in the Jewish–Christian Dialogue and Why[1]

JOHN HOWARD YODER

The theme of this collection of essays, namely defining the correction needed in Jewish–Christian relations, has normally (i.e. predominantly, typically, statistically) claimed the attention and commitment of people on either side who were on the edge, usually the 'liberal' edge, of their respective families.

From G. E. Lessing to Reinhold Niebuhr to Roy Eckhardt, the Protestant Christians who most effectively made room for *dialogical respect* for Judaism, and who were first to oppose political anti-Judaism, were often those who at the same time were relatively least bound to the classical core of their respective confessional traditions. They tended also to be less bound to the folk components of their own traditions, where much of the inchoate anti-Judaism of any culture is lodged.

Especially once American denominational pluralism had made room for many communions to recognize one another non-judgementally and to flourish side-by-side, these liberal Protestants could see in Reform Judaism a sister communion with whom they had more in common than with some Christians.

On the other hand, the Jews, from Felix Mendelssohn to Martin Buber to Will Herberg, who most uninhibitedly 'talked back' to the Gentile establishment, were not the Hasidim, the ghetto merchants, or the *shtetl* farmers who constituted most of Jewry, nor the Anti-Defamation League and other defence agencies articulating and defending Jewish identity from the inside, nor the Zionist militants.

This is not to say that the first faltering phase of lowering the tensions between the two faith families proceeded symmetrically. The Jews had to go more than halfway, and the 'liberal' Gentiles still held a power base within the churches. North American society as a whole did not through their efforts become less skewed against Jews, except as western societies as a whole became more 'secular' and developed better civil defences for all minorities.

Few fields of academic endeavour have seen more movement in the last quarter-century[2] than the study of how what we now call 'Christianity' and what we now call 'Judaism' arose from the same cultural soil. A wide stream of literature, some erudite and original, some creatively popular, has opened up the inadequacies of the traditions through which both Jews and Christians have interpreted our differences for centuries. Yet most of the redefinition going on in the vast scholarly literature still is engaged in making adjustments *within* the framework of the received schema. The corrections being made weaken that schema yet without replacing it. What this present study contributes is not another volume of details within those debates, but an alternative perspective on what the problem was and still is.[3] The theme is ready, I submit, for a synthesis that would be informed, though not specialistic, contemporary, yet not trendy.

According to the standard account, we know perfectly well what 'Christianity' and 'Judaism' are. They are alternatives, more or less commensurate and conflicting, answering in partly similar and partly contradictory ways basically the same questions about God and the world and human flourishing. Each is a system of beliefs and rituals, each is a set of institutions. Now (i.e. in the late twentieth century) some of us who are the valid heirs of one tradition, and others who are the valid heirs of the other, are conversing as never before, responding largely to the shock waves sent out by the events of the 1940s. The radical revision reaches back to review many other themes from the centuries of history of Christian anti-Judaism and antisemitism,[4] but at the core there has to be a reviewed understanding of the origins of both movements.

Although I return to the issue later at greater length, here I must already, by way of preface, identify the standard account within which the many changes made by recent scholars have not yet gone deep enough to change everything.

The historical development of the first three centuries of our era ended with the presence, in many of the same places, of two separate, mutually exclusive systems (intellectual, cultural, social) called 'Jews' and 'Christians'. Therefore the standard account claims that this mutual exclusiveness must be assumed to have been inevitable, i.e. logically imperative, even when and where the actors in the story which led to that outcome did not know that yet. Studying history is then the process of showing how what had to happen did happen. The 'had to' is an intellectual construct *ex eventu*. The historian demonstrates his expertise by making that necessity evident.[5]

According to this account, then, 'Christianity' broke away from 'Judaism' (intellectual, social, ritual). Christians interpret this as supersession, whereby the Jews were left behind, no longer bearers of God's story. Jews on the other hand interpret that same separation as apostasy, rebellion. Yet both parties agree on what happened and why. My claim is that they are wrong not where they differ but where they agree.

The new angles on the story in which recent scholarship has been so prolific modify this account in one detail or another. They leave standing the overall outline.

What would be the more adequate alternative picture? I state it first schematically, before returning to restate some of its components more adequately later.

(a) There was no such thing as normative Judaism. Jewry as a population was a great number of very diverse people. Their 'convictions' were scattered across a broad and messy spectrum within which various people projected various normative visions, and many others just went along living Jewishly without asking normative questions, since their own social experience demanded few choices. This diversity had been there for centuries. Some of the bearers of these conflicting normative claims tried to discipline the others, the 'zealous' ones after the mode of Phinehas[6] in fact doing so by the sword, but the people they disciplined were still Jews. That was in fact why the Zealots claimed the right to exercise the discipline.

(b) The collapse of the Jewish governments in Palestine (not only the Sanhedrin administering the Temple but also the puppets of the herodian style running other systems of police, taxation, and courts) meant that the definition of Jewish identity after the year 70 would have to come from somewhere else than from the bearers of civil government. That was not too tragic, since there had not been a completely viable independent Jewish civil government since 586 BCE.

(c) Not until the end of the second century of our era can the historian say that there existed a single definition of Jewishness claiming normativity. It acquired an institutional definition in the networking of the rabbinate, and an intellectual vision in the codification of the *Mishna*. It is intellectually possible to stretch back to say that this identity definition was the fruition of a process which had begun in the age of Akiva (*c.* 135), surviving the failure of the Bar Kochba revolt. One can even claim that the seeds for that kind of rabbinate had been sown in the age of Jochanan ben Zakkai (*c.* 70), surviving the failure of Menachem's revolt. Yet those beginnings, whenever we say they began, were smaller in constituency and weaker in terms of inner coherence than were the 'Christians' at that time. Even once codified, the *Mishna* was not immediately 'received' (in the strong technical sense[7]) from Babylon to Barcelona. It needed to be propagated and to make its way in the synagogues, just as the Christian gospel before it had had to do.

I shall show elsewhere that this standard picture, highlighting Akiva and Jochanan as forerunners of the rabbinic movement, is itself partly in error in that, being palestinocentric, it undervalues the earlier progress in Jewish self-definition already represented by Babylon.

(d) 'Paul' did not leave Judaism. I put the apostle's name in quotes here, because in order to go on with the story we need not resolve the enormously messy discussions which pull apart the man who really existed, the probably authentic writer of some of the epistles, the stylized hero of most of Luke's book of Acts, and the otherwise stylized author of Ephesians and Colossians.[8] There is as much room for differences in the fine points here as there is in the debates about the Jesus of history; yet for our purposes those debates do not matter. In what is essential for our present purposes they all agree.

What Saul or 'Paul' did was not to found another religion but to define one more stream within Jewry. More narrowly, he created one more stream within *Pharisaic* Jewry. His stream differed from some of the other streams in taking (some strands of) *halakhah* loosely, but that was not new. Many other Jews were loose about those rules too. It differed from (some of) the other strands of Jewry in being open to Gentiles, but that was not novel either.[9] Paul's stance differed from (some of) the others in the *mode* of integrating Gentiles. Others would affirm that Gentiles who keep the laws of the Noachic covenant would have a place in the world to come.[10] Others would accept their presence as 'God-fearers' in the synagogue but not at the table.[11] The policy of 'Paul' was marginally more open on these matters than the other contemporaries we know of, but still it was only a little more of the same thing. That openness was explained by 'Paul'[12] on the grounds that the messianic age was beginning, an argument meaningful only in a Jewish frame of reference. To use the name *meschiach* for the person in whom the new age begins is only possible in a Jewish setting. This 'pauline' stream should be called 'messianic' Judaism, and it continued to survive as a stream *within* Jewry for centuries. The Romans saw it as such for generations. 'Paul' never granted that the having-come of 'the age to come' made him or his communities less Jewish. All his life he kept attending the synagogues, and (when in Jerusalem) the Temple. When they told him to 'get lost', he pressed himself on them to the point that they disciplined him as a Jew. He kept provoking that discipline by refusing to leave quietly.

I state this argument defensively here, in terms of the palestinocentric debate which has dominated the recent revisionist literature. The story would look a little different if there were more adequate awareness of the extent to which the phenomenon of 'Paul' had been prepared for by the phenomenon of 'Jeremiah', i.e. by the acceptance of *galut* (or exile) as mission centuries before. Jeremian/Babylonian Jewry was already bicultural, bilingual, long before 'Paul' came on the scene. It was already making proselytes (of all degrees from the 'God-fearers' staying on the edge of the synagogue to full integration through baptism and circumcision) long before Paul came along. Other synagogues may very well already have worked out wise modest compromises about table fellowship, like those spelled out in Acts (15 and 21) and 2 Cor. 8–10.

There are references to 'persecution of Christians by Jews' in the New Testament and some other early sources.[13] Yet none of these accounts may properly be taken as indicating that the 'Christians' at that time were not Jews. In fact the term 'Christian' was not used at first.[14] Nor can 'the Jews' in question be identified with anyone whom today's Jews would acknowledge as speaking for them.[15] It is precisely because they were Jews that local Jewish authorities applied to 'the Christians' the standard Jewish disciplinary measures. Even in the Roman province of Palestine, where the Sanhedrin structures had some quasi-civil prerogatives, they applied only to Jewish subjects. Everywhere else, and in Palestine after 70, the only authority which Jewish community leaders had over any individual was under the conditions of the voluntarily consenting sub-culture. Paul would never have had to undergo the standard ritual chastisement of 'Forty lashes less one' (2 Cor. 11.24), if he had not insisted on claiming Jewish identity and demanding a hearing in the synagogues he visited.

Jewish community authorities could tolerate looseness in the application of halakhic detail, on the part of ordinary members of the synagogue community, when this was going on in settings of toleration under the surrounding Hellenistic culture, where they got along with their neighbours and sold their goods and services. What they could not tolerate was the way Paul and his kind made a normative case for such looseness, not by keeping the rules less carefully himself (Paul made a point of being halakhically faithful when among Jews) but by teaching that messianic Jews could and in fact should eat with Gentiles who (for their part) would not have to keep the rules. So the offence was double. There was a concretely lived-out widening of table fellowship (the aphorism is well worn: Jews did not mind the Gentiles having a place in the world to come; they just did not want to give them a place at the table); and there was the claim that the *reason* for this ingathering was the inbreaking of the messianic age.

What Paul added to all of the above was the pastoral and political power of a strong mind and will, with which he founded and led messianic synagogues in this already available style. He led by the authority of his presence and the power of his ideals. His complex *ad hoc* arguments about what the Law can and cannot do, his appeals to Moses and Adam, whether those arguments be very personal (in the numerous references to himself) or very complexly intellectual (in the style of proof-texting argument which Protestants tend to call 'rabbinic'), all served that pastoral goal. The concrete commands which Paul formulated were not the beginning of state-supported canon law, but *ad hoc* pastoral wisdom. The abstract arguments he spun out were not the beginning of systematic theology but *ad hoc* pastoral wisdom, all of it vulnerably subject to the readers' reception.[16]

(e) What it did mean for Saul to become 'Paul' is currently the subject of an over-done debate, precisely because the debaters are in different ways trying to explain the beginning of something non-Jewish. Alan Segal calls it 'conversion',[17] reacting to the interpretation of Krister Stendahl, who had called it a 'call'. The argument would not be so hard (to follow? to take seriously?) if the labels were not distorted by alien definitions. Stendahl is right that what made the man a 'missionary' was not a pietist conversion centered on guilt.[18] Segal is right that Paul was called into a whole new world. He was changed from a Pharisee who (because *meshiach* had not come) defended the halakhic boundaries of the community, to a Pharisee who (because the age to come had begun) celebrated the ingathering. That is to say, once again, that what has changed is not the man but the world.[19] The messianic 'Paul' is no less a Jew, no less a Pharisee, than Saul. What has changed is that a new age has begun. It has begun with the Resurrection, which only a Pharisee could believe in.

This coming of the new age did include for Paul a visionary experience, as Segal emphasizes, but Paul does not interpret that as a private privilege, nor as any kind of pattern for others. It was rather (1 Cor. 15.1ff.) a way for him to get into the procession of resurrection witness, joining ('as one born out of due time', i.e. as a straggler let into the parade after it had begun) the others who had claimed (or needed) no such mystical accreditation. Paul's stance also included rational argu-ments about the fulfilment of prophecies (as with Matthew and the 'Paul' of Acts). It also included making sense (*after the fact*) of the phenomenon of Gentiles' coming to messianic synagogues, reported as happening already in Acts 9 before Paul came along.[20]

The full meaning of this coming of the Gentiles is claimed as his personal 'mystery' by the 'Paul' of Ephesians. Even that late, assuming that Ephesians is among the latest writings in the 'pauline' corpus,[21] there is nothing Gentile about the message. It is about how people who were 'far', 'without God and without hope', namely Gentiles, were brought 'near' by being integrated in one new humanity, breaking down the wall between them (Ephesians 2.11–21).

The reader will already see that the theme of my study, thus briefly sketched, is not a prolongation of the liberalizing process (of main-line Protestants such as Reinhold Niebuhr) described at the beginning. I rejoice in the refinement of the dialogue already going on between the liberal edges of the two communities, but it is not something to which I have anything to add. I rather come at the topic from the other side. While rejoicing in and benefiting from the liberties which western democracies in the last two centuries have come to afford to more people than before, liberties from which my ancestors as minority Protestants (fár less numerous and less threatening than the Jewish minority) also benefited, I am responsible for interpreting and applying a different vision, namely a criticism of past 'Christendom' practices, from the centre of Christian identity rather than from its liberal margin.

Christianity *as a cultural political establishment*, perhaps better designated as 'Christendom',[22] which was its primary image from the fourth century to the twen-tieth, under which Jews suffered, should be challenged for its own sake. It should not be found wanting only from the perspective of the Jews whom it mistreated,[23] but also for the sake of Jesus whom it claimed to serve and thereby defamed.

The core provocation of this project arose in the early 1970s. The late Rabbi

Marshall Meyer, then heading a rabbinic seminary in Buenos Aires, and José Miguez Bonino, outgoing rector of the Evangelical Theological Faculty there invited me in 1971 to project what a contemporary perspective drawn from the 'radical reformation' tradition of Christianity could contribute to the Christian/ Jewish conversation.[24] I found there more than I expected. My writing out what I found has been delayed by the awareness that the conversational field is complex and crowded, and becoming more so as time passes. It was reasonable to hesitate to publish in an area well worked by many more erudite people. Yet the more expert people are investing their greater expertise in other themes than the one I am presenting here. I have therefore resolved after all to submit to the reader a thesis which I have not the special skills nor the time to expand into a *summa*.

Karl Barth began to publish theology in the early 1920s, saying that he had no intention to cover the field. All that was needed, he wrote, was one foundational corrective. Yet before death cut him off, Barth's nearly-complete *Kirchliche Dogmatik* was the nearest thing Protestant theology had seen to a *summa* in centuries. That provides an interesting contrast to Karl Rahner who, although dealing all of the time in what he called 'fundamental' issues, wrote not a *summa* but a shelf full of *Quaestiones Disputatae*. So did Martin Luther, whom Barth described as an 'occasional' rather than a 'systematic' theologian. The fragments which follow are sure not to expand even into one real book; yet their intent is something like what Barth said his was. I seek here to articulate one basic alternative perspective, which if correct will call for redefinitions all across the board, even though it cannot be my task to do all that redefining.[25]

I have been taught much by numerous Jewish friends, but by no one else so much as by Steven S. Schwarzschild *ztz'l*, to whose memory this collection is dedicated.

Summer 1996

Notes

1. [Editors' Note: This essay was the 'second preface' in the 1996 *Shalom* Desktop distribution of the 'package' of essays on *The Jewish–Christian Schism Revisited*. The text has been edited for style and clarity, but the substance remains. See note 25 for material originally included between the last two paragraphs of Yoder's Preface.]

2. This essay gathers material previously presented:

   – in a contribution to an ecumenical seminar at the Seminario Rabbinico in Buenos Aires in April 1971;

   – in a lecture at the Ecumenical Institute for Advanced Theological Studies (Jerusalem, West Bank) spring 1976;

   – in a lecture sponsored by the Theology Department at the University of Notre Dame October 1977;

   – in a lecture series presented at Bethel College (North Newton KS) 31 October and 1 November 1982, and again at Earlham School of Religion (Richmond IN) April 1985.

None of that material saw publication, partly due to my sober awareness of the complexity of the field. Much of what I said then has now become the predominant wisdom, but the challenges I had to address to the frame of reference of the debate as a whole are still entire, and therefore seem to me still to justify this further distribution of these materials.

3. If this were a volume for scholars, needing self-attestation by the proof of my having done all the homework, there would have to be many side glances to the writings of Krister Stendahl, Lloyd Gaston, Alan Segal, John Gager, James D. G. Dunn, E. P. Sanders and James Sanders. I do not pretend to that level of thoroughness. The pertinence of the alternative perspective I here advocate does not depend on my having finished that debate with all of those wiser people, most of whose major contributions are more recent than this material, though final 'proof' perhaps would.

4. Some participants in the debate make much of the difference between 'anti-semitism' and 'anti-Judaism'. I recognize the issues at stake in making such distinctions, but they are not adequately served by attempting to impose one's own word usage on one's interlocutors in the midst of a conversation.

5. This notion of logical inevitability was first challenged at length in my lecture 'Tertium Datur' (see Chapter 1 below); I have also pursued it into other fields, as a general historiographical error, in my paper 'The Burden of Evangelical Revision' in James Juhnke (ed.), *Nonviolent America*, North Newton, KS: Bethel College, 1992, 21–37.

6. In Num. 25.7 Phinehas acted as the executioner of idolaters; in Num. 31.6 as military commander. Ps. 106.30 shows that he had already become the prototypical zealot.

7. 'Reception' is a technical term in law, in canon law, and in the study of the development of doctrines. It means that a phrase, an idea, a law, or a text, first formu-lated or promulgated centrally, is validated by the way its constituency appropriates it. Especially if propagated across cultural boundaries, such 'reception' can significantly modify meanings and/or delay implementation. Especially in the absence of military coercion such appropriation of a body of moral guidance can and could take generations.

8. To say nothing of the still more stylized patron saint of Lutheran antisemitism. While the total study that follows is already a quarter-century old, this prefatory formulation was provoked by the scholarly conversation provoked more recently by Alan Segal's *Paul the Convert* (New Haven, CT: Yale University Press, 1990).

9. For centuries Gentiles had been coming to the synagogues, and had been welcomed in various ways. How to welcome them, what to require of them, was a standard rabbinic discussion theme.

10. Many assume that this notion of the second 'Noachide' stream of salvation, whereby Gentiles could have a share in the world to come by keeping a more general law without the Mosaic details, is as old as Rabbinic Judaism, but it is probably much younger. Cf. Chapter 3, n.8 in this volume.

11. Some scholars hold that 'God-fearers' were a standard, quasi-canonical category; others deny that such a category existed. Considering the expanses of space and time we must consider, it is quite possible that both are right.

12. I use the 'scare quotes' here to avoid, rather than trying to resolve, discussion about the difference noted above: the authentic author of some letters, the eponymous author of some other letters, the hero of the book of Acts, and the 'real historical' person behind them all.

13. Douglas R. A. Hare, *The Theme of Jewish Persecution of Christians in the Gospel According to St Matthew*, Cambridge: Cambridge University Press, 1967.

14. It is used three times in the New Testament, each time as a characterization by outsiders, in texts written long after the events (Acts 11.26; 26.28; 1 Peter 4.16).

15. This will be spelled out further in Chapter 1 below.

16. Occasionally his letters make it explicit that he is dependent on his readers' 'reception' for his guidance to be implemented.

17. These comments were provoked by a presentation by Alan Segal at the Society of Biblical Literature, based upon his book *Paul the Convert*, New Haven, CT: Yale University Press, 1990.

18. Krister Stendahl, 'The Apostle Paul and the Introspective Conscience of the West', *Harvard Theological Review*, 56, July 1963, 199ff.

19. 2 Cor. 5.17 describes a 'new creation' or 'whole new world' which is not a born-again individual but a transformed cosmos. Cf. my 'The Apostle's Apology Revisited', *The New Way of Jesus,* ed., William Klassen, Newton, KS: Faith and Life Press, 115–34.

20. According to the witness of Acts, it was precisely this ingathering which Saul opposed; not some other idea about Jesus or the Law. Far from creating 'paulinism', he was dragged into it against his will.

21. For some scholars it is very important to know who wrote which epistle. For our purposes it is not. In fact, to have Paul's special ministry described as Ephesians does would be even more worthy of attention if a later admirer wrote it.

22. Sometimes this established Christianity is described as 'Constantinian', because of the importance of the fourth century in its taking on this shape. Yet our present concern is with mistakes that were made earlier than that.

23. To say nothing of the many other colonized peoples around the globe. These lines were drafted in the wake of the centennial celebrations of 1992, when the hemisphere remembered how odd it is to describe the imperial subjugation of this hemisphere as 'the spreading of Christianity'.

24. I was a guest instructor at Miguez' Instituto Superior de Estudios Teologicos. The two men had become friends when both were graduate students in New York.

25. Since I was first led to this theme, once in 1971 and again in 1977 at the University of Notre Dame, it has been clear to me that there is important unfinished intellectual business to be worked on at the intersection of two themes:

> 1. the 'believers' church' critique of how the meaning of Christian discipleship has been denatured by the historically dominant deformations variously designated as 'establishment', 'Constantinianisation', or 'patriarchalism';
> 2. the critical revision of Jewish–Christian relationships especially since 'the holocaust'.

Despite the exponentially expanded bulk of meetings and writings on the theme of correcting the Jewish–Christian conversation, some of it led by concerns related to my own, it as yet has not directly duplicated as a whole the re-reading of the meaning of the Jewish–Christian schism which I propose. Some of the things I said twenty years ago have become common currency, but the frame of reference of the debate still largely remains where it was, so that my critique is still called for.

The field remains so full of communication and of tension that I cannot hope to make a major statement without 'covering my flanks' with considerable dialogical cross-reference to the recent debate. Much of the 'revision' which is going on backs away from explicit Christian loyalty; and thereby makes careful debate delicate. Much of the needed revision cannot avoid being somewhat abstractly methodological, argumentative.

That is why, ever since the lectures in Bethel and Earlham, I have considered the prospect of a major effort in this area to be unlikely, even though I am sure there is a message here needing to be articulated. I have nevertheless been moved to reopen the file by the coinciding of several considerations:

1. the fact that after twenty years some of what follows still needs to be said;
2. the recent renewed expression of interest by several friends;
3. the awareness provoked by ageing and accident that I need to be more careful in contemplating what I might still get done in the next few years of scholarship;
4. a certain flowing together of this concern with other themes (missiology, history of pacifism, radical reformation, ethical methodology) in which I am interested.

Rather than beginning from scratch to draft new chapters, each of more or less the same size and shape, I shall stay for the present with the form in which the texts already have, editing only for clarity and continuity, and to decrease repetition. The oldest and longest text, presenting the core thesis, shall be presented in its fullest form, without all of the updates that might be added. It shall then be followed by the several side views that were presented as separate lectures at Bethel and Earlham, where the special concern was 'believer's church' or 'radical' Christianity, not normally considered by Jews as their interlocutors.

Commentary

PETER OCHS

Yoder's Preface anticipates some of the wonders of his overall contribution to Judaism and to Jewish–Christian theological exchange today. It also anticipates some of the burdens of his approach. I will therefore begin this, the first of eleven commentaries on Yoder's chapters, by outlining all of what I take to be the wonders and burdens of Yoder's approach to Jewish–Christian relations. This will remain the unwritten outline for each of my subsequent commentaries. In each of these, I will comment only on ways in which, in a given chapter, Yoder's writing illustrates some number of these wonders and burdens. Again, I will always respond from out of the movement of the post-liberal Jews who share in or support the approach of the Society for Textual Reasoning.

1. *The wonders. Overall, Yoder presents a Scriptural post-modernism that offers hopeful change for each of these two scriptural traditions (Jewish and Christian) and also for each in relation to the other.* Contemporary Jews, and Textual Reasoners to be sure, have reason to thank Yoder for his contributions not only to Jewish–Christian dialogue, but also to philosophic-theological resources for strengthening Jewish as well as Christian religious life and thought after the demise of modernity. More specifically, the wonders include:

(a) *A new kind of Christian openness to dialogue with Jews and Judaism.*

(b) *A post-liberal openness to dialogue.* This means an openness stimulated by the demise of the modernist, liberal paradigm of knowledge – religious as well as scientific. 'Post-liberal' is a term often applied to what some call the 'Yale School' of Christian theology and cultural criticism. The most visible teachers of this approach were George Lindbeck and Hans Frei and their student-colleague Stanley Hauerwas, with earlier roots in Karl Barth and in efforts to return to what they consider the radical visions of Luther and Calvin as well as of Thomas Aquinas. Hauerwas is the direct link here, since he was also a close colleague of Yoder's and studied his work very closely. Hauerwas' own version of Christian ethics could be dubbed 'Yale School Free Church', or an

Anabaptist (radical Methodist in this case) variety of post-liberalism. Semantically, the term 'post-liberal' refers to the effort of university trained scholars of Christianity to re-ground their scholarship in doctrinally warranted and community-based readings of Scripture, in particular the plain-sense narrative of the life, death, and resurrection of Jesus Christ. The post-liberals retain their academic skills of text-historical study and of philosophic discipline, but as instruments of the truth and of the behavioural rule of the gospel narrative. They direct their primary criticisms at 'liberal' theologians, meaning Christian theologians, since the Neologians, who have proclaimed a gospel that is made subservient to western paradigms of reason and of socio-economic-political organization. 'Western' refers here both to the cultural programme of the modern secular West and to the political-cultural programme of what they call Constantinianism. They envision a post-Constantinian Christianity that accompanies Christians in their new-found minority status in the West, detached from goals of political governance. This vision is non-liberal, where 'liberal' is glossed as 'intentionally or unintentionally supporting the secular values of modernity'; it includes western 'conservatism', and therefore has nothing to do with distinctions, in the United States, between 'liberal and conservative', or left- and right-wing politics. In contemporary American terms, post-liberals may tend to be 'conservative' in the sense of being loyal to the task of imitating Christ, but often radical in their political-economic judgements. Against the grain of both liberal and pre-modern Marcionites, post-liberals read the Gospel narratives as meaningful only in relation to the Old Testament narratives and, therefore, as extending our understanding of God's enduring covenant with Israel. Frei and Lindbeck also adopted Rabbinic Judaism as a model for Christian life now as a minority religion. The Society for Textual Reasoning emerged in close dialogue with the founding post-liberal theologians.

(c) *An openness at this particular time in history. But what marks this time as the time of a new paradigm shift, or a new epoch in Jewish and in Christian history?* For post-liberal Jews, the new epoch is dated from the Shoah, as an ultimate symptom of the failings of both the modern and pre-modern paradigms of Jewish–Christian relations as well as of knowledge.

(d) *A post-liberal rediscovery of scriptural study as the basis of our knowledge of how to act in the world.*

(e) *A post-liberal rediscovery of community as the context for this scriptural study.*

(f) *A post-liberal practice of 'depth historiography', as a way of reading not only the plain sense of scriptural history, but also the deeper sense that directs the Word of Scripture directly to our own context of interpretation* (we will explain this in the commentaries to follow).

(g) *The vagueness and fluidity of normative Jewish identity in the first century and beyond, including the Jewishness of what Yoder calls 'messianic Judaism' (the followers of Jesus);*

(h) *An appreciation of the lateness of Rabbinic Judaism: that Rabbinic Judaism is itself a commentary on the religion of Biblical Israel;*

(i) *The correlated virtues of later Judaisms and Christianities: that both have overlapping sources in the exilic religion of Rabbinic Judaism.*

2. *The burdens: Yoder's work is also burdened with some tendencies that post-liberal Jews may find problematic. Among them:*

(a) *A modern tendency to mistrust all inherited traditions, which means, in Cartesian or Lockean fashion, to place excessive trust in immediate or direct disclosures of knowledge (Post-modernists, since Wittgenstein, have called this a 'foundationalist tendency').*

(b) *A related tendency to draw stark distinctions between true and false judgements and to assume that what appears to be the contrary of a true judgement must be a false judgement.*

(c) *A related tendency to uncompromising judgements, which tendency both reinforces and is reinforced by a doctrine of fulfilled or messianic time: that in Jesus Christians have the potential to live in fulfilled time.*

(d) *A related tendency to an unintended form of supersessionism and of religious exclusivity.* This tendency is illustrated in Yoder's effort to identify the essence of Judaism with the strictly exilic dimension of 'Jeremiac Judaism' and its Rabbinic and messianic successor.

Part I

TERTIUM DATUR

To Rabbi Steven S. Schwarzchild
of Blessed Memory

'It Did Not Have to Be'[1]

A. Re-thinking the Way We Read the History of Christianity

The first mistake Christians have tended to make – for the last thousand years when thinking about Jews – is to forget the 'Jewishness' of Christianity, in such a way that we take for granted that the relationship between the two faiths, the two streams of history, could begin with their separateness.

I contend that the valid reading of the history of Jews and Christians must begin with one movement. We can best begin our open search for new light on the Jewish–Christian schism of the second and third centuries (not really of the first) by clarifying an indispensable corrective emphasis concerning historical method. That is the historian's axiom: *It did not have to be.*[2]

There is no error more natural, and perhaps there are few errors more damaging in the reading of history, than the assumption that events had to go the way they did. When the historian tries to 'make sense' of an event, it is natural that the effort should proceed by way of understandings of causation. We seek to enlarge our grasp of all the factors that were present in the situation. The more carefully we look, the more naturally we see how those factors which we have found to be important pointed in the direction of what finally happened. We feel we have adequately explained an event when we have constructed a line of 'causation' such that we can now see that it could hardly have gone otherwise.

As natural as that explanatory task is for the historian, it does a fundamental disservice to real understanding of what was going on *then*. For the people in the period we are talking about – whatever period,[3] who knew much more than we do about all of those facts, did not at all know that things were going to have to go a certain way. Some of them were quite conscious that they were making decisions, sometimes agonizing decisions, about which way things would go. Others felt powerless in the face of forces pushing them in the wrong direction. Some feared or hoped or prayed about the outcomes, later finding that some of the fears and some of the hopes were actualized. At other points, they were surprised by outcomes which they would not have expected or even considered.

We therefore do violence to the lived reality of history as it really was, if in our concern to make sense of it after the fact we let our explanatory schemes rob its actors of the integrity of their indecision as well as of their decision-making.

For simplicity's sake, I state this with regard to specific event-decisions which we can talk about as if they were made at identifiable points in time. The same is even more true if we can seek to narrate the kind of decisive developments which, although utterly conclusive once they have reached an end point, took years or even generations to 'happen'. Our particular theme, the Jewish–Christian schism, was this kind of development. There was never a single event by that name. After it had conclusively taken place, it seemed to everyone to be utterly natural that it should have come to pass. Yet there was a space of at least fifty years – twice that in most

respects, during which it had not happened, was not inevitable or clearly predictable – and was not chosen by everyone, not even by everyone who finally was going
to have to accept it.

We do violence to the depth and density of the story if, knowing with the wisdom
of later centuries that it came out as it did, we box the actors of the first century into
our wisdom about their children's fate in the second. We thereby refuse to honour
the dignity and the drama of their struggle, and the open-endedness of their questioning and the variety of paths available to them until one answer, not necessarily the
best one, not necessarily one anyone wanted, was imposed on them.

Even more do such interpretations of the inexorability of what actually happened
fall short, if as biblical faith does, we take seriously the conceptions of sin as something that shouldn't have been, and the trust in God's capacity to bring to pass the
unexpected.

I do not mean to disparage the labour of historians who try to get the facts straight
and to make sense of things having happened as they did. It is better to know than
to not know how it is that the American Revolution, or the war between the States,
or the First World War, or Auschwitz, actually happened. But it is a more promising exercise, more hopeful and more repentant, as well as more complex, to seek in
addition to that to put ourselves so effectively into the psychic skins of the actors of
those days that we can say that the history looks open; it could have gone otherwise.
It did not have to be that way. There did not have to be an American Revolution, as
Canadians have often argued. There did not have to be an American civil war. Even
professional military scientists on both sides tell us that there was no valid political
or military reason for the First World War. Better statesmanship, on quite reasonable (non-pacifist) grounds, could have avoided that disaster. At least some
Christians in Germany were ready to say that there did not have to be Auschwitz.

That more repentant and more hopeful perspective on what *could have been* is
not 'realistic' in the sense of positivism; it refuses to let 'the way things are' have the
last word. It is, however, realistic in a *deeper* sense. It pushes us to ask far more
ambitious and complex questions about all of the forces which were at work, and
about how things could have been otherwise, in order to discern options which
might have been really available if someone had had the information, or the
courage, or the organization to reach them, distinguishing these from other kinds of
wishful thinking, and from wasteful or resentful utopias. It drives us to take stock
carefully of the powers and resources which were there but were not tapped, or
which were at work but did not win out. It drives us to reconstruct the processes of
decision operative within the minds of major actors, within the deliberations of
groups, within the interactions of structural pressures, so as to liberate those events
from the deprecation which is involved in saying that they were fated, and thus to
restore to them their authentic worth as real, flawed, yet sometimes noble human
searches and decisions.

As I re-visit the story of the Jewish–Christian schism, I shall not be seeking to
produce any heretofore unsuspected information, although it is constantly surprising how much of what we do know about that hinge century we have not really
thought through and profoundly remembered. What I am seeking to do is to
illuminate from a different critical perspective some known but less-noticed facets
of that experience of primal schism in the Jewish–Christian community of the first
centuries, by accentuating this reminder about historical method.

B. The Criticism of Unfaithfulness in Radical Protestant Identity

Doubting that things had to go as they did *way back when* correlates logically with doubting the rightness of how they continued to go later. Our present concern is thus appropriately at home within that strand of the western Christian story, which we call 'free church' or 'radical reformation'. Mennonites and Friends, Methodists and Disciples[4] are the heirs of leaders who in other ages took risks to be critical, after the fact, about events in history that should not have happened. There are strong grounds, which have been operative in the origins of these movements, to be critical of what had gone wrong in Church and world even when they were not themselves its victims.[5] There are values which justify remaining in minority status even when given the chance to assimilate. There are causes other than the defence of one's own separate identity which would render morally imperative a counter-cultural commitment.

There are those for whom the criticism of 'establishment' Christian cultural models has become obsolete in our own world, partly because the battles (e.g. religious liberty) are over, partly because the communities who are heirs to the earlier radicals (e.g. Mennonites and Quakers) have lost their wonted *élan*. Does the loss of separateness or the loss of nerve or the end of persecution, as experienced by the sectarian Protestant minority, not now mean that the inclusive Catholic or Protestant majority was right, and the 'sectarian' posture has been refuted by its loss of confidence? Or does it only follow that the foundation from which the critical minority witness had been stated during the time of isolation had been too thin or shallow? Then we should look for alternative fulcra to provide critical prize. We would find that there are such theologies in our time, newly focused resources for critique responding to the major new defeat experiences of the age.

One of these new potential sources of insight is the theological response to the complex of tragedies coming to be referred to by the code term 'holocaust', demanding deep theological revision both among survivors within the Jewish people and from Christians who confess that they stand in some kind of complicity with the perpetrators. Another source, mostly seen as coming from Latin America but with analogues representing other victim cultures, is coming to be know as the theology of liberation. A third, less adequately formulated and known thus far, comes from eastern Asia, and is the called the theology of *min-jung*.[6]

Here I do not undertake to set out at length the dimensions of the overlapping interests which should lead those heirs of the older 'reformation' communities to make common cause with contemporary prophetic minority communities. It suffices to note that both kinds of criticism of Christendom from within – the classic 'radical reformation' and the current 'liberative'– should have a stake in recognizing the challenge that the Jewish community, standing over against dominant forms of Christianity, represents to critics from within. Both Jews and radical reformers accuse established Christian religion of unfaithfulness to its original mission. Both thereby let their particular historical origins define a mandate for separate survival. Each begins by accusing the 'main-line' party of denying the faith utterly.

This critical vision is not like the difference between Scandinavian Lutherans and British Anglicans, who although favouring different doctrinal or liturgical formulations never split off from each other. They can with relative ease recognize that their differences are contained within a common 'high church' Christian stance. Even less is it like the difference between American Anglicans and American Lutherans, who understand their inherited differences more in terms of contrasting ethnic folklore than of issues of truth on which the Church will stand or fall. Such 'main-line' church groups can with deceptive ease assume that the ecumenical challenge is a matter of bringing people together who are separated by nothing really important.

The readiness to accept minority status and persecution (especially when coupled on the other side with the readiness to inflict it) has created and still creates schisms of far more painful quality; these issues are harder to handle within the ordinary good-mannered conciliar ecumenical style.

The common painful memory of having had to face schism with deadly seriousness may protect us against trying to get truth questions to fade into a fuzzy pluralism, as is thought by some to be an imperative of ecumenical style. The differences we need to take stock of are too fundamental to be 'outgrown' by merely regretting that someone once took them too seriously.

When Jews describe what they reject in Christianity, the list of unacceptable elements will include the linkage of religion with an oppressive political and social system, uncritical assimilation to pagan styles of culture and morality, centralization and sacralization of the man Jesus as competitor for the glory of God. Movements of reformation and renewal within western Christendom – Anabaptists and Friends among them – had some of the same complaints. Might it then be that our articulation of what has gone wrong with Christendom, from within our own setting of post-Christian modernity, could be fostered by looking more closely at the sister community which first raised the same objections?

The same marks of classical Christendom, which have long been challenged by Jews and radical reformers, are today as well losing their credibility for people in the mainstream churches and people outside them: Byzantine dogmatics and episcopal politics, ritualism and establishment, are the mainstream mistakes most easily identified by the cultured critics of religion in our time. If then there should be some new wisdom to be harvested in the encounter with Judaism, that might well be the key to a renewed modernity in our witness.

The task of inventory undertaken here is that of an amateur, which all interdisciplinary and interfaith conversation must naturally be. An expert is a person who shares her or his colleagues' axioms. The amateur asks why they have become axiomatic. To the story as told by the historians of the first century, and to the interpreters of the dogmatic definitions of the fourth, I bring questions sharpened by the study of modern western Christian history and contemporary social ethical concern.[7]

C. Tertium Datur

These background remarks about the shape of the debate may help to prepare us to return to the question 'did it have to be?' by restating the 'standard account' with which clarification must begin. Our inherited, unquestioned definition of the problem of Jewish and Christian identities, and therefore of the problem of Christian antisemitism, derives from a time when the definitions of normative Christianity and normative Judaism as mutually incompatible religions were perfectly clear and there was no mediating possibility.

Historians project that later clarity into the early situation, when they look in the earlier texts for explanations of the later polarization. But the fact that we are looking for such explanations to answer a later question ('why the inevitable schism?') itself distorts our capacity to read the story for what it itself wants to say. We find issues back there which the actors at the time did not experience that way. Perhaps the purpose of those living that story then, or the purpose of God in letting it happen, was not to explain (or even dictate) a later tragic division, but perhaps even to offer some other option. If God's purpose might have been to offer a different future from the one which actually came to be, then we do not do total justice to God's intent in the story by reading it as if the outcome he did not want, but which did happen, had to happen.

In order to be able to argue its limits, I will summarize the basic theses of the inherited position:

1. There was first of all a base line of 'normative Judaism'. We can draw from the documents what that was. It was essentially the same as that codified two centuries later in the *Mishna*, except for its being at home in Palestine. For these purposes 'Judaism' means both a *position*, i.e. a religious synthesis of beliefs and practices, and a *population*, which we might more precisely call 'Jewry'. Both the positions and the population were relatively homogeneous.

2. Jesus rejected normative Judaism and was rejected by it. That reciprocal rejection is not a misunderstanding or a tragic fluke, but a proper and necessary response, befitting the real positions of both 'sides'. There was a necessary antagonism between what Jesus was saying and the Judaism which he attacked.

3. The apostle Saul/Paul again rejected Judaism and was rejected by it.

4. Christianity as such is defined by these two successive rejections, not by its commonalities with Judaism. The many convictions which were still held in common by Christians and Jews around 100 CE. (regarding for instance the uniqueness of the one God creator and sovereign, God's rejection of idols and polytheism, his law and God's world vision, God's loving kindness), do not contribute as fundamentally to the definition of Christianity as do the points involved in the double rejection summarized above. The rejection is *doubly* double: Jesus and Paul rejected Judaism, and Judaism returned the compliment.

If we had the time and the erudition to proceed slowly and sceptically,[8] we would find problems in the fact that after Jesus and Judaism had already carried out the first mutual rejection in the period of his earthly ministry recorded in the Gospels, Paul and the same Judaism would by this account have had to go through the same division again as recorded in the book of Acts and reflected in the Epistles. Why did it have to happen twice and why only twice?

Though brief, the above characterization of the standard account is not unfair. It encapsulates the ordinary view of how far back the schism goes. On looking more closely, however, one cannot explain the timing, the subject matter, and the external form of the two reciprocal rejections as simply as the uncritical customary account assumed. Here, however, I cannot pursue those details; a simpler, direct challenge to the theses as stated will need to suffice.

1. Hereby we are able to formulate the first corrective: *There was no such thing as normative Judaism in the first century of our era*. That standard definition against which first Jesus and then Paul are supposed to have reacted had not yet as a matter of fact been defined. Brown University historian Jacob Neusner has the special merit

of having made this historical awareness much more conscious in our generation. [9] Christians, guided by their experience of later authority models (i.e. episcopal hierarchy, ecumenical councils, the creeds, governmental pressure for conformity) understandably ascribed to the Jews of the time of Jesus patterns for defining what is 'normative', somewhat like those which existed in the experience of those later Christians, but patterns which in fact were not present in the Judaism of the age before the *Mishna*. The function of a fixed liturgy, that of a creed, that of a bishop, that of a written canon law, that of a godly sovereign, the definitional effect of ethnic solidarity within an enclave – all of these resources for self-definition could later easily be ascribed to first-century Palestinian Judaism by Christians whose own identity was taken-for-grantedly defined that way – yet in fact, they were not there.

What really happened in the age of the Second Temple was much more confused. Within Jewish society there were several competing authority structures. There were the rabbis, the most respected of whom we identify with the position known as Pharisaical. Their authority depended upon the voluntary loyalty of their disciples. In no sense were they like bishops, nor was the greatest among them like an archbishop. There was the constituted authority of the Sanhedrin, indisputable at the point of having arranged with the Romans to have charge of the management of the Temple, but – partly for that very reason – not enjoying the respect or the adhesion of all the population. Other authority models – the Dead Sea communities, other seers and preachers, freedom fighters – established their claim to speak for 'the Jews' on still other grounds and were accredited by still other constituencies. There was no power authorized to impose uniformity, and if there had been, its focus would have been *halakhic*, i.e. concerned with behaviour, not with ritual, doctrine or piety.

It is a disservice to understanding to think that one of these groups was more adequately, more validly or more normatively Jewish than the others. They were all there. So was the utterly Jewish Jesus, with his crowd of almost exclusively Jewish listeners. The confusion was heightened by the being in their own land rather than in a ghetto, and the absence of political sovereignty in the ordinary sense.

After the collapse of the first Zealot revolt in the year 70, and especially after the collapse of the second revolt 65 years later, the situation became more clear, but only gradually. The Sanhedrin structures fell away, together with the Temple which had been their reason to exist, destroyed by the same Roman authorities which had once supported them. The Zealot definition of authority was still thinkable, but after two more resounding defeats it was no longer credible. Simply to be Jewish by virtue of having been born in that land was no longer a self-evident identity. What was left had to be a way of being a believer without the Temple and without the turf. This meant structuring a confessing community on non-geographical grounds, an identity that could be voluntarily sustained by a minority of people scattered in lands under other sovereignties. There were two groups who did this successfully, as Neusner says it. There were the messianists, later called Christians, and there were the rabbis.

Both of these movements were Jewish. Neither was more Jewish that the other, although the 'Christian' side of the tension had been crystallized earlier. They had almost the same moral traditions, almost the same social structures. They differed from one another only about one very Jewish but also very theological question, namely on whether the presence of the Messianic Age should be conceived of as future or also already as present. The Jews who affirmed the messianic quality of their age (something only Jews could do), by confessing Jesus as risen, were *no less* Jewish than those who rejected that confession (or who may have lived in some region of the Dispersion where they had not yet heard the report). They did not differ about whether to accept Gentiles into their membership, although with time differences developed about how to regulate that openness and how many people would take advantage of it.

But if then the very notion of a 'normative Judaism' as backdrop and interlocutor for Jesus and Paul does not hold water, the whole picture must be redrawn. This calls forth our second corrective.

2. Second Corrective: *Neither Jesus, nor Paul, nor the apostolic communities rejected normative Judaism.* This is true first of all, of course, on the superficial level, with all the semantic clarity of tautology. If there was no such thing as normative Judaism no one could have univocally rejected it or been rejected by it. But the point is far more fundamental. What Jesus himself proposed to his listeners was nothing other than what he claimed as the normative vision for a restored and clarified Judaism, namely the proper interpretation of the Jewish Scriptures and tradition for this present, in the light of the New Age which he heralded. Jesus rejected certain other teachings, and he scolded certain other people, as did all Jewish teachers, but he never granted that the traditions and the people he was challenging or reprimanding were qualified interpreters of Torah. He claimed that he himself represented that, and that those other teachers were misled and misleading in their contrary efforts to interpret the tradition.[10]

There is in the Gospel accounts of the ministry of Jesus nowhere a rejection of Judaism as a stream of history or a group of people. With regard specifically to the law [Torah], Jesus' attitudes are all affirmative. He said he had come not to destroy the law – or even relax it – but rather to *fulfil* it. He claimed to defend its intent against interpretations which would destroy its meaning or dull its edge. He appealed both to the historical experience of Jews and to their canonical writings to authenticate and illuminate everything he taught. He placed himself completely within that history, with no reference to other histories or sources of wisdom like those from which syncretists or a Jewish philosopher like Philo would borrow.

At points where Jesus entered into debate, it was a debate about the proper meaning of the Jewish Scriptures and traditions, never an effort to relativize or deny that heritage. Within the debate on the meaning of the tradition, which is part of the ongoing identity of any living human community, his preference was for return to the 'original' or the 'radical' meaning of teachings on the sovereignty of God and the imperative of obedience. Sometimes in dialogue Jesus reached back to what he claimed Moses really meant. In one case (Matt. 19, about divorce) he reached back beyond a concession 'Moses' had made to human frailty, to restore the original intent of creation, but he always did this within an absolutely Jewish context and in Jewish terms. The freedom he claimed to redefine[11] was *no greater* than the freedom taken by the earlier prophets and canonical writers as they each in their time had also reworked living traditions, or than the freedom taken by later rabbis.

Similarly, the Apostle Saul/Paul never surrendered his claim that a true child of Abraham must share the faith in the son of the promise made to Abraham. Those Israelites who had not yet seen Jesus the Promised One were not thereby for Paul main-line Jews, or authentic Jews, but rather Jews not yet accepting the fulfilment of the promises made to their father. In all of his polemic against people who were making what he considered to be a wrong use of the values of the Hebrew heritage (the law, the ritual, circumcision, *kashrut*), Paul never suggested that his adversaries were typical Jews, or that the values they were using wrongly were unimportant, or that he wanted his own disciples to be anything other than good Jews.[12]

Paul debated head-on against certain ways of applying the Jewish heritage to the diaspora situation, especially with regard to how much of the Jewish lifestyle should be expected of proselytes and of God-fearing adherents of the synagogue who did not become full Jews. That was a debate which had been going on already generations earlier, a debate provoked within Diaspora Judaism before Jesus, by its extensive success in attracting to the synagogue community sincere seekers of non-Jewish blood, which had been the experience of the synagogues for decades already. Paul's advocacy of a relatively liberal attitude toward these people without a Jewish ancestry was one of the positions which had already been taken in those earlier discussions. It was in no way an un-Jewish or anti-Jewish position. Paul was the great Judaizer of the Gentiles (we'll return to that). He could weave Aramaic liturgical language into his letters to non-Jewish believers at Rome and Corinth. This means that he or someone else with similar orientation had taught Aramaic prayers to Gentile believers. He collected money to carry back to the poor in Jerusalem. He himself returned to Jerusalem to fulfil vows he had made committing him to Temple worship.

We do find in the New Testament, especially in John's Gospel, a series of texts speaking negatively of 'the Jews' as being wrong, hostile, reprobate. The problem those texts pose for us is not set aside by saying that they appear only in a small portion of the New Testament (though that is true). It is not sufficient (though some scholars with a more cavalier attitude to Scripture may be satisfied by it) to say that some of the harsher references might have found their way into the text in the course of its later transmission over the generations, or might not all have been in the original text, or that still fewer might be directly indicative of the thought of Jesus himself (all of these explanations also being possible). What counts more is to note that even in there critical cases, the people being talked about are not Jewry as a whole, not the bulk of the people in Judaea, but a particular set of authorities, the people who today would be called 'the establishment', a relatively small group of men wielding institutional power. This becomes quite clear if one asks about the actual social referent of the mentions of 'the Jews' or even 'the Pharisees' in the Fourth Gospel. Not the crowds, nor the poor, nor the 'nation', nor the synagogue congregations can be meant, but a few rulers, the decision makers.[13]

This can be well illustrated by what took place two decades ago when the critics of our Vietnam war talked about 'the Americans' in south-east Asia. They did not mean all the American people, or the bearers of valid American moral values, or even the journalists and church related service workers in Vietnam, who were also American citizens, and were doing other things in Vietnam. They meant the power bearers of the diplomatic and military presence of the Washington government. The same is often true in ethnic-based controversy. One often grants by a linguistic convention what one really intends to challenge on the level of principle, namely that the power elite or decision-making minority is in some sense, or represents (or ought to be made accountable to) 'the people'.

So when John's Gospel speaks of 'the Jews' (always translatable literally 'the Judaeans'), in almost every case the actual reference of that narrative is to a mere handful of people who had major decision power in the Judaean society of the time.[14] Empirically, visibly, they are in control. Yet Jesus does not grant the validity of their definition of Jewishness. By no means does he grant that they are more Jewish than he. After the year 70 they no longer exist.

3. These two revisions demand a third. *The Jews did not reject Christianity.* Again this thesis is true far more deeply than in the superficial sense that it is the sum total of the other two. Jewishness or Judaism as a system of beliefs and practices did not reject Christianity as a belief system. Nor did Jewry as a body of people, or most of their institutions, reject believers in Jesus as a people. The Temple at Jerusalem was open to believers in Jesus until its destruction. The experiences of clash reported in the book of Acts are not typical, few of them are official, and they did not interrupt the continuing participation of believers in Jesus in Jerusalem in the life of the Temple, in the celebration of the Jewish week and year and the observance of a Jewish lifestyle.

Outside of Jerusalem the social context of the believing community was the synagogue. Until the end of the first century (at the very earliest hypothesis) there was no general expulsion of Christians from synagogues. In fact no specific expulsion of the Christians from particular synagogues is recorded that could be taken as representative or as setting a trend. The few cases we can find, or any grounds for thinking that such expulsions happened, are at the earliest from late in the century and it is not clear that they are representative. The reports in the Acts of the Apostles describe synagogues which were torn by debates, or which divided, as diaspora synagogues were prone to do: but both parties after such a split constituted synagogues. Neither party in such a case was more Jewish than the other. There were no disjunctive options – such as later history had always told us we must expect to find there – between which a believer in the God of the Jews and in Jesus in the year 50 or 65 or 75 of our era would have had to choose, one of which would have been other than Jewish. To be a Jew and to be a follower of Jesus were not alternatives. *Tertium datur.*

But is there not a record of the earliest Christians being persecuted by the Jewish authorities? Is not most of the New Testament story under the shadow of an already irrevocable rejection of Christians by Jewish authorities and the community at large? When we read the New Testament story with the glasses and the glosses of later experience, this already polarized mood is present. But a closer scrutiny of what the stories themselves actually say represents a situation which is much less decided and much less divided.

The accounts in the New Testament of what could authentically be called persecution of believers in Jesus by Jews are very few. In the cases we do have, the agents of such mistreatment are generally not the most morally qualified representative leaders of the Jewish community. Often the action they take has no official status, and even when such action is taken it means that the believers in Jesus are being dealt with as Jews subject to the internal discipline of the Jewish community, not as Gentiles or as irrecuperable apostates.[15]

For the purposes of this argument, I shall not attempt to make much of one additional consideration which is important to most historians, namely the assumption that, by the time the New Testament writings took their present form, the way in which they tell the story had probably been significantly modified by much later events. Such arguments would provide additional support for my argument.

D. But What of the Anathemas?

One interpretation of how the division took place appeals to some scholars because it pretends to build a floor of verifiable scholarly confirmation under the earlier assumptions. In the standard Jewish morning prayer, the *amida* or 'eighteen blessings', there are actually nineteen verses. Legend has it that the nineteenth was added in order to shut the Christians out of the synagogues. In this prayer, the believer calls upon God to judge the *minim* (the apostate). Legend has it that the addition was drafted by one Schmuel the Lesser, at the behest of his teacher Gamaliel II, the leading spirit behind the consolidation of the second generation of the school of Yavneh. This would put it at about the year 85 CE. The 'blessing' read something like this:

> Let there be no hope for the apostate;
> root out and destroy in our time the arrogant kingdom:
> let heretics disappear like a moment,
> Praised by you, O Lord, who dost destroy the sacrilegious
> and humble the arrogant.

There is no reference to Christians in the earliest documented forms of this text. What does exist is circumstantial evidence from Christian writers, the earliest of whom is Eustathius (*c.* 355) and there is Jewish manuscript evidence from the third century, that in the usage of *some* synagogues the term for 'Christians' (*nozrim*) had *by that late date* been added in the third line to that for 'heretics'.

The suggestion that the origin of the twelfth blessing was intended (as the legend about Gamaliel II and Schmuel does not in fact say at all) in order to provide a specific measure of defence against Christians, a measure taken at Yavneh and communicated officially from there to all of Jewry[16] was apparently first made in the 1890s. It has cut a wide swath among scholars since then, especially since being expanded by Louis Martyn in 1968.[17]

John's Gospel reports concerning the man born blind – whose healing by Jesus is the theme of the ninth chapter of the Gospel – that his expulsion from the synagogue was first threatened and then carried out by 'the Pharisees (13, 15)' or 'the Jews (18, 20)'. It is not otherwise known what 'expulsion' from a synagogue would have meant in the third or fourth decade of the first century. There is no rabbinic literature, nor is there anything else in the New Testament, to interpret how it could be done or with what effect. Scholars have therefore doubted whether the story could be historically authentic, and have sought for other explanations of how John, writing much later, would have invented such an account.

Now Louis Martyn has suggested imaginatively a new answer, he hypothesizes that the legend of Gamaliel and Schmuel is historical, and that John is responding to that event, i.e. to its impact in the synagogues after 85 CE. About that time, he suggests, synagogues first began expelling Christians. John then read that situation back into the time of Jesus, thereby giving us a new handle for dating the redaction of the Gospel, and clarifying the author's pastoral intention.

Further conversation with Martyn would belong in the realm of speculative New Testament scholarship. In that framework it would be challenging, but it would not help us here.

1. It would hardly render credible a total scepticism about the Gospel accounts' having any historical value because they were fabricated from whole cloth to serve a polemic purpose in the ninth decade of the century;
2. It would affirm that for two entire generations, from about 35 to about 86 CE, the two communities were not separated, which would confirm my present argument.

In the interest of a less imaginative appropriation of the challenges posed to us by such stories, it makes more sense to assume for this account, as for the handful of cases where Paul is reported as having similar difficulties in synagogues (Acts 13.45ff.; 14.2f.; 17.4f.; 18.6f., 9f.), that the events reported are the natural *ad hoc* defensive responses of local community leaders, with no foundation in rabbinic law stated, claimed or needed, and no effect in taking away the Jewish identity of those excluded.

The legend of Schmuel would also be worthy of more analysis, but for the present it suffices that I note why the most careful more recent scholars – including Geza Vermes, Peter Schafer, and Asher Finkel – sweep away the entire construction.[18] The 'school' of Yavneh – also transliterated *Jabneh* – was not what we call a school. Even less was it a Vatican from which encyclicals or pastoral letters or messengers could be sent out to all the synagogues of the world.

The task of the rabbis conversing there was to clarify, unify, perhaps implicitly to codify their heritage (but not literally; codification proper was not done until generations later, with the work of Judah Ha-Levi) in a form which could survive without the temple and without any imminent prospect of national restoration. The process of redefinition has never ended, but it did reach a first rounding-off in the redaction of the *Mishna*. Before the compilation of the *Mishna* no rabbi could send out pastoral letters. That was not a part of his office. After the compilation there was no need to do so. Only projecting onto Jochanan ben Zakkai and Gamaliel models of polity which Christians developed only much later could have permitted Christian historians thus to misunderstand the legend about Schmuel, whose concern is with other matters, such as whether a person leading in prayer should be removed for making a mistake. Likewise the Christian interpretation of there having been a 'synod' or 'council' at Yavneh to settle upon the canon of the Hebrew Scriptures must be abandoned.

The normal meaning of *minim* (the term usually translated 'heretics') does not cover a Jew who thinks Messiah has come. The primary focus of the maledictions is the 'arrogant Kingdom', i.e. Rome.[19] But even if the Martyn thesis of the 'encyclical from Yavneh' were to be tenable, my historical point, from which a theological point follows, would still stand. It still leaves intact the first fifty years of Jewish–Christian common life, during which such a measure had not been taken. During this half century (*at least*) the fact is undisputed. Therefore it is also theologically undeniable, that it was possible that a person could at the same time be a fully faithful Jew and a believer in Jesus of Nazareth as the Anointed One. What happened *historically* cannot be excluded *theologically*. If it cannot on historical grounds be excluded for then, it cannot on theological grounds be forbidden for tomorrow.

For a half-century, at the very least, these two commitments were thus not incompatible. Their mutual compatibility was lived out Sabbath by Sabbath by hundreds, perhaps thousands of people, in Jerusalem for the first two thirds of this period and in the diaspora beginning with the ministry of people like the apostle Paul. Of course there were soon some believers in Jesus who were not born Jews, and how they related to the Jewish believers was an ongoing problem, to which we shall return. Of course there were also Jews who did not believe in Jesus. Paul made a special point of not giving up on them. But the significant datum we have been taught to undervalue is that it was completely possible, subject to no necessary disciplinary measures, according to the best traditions of both communions, for the same Jew to be both 'rabbinic' and 'messianic' (or, in later anachronistic terms, both a 'Jew' and a 'Christian').

The incompatibility of those two commitments thus must not be interpreted as the definitional base line, from which two separate communities evolved independently, organically, so that we should already read the ministry of Jesus and of course that of Paul as carried out under the shadow of an already inevitable schism. This incompatibility is rather the product of historic development which took at least a half-century (really much longer for most[20]) to turn its first corner.

The incompatibility of faith in Jesus with Jewish identity is thus not the point of departure for the problem of Jewish and Christian relationships. To assume that disjunctive incompatibility is the fundamental mistake of pre-critical historians. The development of that incompatibility represents rather a departure from the original, tense but tolerable, overlapping of Jewish and Christian identities.

Our landmark for the first clear presence of the other view is Justin Martyr (*c.* 135). Justin reports that Jews regularly curse Christians in their synagogues, although he does not specify the *birkat ha-minim* (which is not primarily a synagogue prayer). Nor does he report any specific usage which can be confirmed from Jewish sources. He also reports it as a fact that there are Jewish Christian believers who are not thus rejected by the synagogues. He disproves of them, but he does not deny either that they are numerous or that they live their faith with a good conscience. Justin is thus engaged, a century after Pentecost, in driving a wedge between two kinds of Christians: those who, following the counsel and the theology of Paul, invest in keeping the border between them and Jewry open, and those like himself, whom we have since come to call 'apologetes', who turn their back on the Jews in the interest of making more sense to the Gentiles.

Justin counts as the first major figure among the so-called 'apologetic fathers'. It is here, as far as the Christian side is concerned, that the schism may be said to begin *as a doctrinal position*. Yet Justin himself testifies that he is not authoritative, and that there are 'Christians' who hold to the view he decries, still attending the synagogues. He proves my point, although he disapproves of its being true.

But did not the Christians claim that Jesus was the Christ, the Messiah? Was this claim not the heart of the offence? To take this for granted is itself also a product of the later polarization. There was nothing wrong in the first century with thinking that some particular person was an anointed one or even the Anointed One. As Jesus himself is recorded as having predicted, candidates for that dignity arose several times in later Jewish experience. People who took that risk were received critically, but not excommunicated. The Jewish population tested such pretenders, and ultimately found them wanting, but not *a priori*. They were not told that they were not a Jewish possibility. To ascribe the status of 'Anointed One' to someone might be a *mistake* (it always has been so far) but it was not heresy. Some historians believe that Rabbi Akiba was ready for a time around 133 CE, to recognize Bar Kochba as Messiah. He was wrong, and everyone was sorry, but during the period when he could make that affirmation about a particular man, nothing about that recognition made him less Jewish, or less a reputable rabbi. His error on this point did not keep him from going down in history as one of the major figures in the formulation of the rabbinic heritage for his generation. Other Jews, on into early modern time, have taken the risk of accrediting other messianic claimants.

More than this there were other rabbis, active during the first century, whose sayings have entered into the Talmudic collections, who seem to have been ready not merely to recognize that some particular human being could be Messiah but even that Jesus of Nazareth may have been that person. Of course the sources are hard to interpret, but there is some indication that perhaps Eliezer in the age of Gamaliel II, or Ben Soma in the age of Aqiva, might actually have continued to hold the opinion, certainly a minority view but not an impossible one, that Jesus had been the Anointed One and/or that the reports of his resurrection might be credible. These men did not need to break faith with the other rabbis because of this kind of question. Eliezer did for a part of his career experience rejection by his colleagues, perhaps for this reason, but that isolation did not deprive him of the status of Jew or even of rabbi.

Thus it is not true either in theory or in actual experience that to affirm the messianity of a man made anyone less Jewish, in the first or second centuries. So this reason, which ordinary Christian thought assumes would automatically have driven Jesus out of fellowship with his neighbours, and all the Christians out of the synagogues, did not actually function that way then.

But then advocates of the standard view of the Jewish–Christian schism rephrase their objections. Did not the Christians call Jesus the Son of God? Was that not logically impossible and morally inadmissible for 'the Jews'? Again, the argument is circular. If the title 'son' has to be taken with the meanings defined in the course of the controversies of Gentile Christians in the fourth century, that would seem to be true. But we aren't in the fourth century yet. In the first century that term could not mean that. In the second Psalm the name 'Son of God' is a title applied to the King. In Jesus' temptation, it is another word for the claim which Satan wanted Jesus to make to be a Zealot king. Obviously such a title was an offence to anyone who did not want Jesus to be King; but not because it was either metaphysical nonsense or blasphemy.

Here lies the flaw in Rosemary Radford Reuther's nonetheless epoch-making work *Faith and Fratricide*.[21] She derives the Jewish–Christian split from christology. Yet in order to do so she must project back into first-century messianic language meanings which those phrases could not have had (then). Their original meaning was just one other form of words, chosen by first-century Jews, to make a Jewish point. Martin Hengel has renewed the demonstration that this kind of 'Son' language must have developed very early in *Jewish* Christian congregations,[22] where it cannot have had the kind of meaning that it later had, when it underwent redefinition so as to become categorically offensive to any Jew.

This question must be distinguished from a further one, namely whether the 'high Trinitarian' language of the post-Constantinian creeds and the Athanasian theologians should in principle be regarded as counter to monotheism and as offen-sive to Jews, if properly understood. Later Jews certainly took them that way, as did Muhammad later, but were they conversing with the most careful theologians, who argued most carefully to distinguish Trinitarian monotheism from tri-theism? Or was the clash not rather one between popular oversimplifications and distortions on both sides? May the strictly theological polarizations not often – as in intra-Christian divisions – have been more the results than the causes of conflicts arising first on the plane of personalities and power struggles?

There are yet two further ways in which we carry back into the interpretation of ancient debates assumptions which we would more clearly see are inappropriate, if we were more responsibly involved in conversing critically in our own time. One is that any pair of ideas which appear contradictory to us could not be held by the same people, or could not be held by different people in fellowship with one another. Intellectual historians are especially prone to sniff out necessary divisions where only paradox, or inconsistency, or tolerable diversity, inconclusive debate, or amusing variety really existed.[23] The rabbis were especially skilled at managing contradictory views within the one social process. The fact that people argue against one another does not prove that they are in incompatible movements: it may prove just the opposite.

Any human community is marked by internal conflict as well as by conflict with the outside. One of the marks of the importance of any group identity is in fact the special virulence and dramatic weight which it imparts to intra-group conflict. There was always conflict within Jewish identity. It is recorded within the Hebrew Scriptures. It is a necessary implicate of a vision of God which includes person-like will and historical sanctification. Priestly religion and imperial religion can avoid this kind of internal diversity, i.e. can rule it out by authority. The notion of apostasy – uncomfortable for mainline Christians – is routine for the Hebrew prophets. Conflict marked post-*Mishna* Judaism through the centuries, and still does. This is one of the specifics of Jewish identity, characterized as it is by a revelation claim ceaselessly standing over the empirical ethnicity. When we take account of the existence of conflictual materials (attitudes, vocabulary, actions, institutions) within the first-century story, we must recognize the need for a much greater degree of sophistication in definition which will enable us to distinguish between the *kind* of conflict which is an affirmation of the common identity of those who are in tension with one another, and other levels of tension or conflict which imply the denial of the destruction of the other. No one scolded the Jews more rude-ly than their own prophets. Does that make them anti-semites?

We are then still searching for the explanation for the actual development, whenever it came, within the synagogues, of a rejection of the messianic believers by the synagogues. Another set of historians would link it with the failure or refusal of the 'Christians' to stay with the Zealot defenders of Jerusalem until it fell in 70 CE; but Jochanan ben Zakkai, founder of Yavneh, also deserted Jerusalem at the same time, and accepted some kind of understanding with the victorious Romans. Most other Jews were in any case never deeply devoted supporters of the Zealot cause, especially after its failures.

The same hypothesis, subject to parallel refutation, has been suggested regarding the Christians' not having supported Bar Kochba, the would-be Messiah of the years 130–135, either on the grounds of the rejection of violence or because since they reasoned that Jesus was 'Messiah' Bar Kochba could not be. Others think it was because Jews began to be distinguished from Christians as victims of the persecution by Hadrian, or because Christians (like Justin Martyr later) pointed to the outcome of the two Zealot wars as proof of divine judgement on the Jews. The latter idea could have been an argument for most of the rabbis of Yavneh and the diaspora, since they had not supported Bar Kochba either.

For now it will suffice to note that there is no clear answer, and that *for present purposes* there need be none. That is in fact the point. All serious historical hypotheses place the *beginning* of the implementation of the division from the rabbinic side no earlier than 135 CE, a full half-century later than the guess based on the legend of Schmuel the Lesser and a full century after the Pentecost recounted in Acts 2. Other historians would make it still later.

Whenever the initiative was taken to make the breach irrevocable, and by whomever, the fact stands that the non-schismatic stance and the non-split sociology, the stance of Paul and the New Testament and of the Jewish society which tolerated the overlap, had stood for at least a full century. Even after the polarization had been institutionalized, simple common sense will know that it must have taken generations for the polarization to generalize, and generations more for the middle party to die out.

The effort cannot be made here, and cannot be carried out easily even by the most expert scholars, to determine in detail which of the many steps, which finally separated the two sister communities was taken first, and by whom. Even when some synagogue leaders had decided to formulate a clear rejection of the *nozrim*, we cannot know how long that usage took to be received and to become standard usage. It cannot have been immediate. Even when some Christian writers or bishops had espoused anti-Judaism, or had enunciated implicit theories of supersession denying the right to existence of Jewry after Pentecost, there were still other Jewish Christian communities which did not hold that theory, or who if they held it as theory did not implement it by rejecting their own Jewishness or adopting Hellenistic Gentile forms of church life.

One can suspect that the division was not final until Christians in the fourth century came into political power, and thereby changed not only the resources at their disposal for dealing with adversaries, but also the social meaning of their own faith. Groups called 'ebionite'[24] or 'Jewish Christians' by their critics survived for centuries more, despite the attacks of the 'orthodox' bishops who had the support of the Roman authorities. Historians have tended to talk as if that middle group had actually disappeared; yet their traces can be found for centuries. The notion of their 'disappearance' means only that later historical memory had no use for them, not that they were no longer around. It was the Hellenizing apologetes who produced more literature, and who later became recognized as the 'orthodox fathers', at least partly for non-spiritual reasons. Although it is not surprising that later Gentile Christians accepted the idea that those 'fathers' define 'orthodoxy', it is striking that the earliest documentation of the position they represent comes at the earliest a whole century after the writings of Paul.

One can never adequately recuperate the narrative of communities which ultimately died out. The reminder of the 'middle party' experience, as historical fact and therefore also as theological datum, can nonetheless be salutary, if it awakens the awareness that the 'main-line' perspective which we know the best, because its heirs came to dominate our culture, was not thus dominant at the time. At the same time when the first Hellenized Christian exegetes were beginning to deny to Judaism any place in the ongoing purposes of God, and when the first most antagonistic (but unrepresentative) rabbis were beginning to restructure their theology to build into it a corresponding rejection, not only of the messianic Jews who were their contemporaries (i.e. the 'Christians') and were still in their synagogues, but of messianism as such, there were still, for several generations more, a number of messianic Jews, (i.e. 'Christians'), at first in fact a larger number of them, who had not broken fellowship with their non-messianic cousins, nor ceased to attend the synagogue, nor been told that they should, nor ceased to observe *kashrut*. There was a considerable number of God-fearing persons of Gentile blood who took on willingly the restraints of the apostolic decree (Acts 15.19ff. and 21.25)[25] in order not to create a barrier between them and the others for whom also (to use Paul's language) Christ had died.

To recapitulate our argument thus far: The story of the interaction of Jews and Christians in the first century must be retold in the awareness that it has been misused for ages. Any reformulation of the narrative of 'the Jewish–Christian schism' is unsure, when all of the available language has already been used wrongly. All of the identifiable issues have already been misdefined, for so long that we have very little trust potential left for the possibility that serious dialogue can ever take place between Jews and Christians without falling back into the gaping ruts.

E. Is There Another Way? Could There Have Been?

The alternative construction begins where we already were, with the record that in the first century of our era Jewry existed but *not Judaism*. That is to say: there did not exist one standard definition, either intellectually in a body of concepts, or institutionally in an agency, qualified to define Jewish identity in a normative way, as the rabbis could two centuries later. One Jew can contest a fellow Jew's faithfulness to the Torah, but one Jew cannot tell a fellow Jew that he/she is not Jewish. Jewry is defined partly territorially, in that the centrality of Jerusalem and the Land can never be challenged, and yet that territorial definition is not precise and essential as for a Swede or an Afrikaner. One can perfectly well maintain Jewish identity for several generations of life abroad, while the attachment to Jerusalem is only symbolic and liturgical. Certainly Jewry has an ethic definition, because a Jew is normally a child of a Jewish mother, yet by virtue of their success in proselytizing, to which already Jesus referred, and because of their voluntary and involuntary mobility, there was probably less genetic purity among Jews than among most other ethnic groups.

Thus the stream of Jewish population and culture is not firmly definable by any of the standard criteria. It is ethnic, but more than that. It is geographic, but more than that. It is ethical, but with considerable leeway in details of compliance. It is gathered around community practices of prayer, Scripture study and preaching, yet less concerned about the proprieties of ritual or dogma than most other religions (including most Christianity) which we are accustomed to define in terms of their cult practices. Yet the inadequacy of each of these definitions does not mean that Jewishness was vague.

It is into this ill-defined but powerfully self-aware pool of people that the message of Jesus fell, alongside many other catalytic messages, charismatic persons and organizing principles, among which the Pharisees, the Essenes and the Zealots were the most nearly analogous. The message and memory of Jesus persisted in the form of an organized sub-group within Jewry, perhaps somewhat more firmly organized than some of the Pharisaic *chabouroth*, less firmly than an Essene commune, certainly differently organized from the Zealot bands, but hardly fundamentally different from those other sub-groupings at the point of being recognized as an entity fully at home within Jewish population and culture. What we know about the first generation of this movement gives us no basis for projecting how it would have to break with the rest of Jewry.

Our present analysis need not be concerned with knowing the *size* or even the duration of the survival of the middle range of believers, fellowshipping and debating both with Jews whom their presence embarrassed and with Gentile Christians previously culturally inclined to anti-semitism. What matters for theological purposes is that such a position could exist at all, and that it could be held for generations, if not for centuries, by living communities.[26]

The real division had to come much later because it *could* only come in the diaspora situation, only after Bar Kochba and only after further developments within rabbinic thought and social forms. Here too (in the post-Kochba diaspora) most 'Christians' were Jews and the 'Christian' community was part of the Jewish community. The 'Christians' did not differ at the point of keeping the law, because as we can tell from the writings of Paul[27] they did keep the law, although with their own understanding of just why.

They obviously differed at the point of specific beliefs about Jesus, but that was a difference which was tolerable within Jewish pluralism (and had been for generations already). They did not differ by being less concerned for Jerusalem. The difference was a very thin line between degrees or tonalities in the attitude towards the incorporation of the Gentiles into the faith of Abraham. Should that widening of the covenant be permitted, or even encouraged to proceed so wholeheartedly and so rapidly as to shake the structures of the diaspora minority community? Or should it be expected and permitted to happen only around the fringes of the community, in such a way as to leave its core leadership among the old ethnic families? This is a most natural structural issue in any growing human movement. It is no surprise that it should have threatened and divided the Jewish community in every city where the new Messianic movement came with some vigour.

But even then, even when local synagogues broke asunder, that breach was not a basis for creating two movements, separate from each other, and each united within itself. The Jews at Ephesus or at Corinth or at Beroea who did not accept the messianic message did not thereby acquire a distinctive theological identity and become 'normative Judaism'. They are defined thus far only at one point, negatively, by their not having moved (yet) into the next phase into which the messengers of Jesus say all Jewry is invited. They did not thereby have (or think they needed) a rationale or a structure for being non-Christian Jews. That rationale and structure could be developed only gradually, as the refugee school at Yavneh, later at Usha, could go on to establish its prestige and spokesmanship, as the lessons of the collapse of the Herodian and Sadducean strategies could sink in, and as the Zealot strategy's having failed not once – but once again – could be thought through.

Only after that sifting process, which could only enter its final phase after 135 CE, can we begin to affirm a discernible (non-or even anti-messianic) Rabbinic Jewish identity. Only after that will the rabbinic patterns of guidance, instead of representing one cultural stream among many, settle into being the backbone of their people's self-understanding. Only after that could safeguarding the chains of oral identity become codifiable.[28] Even this much later, even in the jelling of the *Mishna*, that vast corpus of traditions was never to become 'canon' as is the Hebrew Bible, or like the New Testament for Christians. The *Mishna* is too large, and too complex to function that way, even if the rabbis had wanted it to, and they did not.

Where does this leave us systemically, i.e. in terms of what 'could possibly have been'? In the very earliest sense we can begin to see 'normative Judaism' as a possibility after Bar Kochba. In another sense, it can be seen as a reality only at least a century later, with the redaction and reception of the *Mishna*. Whichever be the date, Judaism *so defined* is younger than Christianity.

In sum: the standard account with which we began is *wrong on all counts*. Nobody withdrew from anybody; neither 'religion' ejected the other or left the other; but later Judaism is more marked by its rejection of the messianic Jews' claims than the New Testament is marked by any rejection of what the other Jews stood for. The Christian 'New Testament' includes significant sections – most of James and the Apocalypse as well as some sections of the letters of Peter (as at the other end, most of the teachings of Jesus) – which are not uniquely messianic and could have been written by non-Christians.[29]

Nothing in the Christianity of the apostolic canon is anti-Jewish, or even un-Jewish or non-Jewish, unless it be read in the light of later Christian prejudice. *Christian anti-Judaism* arose well *after* the apostolic/canonical period, from causes running counter to the apostolic experience and witness. Thus 'normative Christianity', when defined by the Christian canon rather than by the fourth century and its anti-Jewish precursors, was documented, as a Jewish movement, before the Jewish–Christian split. The apostolic writings do not call for or legitimate such a split; whereas the documents of specifiably non-Christian Judaism come in their written form from long after the split. The Judaism of the *Mishna*, being post-schism, is committed (in some but in fact very few of its parts) to being non- or anti-messianic, whereas the Christianity of the New Testament is entirely committed to being Jewish.

The adjustment of Judaism to the division, which by the nature of the case can only have been experienced after 150, then came to be concretized by developing a firm doctrine, according to which Jews do not look forward to the ingathering of the Gentiles and therefore need to give some other interpretation to the prophetic texts which seem to promise that. The rabbis came to need, as they had not needed it before, a way to affirm that the Gentiles can please God in other ways than by keeping the law and gathering in synagogues. That position developed in the form of an appeal to the covenant of God with Noah. It is doubtful that the rabbinic texts which hold out another hope for Gentiles to have a place in 'the world to come' can be dated earlier than the second century.[30] Before the schism, texts like Isaiah 66.23: 'all flesh shall come to worship before me, says JHWH', probably meant, to any Jews who thought about it, that in some future time, the praise of JHWH/Adonai, alone, and its expression in Jerusalem through Temple ritual, would be the belief and practice of all peoples. After the schism, on the other hand, the way in which the *goyim* can serve the true God is different, and it is specified. To keep the Noachic law is enough to give a Gentile a share in the world to come.

This notion of the adequacy of the Noachic covenant has to be a speculative construct after the fact. We cannot well imagine a Jew either informing a Gentile that what really matters in preparing for the age to come is that set of six or so rules, or demonstrating by a survey of what Gentiles already know that such information is a legacy of Noah's age which is still common to them all.

As long as neither polar party disposed of the power of the civil sword, as long as neither community was administered by a theologically justified centralized hierarchy, and as long as social communications were informal, there was no force in the world to make it impossible for a person, or for many persons, to be in communion at the same time with the rest of the Jews and the rest of the Christians, and to live in the overlap between the two populations, maintaining social relations and attending worship events with both.

By 'being in communion' I obviously do not mean that such persons would have defined their fellowship 'in both directions' in terms of centralized hierarchy or systematic theology: such criteria did not exist then. Nor do I mean being in full agreement with everyone on 'both sides'. Both what later historians were to call the Jewish community and what later historians were to call the Christian community were divided all the time by parties, splits and sects. Each of the two major streams was torn by 'internal' divisions just as fundamental as the difference between them. Yet the total social stream in which these divisions operated – and within which people saw one another as fellow-believers worthy of debating with, worthy of dividing from over issues of truth that both cared about – was still the wider stream of missionizing Judaic culture which *both* the non-messianic rabbis and the messianic *didascaloi* and prophets and elders were trying to lead.

We do not know *for sure* of *any* rabbi trying to drive a wedge between himself and the *nozrim* before Justin began driving his wedge between himself and the Jewish church. If Justin's need for Gentile respectability had not lead him to be ready to split the church, we cannot be sure the rabbis would have reciprocated in kind.

F. The Contemporary Value of this Review of the Ancient Schism

Why should it be of interest in the twentieth century to restate, in order to refute them, the inherited standard accounts of the history of the first four centuries? Can that be ever of more than archaeological interest? It certainly can. In this day, even in the post-Auschwitz renewal of Christian understandings of the Jewishness of the apostolic community, and even in the contemporary rabbinic renewal of the understanding of suffering and defeat in a world under God (to speak only for now of theologians), the old accounts still control us.

Whether in the investment which some Christians are now making in seeking a new relationship to the Jewish community in the western world, or in the highly original work of Jewish thinkers coming up from under the shadows of their own conversation with European accommodation, it still continues to be assumed, on the several sides of the contemporary discussion – even on the part of those parties the most interested in innovation and in dialogue – that there was from the outset a structurally ineluctable incompatibility between Jewish identity and the recognition of Jesus as Messiah. Yet we know that such an incompatibility was culturally impossible in the year 20 or the year 60 of our era. Even in 140 or 160 CE it would have been an odd idea to most. That divisive second century of our era thus remains foundational for all of us in such a way that to reread it with new vision, especially if in so doing we should come to see some facts afresh, or to see some paths as having turned out later to be very wrong, is to redefine ourselves, i.e. to repent. Christians need that.

It does make a difference, even for today, if as a matter of fact for generations non-messianic and messianic Jews and messianically missionized Gentiles could continue to read the *Tanakh* together, to pray together, to break bread together, and to consider themselves as part of one people of God, however strained and threatened, one family of Abraham under the heels of the emperors of Persia or of Rome.

According to the standard later western account of these matters, which is not deeply challenged even by much contemporary theological re-interpretation, that *could* have happened. Yet according to the record, *it did*. If that is the case, then there must be something wrong with the standard account. If then there is something wrong with this standard understanding, as an inadequate explication of several centuries of our early common history, it ought to follow that our coming to grips with that misperception might contribute something to our continuing search for who we want to be together.

It might be that an effort to reconceive the meaning of the original division could cast significant light on the meaning of ongoing debates within both contemporary communities, as well as on the options and openings we might hope for between them. The promising initiatives which have arisen in the past generation, in the direction of dialogue between Christians and Jews, have been understandably marked by a fear of putting truth questions.

Christians have tended to accept the blame for the 'mainstream' western history, and have begun to see at which points repentance occasioned by that history could change their own manners or their own theology. Jews have so recently come from under the shadow of Auschwitz that they did not need to open before Gentiles the full spectrum of intra-Jewish debate about their own identity. Now that in the State of Israel the Judaism of our century has again had a founder, David Ben Gurion, and again a zealot, Menachem Begin,[31] again its own experience of establishment and of empire, so that there has arisen a new spectrum of non-ghetto Jewish stances, perhaps the conversation can begin on other terms, with a different ethos from that of the first modern generations.

There are Christians who never approved of establishment and empire, and there are Jews who never experienced Auschwitz. The spectrum of differences *within* each of the faith communities is now broader than the distance between their centres; the terrain of their overlap may again become substantial.

I have been telling the story thus far in terms of communal cultural experience, or what might be called the historical sociology of the Christian–Jewish relationship. Yet the ultimate intention of this study is theological, interpreting the notion of 'theology' especially in the ethical and pastoral modes.

Most of the argument I have been making here appeals back to the original documents and the earliest history. It can however also be supported strongly with reference to recent developments, whereby the data of the debate have been reori-ented from quite different angles.[32] Numerous Christians in recent centuries have adjusted in most varied ways to their conclusion that in Jesus the Messiah had not come after all, in the sense in which the earliest Christian believers thought that to be the case. Does that in some sense make them 'Jewish'?

Still more numerous western theologians have worked out, in ways that they believe to be intellectually responsible, their conclusion that Christians should not look forward to a 'coming of Christ' in the way the early believers did. That should by all logic then re-open the question of what difference it made in the first centuries to be messianic or not. If they do not confess Jesus as Christ then in what sense are they 'Christian'? Would not that make them either pagans or Jews?

The same can be said *mutatis mutandis* for the shaking of the intellectual foun-dations of twentieth-century Judaism. Some Jews have come to believe that some of their fathers had been wrong in hoping in early modern times for an increasingly peaceable and fruitful assimilation into the culture of the *goyim,* and that others of their fathers were wrong in the certainty that there would be no restoration of civil Israel before the coming of the son of David in some transhistorical sense. The hopes which Jews had developed in the west in the previous centuries for the gradual coming of a peaceable kingdom somehow within the western experience were smashed (not for the first time, but more brutally than in earlier pogroms) by the Nazis. On the other hand, the perennial but unhurried expectance, typical of the rabbis for centuries, with regard to the renewal of an earthly kingdom around Jerusalem, has been reversed by the impact of geopolitical forces beyond anyone's calculation, but also by the leadership of great personalities with the portentous names of Theodore (i.e. Jochanan), David, and Menachem.[33] Jews today live in an age of fulfilled promises, yet they are the heirs of those who in the second and third centuries took the other side, saying that the promises were not fulfilled (some saying even that they never would be).

Thus from both sides of the wall, what it means to be consistently messianic (i.e. 'Christian') or non-messianic is once again up for grabs in both communities. Is it not then even more odd that thinkers in both communities should seek to stand by the thesis of an ineluctable incompatibility which is supposed to have settled every-thing negatively as soon as Jesus was once called 'Anointed' by some Jews? The preceding argument has made the case that we must dare to revise our understand-ing of this history. After all, it did not have to be. *Tertium datur.*[34]

Notes

1. [Editors' Note: This essay originated as a lecture given by John Howard Yoder (Oct. 1977) as one of a series of campus lectures sponsored by the University of Notre Theology Department. Some fifteen years later, Yoder revised the essay (1992) based on the version he presented in the first of his Menno Simons Lectures at Bethel College, North Newton, Kansas (1982) and the first of his Huff Lectures at Earlham College (1985). The revised draft found its way into the 'Shalom Desktop packet' of essays (1996) which is the basis of this collection. In preparing the text for publication, the editors have restored some of the notes and allusions that were found in the earliest version of the essay. Also, in order to create a more readable text, the editors have

deleted those references that were specific to the audiences of the later version; however, the substance of the argument has not been altered.]

2. The same point was made by the title of the earliest presentation of this lecture at the University of Notre Dame: *tertium datur*.

3. I have since had to make the same point concerning ways of reading the history of the conflicts of the early Protestant Reformation with too much information of how it had to go. Cf. my 'The Burden of Evangelical Revision' in James Juhnke (ed.), *Nonviolent America*, North Newton, KS: Bethel College, 1992, 21–37.

4. My first lecture on this theme, at Buenos Aires in 1971, was undertaken as indicated in response to an invitation to articulate a 'free church perspective' on the Jewish–Christian dialogue. For more background on the 'free church' or 'radical reformation' perspective, cf. Donald Durnbaugh, *The Believers' Church*, New York: Macmillan, 1968 and also James Leo Garrett, Jr., (ed.) *The Concept of the Believers' Church*, Scottdale, PA: Herald Press, 1969. Yet the notion of biblically guided reformation is not the property of 'radicals.' More broadly, the same is the case for Protestant movements in general.

5. Many dissenters have called for freedom of religion for themselves without being equally committed to the same liberties for others. The authentically 'radical' reformers however did not accept 'establishment' even for their own truth. Roger Williams and William Penn exemplified that renunciation.

6. Cf. John Howard Yoder, 'The Wider Setting of Liberation Theology' in *The Review of Politics,* 52, Spring 1990, 285–96.

7. [Editors' Note: In the earliest version of this essay, Yoder followed up this identification of himself as an 'amateur' with this remark about some of his 'local' conversation partners in the Theology Department at the University of Notre Dame: 'I must lean very heavily on the wisdom of many others who have supported my right to ask these questions, and who in the realms of their respective expertise have confirmed the validity of my search for alternative frameworks . . . I must especially acknowledge the encouragement of colleague Charles Primus, whose perspective on early post-temple Judaism is crucial to my hypothesis. I also have more to learn from colleague Robert Wilken, who has surveyed the same topic for a period just a little later.']

8. When I first opened this theme informally in Buenos Aires in 1971, and in informal lectures at the Tantur Ecumenical Institute (West Bank) in 1976 and then at the University of Notre Dame (Indiana) in 1977, these methodological suggestions appeared somewhat original. In 1996 that is hardly the case. The argument which was new then is on the way to becoming a generally accepted wisdom though many do not draw from it the lessons I do here.

9. [Editors' Note: The original text of this essay does not provide a citation for this reference to Neusner's argument about Judaism after the destruction of the temple in 70 CE. Yoder probably has in mind Jacob Neusner's study *Method and Meaning in Ancient Judaism* (Missoula: Scholars Press, 1979), which he cites in a similar context in chapter ten of this collection of essays.]

10. This is the theme concerning which the accumulation of scholarly confirmation has been most impressive in the quarter-century since I first stated the thesis: Notable are the works of Lloyd Gaston, Neil Elliott, Alan Segal, Mark Nanos.

11. The strongest term for Jesus' attitude to the law is 'fulfil', that provides leverage for his critique of the righteousness of 'scribes and Pharisees' who 'loosened' some of its provisions.

12. At the time (1977) I wrote the first version of this essay this was a debatable thesis. Since then it has come to seem much less daring, thanks to the work of Krister Stendahl, Lloyd Gaston, Alan Segal, and Mark Nanos.

13. When I first wrote, the nation that *ioudaioi* in John should best be rendered 'the Judaean establishment' had first been argued in a dissertation of which Prof. Markus Barth spoke to me. Now a wide body of scholarship pointing in that direction is summarized by Urnab C. Von Wahle, 'The Johannine "Jews": A Critical Survey' in *New Testament Studies*, 28, 33–60. Cf. Also David G. Burke, 'Translating *Hoi Ioudaioi* in the New Testament, *Explorations 9/2*, 1995, 1–7.

14. One of the more trendy new translations renders the term simply 'the authorities'. [Editors' Note: Yoder appears to have had the New English Bible in mind here.]

15. Cf. Douglas R. A. Hare, *The Theme of Jewish Persecution of Christians in the Gospel According to Saint Matthew*, Boston, MA: Cambridge University Press, 1967. The apostle Paul wrote (2 Cor. 11.24) that he had twice been scourged with 39 strokes of the lash. That is a discipline of the synagogue. His receiving it proves that both he and the synagogue leadership considered him as a Jew under their jurisdiction.

16. One Catholic historian used the term 'encyclical' to express his notion of a letter going out from the rabbinic academy of Yavneh [also transliterated as 'Jabneh' or 'Jamnia'] to instruct all of world Jewry to add this new line to the *amida*. Every word in that statement is an anachronism; Yavneh was not an academy and it sent no encyclicals. This is an excellent specimen of the misleading application to the rabbinic world of mental habits from the Vatican.

17. J. Louis Martyn, *History and Theology in the Fourth Gospel*, New York, NY: Harper & Row 1968. I reported above how Louis Martyn made much of the notion that around the year 85, under the leadership of Gamaliel II, a 'blessing against the heretics' was added to the daily prayer formula, the *amida* or 'eighteen blessings'. The hypothesis killed several birds with one stone. It offered an explanation of the origin of the apparent 'anti-Jewish' tone of the Fourth Gospel, at a late enough date that the first-generation gospels would not bear that burden. It thereby located the responsibility for Jewish rejection of Christianity on the side of the rabbis. Yet as I already indicated in the earlier setting, the hypothesis makes impossible assumptions. The rabbinic 'school' of Yavneh was nothing like a Vatican. It did not send out encyclicals. There is no documentation of any policy of hostility toward messianic Jews on the part of rabbinic authorities before 135. Most likely if conflict arose then it would have been as a result of their not supporting Bar Kochba in his military venture.

18. For more on this theme see Chapter 5.

19. The clearest evaluation of the Martyn hypothesis is that of Reuben Kimmelman 'Birkat ha Minim and the lack of evidence for an anti-Christian Jewish Prayer in Late Antiquity' pp. 226–44 in E. P. Sanders (ed.), *Aspects of Judaism in the Graeco-Roman Period*, Vol. II of *Jewish and Christian Self-Definition*, Philadelphia, PA: Fortress Press, 1981. Certainly no Jew in the first two centuries could have understood the term 'arrogant *Kingdom*' to mean Messianic Jews.

20. I shall attend later to the efforts of some scholars to date the 'parting of the ways' around 135 or a century later. That project is however vitiated by the variety of meanings of the question.

21. Rosemary Radford Ruether *Faith and Fratricide*: *The Theological Roots of Anti-Semitism*, New York, NY: Seabury Press, 1974.

22. Martin Hengel, *The Son of God: The Origins of Christology and the History of Jewish–Hellenisic Relations*, Philadelphia, PA: Fortress Press, 1976. Likewise Willi Marxsen's *The Resurrection of Jesus of Nazareth*, trans. M. Kohl, Philadelphia: Fortress Press, 1970. In fact such language would make sense only in a Jewish setting. Several of the papers in Alan Davies (ed.), *Antisemitism and the Foundations of Christianity*, New York, NY: Paulist Press, 1979, identify more fully this flaw in Ruether's account.

23. This points back to the methodological rigidity which I denounced at the outset of this essay; one of the strongest angles on the argument that some specific split had to take place somewhere in the past is derived from the claim that two positions cannot be reconciled.

24. [Editors' Note: Yoder provides the following explanation of the ebionite understanding of the significance of Jesus of Nazareth in his book *The Politics of Jesus*, Grand Rapids, MI: Eerdmans, 1972, 100. To see Jesus through 'ebionitic eyes' is to limit 'his relevance to that which one chooses to attribute to his human status as a radical rabbi' (100). In the first chapter of *The Politics of Jesus*, Yoder engages those who doubt the possibility of a 'messianic ethic' with the following sequence of questions: '. . . what becomes of the meaning of incarnation if Jesus is not normative man? If he is a man but not normative, is this not the ancient ebionitic heresy? If he be somehow authoritative but not in his humanness, is this not a new gnosticism?' (22).

For a more systematic and very perceptive discussion of Yoder's christology and the ways it diverges from the ebionitic view of Jesus, see Craig Carter, *The Politics of the Cross: The Theology and Social Ethics of John Howard Yoder*, Grand Rapids, MI: Brazos Press, 2001, 50, n. 91 and 65–6.]

25. See Chapter 3 n. 8 for a more detailed discussion of both the 'God-fearers' and the 'apostolic decree.'

26. To judge by the series of sermons preached by Chrysostom against the Jews, the phenomenon was still present in the fifth century. St John Chrysostom, *The Eight Discourses against Judaizing Christians*, trans. Paul W. Harkins, Washington: Catholic University of America Press, 1977.

27. This is not to claim that Paul was representative, or dominant. He clearly was neither, at the time. His is however a coherent and credible voice, which the much later formation of the canon somehow ratified.

28. It is part of the standard paradox. Both for the rabbis and later for Rome, the way to clarify the status of the 'oral Torah' was to write down both its content and its authority claims.

29. Dr Charles Primus, my colleague at Notre Dame when this lecture was first presented in a departmental seminar in 1977, often said that the New Testament is the most reliable, least-edited, most datable extant source of historical information of Judaism in that century.

30. Cf. Chapter 3, n. 8 below.

31. [Editors' Note: Here Yoder refers to two twentieth-century Israeli political leaders. David Ben Gurion was the first prime minister of the State of Israel. Menachem Begin was the name of the Likud politician who served as prime minister from 1975–1981, and who, along with Egyptian President Sadat, signed the Camp David accords in 1978.]

32. See Chapters 7–9 below.

33. [Editors' Note: Here Yoder's wordplay has in view Theodore Hertzl, the person who articulated Zionism and called for the founding of the nation state of Israel. See note 31 for clarification of the references to David Ben Gurion and Menachem Begin]

34. [The final two sentences of this chapter have been added to the original text by the editors as a means of reiterating Yoder's primary thesis in this essay.]

Commentary

PETER OCHS

Yoder's overall vision that 'it did not have to be' is an ultimate prototype for what it would mean to be open to dialogue with Jews and Judaism (p. 43). His argument is based on what we have called 'depth historiography', criticizing any effort to reduce all history to its plain sense: 'We do violence to the depth and density of the story if, knowing with the wisdom of later centuries that it came out as it did, we box the actors of a first century into our wisdom about their children's fate in the second' (p. 44). Yoder assumes we need to begin with plain sense history ('to get the facts straight'), but that we must seek, in addition, 'to put ourselves so effectively into the psychic skins of the actors of those days that we can say that the history looks open: it could have gone otherwise' (p. 44). This is no mere effort to replay Schleiermacher, since we are not claiming as plain sense historians to know the ancient actors 'better than they knew themselves'. We are claiming, instead, to learn about ourselves now by imagining ourselves in their skins then. I trust that this is, indeed, a lesson that both Christians and Jews need to learn: to overcome the presumption that there was 'one Judaism' and 'one Christianity' back then and that they were separate and, to a great extent, mutually exclusive. With appropriate warrants in more recent rabbinic scholarship, Yoder argues that the Judaisms of the Roman era were pluriform and that proto-rabbinic Judaism competed for religious authority among several other forms, including the Nazarenes (or followers of Jesus) and other messianic movements (pp. 46 ff.). There is, therefore, no evidence of a single, 'normative Judaism' in this era. Yoder's broadest conclusion is compelling as well: that the evidence does not warrant the conventional assumptions that early Christianity rejected 'Judaism' and that first- and early second-century Judaism rejected 'Christianity' (pp. 49 ff.). Jesus' work takes place within the people Israel and within the Judaisms of his time (p. 49); Paul extends a messianic Judaism to the Gentile nations as his way of practising Judaism (p. 50); and the Gospel of John did not seek to condemn 'the Jews' in general, but only a certain part of what he took to be the Jewish 'establishment' (pp. 50–1). What we take to be early Christian–Jewish invectives were, therefore, intra-Jewish invectives, typical in energy and acerbic tone to intra-Jewish debates of this period. This means that it would be anachronistic to claim that 'the Jews rejected Christianity' (p. 51). Many Jewish movements rejected the claims of many other Jewish movements, but without rejecting the membership of the other claimants in the people Israel.

There is also appropriate scholarly warrant for Yoder's next broad claim: that the Jewish–Christian schism emerged gradually, and, first, for political reasons, after 135 CE and the Roman Wars and, definitively, only after the emergence of Constantinian Christianity in the fourth century (pp. 56 ff.). Historians will, appropriately, continue to debate plain-sense evidence about the precise dates and contours of the Jewish–Christian schism, but Yoder shows us where the clear evidence is not what we may customarily think and where the historical reality may have been so complex and fluid as to warrant our reading it with much more imagination. His strongest two contributions are, first, to criticize conventional tendencies to read the later separation of Judaism and Christianity back into the plain-sense evidence of the first two centuries; and, second, to argue that the historical evidence warrants our imagining a past pregnant with much more unexpected possibility than we customarily allow.

Yoder's argument is burdened, however, whenever he appears to forget his own generalization: that the identities and borders of these religious movements remain vague in the early centuries and that, therefore, we should expect to find conflicting evidences. Yoder's openness to new forms of Jewish–Christian sharing is closed down when he claims already to know in advance what that sharing should be. We have reason to applaud Yoder's claim that early Christian (Nazarene) Judaism was just as Jewish as early Rabbinic Judaism (pp. 47–9), since he reminds both Christians and Jews that what we call early Christianity was a messianic movement within first-century Judaism. We have reason to be wary, however, of his use of this claim to equalize the legitimacy of the Jesus movement, as if Jesus and then Paul's followers were as central to the normative centres of first- and second-century Judaisms as the followers of Hillel and Akiva. Here he is reading his understanding of a later Christianity back into the early centuries.

We should be troubled, for example, by Yoder's claiming, on the one hand, that we cannot 'recuperate the narratives of communities which died out' (p. 57) and that there was no single Judaism in the first century (p. 58), but, on the other hand, that we should recognize diasporic, 'Jeremiac Judaism' as the essential thrust of first-century Judaism (the claim of his later chapters). There is the potential here for a supersessionist strategy. I read these contradictory tendencies in Yoder's Jewish–Christian writings as signs of a pioneer's work: both reproducing the old order that nurtured him (the supersessionist order) and generating a new order (beyond supersessionism). He has made his contribution; the challenge is for his students to continue the new order he introduced, and let go of the old one.

2

Jesus the Jewish Pacifist[1]

A. The Standard Anti-Jewish View of Jesus

We have learned that instead of thinking of 'Christianity' and 'Judaism' as systems, existing primordially in a 'normative' form, and instead of thinking of 'Christians' and 'Jews' in the early centuries as separate bodies existing over against each other, we must think of two initially largely overlapping circles. The circle 'Church' and the circle 'Jewry' overlapped for generations, in the persons whom we may call either messianic Jews or Jewish Christians, who for over a century at least stood in fellowship with both wider circles. They were not split apart from one another by Jesus' being honoured as Messiah, nor by anyone's keeping or not keeping the law.

The split which was ultimately to push the circles apart began, we saw, not in the first century but in the second. It began not as a cleft between the two larger circles but as a schism within each of the communities. People like the 'apologetic father' Justin began splitting the Church over the issue of respect for Jewish culture, and some rabbis began pushing out the *nozrim* who wanted to stay in their synagogues. 'Justin's wedge' is dated about 150; the 'rabbis' wedge' returned the insult at least a generation later.[2]

But is there not a clash between the two on the level of ethics? It is that question to which we now turn. We turn to the place where, according to the standard account, there should have been such a dichotomy. We have routinely been told that the reason 'the Jews' refused to accept Jesus was that they desired an earthly kingdom, which Jesus did not provide. His 'kingdom' was 'spiritual'; their desire was for a political national renewal. Therefore they rejected him, and he them.

This account is difficult to connect with the fact that the people most opposed to Jesus were the ones who wanted no national renewal, since they (the so called 'Herodians' and 'Sadducees') were already getting along quite well with the Romans. It is also difficult to reconcile with the fact that the people most attracted to Jesus were the disinherited and the nationalist freedom fighters of his time.[3]

Secondly, the standard account says, Jesus' pacifism is a rejection of the Old Testament story, with its holy wars and righteous royalty. Thus the position Jesus is portrayed as taking was anti-Jewish. Three times in Matt. 5 his phrase, '. . . but I say to you . . .' identified within the old regime issues of violence and the treatment of enemies. Love of the enemy is frequently characterized as the point at which Jesus is most original over against 'the Jews'.[4]

Thirdly, Jesus' pacifism is thought to be the product of mental moves, or moral insights, which we might call 'individualization' and 'interiorization'. We think of his saying that angry thoughts or language are as bad as killing, or lustful thoughts as bad as adultery. Jewish morality, it is held, was external and communitarian. Or, others will say, Jesus was apocalyptic, impatient, expecting divine intervention in history, whereas 'the Jews' were more realistic about the world's regularities.

This view has been held, not surprisingly, by Christian pacifist minorities, who could use the 'but I say to you' passages as an answer to others' arguments about wars having been morally legitimate in the Old Testament. More surprising is the fact that non-pacifist Christians often include Jesus' rejection of militant nationalism and violence as part of the reason for his being rejected by 'the Jews', even though they do not take his teaching on those matters as normative for themselves now.

This illustrates the way in which, once western Christians have had it decided for them that 'the Jews' are to serve as a foil, to be accused of whatever counter-view will serve to make the Christians look better, then 'the Jews' can be described in ways quite unjustified by the record.

In the Gospel accounts Jesus is rejected by many individuals and sometimes by the leaders of groups of people, for various reasons, but his nonviolence is not given as a reason. Neither is his calling for the law to be 'fulfilled'. Thus the first thesis of the 'standard account' is wrong. Jesus did not reject anything Jewish in calling for love of enemy, and those who reject what he said on that topic do not reject it because they are Jewish.[5] Most who reject what he said are not Jewish.

Jesus' own statement of the point of the contrasts in Matt. 5 was that he was bringing not rejection but fulfilment of what the Torah had really always intended. His preface to the six contrasts was: 'Do not imagine that I have come to abolish the law or the prophets.' His call was for a 'greater righteousness' than that of other teachers, marked by none of the commandments' being 'dissolved' or relaxed. This stated intent is confirmed when we analyse the substance of the contrasts. The intent of the original Torah is broadened, or intensified, or interiorized by the antitheses: never diverted or negated.

There must then be, in the mind of the Jesus of Matthew, an original intent which we can discern as having been within the Torah itself, which points toward the renunciation of violence and the love of the enemy. Without having got that far, the Law and the Prophets must have been reaching, pointing toward that fulfilment. The last words of the same chapter say that in yet another way. There Jesus says that our loving our enemies is the imitation of the limitless love of the heavenly Father, who first loved his enemies.[6]

B. How first-century Jews should read Israelite history

The standard account is wrong, secondly, in fusing the Jewish nationalism of Jesus' time with the memory of the ancient wars of JHWH. Christians' understandings of the import of the wars of the Hebrew story have been skewed by the use of the example of Joshua or David by Christians since Constantine, who have made it part of their argument against the ethics of Jesus.

Readers of the same *Tanakh* (Hebrew Scriptures) in the first century had another perspective. Without denying in the least the nation-forming events at the roots of their identity, Jews knew that their story had moved far beyond there.[7]

Already in the histories of the age of Gideon and Jotham, Samuel and Saul, the recognition of JHWH as a warrior and king had led to rejecting, not accepting, the notion that Israel should adopt the institution of kingship 'like the other nations'. The later review of that national story by the prophets became still more critical of kingship. National independence was forfeited, first in the North and then in Judaea as well, because of the unwillingness of the kings and the people to trust God for their national survival. With Jeremiah God abandoned kingship as a vehicle of his people's identity. With Ezra and Nehemiah the return to live and worship in Judaea was brought about without political independence or a king.[8] The Maccabean adventure, although militarily successful for a time, ultimately further discredited the holy war vision. The texts of Esther and Daniel (whatever be the historical value of the reminiscences behind them), fill out the picture of the faithful life that can be lived under pagan kings.

Jesus' realism about the claims of 'the kings of the nations' to be 'benefactors,' and his projecting a different path for both himself and his followers (Luke 22.26) may well represent a widespread current of folk wisdom about royal benefactors whether Jewish or Gentile, already current among his audiences.[9] Jesus thereby prolonged the critical stance which previous centuries of Jewish experience had already rehearsed.

What the folk culture senses, modern scholarship can spell out with greater sociological detail. The cultural meaning of 'covenant', as the way to be God's people, was in its Ancient Near Eastern origins anti-royal and egalitarian. This has been increasingly clarified by the research of George Mendenhall and Millard Lind, Norman Gottwald and Walter Brueggemann. The covenant was in its origins an alternative both to the Mesopotamian and to the Canaanite models of 'kingship', as one can see already in Judges and 1 Samuel. Israelite identity was not defined first by a theoretical monotheism, by cult or *kaschrut*, nor by the decalogue. It was rather defined by the claim of the tribes to 'have no king but JHWH/Adonai'. One strand of Judges/Samuel rejects even the notion of kingship. The other side of the narrative then goes on to prove how right the elders who wanted a king had been, when they got what they asked for.

'Holy war'[10] was thus not a precedent for national war in our time: it was an alternative to the wars of the king, differing from them in cause, means, and outcome. Deuteronomy accepts kingship under conditions (17.14-20) which amount to a condemnation both of the Mesopotamian and Canaanite models and of the way the Israelite history actually worked out.

Chronicles reads the whole history in this light. 'Trust in JHWH/Adonai' is what opens the door to his saving intervention. It is the opposite of making one's own political/military arrangements. Jeremiah's abandoning statehood for the future is thus not so much forsaking an earlier hope as it is returning to the original trust in JHWH.

According to Luke 22 Jesus said he expected to live out the fate of the suffering Servant of JHWH in Isaiah 40-53. Whether this expectation on Jesus' part was the thought only of the evangelist or already of the historical Jesus, and whether the Isaiah text was describing an historical prototype or a purely prophetic hope, is immaterial for our purposes, as is the fact that rabbinic or apocalyptic thought had not otherwise linked the Servant with the messianic age. Already earlier in the Luke's account Jesus had described his own vocation as continuing the line of prophets dying at the hand of and for their own people (Luke 13.33). He thereby moved the understanding of his suffering from the level of ethics alone to that of redemption, tightening the linkage of non-violence with martyrdom, and the linkage of suffering with salvation, which one finds as well among the early Christians, the later Jews, and the (much later) pacifist minority Christians.

Jesus affirmed the opening of a new range of possibilities for obeying the will of God. Jeremiah (31.31) had promised such a new beginning under the designation 'new covenant' and described the renewal of the human heart. John the Baptist had announced its imminence in the form of a washing by the Holy Spirit. Jesus followed John in saying that the kingdom had come near. Later apostolic writers say the same thing in terms of 'new birth' or 'resurrection', or 'Holy Spirit'. This new possibility frees the followers of Jesus from the manipulative consequentialist reckoning, within the assumptions of a closed causal system, which modern 'realistic' Christians use to explain their rejection of his pacifism.

Jesus inserted his call to a new kind of life into the announcement that the kingdom of God was at hand. In whichever way we take that announcement, from something purely future to something already realized, but even more appropriately if, like most readers, we take it in one of the mixed or mediating ways which Gospel scholarship would favour, it grounds Christian behaviour in a new world reality which, however incomplete its implementation still is, nonetheless constitutes an alternative to the way other people are living and their reasons for living those other ways. That kingdom presence is justice and peace. It is imperative but it is also empowerment. One does not then ask why one should behave that way, or whether, if one tries to, one can bring it off, or whether, if one does do it, it will be successful. One has entered into another world which just is that way. We are liberated from enmity as part of the law of the old world.

We could extend further the list of elements within the teaching of Jesus which undergird his rejection of bloodshed and his affirmation of reconciliation. The items just named are those which make the most difference:

– fulfilling the Torah which already in its earlier phases limited enmity;
– imitating the divine nature;
– the new power for deliverance from old patterns;

but there would be more. There would be God's announced purpose of ultimately pacifying the nations. There would be the explanations of the origins of violence and the state provided in the stories of the Fall of Adam, the sin of Cain, and the Covenant with Noah. All of these are, within the world and the backgrounds of Jesus, specifically Jewish ways to reason.

It is not enough, as we seek to understand the way in which the peace commitment of Jesus was Jewish, only to lift from the Gospel accounts those elements of Jewish heritage which throw direct light on moral decision-making. We shall see yet more if we proceed backward, unrolling the history from the perspective of the later non-pacifist (Gentile and Constantinian) Christianity, since it was in the process of becoming non-Jewish that Christianity also became non-pacifist.

C. The Loss of Jewishness as Christianity Became Roman Establishment

When Christianity became the established religion of Caesar's realm, it seemed to those who were at home in that imperial culture that 'the whole world' had been taken over for Christ. Yet on the world scale the Roman Empire, although enormous, was a province. It excluded known civilizations to the north and south and east, including (older and more developed) civilizations to the south and east where Jews had been living for centuries, and Christians for generations. The Jewish world vision was *in lived experience* wider than was the Roman Empire.

This social fact parallels the fundamental notion of monotheism. If there is but one God, then his dignity and power must somehow hold sway over other nations too. Other nations were not merely hypothetically imagined, in the sense that there must be someone out there beyond the confines of the Empire. Jews had cousins living there, worshipping in sister synagogues, and (for the case of Babylon) Jews around the Roman-ruled world received moral guidance from those centres outside Roman control. Likewise the way in which monotheism demanded detachment from civil religion was a safeguard of a wider world-view than the imperial one.

We have been thinking so long of Jews as being in the ghetto and of Rome as being the whole world, that it takes a special mental effort to be able to come to terms with the fact that it was really the other way round. Roman imperial loyalty was a provincial loyalty, albeit on a very large scale, in contrast to the world vision, which Jews were experiencing concretely by being scattered, and which they were confessing theologically by being radically monotheistic, confessing in their regular prayers that their God was not only the object of their reverence but also the maker and sustainer of the cosmos.

In pagan empires, justice was the word of the king. In the Hebrew experience, that was not so. Justice could not be above the pagan emperor since it was he who edicted it, and the priests celebrated his empowerment to do so. For Jews, justice was knowable otherwise: by the oral Torah, by prophets, later by Scriptures. None of these were dependent upon the king. When there was an Israelite king, he stood under, not over the words of JHWH, and it was because Israelite kings did not obey those words that the two Israelite kingdoms did not last. Social value and institutional legitimacy were located in other structures and functions than those the king administered. One could be socially useful by taking care of widows and orphans, and by showing hospitality to outsiders, not only by praising the royal house. Thus both in doctrine and in sociology the king is relativized. He is at best the servant of divine righteousness, not its origin.

When we view the Constantinian shift from the vantage point of that Jewish world, we note that the shift does not only mean that Christians entered a new situation where the ruler was supposed to be one of the believers. It also meant accepting a setting in which the objectivity of the Torah of God as moral norm was replaced by the judgement of a general,[11] within the causal system of political realism, of how best to achieve those of his purposes which he considers to have been entrusted to him by God.

Against this, the Jewish sense of Torah, which is revealed 'from above', i.e. confessed as transcendent, coming from beyond our system and from above our king, provided the defence against sacralizing the aristocracy or the ruler. Constantine represents a 'Fall' from a moral life founded transcendently to one rendered serviceable to the present power structure.[12]

A morality of Torah is structurally an alternative to a morality of 'utility' or of 'prosperity'. To obey the revealed will of God will generally be for our good: that is why, when we obey God, we need not fear in the long run for our survival, or that of good causes. Obedience may however include suffering: suffering may be understood as chastisement, which we willingly confess our sins may have brought upon us, or as moral training. It may also include suffering without moral culpability, because such costly faithfulness is one way to 'sanctify the name' of God. One is therefore protected from a vision of morality, which proceeds by calculating effectiveness in reaching desirable selfish goals for either persons or groups.

What it had meant to trust God for one's survival in the formative period of Israelite national origins, as we saw, was derived from the experience of holy war. When the Israelites did not defend themselves, JHWH defended them. As that truth was transmitted, transposed, into the Jewish experience of the exile, to trust God came to mean believing that there can be survival even through suffering, even in and through the loss of the homeland. Our fate is not in our own hands. We have not been called to undergo any testing without there being a way of escape. That confession (1 Cor. 10.13) is not optimism about our wisdom or our luck. It is Jewish confidence in the power of the God who saves. Both affirmative interpreters of the Sermon on the Mount, like Tolstoy, and critical ones, like Reinhold Niebuhr, have pointed out that love toward the enemy in 5.43ff. is parallel to the renunciation of laying up treasures toward one's future security in 6.19–25. Both assume that trust in God's saving intervention makes obedience 'realistic'. Such trust is what Hebrews 11 calls 'faith', and sees as being rooted and perfected in the sacrifice of Christ.

If then we trust God for the defence not only of his large concerns but also of our own authentic welfare, we shall not be enticed by the kinds of reasoning recently called 'realism' or 'responsibility'. We shall not usually ask 'what would happen if everyone acted the way we think we must?' because being a disarmed minority we know they never will. Our action should be paradigmatic for the coming kingdom, not for how unbelieving majorities can act.[13]

While pursuing further the commonalities underlying Jewish and Christian moral thought in general and Jewish and Christian renunciation of violence in particular, I have left aside for the moment the original description of how Jesus was thought to be non-Jewish or anti-Jewish. Returning to that background theme, I next note that the standard account is also wrong in thinking that the ethic of Jesus is not practical nor socially responsible.

The readiness to be atypical, to be non-conformed, of which I have just been writing, is strengthened by one further turn of the argument in which Jewish thought had already taken the path which Jesus followed further, and which later rabbis took still further. This is the preference for the concrete case. *Halakah*, the tradition about specific behaviour, is clarified and codified sooner and more firmly than *aggadah*, the vision of things in a world under God which makes such behaviour reasonable. The concrete shape of the culture of faithfulness is more crucial to a people's commonality of commitment than is the piety with which it is filled out, kept alive, personalized, and explained to outsiders.

Imperatives like 'go the second mile' or 'first be reconciled with your brother' or 'swear not at all', or reality readings like 'whoever marries a divorced woman commits adultery' or 'if you do not forgive others God will not forgive you' are more trans-culturally translatable, and more foundational in defining a community's identity, than the more abstract 'first principles' from which academics would like to say they are 'derived'. We moderns would like first to say something formal like 'so act that your behaviour could be a rule for everyone'. Then we would like to say something substantial but broad like 'the nature of marriage is . . .' or 'every person has a right to . . .' Only a few logical steps later would we then be willing to get down to specific duties and decisions.

Jesus, Jewry, and the minority churches do it the other way. They first name representative acts that are imperative or excluded. This is *halakah*.[14] Then *aggadah*, 'spirituality', considers why such judgements make good sense.

The tilt toward concreteness can be overdone, of course. It has shortcomings in the face of rapid cultural change, or in the face of ecumenical challenge. It can become 'legalism' in the bad sense of that term. It can build a barrier in the way of cross-cultural communication or service. Here however, we are discussing what originally made a commitment to love the enemy and to renounce violence credible and viable in its challenge to the ethos of establishment.

D. 'Peace' as Good News, as Mission

It was the Jewishness of Jesus, the rootage of his message in the particular heritage of Abraham, Moses, and Jeremiah, which as we have seen made it good news for the whole world. There were other peace philosophers and peace prophets in the Ancient Near East. Only the Jewish world vision, effective in Jochanan and the entire stream of non-Zealot rabbinism, which he catalysed, could make of accepting powerlessness not only a viable compromise but an identity, to make Jewry, beyond the collapse of the Jerusalem polity, into a new kind of culture viable without a state. Only the Jew Jesus, by announcing and accomplishing the fulfilment of God's promises to the Jews, could send out into the world a people of peace open to the Gentiles. Only the Jewish claim that the one true God, known to Abraham's children through their history, was also the Creator and sustainer of the other peoples as well, could enable mission without provincialism, cosmopolitan vision without empire.

How Judaism Since Jesus Went on Being a Peace Church

A. Defining Judaism in Its Own Historical Terms

We open up this other side of the story by reviewing the necessary clarification of language. We have begun to see through the confusion created for us by thinking that 'Judaism' is the religion of the Old Testament, unchanged since before Jesus, which by rights should have gone out of existence by the end of the first century, because it had been superseded by 'Christianity'. That orientation preprogrammes us to assume that 'Judaism' today is still what it was back there, with its commitment to the land, to holy warfare, to dietary regulations and its festival calendar drawn from the Old Testament and unchanged since then. That picture was so dominant that for a while reputable Christian scholars would talk about 'late Judaism' when they meant the period stretching more or less from the Maccabees to the fall of Jerusalem.

This is but a part of a much more widely represented tendency which we all have, to violate the reality of history by projecting identities backward behind their point of origin. To think of the Old Testament as 'Jewish' is representative of this. Abraham was neither a Jew nor an Israelite. The name 'Israel' cannot be used to designate a body of people before the sojourn in Egypt. The noun 'Jew' is without meaning until at the very earliest the time of the division under Rehoboam, and is not really functional before the Exile.

A geographically based name only really makes sense to describe an ethnic group if the group is no longer at the place described by the name. Some people in Europe in the sixteenth century were called 'Swiss Brethren'; the term was meaningful in Alsace or Moravia as it would not have been in Switzerland. Later in that century dissident communities in Holland were divided among tendencies called 'Frisian', 'Flemish' and 'Waterlander'. The terms, although originally geographical, were useful because the people they described were all living in the same places, and not in the places for which they were named. In the same way, 'Judaism' is first a functional designation when it denotes a people who are surviving outside of Judaea. It properly begins to serve with that meaning in the age of Jeremiah.

What we mean today when we speak of 'Judaism' as part of our world, should most precisely be identified by the further adjective 'rabbinic.' Rabbinic Judaism, as we noted briefly before, is younger than Christianity. It is also in some ways less close to the Hebrew Bible than Christianity is. Its definitive documents came into being later than the Christian New Testament, namely around the year 200, when the massive collection called the *Mishna* was codified by Judah the Great. Because of their particular thoroughly reworked literary form, gathering together by *halakhic* topic the memories and arguments of many earlier rabbis, these documents are historically less reliable, less interested in history, than is the Christian New Testament. They include no epistles, or gospels. The narratives they contain are very brief case descriptions and anecdotes about rabbis with their pupils. The collected accounts of what rabbis are reported to have said have gone through so many hands that the most informed and critical scholar of our generation, Jacob Neusner, warns us to be very careful about whether anything can be sure to have been said at the time of the rabbi to whom it has been attributed: and if it was, knowing this still would add only the barest historical or narrative dimension to the statement.

The *Mishna* is far more voluminous than the Christian New Testament. To know it well, as a bridge between the Hebrew Bible and the present, is a much more demanding discipline than is familiarity with the Christian New Testament. This makes the rabbi reading a text proportionally more important in the mediation of whatever it is about Hebrew Scriptures that will matter to the faithful in our time than the Christian teacher seeks to be.

Other characteristics of the *Mishna* as literature make this even more evidently the case. As the *Mishna* was interested in being inclusive rather than definitive, it often reports both sides of a question, without coming to a conclusion. It cannot be a 'canon' in the sense, which Christians are accustomed to thinking of their Bible as a whole as a 'Rule of faith and life'. It is rather a quarry from which all kinds of resources can be drawn.

The creation of Rabbinic Judaism, subsequent to the formation of the messianic Jewish communities later called 'Christian', occurred as we saw subsequent to the impact of Jesus upon the Jewish people. Yet most Jews of those centuries never 'rejected Jesus'. Living in faraway corners of the diaspora, many of them never heard of Jesus until it was too late for the message to be 'new' for them; i.e. until the message had been de-Judaized by the 'apologetic fathers' and anathematized by the more defensive rabbis. Thus most diaspora Jews kept on living the life set up by the generation of Jeremiah, which Jesus said he had come to 'fulfil' (i.e. confirm), without ever being faced with a chance to accept or reject that claimed fulfilment.[15]

A first definitional mark of rabbinic Jewish identity is its coming to terms with life without Jerusalem and without the Temple. This meant both absence from the Land and loss of the forms of worship tied to the Temple. This is the arrangement initially established for most Jews at the time of Jeremiah and portrayed dramatically in chapter 29 of that prophet's book.

At that time there were prophecies and counter-prophecies concerning the meaning for all Jews, both for those who had been carried off to Babylon and for those who were still back in the land of Israel, of the new situation into which they all had been placed by the destruction of the Temple, the fall of the royal house and the exile of most of the community's leaders. There were prophets, Hanania son of Azzur in chapter 28 and Shemaiah of Nehelam in chapter 29 among them, who were encouraging the people still in the homeland to set up a rump regime, and promising the exiles in Babylon that they would be back within two years.

Jeremiah (i.e. JHWH speaking through Jeremiah) rejected these promises as 'lying dreams'; he threatened prophets and people with further judgements, and called the entire people of Israel, both those already in Babylon and those left behind in the devastated homeland, to see that the course of saving history had now moved to Babylon. That is the place where they should settle down, buy land and plant crops, make money and marry off their children.

The culminating imperative is: 'Work for the good of the country to which I have exiled you. [The Authorized Version says 'Seek the peace of that city'.] Pray to JHWH on its behalf, since on its welfare yours depends' (Jer. 29.7).

The return from exile will come in seventy years, Jeremiah says; but that figure (although it will be looked to later as a literal promise) means on a deeper level 'a long time', so long that present plans should not be based on the idea of return.

From then on until 135 of our era there were many projects of military national renewal, but they all failed. Three of them got as far as a temporary military success, but God did not ratify them with prosperity. Once they had all failed, it became clear that Judaism already had an alternative identity, and an alternative historical vision, away from Jerusalem, which most Jews ever since Jeremiah had been living with, even though the myth of a return to Jerusalem had dominated their hope. Thus the culture of exile already had a momentum of seven centuries when the rabbis after 135 began to face the fact that that was the way it was going to have to stay for a long time.

Rabbinic Judaism is thus the way of life, which makes sense of exile as the way it is going to have to be. The rabbis in Galilee after 135, and the House of Assembly later established at Usha, needed the support of the Babylonians to resume their work, and continued to draw their leaders from there. We can say that 'Rabbinic Judaism' begins *c.* 200 (redaction of the *Mishna*, 135 (defeat of Bar Kochba)), or 70 (loss of the Temple) or still earlier (foundation of the school of Hillel?), depending on the variables we consider important, but the way of life which the rabbis define has been going since 586 BCE.

Jews had already discovered in the diaspora situation, long before Hillel, that there was within their tradition more of what it takes to survive than they had been aware of while they had been focusing their hopes on an imminent return to

Jerusalem. There was for instance the set of hero stories stretching from Joseph through Esther to Daniel and his three friends. These Israelites in pagan courts had all stood up victoriously for the one true God, disobeying non-violently, amidst a hostile pagan culture. Regularly these non-conformist Jews had been helped by God, saved from the designs of godless enemies. Regularly the Gentile sovereigns came to confess the true God, and called (for their own survival) on the wisdom of the Jew who had run such heroic risks, to share with them from then on in the management of the realm.

In the absence of access to a Temple where proper sacrifices could be celebrated, Jews in the diaspora developed a new form of worship. It is of enormous importance that, precisely because of the mythic centrality of Jerusalem, there could be no question of setting up another place of priestly, sacrificial worship in the exiled communities. Therefore the Temple was to be replaced not by another Temple but by a house of prayer, a synagogue, a gathering of believers around the scrolls of Scripture. Thereby a community was created which needed neither priest nor Temple; sociologically speaking perhaps the most fundamental innovation in the history of religion. This change protected the Jews providentially from further evolution in the forms of outward religion, and thereby channelled their energies into forms of community maintenance (one can even ask whether 'worship' in the ordinary Gentile sense is the right label) gathered around the Scriptures.

Unfortunately, later Christians did not have the same providential protection against falling back into 'religion'. Christians began with the same social form, that of the synagogue, but once they stopped respecting the Jewish sobriety about religious banquets, the meals of the Christians could become 'sacraments', and the slide into 'religion' as a special sacerdotally validated ritual set apart from ordinary life had begun. Not possessing the specific backhanded protection represented by a set of instructions prescribing a kind of priestly ritual which could only be celebrated somewhere else, Christians had no defence against slipping back into a 'religious' understanding of what their meetings were about. Their reconciliation became absolution, their presbyters became sacerdotal celebrants, their gatherings came increasingly to be organized around image and ceremony, less and less around the Scriptures, and the way was open to the gnosticization of 'true religion' as otherworldly.

What Scriptures mean in the life of a community is that people can gather around the physically tangible representation of the fact that they are not taking orders from contemporary authorities alone. In this sense a book represents transcendence, far more than does an ecstatic utterance or a voice from heaven or from the tomb, or an ancient ritual.

It does not matter so much exactly what the book says. In both Jewish and Christian experience, it has often been the case, sometimes with some embarrassment but other times with no apology, or even with a certain glee, that there has been considerable difference between what the words of the holy book actually said, or would be taken by experts in literary interpretation to say, and what was being believed or done or confessed by the people gathering with the scroll or the book before them.

For some purposes, especially for the purpose of radical renewal within a community, it can be of great importance to clarify just what the text of the book says. That explains how later generations become 'scholastic' about exactly what the book means as revelation. It would however appear that more often, especially when the believing community is a beleaguered minority, what matters is rather that the book or the scroll is there, as the inescapable symbol for the axiom that our identity and our marching orders come from before and beyond the society in which we live, and as testimony to the past story which defines the community.

In another sense it does matter what the book says. It matters that the book, which certifies the authority of Jewish and Christian identity is at the core a narrative. It is not a mythic or a dreamed story but one naming persons whose descendants live among us, and events that really happened at places on a real map (even if we cannot go there). When we look at the function of 'sacred story' as a sociologist of knowledge does, it matters profoundly, in contrast to Asian and gnostic visions, that the past from which we claim to draw our identity is a real past.

It also means something important that a community understands itself to be bound effectively to other people in other places who are also heirs of the same story. Many migrant peoples over the centuries, especially refugee peoples, including in our days Armenians, Mennonites, South-east Asians, and many others, have become unintentionally communities of a transnational character, depending on the grace of the nations, which have given them refuge, bound to relatives in other lands. Jews have been living that experience not for two generations, like the Armenians, or for a century or two, like Mennonites and Chinese of the dispersion, but for millennia. Travel, commerce, intermarriage, consultations about *halakah*, a prestigious rabbi being sent or invited from Babylon to Palestine, or from Spain to Egypt, or from Lithuania to Brooklyn create an authentic sense of world culture, for which the term 'cosmopolitan' is too snooty. Every foreign land can be home: every homeland is foreign. World awareness is not (as for most of us in monolingual middle America) an educational privilege. It is identity.

Thus the formative value of the experience of Babylon, for Jewish identity as such, and therefore also for Jewish pacifism, is important far beyond the mere fact of accepting exile and the pressure to develop a pattern of common life around a book. That historical background created for Jews a permanent awareness of not needing to assimilate. Even though much of the rest of Jewish history that matters to us took place in the West, the awareness of a long previous history centred in Babylon, and the continuing weight of the fact that the Babylonian Talmud was preferred to the Palestinian one, maintained for those Jews who were driven about from the Rhine Valley to Spain to White Russia that sense of not needing to fit in which became permanently a component of the Jewish experience.

A theology for diaspora existence was thus not, as some would have us believe, developed as a merely pragmatic expedient, out of the collapse of Jewish nationhood after the year 70 or 135. Those vital tragedies only settled and restated what had existed already in the messages of Jeremiah and Ezekiel, and in the ministries of Ezra and Nehemiah. The defeats of 70 and 135 only clarified and made sense of what most of world Jewry had already been living for seven centuries.

Because a theologically and sociologically coherent strategy for renouncing civil kingship as the instrument for the renewal of the people of God was already present in that heritage, it was no surprise that Jewry could disengage itself from the Maccabean/Zealot adventures and proceed not only unshaken but renewed and refined by those collapses. What happened in the years after 70 and again finally after 135 was not the creation of a new system, either social or intellectual, to make diaspora existence (including its non-violence) acceptable as acquiescence to an unavoidable loss of power.

What happened was rather the demise of the other views that had been live contenders. The communities bearing those other visions had had some strength, until they were swept away. Both Saducean accommodation and Zealot insurrection had represented efforts to renew and prolong the Davidic vision, by adapting it in one of two possible ways to the tyranny of the *gittim* (originally the Hittites, now the Romans). By letting the shape of the challenge of the *gittim* (namely military power) dictate the form to which they adapted their own counter-hope, both of these groups (as the rabbis increasingly came to see them) were unintentionally selling out other important values.

The critique which the rabbis (not only Jesus) addressed to both of them was based upon those Jewish elements which the critics saw being sold out. Yet as long as there continued to be a political and economic base for those strategies, the rabbis' spiritual insight could be shouted down. When both of those other strategies collapsed, the rabbis held the field. Their acceptance of weakness turned out to be viable.

It should thus be no surprise that the social base for the redefinition of world-wide Jewish identity after Bar Kochba was not just any one of the other major Mediterranean cities where there were large Jewish communities, and not Syria/Palestine, where some Jews survived and more soon trickled back in, but Babylonia, through which the canonical prophecies of Jeremiah and Ezekiel had proclaimed the mandate to preserve the vision.

Now we see why, although most of the Jewish history with which we have occasion to deal is western, and has been living under the same governmental and cultural roof with Christians for over a millennium, it is of structural importance that from the second century to the fifth that was not the case. The Jewish world had its real centre in Babylon throughout that period. In point of fact the effective centre was in Babylon since Jeremiah, but it was only the collapse of the Palestinian establishment under the post-Zealot backlash which made that pre-eminence irreversible and visible. That is why it was not only possible but natural that while Christianity was entering into the Hellenistic–Roman synthesis, Jewry was surviving and evolving on another quite different track, in a different non-Roman world.

It is not unimportant then that the Talmud is from Babylon. It provides Judaic culture with an anchor which through over a thousand years of living with and under 'Christians' all over Western and Central Europe kept the Hellenistic–Roman world culture from ever seeming to Jews to be the 'real' or the 'larger' or the whole world, and kept its pagan philosophical assumptions from being admitted as self-evident or 'natural'.

Having a base outside the Roman Empire preserved Jews from ever thinking, as Christians did a little since the second century and widely since the fourth, that Caesar was ruling the world.[16]

What the Babylonian Talmud does for Jews, the canon of apostolic writings is supposed to do for Christians. It can provide a fulcrum, or a fixed star, outside the Hellenistic–Roman system, morally and philosophically, although within it politically and geographically, whereby to evaluate both acceptable compromises and unacceptable betrayals, while one critiques what has come of Christendom. That is what the notion of 'restoration of original Christianity' or of the New Testament as rule for renewal has meant in western Christian experience. But it can only do that effectively if there is also some experiential base for the awareness of 'otherness'. This is what Christians largely lost when they settled into provincial establishment. They lost it in terms of social base by becoming imperially provincial; that freed them to lose it intellectually by becoming theologically provincial. What Christians borrowed from Plotinus through Augustine, and from Cicero through Ambrose, nailed shut the door which Justin had begun to close.

What Jews bring into the context of later western history is a sub-culture and a sub-community, or a counter-culture and a counter-community, protected by its peculiar historical experiences (as well as by the spiritual guidance of its rabbis) against repeating the mistakes which Christians began to make with great conviction in the fourth century. Judaism is a religious-cultural movement named for a land which only a few of its members can inhabit, even they only as sojourners under the civil control of others. It is a community ostensibly awaiting some future time when animal sacrifice in one central place shall again be established by divine intervention; in the interim it gathers around the record of the ancient revelation of the Torah and engages in unending study of the meaning of that law for their present time. Sometimes favoured almost to the point of quasi-'establishment' under friendly monarchs, sometimes persecuted to the point of extinction in any one place at one time, it is a people whose common identity can by definition not be guaranteed by any central hierarchy, but only by the constant network of communications among its most noted sages. It is thus no surprise that in this situation it was possible to draw out of the lessons of the past, against the background of a permanently insecure present, an abiding understanding of the requisites for communal survival which included renouncing any more attempts at the violent restoration of a national homeland, or any unquestioning or unqualified alliance with any particular Gentile regime.

It is thereby established by simple sociology, without our yet having needed to enter into the substance of ethics, or speculative theology, or spirituality, that Judaism within Christendom since Constantine has the *shape* which historians will later call 'radical reformation' or 'peace church'. Jews expect and accept minority status. They deny ultimate loyalty to any local nation or regime, which is what war presupposes, while they provisionally accept its administration. They look on past and present righteous violence and religious nationalism, including that of their own ancient history, as mistaken. It is evident how this *sociological* distance from the Christendom synthesis frees one for pacifist moral insight.

What I here have described formally would be much more interestingly pursued narratively. For two millennia Judaism has lived its ages of toleration and its ages of renewed exile or even martyrdom, sometimes within and sometimes outside the 'Christian' empires of East and West, but never have they reached for the sword. Their literature never justified violence, and in fact created a special genre of literature, the rabbinic rhapsodic 'praise of Peace'. Occasionally privileged after the model of Joseph, more often emigrating, frequently suffering martyrdom nonviolently, they were able to maintain identity without turf or sword, community without sovereignty. They thereby demonstrated pragmatically the viability of the ethic of Jeremiah and Jesus.

In sum: for over a millennium the Jews of the diaspora were the closest thing to the ethic of Jesus existing on any significant scale anywhere in Christendom. Simple social analysis tells us this; now it is fitting that we move to the level of ideas.

B. Why Jewish Pacifism Makes Sense

Since *halakah* precedes *aggadah* and life precedes theory, it was fitting that we should read the Jewish story before attempting to understand Jewish thought. Now we must however move to the 'thought'. The 'pacifism' of Talmudic Judaism has seldom been thoroughly exposited under the heading 'pacifism', and of course even less often under the more modern heading 'non-violence'. That lack of a synthetic statement in an abstract intellectual form is a characteristic of Jewish culture on many other subjects as well. It is not a weakness. The way Jewish culture did what western academics call 'ethics' was not, and in its most authentic forms today still is not, to produce synthetic statements. It must therefore be a part of my reporting that I should seek, as a respectful but amateur outsider, to explicate the mental structure of Jewish non-violence. Yet amidst this descriptive task, our interest goes beyond the historical awareness that such a position existed and exists, to the deep meaning which its persistence has for our understanding the ways of God in his wayward world.

How such a stance is stated, how it is stated differently because Jewishly, is as important to understand as is the *fact* that a riskily outspoken Jewish pacifism exists at all. The form of this summary is my own.[17]

1. Blood is sacred. Blood is the life and belongs to God. The blood of an animal must not be shed except in a ritual context and then may not be consumed. The shedding of human blood is the fundamental denial of human dignity (stated in the strongest possible terms as 'the Image of God'). It is the root social sin from which all the rest of the structured evils of society evolve (Gen. 4). The sacredness of blood goes all the way back to the Fall. Bloodshed was Cain's primal sin, and God promised to intervene to protect him against blood vengeance. The 'Image' of God in man in Noah's covenant was protected specifically at the point of bloodshed.

> It has been taught [by R. Jonathan b. Saul] that if one was pursuing his fellow to slay him, and the pursued could have saved himself by maiming the limb [of the pursuer], but instead killed his pursuer, the pursued should be executed on that account. (*bab.tal.sanh.*74a)

Those points in the Torah where exception can be made to the wrongness of shedding blood are in the context of the Noachic prevention of murder, the Mosaic provisions for civil administration or in the holy war narratives. *At the most* such room for killing would apply to a pre-exile Israelite state. Even there, they would not apply rigorously, if the Israelite states in Palestine had not gone into exile, since Judaism assumes an evolutionary process moving toward greater grace and humaneness.

2. The Messiah has not yet come. If anyone could have a right to restore the patterns of divine vengeance, or of national policing, which alone could justify the shedding of blood, it would be the Messiah. Yet we know that when he comes there will be a reign of peace. If the time of his coming will be a time of peace, then we

participate in that hoped-for coming by living in peace already in this world, to the extent to which we can. For some Jews, in fact, living at peace is a part of contributing to his coming. If on the other hand any 'ruler' would have the right to reinstate 'kingship' structures, it would only be the Messiah. It is on this ground that the *neturei karta* and some other very orthodox Jews to this day, while living under the authority of the State of Israel, deny its Jewish legitimacy as a state.

3. Jewish thought is marked by the concern to learn properly the lessons of the Zealot experience. As we already saw in the historical survey, this experience came to its final catastrophe in 130–135 with Bar Kochba, but the earlier catastrophe in 66–70 and the still earlier Maccabean drama all represented the same strategy, and all failed. They failed at least in part because when the Zealots took power they were unable after all to bring about the righteous and peaceable community they had promised. If anything (in the social ethical realm) is constitutive of rabbinic Judaism, in the sense in which historians speak of it as beginning after 70 or after 135, it is the concern to be clear about having learned the lesson of the wrongness of the Zealot path, which evidently *God had not blessed*.[18] In not ratifying the Zealot option path God is telling us something which he has had to tell us more than once, and should not have to tell us again.

4. The rabbis consistently downplay the wars of the age of Moses, Joshua, and the Judges. They interpret the violence out of the stories of Deborah or even Psalm 37. They do not consider Moses to have been justified for killing the Egyptian. They dismantle and transform the Mosaic legislation, which provides for capital punishment, by tightening radically the rules of evidence and by substituting other forms of retribution. This is part of the theme of the general interpretive pattern called 'refinement', *tzerupah*.

5. The wisdom with which God presides over the affairs of the *goyim* (the Gentile peoples) is not revealed to us in any simple way. We do know that God does rule over the whole universe, and therefore over all the nations. But the *way* that rule over the nations is exercised is not the same as the way he rules over us through the revealed Torah. Therefore he forbids us to draw immediate conclusions about which things going on in that wider world are of his doing and which are rebellion against him. Since he has given us no privileged clues as to his judgements in those matters, it would be presumptuous for us to seek to be the instruments of his wrath, to say nothing of doing ahead of the Messiah's coming what we think he must want done. Especially is this true of acts of judgement we might think necessary, but it applies as well to acts of liberation.

6. There is a place for suffering in the divine economy. That the faithful must suffer under the benevolence of a sovereign God is a mystery not yet clarified in the Jewish understanding of history. Jews have been less inclined than modern Christians to think that the puzzle of theodicy needs to be solved. On the one hand there is a correlation between disobedience and consequent punishment, and between obedience and subsequent prosperity. If we suffer, it may be because we have disobeyed. We should therefore not defend ourselves against that chastisement. Yet this linkage is not automatic, since sometimes the evil prosper. Sometimes the suffering of God's people is beyond explanation. Only those who know less about the past think that the drama of Auschwitz has brought this tragic puzzle to the surface for the first time. In any case some suffering at the hands of the *goyim* has always been expected, and is to be accepted as 'sanctifying the Name' of God.

This cannot *satisfy* our demand for a rounded-out universe, in the sense of a philosophical theodicy; but it does warn us against justifying the violence which we might ourselves claim we should do in order to limit suffering.

7. The survival of Israel is promised by God. There are two ways to take that promise, two conceptions of covenant. One, which Steven Schwarzschild, called 'ethical', says that if Israel disobeys God, the promise is called off, because it was conditional. For Hosea's wife's infidelity, she was divorced. Covenant being reciprocal, it can be rescinded. *We* can break it, and when we do so God lets us do it. [19]

The other view, which Schwarzschild called 'metaphysical', considers the promise immutable. No failure on the vassal's part will defeat the sovereign's gracious purpose. After divorcing Gomer, Hosea will take her back.

Both views are true, dialectically. Connecting them is a major task of Jewish thought. Yet our interest now is not in their difference, or in their dialectic, but in their commonality. The one thing Israel is *not* to do under *either* hypothesis is to take its survival into its own hands. Schwarzschild has the right, as we gentile onlookers would not, to connect this truth to the deep drama of Masada and the Warsaw ghetto uprising; i.e. to the cases of suicidal violent resistance which many in modern Israel consider more noble than the 'weaker' suffering of the vast majority of Hitler's victims.

Two thousand years of Jewish exilic history had taught the Jewish people that the tree planted by the waters could bend its branches to the storm and afterwards rise up again and grow its fruit for the coming season. One has to be an assimilated Westernized secularist to see something dishonorable – as Bialik did . . . and as so may Jews do today – in crouching in cellars until, it is hoped, the beasts have passed by, in order to save one's own and one's family's lives. To be sure, the gentlemanly thing to do is to stand up straight, meet the badman in the open street and get the first draw on him – but then, as Maurice Samuel has put it, we choose to be Jews, not gentlemen . . .[20]

What we have been saying is simply that the survival of the Jewish people is guaranteed by God – that we need not really concern ourselves with it – that to preoccupy oneself with it is a form of sickness, as health-faddists are invariably sick people – that to attribute our survival to human instrumentalities, including and primarily your own, inevitably leads to the acts of *hybris*, which victimize other human beings and result in unending conflict and eventual defeat – and that, to the contrary, the God Who has brought us this far will also redeem His other promises to Israel.[21]

My reporting has hitherto been descriptive, limited to materials narrowly centred upon my topic. Their historical accuracy is subject to little challenge. I now move on to take account of some more novel, and promising, but also more debatable developments in contemporary Jewish thought.

A tiny but growing number of Jews with strong roots in the theology of Jewish existence before Auschwitz have since the beginnings of Zionism seen Israeli statehood in the same terms in which Jotham (Judg. 9) and Samuel (1 Sam. 8) saw Canaanite kingship: not as an absolute evil which it should be possible to reject completely, but as an accommodation, regrettable, to the ways of the Gentiles, an innovation which will disappoint, which will not deliver on its promises. The *neturei karta* are the simplest of these.

There have been some more idealistic strains within Zionism, but the one which triumphed from Theodore Hertzl to David Ben Gurion to Menachem Begin has consciously attempted to be 'a nation like the other nations', rather than seeking to express in the common life of Israel a distinctively Jewish understanding of people-hood and justice.

One of the expressions of that tendency is the reproach of 'double standards' with which Israelis defend themselves against their friends' idealistic criticism. Increasingly during the hostilities of 1982[22] we observed the freedom, coloured even with the reproach of inequity, with which Israeli public figures said they did not want to be measured with a different yardstick than their Arab neighbours. This public complaint about a 'double standard' is an unfair demand, even on the strictly secular level, when we remember that the State of Israel is governed by an immigrant European elite with western social and political visions and commitments, including notions of *noblesse oblige*, and with western economic and military support. Far more profoundly, however, the refusal to admit a call to be different is a denial of the Jewish vision on religious and moral grounds. The whole point of Hebrew identity since Abraham is a call to be doing something else amidst the world's power arenas. It is only by being something different that Jewry in fact has survived; it is only in order to be something morally different that Jewry is called to survive.

It is too easy for me to make these critical though pro-Jewish observations from the safety of distance. They have been made however in costly and therefore far more credible ways by a small but weighty number of Jewish thinkers in creative conversation with western intellectual history, like Martin Buber and André Neher. Some of these critics have been the heirs of the socialist Jewish intellectual creativity which burgeoned briefly in Weimar Germany, like Stephan Zweig in the 1920s[23] or his namesake Steven Schwarzschild until 1990. Some have been less in conversation with modernity, like the *neturei karta* (an Israeli political group) who although living under its *de facto* jurisdiction deny even political legitimacy to the present State of Israel on orthodox theological grounds.

Each of these in its own way rejects the model of western nationalism, triumphalism, and the very notion that Jews should want to be like their neighbours even in external social organization. Since the massacres of September 1982, the number of Jews coming to see that these critics have a point has been increasing.

Jewish identity through the centuries has repeatedly been saved by the toughness of its conservatives, when the more 'relevant' or 'enlightened' elites were first lured into social prominence in the Gentile world and then swept away. The voices of Jewish anti-triumphalism named above were not doctrinaire advocates of non-violence. To be in that way doctrinaire is a Gentile style. Yet they were committed to reasoning from within a world-view where the inscrutable omnipotence and sovereignty of ADONAI makes it inappropriate, if not blasphemous, to claim to save God's cause for him.

All of these people, in various ways, acquiesced in seeing military Zionism go on without their consent. They loved the land and the people as much as the military Zionists, and they could without apology call themselves Zionist. Yet they could not grant that the European-style state and army set up in 1948, especially their military administration of occupied territory since 1967, and their wars, especially since 1982, can be what God wants for their people. A few of them would rather take their chances at living under a non-Jewish government. More would prefer a not-strictly-Jewish form of pluralistic civil government, even though the way to make that vision viable in the Levant will still have to be invented.

The second theme for substantially new contemporary study and debate is the interpretation of 'the Holocaust'. In its scale and style, the Nazi genocidal project surpassed in qualitative impact the many other pogroms and massacres of Jewish memory. It has provoked a round of theological debate such as had not been experienced since the beginning of the age of assimilation.

Only a few thinkers believe that the old answer, namely that the suffering of God's people is 'for our sins', can be stretched to fit this new level of tragedy. The other extreme response is to conclude by denying God's goodness, or omnipotence, or existence. Each of these classical philosophical answers to the God question takes on a special shape when transposed into the Jewish setting and illustrated by Auschwitz. For many segments of Jewish culture this study has pre-empted the energy which previously had been given to discussing the place of Judaism in the modern world, or to the differences between Christianity and Judaism. A genera-tion earlier Franz Rosenzweig and Martin Buber (like more recently Abraham Joshua Heschel in the American context) were engaged in articulating Jewish iden-tity in terms which would be understandable to the western intellectual, whether Christian or not, and would therefore also contribute to communal self-respect on the part of partially secularized Jews.

That is what has changed, partly, since Auschwitz. The value of that preoccupa-tion with the enlightenment edge of Jewish thought has been replaced by the challenge of survival at its heart. Even if Christianity as the ideology of oppressive Christendom had not been behind 'the Holocaust', Christianity as conversational partner in the battle for the minds of the children of western Jews has become less interesting.

Thirdly: just when conversation with Christianity or post-Christian secularism had become less interesting to Jews in the West, Jesus has become more interesting to Jewish thinkers in Eretz Israel, and then too, with time, to a later degree, in the West. Historians and Scripture scholars like David Flusser, and writers with other specializations yet interested in first-century studies like Pinchas Lapide, Zwi Werblowski, and Schalom ben Chorin, more recently Alan Segal, have been re-opening the study of the man Jesus, or even the man Paul, in ways that both agree significantly with and differ creatively from what western biblical scholars had been doing. In some cases that rediscovery is intentionally kept separate from, and in other cases it is intentionally integrated with, an interest in conversing about such matters with biblically concerned Christians.

These three elements of very sketchy reporting are on the face of things quite independent of my discussion of Jewish ethics through the centuries. But only on the surface is that so. If the successes and the excesses of Israeli nationalism have provoked a small but clear backlash of anti-nationalistic critique, even in the midst of beleaguered Israeli society, that is a powerful extension of the much older story I was telling about Judaism as the oldest and the toughest 'peace church'. If the priority theological agenda for Jews is no longer dialogue with other moderns, including modern Christians, about the meaningfulness of God language in a secular world, but if what needs to be studied instead is how God can let his people be nearly annihilated, that too is a dramatic reaffirmation of the historic vision of 'sanctifying the Name'. If Jewish historians find a new interest in Jesus as a figure in first-century history, that is certainly partly because that Jesus is more like what Jews have always been like than he is like the Christians Jews have known, especially their Constantines or their crusaders.

My focus in these pages has been selective. I have used as representative the one ethical issue of violence. It serves in a representative way to express and to test a distinctive community stance, wherein Jews and radical reformers distance themselves in similar ways from the culture of 'Establishment'. It shall remain for another chapter to illuminate other analogies from other perspectives within our shared history.

Notes

1. This is the second in a series of lectures presented first as the Menno Simons Lectures at Bethel College, Newton, Kansas, in 1982, and later as the Huff Lectures at Earlham College, Richmond, Indiana, in April 1985. An independent but parallel treatment of some of the same themes is 'The Jewishness of Early Christian Pacifism' (1994) available as a 'working paper' from the Joan B. Kroc Institute for International Peace Studies, Notre Dame, IN 46556.

2. Kimmelman's most careful study indicates it was much later than that, if what we take as an index is the *Birkat ha-Minim*. See Reuven Kimelman, 'Birkat ha Minim and the lack of Evidence for an Anti-Christian Jewish Prayer in Late Antiquity' in E. P. Sanders (ed.), *Aspects of Judaism in the Greco Roman Period*, Vol. II of *Jewish and Christian Self-Definition*, Philadelphia: Fortress Press, 1981, 226–44.

3. When in my *The Politics of Jesus*, Grand Rapids, MI: Eerdmans, 1972, second rev. edn 1995, I reviewed the place of 'the zealot temptation' in the gospel story [pp. 56–8], it was by no means a new idea, but scholarship had been giving it only marginal attention. That has since changed. Scholars of the Gospels differ today about such details as whether the *word* 'zealot' was used in the third decade of the first century, but they do not deny that Jesus is portrayed as needing to relate to the challenge of anti-Roman violence.

4. This notion of a 'new law' replacing or adding to the old has been important for the Czech Brethren, for some Anabaptists and Mennonites, for Tolstoy, and for some dispensationalists such as C. I. Scofield.

5. Here I have taken the issue of violence/enmity as a test, because it is the theme most usually appealed to in this way, and because it meshes with the rest of the present study and the interest of 'historic peace churches'. The point would however not be substantially changed if we were to study some other 'Jewish' identity marker (idolatry, polytheism, diet, Sabbath).

6. That humans should imitate the divine nature was not a new idea in Judaism, though it is not prominent. In the teachings of Jesus this seems to be the only place where it applies; cf. my 'Political axioms of the Sermon on the Mount', in *The Original Revolution*, Scottdale, PA: Herald, 1971, 47 and *The Politics of Jesus*, 119ff.

7. In addition to the Kroc Institute working paper listed above, note 1, I have made the same point in my contribution to Harvey Dyck and Peter Brock (eds.), *The Pacifist Impulse*, Toronto: University of Toronto Press, 1966.

8. This is an understatement. The resettlement of Judaea assumed and ratified ceremonially the legitimacy of the Persian Empire.

9. In my 'The Christian Case for Democracy' I exploit the realism of Jesus' wisdom as a basis for a contemporary understanding of the moral stakes in political structures: *The Priestly Kingdom: Social Ethics as Gospel*, Notre Dame, IN: University of Notre Dame Press, 1984, 151ff.

10. I tend to prefer the phrase 'JHWH War' as a signal that the Israelite phenomenon was *sui generis*. Yet the ethnologists who see such phenomena in many cultures have a right to underline the commonalities. The best overview of the field is Benjamin Ollenburger's Introduction to Gerhard von Rad's *Holy War in Ancient Israel*, trans. and ed. Marva J. Dawn, Grand Rapids, MI: Eerdmans, 1991, 1–33.

11. It is an anachronism to think of Caesars as 'politicians', in any sense of the word that would be accountable to a *polis*. Roman senate politics had long since been hollowed out, to be replaced by pure military dictatorship,

12. Were it our concern here to interpret the Constantinian shift for its own sake, rather than asking how it changes the Christian–Jewish difference, much more would need to be added. Some of the other dimensions of the shift would also relate by implication both to the Christian–Jewish question and to the violence/enmity question:

- the disenfranchisement of the laity within the Church (Judaism has no clergy, and post-70 Judaism has no priesthood);
- the creation of 'nations' aligned against 'nations';
- a dual morality tailoring its demands to 'realism':
- relegating moral idealism to a religious elite;
- ontological dualism leaning on platonism:
- 'religion' as an ahistorical realm thought of as closer to God than is the 'real world'.

Some of these differences, those relating most directly to the shape of ethics, are described in my 'The Constantinian Sources of Western Social Ethics' in *The Priestly Kingdom*, 135ff.

13. This is not to say that Jews in a Gentile world, or Christians in an unbelieving world, have nothing to say concerning the moral issues at stake in the common life. To follow Jeremiah's instructions to 'seek the wellbeing of that city' entails the contrary. We are called and empowered to contribute to the larger society's wellbeing. I have argued this in detail in my *Body Politics* [see 'Baptism and the New Humanity', 28–42] and 'First Fruits: The Paradigmatic Public Role of God's People' in *For the Nations: Essays Public and Evangelical*, Grand Rapids, MI: Eerdmans, 1997, 15–36. Yet our own obedience is not derived from that discussion, nor limited by what it can expect of the other actors in the social mix.

14. The oriental catholic churches from the third century to the fifth continued to shape their moral life in terms like these. Cf. my 1996 resume 'Chapter 1/b: Early Christian Disciplines or Church Orders' Chapters in the History of Religiously Rooted Nonviolence: A publication of the Joan B. Kroc Institute of International Peace Studies, Notre Dame, Document: 7/WP:1, 1996.

15. Cf. my study guide 'Chapter 3: The Nonviolence of Judaism from Jeremiah to Hertzl' Chapters in the History of Religiously Rooted Nonviolence: A Publication of the Joan B. Kroc Institute for International Peace Studies, University of Notre Dame, Document 7: WP:1, 1996.

16. Historians of Christian pacifism have long noted with some embarrassment that although both Origen and Tertullian, late in the second century, retained their pacifism

on the level of Christian personal ethics, they had come to affirm without much thought the legitimacy of Rome's governing the world.

17. I have been greatly aided by Steven Schwarzschild, Everett Gendler, Daniel Smith-Christopher, and the sources they have led me to. Since this lecture was prepared I have been able to extend this list considerably, but I resist the temptation to add that bulk to this text. I have circulated other formulations of the same observations for publication elsewhere (cf. Note 13 above).

18. It was more than a witticism when Steven Schwarzschild wrote me, 'The Maccabees are in your Bible, not in ours.' [The editors have been unable to locate a copy of this document, but Schwarzschild was well known for offering this quip in a variety of settings.]

19. Steven Schwarzschild, 'The Theology of Jewish Survival' in *Central Conference of American Rabbis Journal* Vol. 15, No. 4 (Oct. 1968), 3.

20. 'The Theology of Jewish Survival', 16

21. 'The Theology of Jewish Survival', 19.

22. When this lecture was first presented at Earlham College in Richmond, IN the most recent and most fitting sample was the Israeli–Lebanese war of 1982. Since then of course other more recent versions of the same set of conflicts could be cited.

23. Zweig's play *Jeremiah* [Gesammelte Werke, Vol. 4 (Frankfurt: S. Fischer, 1982); English Translation by Eden and Cedar Paul (New York: Seltzer, 1922)], written in the last months of World War I, coinciding with his turn to a confessional Jewish stance, was his strongest but not his only pacifist writing.

Commentary

PETER OCHS

In my comments to Chapter 1, I suggested that Yoder displays both a pioneering, new Christian approach to Rabbinic Judaism and an old, supersessionist tendency. In 'Jesus the Jewish Pacifist', he introduces his pioneering approach. We should be grateful, first, for Yoder's correcting Christian misperceptions of Jewish 'law', as if Jesus opposed it. Appropriately, Yoder reads this claim of Jesus' in its plain sense: that 'he was bringing not rejection of what Torah had really always intended . . . His call was for a "greater righteousness" than that of other teachers, marked by none of the commandments' being "dissolved" or relaxed' (p. 70, on Matt. 5). Here, Yoder offers the 'depth-reading' that I believe both Jews and Christians need to hear today. He explains that rabbinic law displays Judaism's 'preference for the concrete case', which 'is more crucial to a people's commonality of commitment than is the piety with which it is filled out' (p. 74).

For readers new to Rabbinic Judaism, I might explain that the proto-rabbis of the Roman era and the rabbinic sages of the *Mishnah* and Talmud drew from out of the written and oral traditions of the Torah a body of behavioral teachings (*halakhah* or the 'way of walking [with God]') and of homiletical teaching (*aggadah*, or the 'telling' of the meanings or narratives of scripture). In the wake of the destruction of the Second Temple in 70 CE and of the Roman Wars that ended in 135 CE with diaspora, rabbinic leaders fashioned oral collections of both these teachings, but primarily the legal or behavioural ones. In the second century, Yehudah Hanasi (Judah the Patriarch or 'Prince'), codified the collections of *halakhah* into the *Mishnah*, the primary teaching of Rabbinic Judaism. While presented as a vast collection of behavioral teachings, or laws, the *Mishnah* redacts these teachings in a way that preserves disagreements and minority opinions. The redaction lends the collection the force of a book of discussions about the laws, in that sense a book of behavioural philosophy, spiced with moral claims, occasional narratives and theology. As soon as the *Mishnah* was codified and accepted, the schools of rabbinic sages began to debate it: to review it, explore its meanings, search out its sources in the Torah, and account for apparent contradictions with teachings ('*baraitot*', or 'outside' teachings) that were not included in the *Mishnah* but that had equal authority (see p. 76). Generations of such debates were later redacted into the Babylonian and Palestinian Talmuds: one collection for each centre of rabbinic studies. The Babylonian Talmud, in particular, was replete with *aggadah* as well as *halakhah*, and it served as the centre of Jewish education, thought, and life throughout the years of diaspora (see p. 80). The primary goal of Talmudic study was to inculcate rabbinic teachers and students and, ideally, all members of the people Israel with the spirit and patterns of Torah. This means to learn to study, interpret, imitate, and live the Word of God, not as the word appears in its merely plain sense, but as the ever-renewed meaning that is signified for each community and each generation by the plain sense and its maculations. This meaning is drawn from the scriptural text tradition by the community that studies it, through a process of group interpretation (*midrash*), in the context of the people's historical and literary heritage and memory and as directed by its prayers for the world today. As Yoder teaches well, to live this meaning is to live it in the concrete practices of *halakhah* (pp. 74–5).

We should be grateful, secondly, for Yoder's correcting errant Christian tendencies to identify Jesus' pacificism with his non-Jewish vision, as if 'Old Testament' Judaism were a Judaism of war, opposed to Christianity's post-Jewish peace. 'Jesus did not reject anything Jewish in calling for love of enemy' (p. 70). He was, instead, articulating one version of Judaism as opposed to another: an internal, Jewish debate; and 'most who reject what he said are not Jewish' (p. 70). This continues what Jewish biblical scholars often refer to as the 'Mosaic,' as opposed to the 'Davidic' or monarchical tendency in Israelite theo-politics: displayed, prototypically, in the account, in 1 Samuel, of God's condemning the people Israel for demanding, against the will of Samuel, a king to govern us like all other nations' (1 Sam. 8.4, implicit in Yoder's comments on p. 71). Yoder offers here a vision of Israel's limited pacifism (p. 72). I believe this is, in fact, the dominant way of both Israelite and later, rabbinic peace-seeking. It is not an explicit vow of non-violence (which remains an eschatological hope for the world to come and an individual option in this world, like taking the vows of a Nazirite), but what students of Kant might call a 'regulative ideal': a condition to be pursued within the limits of the earthly needs and realities of a landed people and a political entity. The point, as Yoder stresses, is that Biblical Israel *already* pursued a justice that belonged to God alone, and not to any earthly king or government, except as servants of God (p. 73).

We should be grateful, finally, for Yoder's innovative effort to identify the deeply exilic character of Rabbinic Judaism: its emerging as the religion of Israel precisely in response to Israel's loss of Temple and homeland and its serving, in that way, as prototype for the religion of Jesus' followers. In this effort, however, Yoder also risks replaying some of the supersessionist themes he sought to replace with a new vision of Jewish–Christian understanding. On the positive side, Yoder reverses Christian stereotypes of Judaism as 'the Old Testament religion', explaining that Rabbinic Judaism begins officially in the second century yet draws on 'the way of life [that] . . . has been going since 586 BCE' (p. 77). Explaining how various Jewish sects competed for cultural authority during the years of Roman rule, he draws a line between sects that sought to retain the 'Davidic' – or Temple/King – model of Israelite religion and those that antici-pated Rabbinic Judaism's exilic theo-politics (p. 80). In the former group, he includes both the Sadducees (*tsadukim*, supporters of the High Priest Tsadok, or of the priestly aristocracy in Jerusalem as well as of the foreign empires that ruled by way of them) and the Zealots (who sought to overthrow Roman rule and restore something like the Maccabean theocracy). He reserves the latter group for the sect(s) that inherited 'a theology for diaspora existence' that links the 'messages of Jeremiah and Ezekiel' to the religion of the *Mishnah* (p. 79). Although very recent rabbinic scholarship has complicated the picture, the dominant tendency in the last several decades has been to identify this sect with the Pharisees (named 'Separatists', or *perushim* by the Sadducees), as the proto-rabbis who opposed the Jerusalemite aristocracies and their economic and political power structure; who preached a religion of Torah study, prayer, and pious behavior, rather than of Temple sacrifice; who taught that the meaning of the Torah is to be located not merely in its plain sense, but in the interpreted sense, or *midrash*, that displays the force of God's words for life in the immediate context of the community of interpreters; and who taught, against the Sadducees, that the dead will be resurrected and that there is life not only in 'this world' (*olam hazeh*), but also in 'the world to come' (*olam haba*). Some recent historians argue that the Pharisees' and the Sadducees' theo-politics cannot be separated so clearly. Nevertheless, however ambiguous the strict historical evidence may be, Yoder draws out the value distinction that speaks most clearly to post-liberal Jewish scholars today. It is a value distinction between two potential or imagined trajectories of Judaism, from the Babylonian Exile to today. One trajectory identifies Judaism's world-to-come (and thus Judaism's regulative ideal) with a religion of Temple priesthood and theocracy; the other identifies it with a religion of decentralized centres of Torah study and piety. Both Yoder and post-liberal Jewish thinkers make a clear choice for the second ideal (p. 77).

Yoder's radical thesis is that this 'diasporic Judaism' is the religion, as well, of Jesus, Paul and the Gospel of John. Post-liberal Jews can support this thesis in one sense, but not in another. They can support his claim that what Jews call 'Judaism' today is primarily an expression of the religion of Israel that developed in diaspora. This 'exilic' Judaism is Pharisaic according to the terms we just introduced. Its Torah is not merely a written bible but a tradition of reinterpreting that bible anew so that it displays God's ever-renewed directives for each of the 'wandering Jews'' many homes throughout the diaspora (p. 79). This is the hermeneutic of the people who lives as a 'beleaguered minority', not overly tied to any one immediate homeland, living somewhat apart from their immediate neighbours, but always in touch with other members of the People Israel throughout the lands of the diaspora (p. 81). Yoder characterizes the theo-politics of this exilic people as 'Jewish pacifism'. In a moment, I will suggest ways in which this epithet is troubling, but I will turn my attention first to ways in which it is, in fact, welcome. As Yoder suggests, Rabbinic Judaism does indeed work for peace (pp. 82–5). As he suggests, it regards the shedding of blood as anathema. Its belief that the Messiah has not yet come leads it both to work for the peace that would accompany his coming, while also suspending the aggressive self-certainty that could accompany a belief that he already lived among them. It seeks, indeed, not to reiterate the errors of Maccabean and Zealot militarism, or military nationalism (on which the Talmud looks with great disfavour). It seeks, through its reinterpretations of biblical law, to interpret away the Bible's uses of capital punishment. It deconstructs any political metaphysics that would tempt the Jews into believing they understood precisely how the entire world is supposed to operate politically; it therefore inhibits their adopting an overly clarified plan for the world's own development. (In Yoder's terms, it cannot be 'doctrinaire' in a 'Gentile way' (p. 85)). Visions of empire, or even of a world order according to their imaginings, is out of the question. It recognizes that the righteous may suffer for reasons we cannot understand, which means that, however much it pursues worldly justice, it does not presume that all injustices it suffers could be made right in this world. It trusts that, even when Israel strays, God will not depart from her or from the covenant that binds God and Israel together. This in no way means that Israel can do what she pleases (to the contrary, whatever she does, God will be right there to judge it). But it also means that it need not rely only on itself to secure its future; God will ultimately provide a lamb (to use the image of Abraham's sacrifice of Isaac).

At the same time, Yoder also has a tendency to overstate and reify this view of Exilic Judaism: that is, to describe it in a 'doctrinaire Gentile way'. In this way, he transforms what post-liberal Jews should consider their sages' striving for peace into a conceptually clear and distinct 'pacifism' that will sound to them less like Hebrew and Rabbinic thinking than like Greek and Modern thinking. (I believe this error is displayed as well in Steven Schwarzschild's claim that 'pacifism is the most authentic of classical Judaism', cited below, p. 95.) But Yoder offers only hints of this tendency within this chapter; the doctrinaire view is displayed later.

3

Paul the Judaizer[1]

We took note of the Jewishness of the teachings of Jesus at one particular point in his ministry; namely in the particular texture of Jesus' view of violence and the enemy; what in our age we call 'pacifism'. It was appropriate to centre upon that instance, because that has been one of the places where it had seemed superficially to many that Jesus was doing something else than fulfilling a Jewish vision. If we had chosen other topics, such as his attitude toward the Sabbath or the Temple, the details of the demonstration would have been different. Yet the shape of the overall stance of fulfilment rather than abolition would still have been confirmed.

We appropriately turn now to the other most familiar point at which Christians are accustomed to defining Judaism in a particular way and then to negating it. This is the ministry of the apostle Saul/Paul. Ever since Martin Luther it has been customary for Protestants to identify as their 'canon within the canon' a specific line of argument in the writings of Paul to the Romans and the Galatians. Here the apostle's concern is taken to be with how one can find salvation. The danger, or the error, is to seek to find it by means of keeping the law. Against this danger, Paul is held to be arguing in various ways the impossibility of satisfying the demands of that law. We come to faith, then, not by keeping its requirements but by granting that we cannot, and by throwing ourselves instead upon the mercy wherewith God forgives us purely on the ground of our faith.

This argument in Paul's pastoral writings would make little sense, the standard Protestant argument goes, if it were not the case that the position he is argued against were being seriously advocated by someone in Paul's world: that must of course then be 'the Jews', even 'normative Judaism'.

Paul is supposed thereby to have made of first generation Christianity in Galatia or Corinth something very different from what it had been back in Jerusalem. He propagated his message, formulated thus anti- or at least un-Jewishly, to Hellenistic Gentiles, in terms which they could understand, because they were terms borrowed from or parallel to their own mystery religions. Paul disconnected that message from the particulars of Jewish lifestyle within which the movement had originated, and he facilitated the bridge from one to the other by redefining 'salvation' in terms of a dualism between this world and another world, or between inward and outward reality, as experienced by the individual, rather than as a divine intention carried out within common human history. As Adolf von Harnack could put it, Paul transformed the religion which Jesus had taught, about the fatherhood of God and the brotherhood of man, into a religion worshipping Jesus as a uniquely divine person.[2]

Paul was thus the great Hellenizer. He took a message limited to the Palestinian culture and the Jewish ghetto, and restated it in the language of the wisdom of the Gentile world so that it could become a world religion, at the cost of leaving Jewish substance behind. Or so Harnack argued.

The apostle is debating vigorously against some unnamed adversaries. Those persons, or that party, might have attacked him first, but we don't hear their side of it. As we get the picture through Paul's argument against them, they seem to believe that it is by keeping the Jewish legal system intact, especially by fully observing the ritual provisions concerning foods, Sabbaths, circumcision and purification, that God can be satisfied and believers can be saved. They believe that their own salvation is achieved by full obedience to all the rules, and that this applies to Gentiles as well as to Jews.

The critical conversation called for here, to respond worthily to this modern reading of Paul[3] is complex. It has been rendered no less so by the correctives applied with good intentions by persons seeking to undo past error, but who have aimed their axes elsewhere than at the root of things. We cannot pursue the matter further without unpacking the way it has been formulated.

It is one of the well-kept secrets of contemporary theology that this model is inappropriate for grasping what Paul was about.[4] A few writings which have begun to call it into question have been widely noticed, like one article in 1961 by Krister Stendahl,[5] but it has not been equally widely noticed that a whole generation of younger Scripture scholars, looking at one text at a time, with the ordinary tools of grammar and literary analysis, have been undercutting the adequacy of that total view. Yet the internal critique of one's own prior glasses need not be the only path to progress on a question like this. If we are concerned to learn how we might reconstruct an understanding of Jewish/Christian relations, we will be helped also by noting another shortcoming of that traditional view; it is that persons qualified to understand the mind of other Jewish thinkers of that time report that they do not find anyone advocating what this traditional account says Paul is condemning.

Rather than surveying that complexity down through the years as a full account would need to, let me leap over it to the beginnings of the modern debate. Hans Joachim Schoeps was one of the first widely learned Jewish scholars to revive the conversation about Christian origins, with his 1959 study *Paul: The Theology of the Apostle in the Light of Jewish Religious History*.[6]

Much later Christian theologians like Harnack, as we already saw, have taken Paul's adversaries to be 'the Jews', 'typical Judaism' or even 'normative Judaism', and have not even bothered to read Jewish sources to confirm that picture. Paul should know, Christians assumed, what the Jews believed; had he not been one of them? Thus that debate between Paul and his 'Jews' becomes representative, typical, prototypical, for where Jews in fact did (and therefore still do) stand, and where Christians should stand, and why they must differ, for all time. This one theme is thereby identified as the centre of Paul's thought and ministry, his most original contribution.

To all of this Schoeps objects, strongly and correctly, especially at two points. Since then, his objection has been sustained by a chorus of other scholars, Jewish and Christian.

First, 'the Jews' did not think that way. Schoeps' authentic Jewish sources, i.e. the tannaic or early rabbinic literature, speak of the Law of God as a privilege of covenantal grace, as divine enablement, not as a means for earning (or, failing that, for losing) God's acceptance. The rabbis[7] are closer to what Paul says than to what he is said to be attacking.

Secondly, the rabbis did not ask of Gentiles that they keep the Law, and less yet that they become full Jews. They developed a theory, based on God's covenant with Noah, to explain how Gentiles can be accepted by God in the Age to Come on their own terms, i.e. in terms of their own covenant and its own Law.[8]

'Paul' (when thus understood) is thus misinformed at least. He ascribes to Judaism on both points views which the rabbis did not hold, while arguing himself in favour of positions close to the ones they did hold. Thus Paul – well-intentioned, Schoeps might grant – perpetrated an act of libel, and Christians ever since have perpetuated the same.

Schoeps is right about the perpetuating. That libel is one of the pillars of Christian anti-Judaism. He is less right about the perpetrating. Paul does not say his adversaries are 'the Jews'. Even less does he call them 'normative Jews' or attribute to them leadership in the non-messianic synagogues. They must be either Gentiles trying to act like Jews, or Jews estranged from the deep roots of their own heritage. Schoeps grants that such people may well have existed. They are coming from a pagan world vision.[9] They want to make of Jewish ritual forms a semi-magical, mysterious or superstitious use, analogous to those of pagan ritual, to which they were accustomed. Either they genuinely felt some promise of a saving sacramental effect working though these ceremonies, or they thought that to observe them rigorously would be a way to force their entry into the synagogues.

Paul responds that that is not what those ceremonies are for. Precisely because the messianic age has dawned, Gentiles do not need to become Jews in order to come under the Torah of the Messiah. Yet because Jesus is the Messiah of the Jews, there is no reason either for Jews to renounce their observant custom.

So Schoeps is right; Paul is with 'the rabbis', not against them. Paul is not hardening the Jewish–Christian schism; he is denying or forbidding it. He is combating those who would precipitate schism by forcing believing Gentiles out of their fellowship. 'Normative Judaism' is our concept, and itself does violence to the way Jewish reality was mixed up then, but *if* the term *were* appropriate, it would be for his own view that Paul (like Jesus) would have claimed it.[10]

Steven Schwarzschild was cited above as saying: 'No one can speak for Judaism. On the other hand, I believe, on the basis of intense, lifelong, and professional study, that pacifism is the most authentic interpretation of classical Judaism.'[11]

Paul's claim was of that kind. To believe that the messianic age has begun, and that therefore Jews can share the glories of the Law as Grace with Gentiles, was for him 'the most authentic interpretation of classical Judaism'. Far from being the great Hellenizer of an originally Jewish message, Paul is rather the great Judaizer of Hellenistic culture. He comes with his monotheism into a polytheistic world, with his ethical rigour into a hedonistic world. He teaches Aramaic prayers to Gentile believers and expands the Pharisaic *chabourah* or love feast into a celebration of inter-ethnic unity.

Paul is thus not the pioneer of mission to the Gentiles. Mission to Gentiles had been going on for generations. It was so routine that the different schools of rabbis compared their different rules about how to do it. What is original about Paul's mission is its place in salvation history. In the words of the Letter to the Ephesians – whether the letter was written in Paul's own hand or not makes no difference for our purposes[12] – his distinct missionary vocation unfolds the revelation of a divine purpose, which had been hidden from all eternity, only now manifest in the messianic age. *Because* this is the messianic age, initiated by the resurrection and ascension of Jesus, *therefore* the centuries-old promises of the ingathering of the Gentiles are coming true.

'In that day', Micah had said, '. . . many nations shall come, and say: "Come, let us go up to the Mountain of the Lord"' (Micah 4.1–2).

For generations already, in fact for centuries, the Jewish colonies in most of the major centres of the area stretching at least from Babylon to Rome, maybe already from India to Scythia to Spain, were sufficiently solid and attractive that some of their neighbours were drawn to their lifestyle and world-view, seeing it as more reasonable and morally solid than the various civil religions and mystery religions available in the marketplace. Although we remember that Jesus once spoke of Jews crossing land and sea to make proselytes,[13] we have generally underestimated the extent to which the Jewish culture of the time was self-conscious and aggressive about propagating the faith.

Schoeps in his book on Paul brings together a wide range of evidence in a chapter called 'Jewish expectant universalism'. Some of this 'missionary' aggressiveness was even in fact what one might call 'triumphal' or 'Constantinian'. The Hasmonean kings appear to have put the pressure of the state behind making Jewish the peoples over whom their sovereignty gradually extended in the course of the second century before our era. But more often the missionary successes of Judaism represented the real (and non-coercive) religious and moral superiority of the 'disestablished' Jewish diaspora culture.

This missionary power was correlated with, not undercut by, the belief that there were many people who, without knowing the law, fulfilled what for them was the relevant portion of the law, namely the obligations revealed to all mankind in the covenant with Noah. But Jewish mission did not rest with that. Arrangements were possible for Gentiles to become recognized as 'God-fearers', free to attend synagogue services without observing the full dietary regulations or festival calendar and circumcision.[14] There were also set patterns for the full incorporation of proselytes into the synagogue through baptism and circumcision. During the late period of Hasmonean independence some of the major rabbis actually were proselytes of non-Jewish ancestry. Yet this growth, however aggressively promoted, was statistically a fringe phenomenon in diaspora life. None of the rules for Jews were changed in order to make it possible. It was not expected that people from Gentile background would normally be drawn into synagogue leadership.

It was, however, a part of the messianic expectation that in the age to come all the nations would be drawn in, and would voluntarily want to know the will of God, which they would have to learn by asking Jews or by coming to Jerusalem.

Paul simply puts two and two together. We recognize in Jesus the inbreaking of the messianic age. It is actually happening on a greater scale than before, that Gentiles who hear about Jesus come to the messianic synagogues. Conclusion: the will of God for our age is the active ingathering of Gentiles into a new kind of body. This is said in so many words, in the Letter to the Ephesians, to be a particular 'mystery' revealed to Paul. It had been God's intention all along, but only now has it become manifest.

Schoeps explains the general lack of awareness of how actively missionary Judaism had been by saying[15] that the pro-proselyte attitude of the rabbis 'reversed itself crassly after the Jewish wars and the fall of Jerusalem'. Further he says that 'the successes of Jewish mission fell without a struggle to the younger Christianity'.

It is not clear whether Schoeps means that the Gentiles who previously had been drawn to Judaism by its mission now became messianic Gentiles ('Christians') and thereby discredited the notion of proselyting, or only that from now on the kind of people who previously would have been won by Jewish missionary openness now are attracted instead to the messianic synagogues ('churches').

Here Schoeps seems to me to be making in reverse the normal mistake which others used to make of projecting back into non-messianic Judaism before the schism characteristics which may very well only have developed after the schism, such as the doctrine to the effect that Gentiles can have a part in the age to come by keeping the provisions of the covenant of Noah.[16]

Another standard formulation of the same argument is the concept of 'supersession'. Christianity, it is held, has replaced, 'superseded' Judaism, in the sense that Judaism can or should no longer exist. Rosemary Radford Ruether states the idea most bluntly in her interpretation of Romans 9–11, in her book *Faith and Fratricide*.[17] She seeks in this book to understand the New Testament origins of Christian antisemitism. She finds them already present in Paul, most basically in this section of the letter to the Romans. Paul says, she says, that the mosaic way of knowing God has been cut off and replaced by the Church as God's only instrument. Moses and Torah are not simply added to, in an ongoing organic development, but are cut off. After having said that this is the meaning of Paul, she makes clear as well that this view is theologically unacceptable to her because it leads to antisemitism.

It is not fully clear whether according to Ruether there would be any other way to know the wrongness of that position, if it were not for its alleged negative outworkings in the form of modern antisemitism. Is it in any other sense 'theologically' wrong? Could/should it have been known to be wrong on other grounds?

The projected revision of biblical understandings represented by the work of Ruether is very important as a corrective thrust within the dialectical development of theology. That does not however mean that every step of her argument is intrinsically adequate or convincing. It is generally a questionable method, in the interpretation of any historic cultural phenomenon, to claim to be able to understand it fairly when one knows ahead of time that it is to be rejected. The alternative to that is not uncritical acceptance, but the exercise of at least relative empathy in reconstructing how one might take in the best light the position one is challenging.

The error of this particular passage from Ruether is that she is uncritically traditional in her understanding of the sense in which Paul 'rejects the law'. Like Schoeps, she grants to later Christians that their anti-Jewish use of Paul is faithful to him. Neither the ancient claim of institutional and legal supersession stretching from the apologetic fathers through medieval Catholicism nor the specific Lutheran way of seeing Christ as 'the end of the Law' is fair to what is really being said in Galatians and Romans. What Paul sees happening in Christ and in the Christian Church, like what Jesus had said in Matthew, is the fulfilment and not the abolition of the meaning of Torah as covenant of grace. 'Fulfilment' is a permanently open border between what went before and what comes next. Whenever a Jew says that the Messianic age has not yet come, he or she is saying as well that it might come. That means that such a Jew can never say *a priori* that anyone's statement that the Messianic age has come is unthinkable, but only that it is not yet demonstrated.[18]

Fulfilment must also be an open border from 'this side'. Christians must continue to be claiming as Paul did that Jesus whom they follow is to be interpreted to Jews as the one to whom they still look forward. Christians gave up their messianic claim in its most authentic and original form not when they adjusted to the postponement of the Second Coming (a development which had already begun in apostolic times) but when they renounced their claims regarding the first coming and the Jews: i.e. when they granted to the non-messianic synagogue that it had the right to exclude them, and then went on to give further occasion for the rebuilding of other barriers by forsaking the dietary compromises that had originally been accepted, and by sliding culturally into an increasing Romanization and Hellenization.

There are, of course, modernized forms of Jewish thought that do deny systematically that there is another age to come. I shall comment later on the importance of this phenomenon. But this modern development cannot count as data on the subject of either historic Jewish rejection of Christianity or historic Christian rejection of Judaism.

Notes

1. This essay originated as the fourth in a series of five lectures presented first as the Menno Simons Lectures at Bethel College, Newton, Kansas, in 1982, and later as the Huff Lectures at Earlham College, Richmond, Indiana, in April 1985. It was also included in the 1996 'Shalom Desktop packet'.

2. [Editors' Note: See Adolf von Harnack, *What is Christianity?*, trans. Thomas Bailey Saunders, Introduction by Rudolf Bultmann, New York: Harper & Row, 1957.]

3. 'Modern' for these purposes begins with Martin Luther.

4. This sentence was in my original lecture. The secret is no longer so well kept. Later notes and chapters will demonstrate a growing awareness among scholars of the points which were relatively new when I made them decades ago.

5. Krister Stendahl, 'Paul and the Introspective Conscience of the West' in the *Harvard Theological Review*, 56, July 1963, 199ff.

6. H. J. Schoeps, *Paul: The Theology of the Apostle in the Light of Jewish Religious History*, trans. Harold Knight, Philadelphia: Westminster Press, 1961.

7. The rabbis whom Schoeps is reading are of course significantly later than Paul. That fact however does not weaken his point.

8. [Editors' Note: Yoder offered the following note as an appendix to his book as a whole. We felt it would be most helpful for the reader to receive this note at this point in Chapter 3.]

At numerous points in the above exposition I have noted the understanding, widely held in later Rabbinic Judaism, that the moral will of the true God has two different shapes, one for the Jews and one for everyone else. 'Everyone else' has come to be designated as 'the sons of Noah'. For some, reasoning within a pre-critical traditional vision of revelation and of the scriptural narrative, the covenant with Noah refers simply to the content of the actual narrative of Genesis 9. The father of all post-diluvian humanity was told:

– Be fruitful, multiply and fill the earth;
– You are free to eat both plants and animals;
– Do not eat [animal] flesh with the blood in it;
– If anyone sheds human blood his blood shall be shed by a human.

For his part, God also made a promise, a covenant with all living creatures, never again to destroy the world with a flood, and the 'bow in the clouds' is the sign of that covenant.

Since the Noachide covenant was made with the father of all humanity, and was temporally prior to the covenants later made with Abraham and Moses (and their respective posterities), it is reasonable to consider that narrative as still providing the basis for the relations of non-Jews to the moral demands of the same God who gave the Jews the much fuller and more demanding Torah. (See David Novak, *The Image of the Non-Jew in Judaism: An Historical and Constructive Study of the Noachide Laws*, Toronto Studies in Theology number 14, Lewiston, MN: Edwin Mellen Press, 1983, 257f. See also Ephraim E. Urbach, *The Sages*, Jerusalem: Hebrew University, 1975, 527.) The legend in fact developed later that God had first offered the full [i.e. Mosaic] Torah to the nations. Only when they refused it (Benamozegh 300, 324) did God rule that they should stay with what they had from Noah. But then they were not able (or willing) to observe even that lower level of demands.

Beyond the straightforward reading of the Genesis narrative, the notion of playing off a Noachide covenant for other peoples against the Mosaic Torah of Israel soon took on a broader meaning, less closely tied to the Genesis text. At the latest by the time of Maimonides it was the standard position that there were seven rules. Those seven provisions were functionally equivalent to the Torah in that a Gentile who would 'receive and fulfil' them would 'have a part in the world to come' or 'be regarded as a proselyte of the gate, or a fellow citizen, or as a pious man or sage among the Gentiles'. (According to Maimonides, *The Book of Judges, Kings and Wars*, ch. VIII, the Gentile must affirm these provisions not merely as reasonable but as revealed. Cf. Steven S. Schwarzschild, 'Do Noachites Have to Believe in Revelation?' in *The Pursuit of the Ideal*, Buffalo, NY: State University of New York Press, 1990, 29–60.) Thereby the notion that there is an alternative 'law for the Gentiles' has been cut loose from the text in Genesis. It has become a code reference to everything that one thinks the Gentiles must know. The content which one ascribes to that the law may be drawn not only from Genesis but may also be drawn from other texts in the Pentateuch concerned with the behavior of non-Israelites. ('Jewish law courts were sometimes entrusted with applying the Noachide laws and it was therefore necessary that their decitisons be based . . . on a set of principle . . . the Talmud addresses this question explicitly', Elija Benamozegh, *Israel and Humanity*, New York/Mahwah: Paulist Press, 1995 [orig. 1885], 261.)

In his 1885 work *Israel and Humanity*, the Italian rabbi Elijah Benamozegh (1823–1900) devoted forty pages of his exposition to his understanding of 'Noachide Law'. He frankly abandons the notion that there are precisely seven laws clearly articulated in Genesis 9, or even the notions that the number 7 matters, even though the Talmud in discussing whether the Noachide is obligated, like the Israelite, to accept martyrdom rather than denying the faith, says that 'that would make eight precepts, and there are only supposed to be seven' (TB Sanhedrin 74b). Benamozegh cites what he calls the oldest formulation: 'Our sages have said that seven commandments have been prescribed for the sons of Noah: the first requires them to have judges; the other six forbid sacrilege, idolatry, incest, homicide, theft, and the consumption of a limb taken from a living animal.' (Benamozegh, *Israel and Humanity*, p. 263 citing TB Sanhedrin 46b. In *Image of the Non-Jew in Judaism*, p. 3, Novak says the earliest discussion is found in the *tosephta*, late second century, listing the same seven items.) The vigilant reader will note that already in this ancient summary more is said than in the Genesis account. As the notion that non-Jews can please God without the full Mosaic order was further developed, the difference in content between the Noachic and the Mosaic systems decreased. Almost anything Mosaic could be ascribed to Noah too (Benamozegh, p. 262). Maimonides added that it is not enough that a Gentile should obey the seven requirements; one must believe them to be revealed if one is to have a share in the world to come; in other words there must be a kind of conversion from paganism.

There is in these two most qualified summaries, one early modern by Benamozegh and the thorough scholarly one (below) by Novak, only confirmation for my earlier hint that the notion that Gentiles need not join the Mosaic discipline because they have access to a functionally equivalent revelation though the knowledge of God's will through their ancestor Noah is a post-schism construct. There is no serious idea that such moral knowledge was in fact passed down by Noah to all humankind through his descendants, and no concert to prove just what those laws were. What Benamozegh did in response to the challenges of Enlightenment, David Novak has done in the face of historiographical erudition. It suffices for our purposes to cite his review (Novak, *Image of the Non-Jew in Judaism*).

Rabbinic notions varied greatly as to what these seven rules would be used for. The oldest view may have been that they were thought of as governing the acceptance of a Gentile within the polity of Israel as a 'resident alien' or *ger toshab*. That was an understandable effort to root the notion in concrete Israelite life. Yet such a social category was only relevant before 586, and in addition the Mosaic legislation makes other provisions for those people (for example certain of the provisions of Lev. 17, which refers regularly to 'aliens who dwell among you' as also being bound by purity rules regarding blood). Others have thought that these rules might also be the basis of appeal to govern the acceptance of Gentile 'God-fearers (*seboumenoi*)' as a category of uncircumsized worshippers whose presence was welcome on the edge of the synagogue. (I have noted elsewhere that scholars differ on whether this category really existed. The phenomenon was real, but was it legitimated by 'canonical' provisions?)

Though fascinating in itself as a bit of rabbinic lore, the reason this theme matters for the present study is that it has sometimes been read as correlating with the end of Jewish mission. It has been suggested that the Jews could well turn over mission to the Christians, since there was a second way, beside the Mosaic Torah, for mankind to be saved. Much more recently, they have also been seen as a Jewish functional equivalent of the Catholic notion of natural law, as providing a bases for moral conversation with nonbelievers in the civil polity. There may be some rationality to these interpretations after the fact, yet it cannot explain the roots of the distinction, when we remember:

– that for the earliest readings the use of the seven laws was not to govern inheriting a share in the world to come but the right to reside in Israel;
– that although it seems to have been considered to have been possible from the age of Ararat to that of Sinai, for the Gentiles actually to observe the Noachic law, after Sinai the nations do not even observe that (Novak, 258f.).

This cross-reference to one of the ways Jews in later centuries would speculate about the Gentiles thus confirms my reading from the earlier centuries, namely that by making their peace with the messianic schism the rabbis backed away from the radicality of their earlier commitment to a synagogue polity open to the *goyim*.

9. Neil Elliott, *Liberating Paul*, Maryknoll, NY: Orbis Books, 1994, is among those who say these were 'Gentiles interested in aspects of the Torah' (p. 134).

10. The later we think *Ephesians* might have been written, the more striking it is that its author should ascribe this understanding of the reconciling of Jew and Gentile to Paul himself.

11. Steven Schwarzschild, 'On the Theology of Jewish Survival' (see Chapter 2, n. 19).

12. I have described this vision before in my: 'The Apostle's Apology Revisited' (1980) and 'The Social Shape of the Gospel' in *Exploring Church Growth,* ed., Wilbert Shenk, Grand Rapids, MI: Eerdmans, 1983, 277–84.

13. Matthew 23.15.

14. Some historians hold that there was a quite standardized 'canonical' status for 'God-fearing Gentiles' (e.g. Acts 10.2); others doubt that. Both views may well be right, since we are considering a wide spread of time and space. None doubt that the cases occurred.

15. Schoeps, *Paul,* 233.

16. Cf. Ch. 5. for more attention to the question of whether that 'Noachic covenant' idea was actually current before the end of mission.

17. Rosemary Radford Ruether, *Faith and Fratricide: The Theological Roots of Anti-Semitism,* New York: Seabury Press, 1979.

18. There are of course more modern forms of Jewish thought which will deny systematically that there is another age to come. Yet that specifically modern phenomenon, important in its own right, especially since Auschwitz, does not count as data on the subject of either historic Jewish rejection of Christianity or historic Christian rejection of Judaism.

Commentary

PETER OCHS

This brief chapter extends the helpful comments on Jewish law that Yoder offered in Chapter 2. I won't review this aspect of his presentation here, except to note some of the scholarly sources that may support his view. Yoder mentions Krister Stendahl among Christian scholars and Hans Joachim Schoeps among the pioneers in this area among Jewish scholars. From around 1960 on, both of them offered historical and textual warrants for undoing the false Christian stereotype of Paul as 'rejecter of Jewish law' and of the Jews as legalists. In Yoder's words, these scholars teach us that Paul was, in fact, the 'great Judaizer of hellenistic cultures', not the hellenizer of Jewish culture. Among the many scholars who now extend and strengthen the arguments of Stendahl and Schoeps, readers might begin with the following: Scott Bader-Saye, *Church and Israel After Christendom* (Boulder, CO: Westview, 1999); R. Kendall Soulen, *The God of Israel and Christian Theology* (Minneapolis, MN: Augsburg Fortress, 1996); Robert Wilken, *The Land Called Holy: Palestine in Christian History and Thought* (New Haven, CT: Yale University Press, 1992); E. P. Sanders, *Jesus and Judaism* (Minneapolis, MN: Fortress Press, 1985); Daniel Boyarin, *A Radical Jew: Paul and the Politics of Identity* (Berkeley, CA: University of California Press 1994); Shaye Cohen, *The Beginnings of Jewishness: Boundaries, Varieties, Uncertainties* (Berkeley, CA: University of California Press, 2001); Roland Deines, 'The Pharisees Between "Judaisms" and "Common Judaism"' in Carson, O'Brien, and Seifrid (eds.), *Justification and Variegated Nomism,* Vol. I, *The Complexities of Second Temple Judaism* (Tübingen and Grand Rapids: Mohr Siebeck and Baker, 2001), 443–504; Scot McKnight, *A Light Among the Gentiles: Jewish Missionary Activity in the Second*

Temple Period (Minneapolis, MN: Fortress Press, 1991); Doron Mendels, *The Rise and Fall of Jewish Nationalism* (New York: Doubleday, 1992); A. J. Saldarini, *Pharisees, Scribes, and Sadducees in Palestinian Society* (Wilmington: Glazier, 1988); Lawrence Schiffman, *From Text to Tradition, A History of Second Temple and Rabbinic Judaism* (Hoboken: Ktav, 1991); Alan Segal, *The Other Judaisms of Late Antiquity* (Atlanta: Scholar's Press, 1987).

The new feature introduced in this chapter is Yoder's interpretation of Judaism's mission to the Gentiles. In Yoder's view, which I believe matches the plain sense historical evidence, not Paul, but the Jews of the Roman era, were the first missionaries to the Gentiles (p. 95). David Novak's careful studies of the categories of 'God-fearer' and 'Noachaid' support this aspect of Yoder's claim: that Jewish leaders of this period sought ways of including non-Jews among the at least partial-practitioners of the religion of Israel. There is also plain sense historical warrant for Yoder's claim that the Jewish apprehension about missionary work was largely an expression of their reaction against Christian missionizing. But Yoder freezes this insight into the strongly overstated dogma that 'Mishnaic Judaism' allowed itself to be defined by its rejection of missionizing religion. For Yoder's detailed argument, we need to turn to Chapter 4.

PART II

THE FREE CHURCH VISION
AND
THE JEWISH TRADITION

4

The Jewishness of the Free Church Vision

A. Introducing the 'Free Church Vision'

With the code word 'free church' we have become accustomed to refer to a style of phenomenon diversely labelled by the historians. We name the same phenomenon 'peace church' when attention is given to social ethics. We say 'radical reformation',[1] or 'restitution', or 'restoration' when attending to these groups' critical perspective on the accumulated unfaithful-nesses of historically established Christendom.[2] We say 'believers' church'[3] when concerned for the composition of the visible community. For present purposes the several names can be telescoped.

The concern of this chapter shall be threefold. I shall first seek to describe the early Christian communities, which were of course Jewish, as a 'free church' renewal movement within Jewry. In so doing I shall be particularly concerned with the thought and ministry of the apostle Paul.

Secondly, I shall note those marks of the 'free churches' within the Protestant West, which retrieve certain Jewish aspects of original Christianity.

Thirdly, I shall ask how our picture of the *present* state of relations between Christians and Jews looks different, from the vantage point of a 'free church' critique of Christendom, from the way it is seen by 'mainstream' Christians.

We began by observing the Jewishness of the teachings of Jesus at one particular point in his ministry; namely the quality of his pacifism. It was appropriate to centre upon that instance, because that has long been one of the places where it had seemed superficially, according to the predominant account, that Jesus was doing something other than fulfilling a Jewish vision. If we had chosen other topics such as his attitude toward the Sabbath or the Temple, the details of the demonstration would have been different, but the shape of the overall stance of fulfilment rather than abolition would still have been confirmed.

We next turned to the other most familiar point at which Christians are accustomed to defining Judaism in a particular way and then to negating it. This was the ministry of the apostle Paul. We observed that the notion of a formal rejection of Jewish identity by Paul is a profound misunderstanding, imposed on the first century by readers driven by much later concerns. Paul's vision of his ministry was possible only for a Jew, only understandable in Jewish terms. That leaves us back at the beginning of the conversation about what did not have to be. The 'fulfilment' claim leaves Paul's church permanently open to all of Jewry and Paul's Jewishness permanently open to the nations.

B. Jewish Thought Adjusts to Christianity

We noted before that the Judaism of Jeremiah, of Hillel, of Jesus and of Jochanan ben Zakkai was a missionary faith. It then represented an adaptation to Christianity, when the rabbis by the time of the *Mishna* abandoned their missionary openness, leaving that function to the messianic Jews (i.e. the Christians). What was cause and what was effect in this shift we cannot be sure. For the first time in the *Mishna* inter-visitation between messianic and non-messianic Jews is definitely discouraged, although in the total bulk of that literature it is not an important topic. Then one can shore up the differences by building up more oppositions.

Now, in the age of the *Mishna* (not before), it can make sense for Jews to say that the reason they reject Jesus is that the Christians affirmed that 'Jesus was God' and that 'the Jews' could not accept this denial of monotheism. This has to be a construction after the fact. It does not deal with the fact that all of the 'high' statements about Jesus as the Anointed which we find in the New Testament were made by radically monotheistic Jews and were not, when made, seen by those who said those things to be in any sense polytheistic or idolatrous. Nor is there any record that Jews in the first century rejected such formulations, whether made by messianic Jews or by anyone else.

Only now, after the schism,[4] could it make sense to spell out the argument that Gentiles do not need the Torah because they can make it into the age to come by keeping the rules given Noah.

Whenever and whyever it happened, Judaism did dampen its missionary openness before the onset of serious persecution of Jews by Christians, before Christians had concluded their alliance with the Empire. Persecution of Jews by Gentiles had been endemic to the ancient Roman world. It may be that 'Christians' progressively differentiated themselves from Jews in order not to share in that persecution, and thereby indirectly diverted the anger of Gentiles toward the non-messianic Jews. Yet this would not in itself explain the rabbis' abandoning missionary openness. In fact it could have had the opposite effect. Jews could argue as well as Christians, in fact better from now on, that they had no secrets, that their God was for everybody, that their morality was wholesome and their law reasonable.

In any case, Judaism after the schism turns out to be an ethnic enclave, less missionary than before, if not actually committed to a near rejection of the accession of Gentiles to membership in their community. Thus the abandonment of the missionary vision and action is a kind of backhanded adjustment, not to the Gentile world in general, but to Christianity. *Non-missionary Judaism is a product of Christian history*. For Jews to be non-missionary means that they have been 'Christianized': they have accepted a slot within a context where telling the Gentiles about the God of Abraham is a function that can be left to the 'Christians'. This applies to the development of the theory of the Noachic covenant as a parallel way of salvation.[5] And if the *birkat ha-minim* ever applied to Christians, it is only from this time on that that could be.

If the first stage of the Christianization of Judaism was the abandonment of the Jewish missionary vision, the last stages are the ones we now can observe, in the reciprocal acceptance of the Jewish minority and the Christian 'establishment'. In modern America, Protestantism, Catholicism and Judaism are the three kinds of equally legitimate, socially functionally equivalent theism. They are equally entitled to claim to represent the common 'Judaeo-Christian heritage'. In some circumstances this led also to a degree of theological assimilation, so that Reform Judaism became socially much like liberal Protestantism. Yet the same tripartite division of labour can also apply to Jews who are more traditional.

If assimilation into pluralism signified the rounding out of the Christianization of western Jewry, the development of Zionism is its culmination. The State of Israel models itself on western thinking. It defines Jews in such a way that most of them may be unbelieving or unobservant. The 'synagogue' is one more 'church' in America, abandoning the claim to represent a normative lifestyle. In the State of Israel Judaism is a state but no longer a believing community. Once the state was created, the separateness of Jewishness as an ethnic body is no longer needed as a base for religion or vice versa. Religion in the State of Israel can be just as individualized, just as pluralized, as anywhere in the West. Committed Judaism, i.e. a discernible people ready thoroughly and sacrificially to order their lives around their convictions as to the substance of the Torah, is a minority sect in Israel just as is Christianity, and just as they both are today in western Europe.

C. The Great Apostasy

When the magisterial Reformers (i.e. Luther, Zwingli, Calvin and their colleagues) spoke of the medieval Church as having lost the way, the unfaithfulness they had in mind consisted in the development of the Papacy and unbiblical doctrines of sacraments and Salvation. The deviation they deplored had not taken place before the sixth century, since these 'Reformers' did not intend to abandon the great creeds of the fourth and fifth centuries, or the achievements of Constantine, Theodosius, and Justinian in creating the Christian Empire. The 'radicals' of the Reformation on the other hand dated the 'fall' earlier, beginning at the latest with the persecution of dissenters at the order of Constantine, and perhaps much earlier at the death of the last apostle. For our purposes the exact date does not matter, but we are learning something about how to define the substance of the loss. The first dimensions of the loss to become visible are precisely those traits of early Christianity tied to the Jewishness of the gospel.

Part of the loss of Jewishness was of course the work of the 'apologetes', who reconceived the Christian message so as to make it credible or palatable to the authorities of Gentile culture, be they philosophers, priests, or princes, by sloughing off the dimensions of Jewish particularity. Thereby the faith became an ahistorical moral monotheism, with no particular peoplehood and no defences against acculturation, no ability to discern the line between mission and syncretism.[6]

With its Jewish roots dominant Christianity lost its vision of the whole globe as under God, with all nations (i.e. even beyond the Roman Empire, even including its enemies) seen as having their place and needing to hear their message. With their Jewishness Christians lost their understanding of Torah as grace and as privilege, replacing it with morality as requirements for salvation. With its Jewishness Christianity lost its capacity for decentralized congregationalism and was ready to function as the ceremonial ratification of the Byzantine court.

In our earlier discussion of the place of the synagogue and the sociological meaning of gathering around a book, we saw how Jewish identity was (and still is) rendered flexible by the ability to live without central administration. When both the theology and the sociology for such decentralized vitality had been abandoned, Christianity began to look to Rome for its definitions. Thus in principle, the issues raised by the radical reformers (John Hus and Peter Cheltschitsky, Michael Sattler and Pilgram Marpeck) were transpositions of the old Jewish identity agenda, now restated as an intra-Christian critique. The anti-clericalism, the anti-centralism, the warning against antinomianism, the rejection of national-governmental control of the churches, which had marked early Christianity, were rooted Jewishly just as truly as was the non-violence of the free churches.

D. Sociological Analogies

What we have here observed on the level of the axioms of Christian renewal can also be observed in the later experience of the 'free church' communities.

Whether we use the term 'radical reformation' or one of the other current alternatives ('peace church', 'free church', 'believers' church'), we speak of a critical stance toward what medieval Christianity had become, which considers the short-comings to be structural rather than superficial, and which locates them not only in dogma or moral tone but also in what had happened to the nature of the believing community. My interest here is not in analysing any one of the post-medieval renewal phenomena for its own sake, but for the commonalities of most of them. It is important that we do not single out Quakerism or Anabaptism,[7] but that we claim to speak for a movement both older and younger than your birthright or mine. Yet some of the social traits of the sub-community may demonstrate a greater similarity between Mennonite and Jews than between Friends and Jews, due to a greater commonality of settings.

Radical reformation and Judaism have in common that they see God as active in correlation with historical change and criticism more than with sanctifying the present. For one tack of socio-cultural analysis, it is possible to distinguish 'religion' as that which sanctifies and celebrates life as it is, things as they are, the personal cycle of life from birth to death and the annual cycle of the sun and the culture from spring to winter. Over against this understanding of 'religion', the category of 'history' represents the morally meaningful particular processes, which may not go in a straight line but at least go somewhere; they are non-cyclical, stable, repetitive.

Such a blunt pair of prior categories is far too simple to deal with many impor-tant distinctions we need to make: yet there is something to it. Where it does fit, we will find majority Christianity on the 'religion' side, and on the 'history' side we will find the Jews, radical Protestants, and (today) the theologies of liberation.

This means that God is not only spoken about and prayed to as the One who once acted. God is expected to keep on acting in particular identifiable events within history, in discernible and in fact to some extent even predictable ways. The way God acts will be the same, yet will continue to challenge and to change. Salvation or wholeness or peace will come, often at great cost for God's best friends and at the price of surprise, paradox and humiliation for those who felt the power game was already clear.

It is a part of the self-understanding of both Jews and radical reformers that they find no surprise, and even no embarrassment, in learning that their view is not generally acceptable. They expect to be outvoted. There are ways to appeal, in conversation with people from outside one's own community, to some kind of wider understanding or validation: but that their stance should be, or should have to be made, fundamentally acceptable to outsiders is not expected. There is no dismay at accepting that fact. They are unembarrassed about particularity.

The 'free church' agrees with Jewry in deriving its ongoing social identity, including its capacity to change, from the presence in its midst of a *book*. We need to meditate on the sociology of knowledge to understand how it is that a book can be a stronger power for change than other kinds of forces of critique or promise that arise rootless within a community. Catholic Christianity had the book too, but a screen of clergy and ritual, including a confident explanation of why the book did not have final authority, since it needed the teaching church to make it clear, kept the message of the ancient text from contributing to the Roman Catholic present more than a rubber-stamp function.

Official Protestantism restored the book; yet there was still the screen of professional clergy and state-enforced interpretations to assure that what it would mean would be supportive. By the time the Protestant Reformation became the establishment of the states of northern Europe, special measures had been taken against taking too simply the message of the book. Reading it was the prerogative of a scholastic class authorized by the state. Only the free churches made the book itself and the life of the community it described their fulcrum for historical criticism, making the study of that story the main theme of their meetings.

The first pro-Anabaptist meetings in Zurich and St Gall in 1522–25 were in fact called 'readings' (*lesene*). Their first leaders were called readers or teachers. In creating a new critical sub-culture around the text of their Scriptures, the Anabaptists were doing something more like the synagogue than like anything else going on in Europe at the time. The experience of Friends a century and a third later differed at this point, coming after Puritanism, because in the Puritan setting dogmatic or scholastic proof-texting had come to constitute a hindrance to the Spirit; yet the original Christian story remained the inspiration for George Fox as well.

The free churches were like the Jews in their seriousness about a distinctive moral commitment. They were accused by some of representing a new monasticism or new Judaism, over against the 'grace' thrust of the official reformation. The breaking point between Michael Sattler and the official reformers of the city of Strasbourg, which became in effect (when seen with hindsight) the decision that Anabaptism would be a separate and separatist movement, was due more than any other one thing to the stance which the reformers (Martin Bucer and Wolfgang Capito) expressed by appealing to the text from 1 Tim. 5.20: 'Christ is the end of the Law.' They applied this in such a way as to undercut the notion that any specific moral guidance from the Old Testament or the New is binding upon Christians.

The free churches of the sixteenth century did not see clearly enough to transcend the popular antisemitism of their times. They did not overcome the temptations of a too easy contrast between the two testaments, which seemed to be the easiest answer to the problems of violence in the Old Testament and to the six antitheses of Matthew 5. They did, however, retain, in parallel to Judaism, the affirmative sense of God's holy will being law and grace in one unity, not in contrast or paradox, God's holy compassion being formed in Torah, revealed in God's goodness so that we might find life in doing it, and not only with the intent that we be repentant of our failings or mercifully excused for not having tried harder.

The Anabaptists and Mennonites have been like the Jews geographically, differing somewhat in this respect from some Friends. Every foreign land could be their home, yet every homeland remained to them foreign. For the Jews this meant a recurrent reappropriation of the acceptance of exile, which we saw was the legacy of the age of Jeremiah. Over and over again, when driven from one land, they would settle as tolerated immigrants in another, for a generation or a few centuries, and then be driven on again. For the Anabaptists the migration was sometimes voluntary, but just as often it was undertaken in search of freedom of assembly and worship or freedom from military service.

It followed that Jews and Mennonites could be useful subjects wherever they went. Here again the experience of Friends differed somewhat. Grateful refugees are not always as critical of their hosts as they could be. Jews and Mennonites have sometimes been silent, when they were the guests of the lord of a given province, concerning that lord's sins against his *other* subjects. Part of the cause of the resentment against both Jews and Mennonites on the part of the bulk of the local population (Catholic or Orthodox) was sometimes the privileged status of that hard-working minority population which kept to itself, worked hard, paid its rents and taxes, and was appreciated by the rulers who protected them.

Yet even when tolerated, they never fitted in completely. Even when Mennonites were most at home in the countries which had given them refuge, they still held to adult baptism and usually to their rejection of combatant military service. The Jews, wherever they went, although adapting more or less to the outside shape of the host society, retained their Sabbath and (many) their *kashrut*, thus reminding themselves that they are not fully at home anywhere, at the same time that their family story-telling and their visits from cousins reminded them of all the other places where God's people also are living.

Mennonites are like Jews in facing today a crisis of self-understanding, in the tension between being a community of descent and one of dissent. Both are stretched between an ethnic and cultural identity consolidated by family process and a theological identity meaningful mostly for converted adults. In both communities, although in appropriately different ways, the questions keep surfacing again: is this a community of believing response to transcendent authority? or is it an extended family which celebrates its unity as a divine gift? Neither group has solved the problem by making faith purely spiritual or purely intellectual. Neither of them has solved it by being willing to be at home (as some Catholics and Lutherans have sometimes been) in a purely ethnic self-definition.

There are some who tend to think that the crisis of identity for Mennonites centres at the point of their pacifism, because it is there the most obviously that they say they hold to a position that the rest of the world refuses. Yet Mennonites have seldom been thoroughly or riskily pacifist. Certainly their peace position does not enter as deeply into their spirituality and self-understanding as is the case for Friends.

Perhaps this tension in Mennonite experience has something to do with the agricultural base of the Mennonite culture, even though Mennonites have seldom thought very much theologically about the land and its meaning as created, or as fallen, or as 'natural'.[8] Likewise many Jews have not interpreted expressly why so many of them should be merchants and moneylenders and scholars. In this respect Friends have been sociologically more like Jews. In any case, since Torah is permanently a word from above us, the accommodation to an ultimate 'religions' establishmentarianism can never be the last word.

E. Starting All Over

If we were to bring into the current inter-group conversation all of the unfinished agenda of the past, this would demand reviewing an immense inventory of past conflicts, correctly understood incompatibilities and well-intended misunderstandings. Here we shall have to be satisfied with noticing at what points there may be some hope for new beginnings of self-awareness and readiness for dialogue. Our having reviewed the beginning schism, which 'did not have to be', does not immediately tell us how after all these mistakes the conversation could begin again. Yet our discovery that Judaism as we now know it is in some ways more Christianized than it intended to be, and our ever-growing awareness that Christianity as the dominant cultural power of the West has sold out and needs radical renewal may all open our spirits to let the situation be redefined. Christian shame about Auschwitz is clear, but seldom is it clear what the needed correction is, or why the adjustments that some propose (abandoning christology? abandoning theology? abandoning God language?) would be good news.

For now I must be content with a mere listing of a few of the ways in which the argumentative content of the schism is also up for grabs.

F. When Messiah Comes, Will He Find Faith?

Many who call themselves 'Christians' do not believe any more in Jesus as the Messiah, any more than the Jews do. For many Christians the statement 'Jesus is Messiah' is not meaningful, or is not verifiable, or is not relevant. Some would not say it is not true but would be at a loss to say how it would make any difference. 'Christ' is for most of them simply Jesus' middle name. Any possible definition of what it could have meant for first-century Jews to say 'Jesus is Messiah' would be to them at best meaningless, or if meaningful untrue.

For others it is true that Jesus is Messiah but only in some 'mythical' or 'poetic' sense, which means something under the condition that it not be specified, and which leaves the door open for saying that there are other 'Christs' as well. This use of the label 'Christ' as a cipher designating any affirmation of fulfilment, or of functioning as 'key' is frequent in early post-liberal theology; we find it in different ways in Paul Tillich, Reinhold Niebuhr, and H. Richard Niebuhr (whose word for the cipher function of Jesus was 'rosetta stone').[9]

Still others will affirm the term as meaningful and true, but will deny to it the meanings that it had to the first confessors. They deny its classical implications for mission, or for doctrine, or for piety, or for hope, or for enemy love. They would not know what it would mean to speak of a 'return' or a 'coming' of Messiah.

Many other Christians, embarrassed first of all about any kind of particular faith commitment in the face of the pluralistic and relativizing impact of the Enlightenment, and reinforced in their embarrassment by a sentiment of guilt for their indirect participation in 'the Holocaust', want to see Jews otherwise than as people who reject the fulfilment of God's purpose for them. They do not take this 'accepting' stance on the grounds of the fundamental kind of rethinking proposed in the present study. On the contrary, they thereby prolong and harden the tendency to see western Jewry as just one more equally valid denomination of western Protestantism.

Within the new Jewish interest in Jesus, which I noted in an earlier lecture, some Jewish thinkers have overcome their historically justified resentments and historically conditioned definitions of what Jesus had so long meant to them, as the symbol of their being persecuted. Some of them have done this so redemptively and so creatively as to suggest that no Jew can be sure that, when genuinely the age to come will have come – however that be imaged – that fulfilment then will be different from the kingdom, which Jesus announced prematurely. Then what Christians (those who do) look forward to as 'second coming' may not have to be any different in substance from what Jews (those who do) look forward to as the first.

On the other side there are Jews for whom the State of Israel is in fact the messianic age. Some of those began to think and speak that way with the establishment of the new state in 1948, and still more after the 'Six Days' War' of 1967.[10] Still more such messianic language was current during the summer of 1982 under the heading 'Peace in Galilee', the tactical code name for the invasion of Lebanon. Some of this rhetoric may be cheap demagoguery; but certainly the affirmative claims to the land made by *Gush Emunim*[11] are not less authentically theological than the negative conclusions about God's power, or caring, which others have drawn from Auschwitz.

Our central argument has been to read the history from the beginning, and to discover that according to the way in which Jesus and also Paul expected and intended the Rule of God to proceed, the Jewish–Christian schism was not to have happened. We further sought to loosen up our imaginative capacity by rereading the history of both faith communities with an eye to their overlappings and the ways in which Christianity has misrepresented its Lord.

Now we have had to add a demonstration from the other end: namely by calling attention to the fact that many who call themselves 'Christian' have no commitment to affirm the past-ness of the coming of Messiah, and many who call themselves Jews do not in any traditionally recognizable sense affirm its futurity. Where then has the substance of our schism gone?

The falling-away of the old substance may mean reconciliation at some points, but it can also evoke new conflicts at others. It may reinforce cynical claims that group identity has very little to do with actual beliefs anyway. Its main meaning for the first phases of our reorientation might be a note of promise for those streams from within the Christian story that have attended most carefully to Christendom's failure. The recovery of our sense of the Jewishness of original Christianity and especially of 'free church' renewal should give a second wind to the forces of renewal. Whether the impact be commonality or dialogue, confession of guilt or joy in reconciliation and common witness, to restore the recognition of the sister communion might just call Christians back to their roots as the free church minorities in the West have been failing to do.

G. Bias or Special Pleading? Co-option? First Critical Afterthoughts[12]

The reading of the Jewish story which has been exposed here will obviously appear to some readers – perhaps especially liberal Jews or liberal Gentile Christians – to be 'selective'. I can be accused of finding in that story elements that happen to be compatible with my own convictions. This problem (or, when one feels someone else has solved it wrong, this complaint) is in no way peculiar to the agenda of understanding Judaism. It is an intrinsic part of anyone's reading anyone's history (even one's own). Yet it is fitting that here I should name this question, and wrestle with it for a while, rather than being satisfied with saying (what is quite true) that selectivity cannot be avoided.

Why not let the Jews be themselves? Is it not bias for us even to have an opinion as to who 'the Jews' 'ought' to be? Or who they are? Is it not both bad historical method and bad inter-community dialogue to choose one's own picture of who the Jews must properly be, what image of Judaism one considers representative?

Of course it is: but to take note of that fact is the beginning, not the end of our needing to work at the problem. The error is in thinking that it could be otherwise: that there could be some logical move, or some research technique, which would avoid the problem of bias or selectivity. We must own and struggle with the problem. It will not go away just because we denounce it. Least of all will it be gone if we disavow it or think that some other solution for it is simpler.

The problem is basic enough, classical enough, that people have been arguing about it for a long time. The attempted answers to this challenge are strung out along a long scale from 'objectivity' on the one end to 'relativism' on the other. 'Relativism', when the term is taken the most simply, means the claim that since all observation of any real phenomena is done from a particular perspective, there is no longer any point in claiming to be 'truthful' or 'correct' in understanding any specific phenomenon. This may lead to despair of any truth's being accessible: or it may lash back in the form of the claim that any one view of things is as good as any other. If there is no clear right neither can there be wrong either.

This issue is in no way unique to the specific realm of Jewish experience. There are parallels to other realms of religious conviction. The formula just used, 'any one view of things is as good as any other' is a little blunt. There is however real seriousness in the way the notion is used in a more self-confident form: since everyone else is selective, no one can object to my selecting, from within a given field of data, what happened to fit my own predilections. This is for instance the logic used by James Gustafson in favour of his own christology: since the Christian Scriptures include a great variety of perceptions of who Jesus was, Gustafson will feel free to choose that particular 'christology' which coheres with the rest of his system, which he has chosen on other grounds.[13]

In one sense, it is always that way. Every reader of the Jewish story tailors out of the great variety his/her own Abraham, his/her own Jeremiah, just as every reader of the American story has a specific Abraham Lincoln, a specific angle on World War II, or on Vietnam. But to be satisfied with this sweeping relativity is not enough. It denies the reality of the specific history, enshrining the observer's own identity as a functional absolute.

The other way to seek to respond to the challenge is to work at some specific instrument, some logical move, some statistical method, to sort out two kinds of data. One proposes to set aside on the left the 'particular', the 'provincial' (or if one feels more superior, the 'sectarian'). Thereby one confirms on the right those kinds of observations or convictions of which one can claim that 'any reasonable person' or 'an ideal observer' or 'all reasonable people' will agree. Sometimes these procedures of sorting out and validating are intellectual, focused upon the definition of one's terms, or on an *a priori* narrowing of the kind of data one can entertain.

Particular events, unrepeatable historical phenomena, events formed by specific cultural contexts, will tend to be disqualified *a priori* as not accessible or not convincing to everyone. At other times these procedures will claim to test the credibility of the witnesses we have, or the authenticity of the documents.

This approach to the challenge of particularity is as unconvincing as it is popular. Whether we address our criticism to the *a priori* logic of this 'sifting' approach or to the way it uses witnesses, such methodological scepticism, indispensable in a court of law where the innocent need to be protected, or as an ancillary discipline within the historian's vocation, cuts out most of the flesh of past reality, in the interest of being absolutely sure about the skeleton. It cannot read the past event empathetically as part of one's own world.

Usually the criticism of someone else's bias, from the perspective of this kind of call for 'objectivity', does not apply its scepticism to its own view. The claim to be 'public' currently (a move that is especially fashionable since 1985) characterizes a major stream in the American world of divinity school theology; what it means is to favour a particular level and style of abstraction in theological method. In the effort to assure itself of its acceptability in principle to all reasonable, critical observers, it screens out most of the texture of the reality it doubts, and enshrines the observers' own elite academic world and method as a surrogate church.

Having noted that this set of questions cannot be cleanly resolved in its own customary terms does not mean that we cannot learn something useful, even something essential, by studying the Jewish story as a special object of investigation, and the believing messianic community as a special place from which to read.

The reading of the Jewish story is a test *par excellence* for the problems of being fair with history, precisely because there is not, as for most other ethnic communities and most 'nations', any one central authority within the community to define from what perspective it must be read. Even when there was a royal house in Jerusalem, there were critics of the way the king sought to define his people's identity. Even when there was a temple, the priests' definition of the people's covenant was contested by prophets and neglected both by the non-Palestinian communities and by the *am ha-aretz*. For most of the centuries of Jewish survival the definition of leadership proceeded by the slow, non-violent, dialogical 'competition' of the rabbis for the respect of their pupils, and by the decentralized 'congregationalistic' networking of local synagogues, whereby *any* ten heads of family can establish a gathering under no one's outside governance. No central archive, no central government, no permanent turf: any reading of what can be called 'Jewish' is therefore a debatable selection. We need then to resolve the problem of how to read the story fairly from within relativism, with no claim to have escaped subjectivism in principle.

At the same time and in analogous ways, the perspective of messianic Christian faith is more clearly than some others vulnerable to the challenge of particular perspective. Medieval European imperial Christendom, or Imperial Russian Orthodoxy, or the Enlightenment claims of the French encyclopedists, or the arbitrage today of the news media, or the professional historians, or university academics, have all claimed and can consistently claim that the place where they stand is in some sense more reasonable, more universal, than other places. The missionary messianic community renounces such claims in principle.[14]

The shape of our problem, with neither the object of study nor the reader of the story being subject to irreproachably sure definition, makes it a prime occasion for testing and interpreting the shape of the truth question. How then do we work at being fair, within and not outside of the acceptance of the relativity of both the readers and the read? What are the ways to be more or less fair, when there can be no *absolute* certainty? How can we test the *relative* adequacy of our several construals of 'how things really were', once we have admitted that some older hopes for unassailable accuracy were unrealistic?

Let us begin with a resource we generally wish to be saved from: namely the fact that, and/or the way in which, minorities are misinterpreted by majorities. It is imperative to sense the element of injustice, which is generally vehicled by carica-ture, as anyone with some life experience within a misunderstood minority can tell. Yet one who comes to terms with the fact of caricature will soon become aware that there is no point in fighting back; it cannot be helped. Caricature can also be grace: there are favourable as well as pejorative caricatures, and even the pejorative ones often hide some underlying recognition or jealousy. 'Quakers' have taken a mock-ing caricature and, by accepting it, made it a respectable label. 'Anabaptist' was originally intentionally defamatory, as were 'Dunkard' and 'Quaker' and 'Shaker'. The peace church experience with caricature has as a whole been less tragic than that of which Jews have been victims, but Jews have often, under worse forms of exclusion, known how to turn around as a grace the injustice with which they have been misinterpreted.

People and groups living in the same world cannot avoid doing that to each other. The alternative to each of us having his/her own picture of the other would be to ignore each other and to limit each of us to describing only himself/herself, or to seek a kind of 'neutrality' or 'objectivity' by appeal to some statistical or logical manoeuvre, which would itself be the projection of a particularly small community's assumptions.

So instead of pretending to avoid the danger of seeing the Other in the light of Our own identity, the right way forward must rather be a constructive appropria-tion of the other's identity. We cannot not be selective; we can ask that the selectivity should contribute to reciprocal recognition, finding in the other what one needs, for the sake of one's own integrity, to esteem.[15]

I make then no apology for reading the vast melee of the Jewish experience in such a way that Yochanan is more representative than Menachem, Abraham Joshua Heschel than David Ben Gurion, Arnold Wolf than Meir Kahane, Anne Frank than Golda Meir.[16] What goes on here is *not* that I am 'co-opting' Jews to enlist them in my cause. It is that I am finding a story, which is really there, coming all the way down from Abraham, that has the grace to adopt me.

There are also more objective ways to verify whether the selectivity with which I read my image of someone else's virtues is fair (I prefer the term 'fair' to 'objective', and 'empathy' to 'bias').

(a) There are criteria of literary coherence that confirm that in the drama of prophetic discourse where mercy and indictment intermingle, mercy has the last word.

(b) There are criteria of socio-historical viability, whereby we can see, if we think about it, how it makes sense that the rabbis should outlive the Maccabees and the martyrs should outlive the Nazis.

(c) There are mystical, doxological criteria of coherence whereby the participant in the divine intention discerns the core of God's mode of action, or the deepest vision of God's will, thereby becoming able to discern as well God's nature.

(d) There are criteria of narrative and causative coherence, whereby we see our history and our brothers' and sisters' history as coherent, continuous, pregnant with promise on the way to fullness.

(e) There are criteria of connaturality, congruence, whereby our story and their story demonstrate similarities within their difference. This is the kind of empathy that has been of especial utility in the present study. It would not work in the same way if I were studying the Pentagon or NASDAQ.

(f) There are modes of clarification through conflict and contrast, whereby experiences of oppression and destruction, sometimes of communication or even reconciliation, can tell two very different communities something true and fair about themselves and about each other. This is well represented in our generation by the way in which the memory of Auschwitz has led hosts of Gentiles to encounter things they never would have been open to learn if they had had to hear through the channels of fairness or even congeniality.

These six modes of verification hardly exhaust what is available. They do illustrate, even 'prove', that we are not boxed into a dilemma between relativity, which permits no firm statements and prejudice, which is subject to no validation, or between 'objectivity' so defined as to be unattainable and 'subjectivity' which abandons truth claims. These six ways approach reliable communication and respectful mutual understanding by accepting and moving on through the reality of 'bias' in oneself and past the danger of 'caricature' or 'co-option' of the Other.

It would be more complicated if we were to seek to apply such a vision of understanding between Lapplanders and Buddhists or between Watutsi and Shinto priests. It would also be more complicated to converse between faith and doctrinaire enlightenment,[17] but where the commonalities of historical context and the congruences of social shape are as close as they are between historic Judaism and the peace churches, the room for positive dialogue is promising.

H. Since the Conversation Began

Since the perspective argued above was first sketched, research and publication in the field has escalated beyond what the amateur can follow. The retrieval of the Jewishness of Paul by Alan Segal,[18] Mark Nanos,[19] and others is most weighty. On the general theme of revisiting the schism there is in the work of James D. G. Dunn[20] a wealth of detail that I welcome. What Dunn does not deal with is the basic conceptual adequacy of the metaphor of two 'ways' which part at a particular point,[21] whereas the real cultural reality must have been much more like the branches of the Nile in its delta. Some rabbis became anti-messianic, perhaps as early as 135; and some followers of Jesus became fearful that the Hebrew heritage might turn Gentiles away. Yet there is no evidence at all that most rabbis were anti-messianic,[22] and most Christians were not in that way induced to forsake Jewish values.[23]

These pages have not reviewed the vast bulk of publication dedicated over the past generation to 'Jewish Christianity', nor do historians like Dunn whose basic interest is the first generations. These studies[24] vary enormously as to what documents and what movements they cover; yet all serve to warn us against assuming that the final shape of the schism was already full-blown when the first tensions are documented.

The other point at which Dunn's revision could have been extended is that he takes no account of the component of apostasy within later Christianity, i.e. he does not weave into his rereading of the first centuries a critical perspective on where anti-Jewish Christianity went later, and how the errors of later Christianity (when measured by the New Testament) were at the same time moves away from the Jewish heritage.

Notes

1. George Hunston Williams, *The Radical Reformation*, Philadelphia, PA: Westminster Press, 1962.

2. Richard Hughes (ed.), *The Primitive Church in the Modern World*,Urbana, IL: University of Illinois Press, 1995, is one recent overview of the theme of 'restoring primitive Christianity,' a widespread theme among churches of all traditions, but especially vital in nineteenth-century America.

3. Donald Durnbaugh, *The Believers' Church*, New York: Macmillan, 1968/ Scottdale, PA: Herald Press, 1985; James Leo Garrett, Jr. (ed.), *The Concept of the Believers' Church*, Scottdale, PA: Herald Press, 1969.

4. I accept the term 'schism' because it is already present in the study of the history, but it is not the most accurate term. In later Christian institutional history we say 'schism' when an institutional structure is torn apart by conflict. That is not what we are observing here. Two networking patterns became progressively stronger, initially with considerably overlapping constituencies and shared convictions. As the self-definitions became more demanding and more exclusive, the overlapping was less and less sustainable. But there was never a 'split' at the top, in any way analogous to the later actions of the patriarchs of Rome and Constantinople, or Rome and Canterbury, excommunicating each other, since at that time there existed no such 'top' on either side.

5. Cf. Chapter 3, n. 8 for a discussion of the notion of a different revelation to the 'sons of Noah'.

6. Long after first drafting these lines, I had occasion to review the study of the religion of Constantine, which the historian Burckhardt called a 'dreary monotheism'. Traditional discussions of whether Constantine was converted take on a different tone when one asks what kind of already apologetically Hellenized Christianity he encountered. Cf. my paper 'Constantine and the Conversion of Christianity'. [The editors have been unable to identify this document.]

7. This lecture was presented before a Mennonite audience in 1982, and to a Quaker audience in 1985. For both, the priority of the agenda of pacifism was self-evident.

8. It is in fact a striking oddity, when one considers the cultural and economic power of farming as Mennonite cultural base, that overt ecological awareness remained rare among Mennonites until the 1980s. The Rural Life Movement, like the Mennonite Community Movement, was a conversation of sociologists, not a self-aware drive of the economic mainstream. The Mennonite family farmer is more like a Rotarian than like a peasant.

9. [Editors' Note: Here Yoder is making an allusion to the first chapter – 'The

Enduring Problem' of H. Richard Niebuhr's book *Christ and Culture*, New York: Harper, 1951. Elsewhere Yoder provides a critique of Niebuhr's typology in his essay 'How H. Richard Niebuhr Reasoned: A Critique of *Christ and Culture*' in *Authentic Transformation: A New Vision of Christ and Culture*, ed., Glen H. Stassen, D. M. Yeager and John Howard Yoder, Nashville, TN: Abingdon, 1996, 31–89. Yoder's perceptive analysis of how Niebuhr's fivefold typology functioned in this influential study can be correlated with his analysis of how various typologies of Jewish–Christian relations have functioned as normative arguments masking as descriptive types.]

10. The prototypical and systemic use made here of the notion of messianity is not dependent on naïveté about the place of the word 'Messiah', or related concepts without the word, in the first centuries. As documented by *Judaisms and their Messiahs* (ed., Jacob Neusner, William Scott Green and Ernst S. Frerichs, Cambridge: Cambridge University Press, 1987), one can disengage many distinct Jewish communities and cultures behind the various texts they have left us, and each had a different definition of the bearer of hope, whether personal or not, whether called 'Messiah' or not.

11. The Gush Emunim ('the block of the faithful') emerged after 1967 and adopted its formal name after the Yom Kippur War. It is a movement of ultra-orthdoox and ultra-nationalist Jews who believe that the Bible promised Jews secure life in a Holy Land whose borders include the territories of Judaea and Samaria (the West Bank) and that they were thus commanded now to settle and defend all the land within those borders. While relatively small in number, members of the Gush Emunim have been the strongest lobby in Israel for Jewish settlements on the West Bank. They have also been the most energetic and extreme religious apologists and activists on behalf of these settlements.

12. The doubts identified here were first formulated in response to the presentation at Earlham in 1985. There would of course be more room to extend the discussion to take account of what has been said in the years since then.

13. I characterize this pattern in the argument of James Gustafson in my response 'Theological Revision and the burden of particular Identity' in Harlan R. Beckley and Charles M. Swezey (eds.), *James M. Gustafson's Theocentric Ethics: Interpretations and Assessments*, Macon, GA: Mercer University Press, 1988, 70ff., especially 79f.

14. This principled acceptance of the vulnerability of not being able to force anyone to believe is interpreted in my essay 'but we see Jesus' in LeRoy Rouner (ed.), *Foundations of Ethics*, Notre Dame, IN: University of Notre Dame Press, 1983, 46ff. and in my *The Priestly Kingdom*, Notre Dame, IN: University of Notre Dame Press, 1984. In my 'With Stout Beyond Babble' I argue that the renunciation of coercion, or the acceptance of the status of the vulnerable subculture, is in itself a criterion of transcultural communication and validation. The same point is made in Chapter 10 'See How They Go with Their Face to the Sun' (below, pp. 183–202).

15. This may be compared to what John Dunne, in a very different frame of reference, called 'passing over' as a modality of interfaith dialogue. *The Way of All the Earth*, Notre Dame, IN: University of Notre Dame Press, 1972.

16. I have to do the same for Roman Catholicism when I consider Dorothy Day more representative than Cardinal Spellman, Eugene McCarthy more than Joseph, the Helder Camara of the 1980s to the same man's role in 1950.

17. Yet as I argued in 'But We Do See Jesus'(*The Priestly Kingdom*, 59ff.) the free church vision has nothing to fear from authentic pluralism. Pluralism is the enemy of the establishment and 'realist' visions. It is the ally of Anabaptists and Jews.

18. Alan Segal, *Paul the Convert*, New Haven, CN: Yale University Press, 1990.

19. Mark Nanos, *The Mystery of Romans*, Minneapolis, MN: Fortress Press, 1996.

20. James D. G. Dunn, *The Partings of the Ways*, London and Philadelphia, SCM Press and Trinity Press, 1991.

21. He does signal the awareness of greater complexity by using the plural 'Partings' in his title, but most of his account still assumes the die was cast by 140 CE.

22. James D. G. Dunn follows the generally discredited reading of the impact of the *birkat ha-minim*. The *Mishna* includes the sayings of men suspect of honouring Jesus. This could hardly have happened if there had been a general purge.

23. Origen much later and Chrysostom still later preached on Sunday to people who had been in the synagogue on Saturday. This observation calls for a much greater sociological sensitivity than the history of theology has often shown. When the theologians have to preach against philo-Judaic practice, it is of theological significance that after all these years at least some Christians were continuing to attend synagogues.

24. Jean Daniélou, *The Theology of Jewish Christianity*, Chicago, IL: Regnery, 1964; Jean Daniélou, *JudéoChristianisme. Recherches historiques et théologiques offertes*, Paris, 1972; Richard N. Longenecker, *The Christology of Early Jewish Christianity*, Naperville, IL: A Allenson,1970; Frédéric Manns, *Bibliographie du Judéo-Christianisme Jerusalem*, Jerusalem: Franciscan Press, 1979; Frédéric Manns, *Essis sur le Judéo-Christianisme*, Jerusalem, Franciscan Press, 1977; Hans Joachim Schoeps, *Theologie und Geschichte des Judenchristentums*, Tübingen: J. C. B. Mohr, 1949. In a review on the theme in *Religious Studies Review* 9/3, July 1983, 201ff., Ernest W. Saunders names numerous other scholars.

Commentary

PETER OCHS

The wonder of this chapter is Yoder's introducing his vision of a profound overlap between the Exilic religion he sees within Rabbinic Judaism and his vision of the free church religion of the Anabaptists and Mennonites. But, before turning to the wonder, I will offer a few comments on the burdensome aspects of Yoder's vision of Judaism as a missionary faith (a vision he introduced in Chapter 3). He makes his point quite clear: 'the Judaism of Jeremiah, of Hillel, of, Jesus, and of Jochanan ben Zakkai was a missionary faith'; but the 'rabbis by the time of the *Mishnah* abandoned their missionary openness, leaving that function to the messianic Jews (i.e. the Christians)' (pp. 105–6). On one level, post-liberal Jews might actually find this claim energizing as a claim of depth history: stimulating them, in this age after the Shoah, to help renew Judaism as a mission to the world.

On another level, however, Yoder's readers could also take his claim as a warrant for delegitimating Mishnaic Judaism: judging its legal teachings and its protective care for the people Israel as mere reactions against the ascendancy of Christianity as first a missionizing religion and then a world-dominating mission. Indeed, Yoder infers from his own insight that 'non-missionary Judaism is a product of Christian history' and this 'Christianization' of Judaism culminates, negatively, in Zionism. Post-liberal Jews may observe here the dangers of Yoder's exaggerating and freezing an otherwise helpful insight. Even when it had missionizing tendencies, early Rabbinic Judaism was simultaneously protective of Israel as a separate people, and of Jerusalem as a centre of a landed dimension of Jewish religious life. Yoder may overlook the degree to which early Rabbinic Judaism was free of the bondage of propositional logic and its principle of excluded middle. The Jewish sages recognized that Judaism could be characterized, at once, by the religious ideals of centrality *and* non-centrality, landedness *and* non-landedness, group particularity *and* universality. The wonder of Yoder's insight is discovering that one set of conventional descriptions of Judaism are inadequate (that it is legalistic, merely landed and so on). Tempted, I fear, by the rigidity of modern logic (a temptation he may share with Steven Schwarzschild), Yoder appears to presume that if Judaism fails to display characteristic 'A' (mere landedness, etc.), it must therefore display 'non-A,' or the logical contrary of characteristic 'A' (for example, strict non-landedness). But this is not at all the case. Judaism's life is both: of this world and of the world to come, of land and no land, of home and of exile, of mission and non-mission. Within the logics of Greece and of modern Europe, Judaism cannot therefore be made to appear conceptually pure. There are other logics however, and post-liberal Jewish thinkers are at work right now identifying the non-Greek, non-European logics that may better serve Jewish religious reasoning (since Heisenberg and Einstein, since 'fuzzy set theory' and chaos theory and semiotics, there are many models for such a logic); and Yoder's students might better extend his insights if they were to place them within such logics. I believe Yoder may have seen past the logical paradigms that he had at his disposal. But let us turn back to the wonders of Yoder's vision of the free church.

Yoder suggests that 'the right way forward' to Jewish–Christian dialogue must 'be a constructive appropriation of the other's identity . . . what goes on here is not that I am co-opting Jews to enlist them in my cause, it is that I am finding a story, which is really there, coming all the way down from Abraham, which has the grace to adopt me' (p. 115). Yoder's readers could potentially misuse this intriguing quote by 'appropriating the other's identity' in just the way he warns against. But they could also glean from this quote a wonderful lesson in how to see what has always already been Jewish in the free churches. And, in this seeing, opening free church Christians and Jews today to mutually enriching dialogue. Without abandoning those dimensions of Judaism that fall outside of this area of overlap with the free churches, post-liberal Jews will have reason to celebrate the many dimensions of their heritage that the free churches may share. And they may therefore find in these areas of Anabaptist and Mennonite behaviour highly instructive demonstrations and testings of the virtues of their own Judaism.

5

The Forms of a Possible Obedience[1]

A. The Socratic Challenge to the 'Fall of the Church'

A key historical concept of the radical reformation – namely that of the 'Fall of the Church' – can be seen in the diversity of attitudes which the different branches of Christianity have toward the Jewish heritage of the first century. If as I have contended the 'Fall' of Christianity consisted in the loss of certain elements of the Jewish heritage,[2] I shall logically need to relate the radical reformation to the retrieval of those elements.

The radical reformers were not alone in using the notion of a 'Fall of the Church'. Lutheran and Reformed theologians, and even some Catholics, used it too. They differed as to what they considered to be the indices of fallenness, and therefore as to the date of the 'Fall'. For the Lutherans and Reformed, the errors were a wrong soteriology, sacramentalism, and the papacy. Thus the date of the fall was to be set after the fifth century, saving the classical creeds and the Christianization of the Empire. Likewise when eastern and western Catholics condemned one another, the reasons were different and the dates were still later. I point this out to avoid the thought that the radical reformers ('sectarian' in the sociological sense[3]) were any more 'sectarian' (in the theological sense[4]) than the others.

In the first chapter of this volume, I identified two traits of the Jewishness of Jesus and of Paul, which were legitimate, if not dominant or typical positions, for Jews to hold in that century. The legitimacy of my account was confirmed, more than I could have hoped, by the Jewish colleagues in that meeting. I spoke on the one hand of Jewish pacifism, which Christianity in the age of Constantine rejected, and on the other hand of Jewish 'universalism', rejected by the Christian apologetes of the middle of the second century. We concluded with the question whether 'anti-Judaism' like that of Justin Martyr was not already present in the Fourth Gospel.

In response to the argument of 'It Did Not Have to Be', José Miguez posed a Socratic question: 'You are backing the date of the Fall from the fourth century to the second, and now even into the New Testament itself. Does this not equate "Fall" and "History"? As soon as the church wants to use a language which will be understood (i.e. in this case Hellenistic thought forms) it is unfaithful.' I describe this question as 'Socratic' because I do not know how seriously Dr Miguez means it. It is a valuable challenge.

I shall attempt to explore this question in this address. It contains two components. One is doctrinal or dogmatic, which I shall identify at the outset. The second is practical, and leads me to the theme: 'What would be the form of a possible obedience?'

Before advancing to the dogmatic challenge, I must disavow holding the view which Dr. Miguez' Socratic question attributes to me. I do not grant either that the 'Fall' was immediate, nor that it followed necessarily from 'using language which could be understood'.[5] I reject the Hegelian scheme which dominated German exegesis from Baur to Bultmann, with a Jewish thesis (Jesus) followed by an Hellenistic antithesis (Paul) a generation later. In the 50s Paul was writing his letters in *koiné* Greek; he represented a powerful appropriation of Hellenistic culture well before the Gospels were written. The Jewish roots of the Church, its use of the Hebrew canon and the synagogue forms of worship and lifestyle kept the door open between church and synagogue for a century.

Nor do I accept the idea that the Fourth Gospel counts against my thesis. The Jesus of John's Gospel claims no less than the Jesus of the Synoptics to be fulfilling the hopes of the Jews. Those whom the narrative (especially in John[6]) calls *hoi ioudaioi* are not the Jewish people, but those leaders who opposed the (equally Jewish) openness toward Gentiles which Jesus (like other Jews, like the school of Hillel) proposed. The polemic (not a dialectic) is not between Jew and Gentile or Jewish and Hellenistic but between two kinds of Jews. The difference between John's Gospel and non-missionary Palestinian Jewry is no sharper than that provoked by other minorities, like those of the desert. Nothing says that the hostile *ioudaioi* were authorized or representative spokesmen.

Back to the Socratic challenge; the 'Fall' was not inevitable, nor was it immediate. To label it as wrong does not mean advocating an ahistorical perfectionism, but rather to prefer a different, historically available path, which was taken by some during a century.

B. The Possibility of Obedience

Dr Miguez' challenge can be taken as pointing to a philosophical orientation which I might call 'Augustinian'. In the Augustinian framework, finitude and sin tend to coincide. Faithfulness or 'perfection' is an 'ideal'. The visible, the historical, participates by definition in the fallen state of all creation.[7] Full obedience is by definition impossible, on grounds not of a wrong decision or rebellion but of ontology. No human being, no visible community, can be faithful to the will of God within a fallen history.

Over against this tradition, I need to situate a position which affirms the possibility of obedience within history. I classify Jews, Anabaptists, and Wesleyans[8] as 'possibilist' in this sense: they affirm a possibility in principle – not an achievement in fact – of human behaviour that pleases God.[9]

The Augustinians claim that to affirm the possibility of obedience is to deny historicity, since all historical realization is imperfect. The 'possibilists' respond: we affirm history under God precisely when we confess that God desires and is able to make possible an authentic human existence, or at least particular authentically human actions, within our finitude, in conformity with God's holy will.[10] Aware of this background ('dogmatic') debate, I now advance only hesitantly to the assignment to describe the form of a possibly obedient human community. I know that the collision of different views of historicity makes misunderstanding likely if not sure. My hesitation is not mere modesty, nor the diffidence of an ecumenical guest. It is the fear that an Augustinian grid must misread my 'possibilist' affirmations.

Yet another angle on the difference: for Augustine the true Church is indefectible. Despite all he said about sinfulness there is also something about the empirical

Church that can never go wrong. That is described by means of the *notae ecclesiae*, the traits of what can never be lost. For the radical reformers, on the other hand, the Church, any church, including their own, is radically defectible. The obverse of possible obedience is possible apostasy. This is why some say their vision was not for *reform* but for *restitution*, not a mid-course correction within the presently possible, but for a new beginning in the power of God.

The future of the Church is sure in the sense that God is a God who gives life to the dead. Yet the future of *our* church, that of any given community, enjoys no security. Thus when I distil from the radical reformation's historical witness a vision of the believing community, I do not say that such fidelity is assured, nor that it cannot be interrupted.

C. The Double Scandal

Now I must walk a very narrow path. On one hand, I must continue to offend the Augustinians, represented by Dr Miguez' Socratic question, by seeming 'Jewish', in the apparent pride of thinking it possible to do the will of God. On the other hand I have to offend my Jewish friends, by describing a possibility which could only become real if in Jesus and Pentecost the messianic age in fact began.

In the eyes of those I must offend, the offences are symmetrical opposites. Each side must see me as standing in the opposite camp. The rabbi must see me making unacceptable claims for the uniqueness of Jesus, one more Christian imperialist. The Augustinian will see me as 'Judaizing' or 'Pelagian', negating the need for grace.

Yet from my perspective – and here the introduction concludes – this 'narrow path' is neither a difficult balancing act, nor a tension between two dangers, but a unity. Because the Messiah came and poured out God's Spirit, obedience is possible. The obedience which was a potentiality became a reality in him. Pelagius affirmed (if the biased sources we have can be trusted) that there is something good left in human nature; an affirmation about Man. The 'possibilists' on the other hand are making an affirmation about God. The affirmation that obedience is possible is a statement not about me nor about human nature, but about the Spirit of God.[11]

To protect myself against the danger of using an arbitrary scheme of my own, choosing the elements which I like, I shall now take as my base a text from one of the radical reformation movements, the 'fraternal union' of Schleitheim, February 1527, written largely by the former Benedictine Michael Sattler. This text came with time to be an identity marker for one stream of Swiss and South German Anabaptists.[12] I shall follow its main affirmations as they describe the shape of a possible visible community, limiting myself as much as possible to describing without advocating. I thus walk the divide between the 'rabbis' and the 'Augustinians', not by clarifying a conceptual stand, but by describing a social process.

I am aware that this use of an ancient text as representative may appear naïve, since some of these ideas are common currency today. Yet in 1527 they were so rare as to call forth persecution; what counts is not their acceptability today but what it was that brought them to light then.[13]

D. Situating the Document

Many and varied forms were taken over the centuries since Constantine by the call for a radical reformation. There were medieval orders and third-order communities stepping aside from the *corpus christianum*. The Waldensians of the twelfth and thirteenth centuries and the Czech Brethren of the fifteenth had created independent communities, which the Czechs like to call 'the First Reformation'. The same kind of fermentation goes on all the way to the pentecostals and the 'base communities' of our own time.[14]

Within this panorama the Anabaptism of the sixteenth century bears a certain typical value, thanks to its coinciding chronologically, and clashing socially, with the other classical models of Reformation of that century, which most western Christians are used to calling 'the Reformation'. There were several types of 'Anabaptism' and numerous striking figures. We can take as 'archetypical' the characteristics shared by the three main strands of the movement which survived until 1540: the 'Mennonites' of the Low Countries,[15] the 'Hutterian Brethren' of Moravia,[16] and the 'Swiss Brethren' of the Upper Rhine basin.[17] The 'Brotherly Union' is the first witness to the commonality of the three strands, though it antedates the origins of two of them. We may use it as representative as well for the radicals across the centuries.

1. *The 'Nomic Element'*

Obviously the general effervescence of the 1520s called forth a wave of evangelical antinomianism. Catholics, Lutherans, and Zwinglians all testified to this. Such a loosening of moral discipline was certainly not the intention of the reformers, nor was it the product of their teaching. Nevertheless the rejection of some traditional moral disciplines and the popular preaching of 'freedom' spread more rapidly than did the new Protestant way of rooting the necessity of good works in the preaching of the gospel.

The radical reformation did not escape these same dangers. Spreading very rapidly and without liaison structures, the movement was in danger of disintegrating due to the variety of definitions and the high value ascribed to spiritual independence. We can see the effects of that climate in the words of Michael Sattler:

> A very great offense has been introduced by some false brothers among us, whereby several have turned away from the faith, thinking to practice and observe the freedom of the Spirit and of Christ. . . .They have esteemed that faith and love may do and permit everything and that nothing can harm nor condemn them, since they are 'believers.' Note well, you members of God in Christ Jesus, that faith in the heavenly Father through Jesus Christ is not thus formed.[18]

Yet Sattler's moral concern did not coincide with that of the magisterial reformers. The ethical content, the concrete decisions which obedience calls for, were different. The good works which testify spontaneously to the faith of the Lutheran, of the ethic of gratitude of the Calvinist, found their content in the orders of creation and preservation, with socially conservative implications, supporting the existing governments, economic institutions, the patriarchal family, etc. While the faith to which Sattler calls his readers finds its criteria in the example and the instructions of Jesus, with effects that if not directly revolutionary (because they are non-violent) had to be nonconformist. He rejected the Sword, the Oath, and the state church. What I propose to call 'the nomic element' is therefore epistemologically more important than in the other traditions, since for them the need is only to *motivate* an ethic of social conformity, whereas the Anabaptists' ethic must both motivate *and inform* a costly counter-cultural lifestyle.

The 'freedom' Sattler argues against is thus not only ordinary libertinism, but also the stance of the very tolerant reformers of Strasbourg, Martin Bucer and Wolfgang Capito. They had used the argument 'Love is the end of the law (1 Tim. 1.5)' in a conversation with Sattler[19] in such a way as to set aside his concerns for 'every point; namely with baptism, the Lord's Supper, force or the sword, the oath, the ban, and all the commandments of God'. For them, 'love', i.e. the reasonable consideration of what seems to be good for the neighbour, puts and end to any kind of biblical prescriptiveness.[20]

To reject this kind of suspension of all 'law' need not be done in a naive or literalistic way. Nor need one consider salvation as dependent on obedience as in legalism. Those dangers threaten every ethical position. For now it should suffice to fix on the fact that to appeal to Scripture as higher instance is a part of being a visible community of discernment, confessing its accountability to an objective norm transcending the community's own experience.

2. A Visible Decision

The second important dimension of community is recounted in the introductory narrative, using a very specific turn of phrase; 'we have been united to stand fast in the Lord';[21] not 'we agreed'. The verb is passive; the action of producing unity was God's. The Spirit acted, bringing about a previously absent unity of conviction.

It is the report of this event which 'accredits' Sattler's report. This epistemological assumption of the radical reformation is found as well in the young Luther and the young Zwingli; it is a congregational epistemology. The Word of God is heard in the assembly, known by the unity brought about when the Word is heard.

The kind of certainty which such unanimity provides claims no universality. It does define the obedience which is imperative today. The first 'fraternal union' of this kind (Acts 15) had been described by the words 'It seemed good to the Holy Spirit and to us.' The mark of the Spirit's presence is the gift of unity which reaches beyond the previously present opinions.[22] To become a visible community, what is needed is the concrete experience of having been brought to unity.

3. A Voluntary Community

Baptism shall be given to all those who have been taught repentance and the amendment of life, and who believe truly that their sins are taken away through Christ, and to all those who desire to walk in the resurrection of Jesus Christ and be buried with him in death, so that they might rise with him; to all those who with such an understanding themselves desire and request it from us.[23]

The issue of infant baptism can be posed from the general perspective of sacramental theology (what is required to make a sacramental action valid?) or one can debate the interpretation of particular passages (were there children in the household of Cornelius or the Philippian jailor?). For our present purposes, however, two sociological observations must suffice:

(a) In place of a decision made by one's parents, or dictated by the ethnic setting of one's birth, the integration of a member in this community presupposes a conscious, adult request for this visible sign of faith. The formation of the community presupposes missionary openness and non-establishment. Infant baptism is wrong not because a baby cannot have a born-again experience, but because only an adult can enter a covenant.

(b) The membership request includes a doctrinal and moral commitment. By virtue of the fact that the request is made freely, it does not bring with it the same dangers of alienation or later oedipal rejection which today attack traditions opposed by authority. For a community to be visible, the adhesion of each member must be freely responsible. For such a community to be an instrument of the will of God, it must offer to all men and women the possibility of such adhesion. Thus Anabaptism had a missionary stance in its century, by definition.

4. A Community with Borders

The ban shall be employed with all those who have given themselves over to the Lord, to walk after him in His commandments; those who have been baptized into the one body of Christ, and let themselves be called brothers or sisters, and still somehow slip and fall into error and sin. The same shall be warned twice privately and the third time be publicly admonished before the congregation according to the command of Christ.[24]

To the possibility of entering the community freely there corresponds the possibility of leaving it or rejecting it. The reconciliation process described in Matt. 18.15–20 is a series of conversations with the objective of 'winning your brother', not a chain of juridical procedures to castigate him. Implementing this 'rule of Christ' is very different in character from the so-called 'church discipline' of the Puritan traditions. The possibility remains open that the brother or sister, contradicting her/his original baptismal covenant, will not accept being reconciled with the community. The church will respect this rejection, and will ratify in the form of excommunication. For there to be a visible community, there must be a procedure to identify who is no longer its member.

5. Unity in Worship

In those years 1523–27 the debate between Zwinglians and Lutherans about the meaning of the Lord's Supper was beginning. Yet when Schleitheim speaks of the breaking of bread, its concern is not about alternatives to trans-substantiation. Here the concern is to safeguard the authentic unity to which the ceremony is supposed to testify:

all those who desire to break the one bread in remembrance of the broken body of Christ and all those who wish to drink of one drink in remembrance of the shed blood of Christ, must beforehand be united in the one body of Christ, . . . whose head is Christ, and that by baptism.[25]

Negatively, there needs to be a separation from the world of unbelief; positively the commitment of baptism. The Communion is not a resource offered by the Church to everyone who might want it, but the celebration of visible community by its members. To be a visible community, there need to be specific shared cultic actions.

6. Nonconformity to the World

In a situation of persecution, a community's survival will depend on their capacity to define together the borders of fidelity.

We have been united concerning the separation that shall take place from the evil and the wickedness which the devil has planted in the world; simply in this, that we have no fellowship with them, and do not run with them.[26]

Every living society has its limits, its *damnamus*. For Anabaptism, the limits are less dogmatic than sociological. They do not condemn heretical doctrinal formations (as do the Protestant creeds) nor specific personal practices (like the so-called 'pietist ethic'), but rather the expressions of wrong community; apostate worship, alcoholic partying, commitments of bad faith,[27] and violence.

7. Autochthonous Leadership

The shepherd in the church shall be a person according to the rule of Paul . . . who has a good report of those who are outside the faith . . . in all things to take care of the body of Christ, that it may be built up.[28]

The very first Anabaptists tended to recognize only the leadership of the itinerant apostle. Yet within two years Schleitheim has come to call for a local shepherd.[29] He is marked by his rootage within the local community which calls him to serve. No academic formation is needed to qualify him, and no authorization by government or 'ordination' by some ecclesiastical agency from outside. This is not to argue for a doctrinaire 'congregationalism' which would negate the reality of 'Church' beyond the locality; Schleitheim was the first Protestant synod. To be a visible community there needs to be leadership responsible primarily to the community itself.

[A minor polemic parenthesis. It is often argued that the recourse of the 'magisterial' Reformers to the support and control of their respective states, while regrettable, can be explained and justified by the need to organize new viable ecclesiastical structures, over against the old Roman Catholic order, as quickly as possible. Yet by 1527 there existed no official Protestant ecclesiastical structure. There were as yet no Reformed synods, no Lutheran consistories or visitations. Yet at Schleitheim and a few months later in Augsburg the Swiss and South German 'brothers' were able to formulate and fortify their faith unity, which would be respected throughout the triangle Bern/Worms/Tyrol, capable of surviving, maintaining its identity, and propagating itself in the face of the opposition of both Protestant and Catholic governments.]

8. Cross or Sword

The 'pacifism' of the Anabaptists did not promise a peaceful world. Their rejection of 'the Sword' was derived from their loyalty to the teachings and example of Jesus. It cannot be imposed on a world without faith. It represents a minority lifestyle in the midst of a violent world that the Church cannot dominate.

> The sword is an ordering of God outside the perfection of Christ . . . But within the perfection of Christ only the ban is used . . . without the death of the flesh.[30]

This does not imply a rejection of concern for public life. This article rejects participation in ruling (*Obrigkeit*), but feudal lordship is not all the public life that there was. The suzerainties of the time had no democratic base. They were hereditary (in the Lutheran princely territories) or corporative (in the city states of the upper Rhine basin which became Reformed). They did not provide community services (health, schools, roads, post) but concentrated the use of their arms on the maintenance of their social control, the punishment of common crimes, and the persecution of Anabaptists. It is that kind of government in which, says Schleitheim, there is no place for the disciple of Jesus. Nothing is said on the other hand to exclude participation in other kinds of services under other kinds of regimes.[31] Nor does it call for unconcern even for the governments of the time. Even without any elective voice, Anabaptists took positions about the taxation systems, usury, the death penalty, on the civil wars provoked in Switzerland by the Zwinglian movement, and on the potential crusade against 'the Turk'. Thus renunciation of 'the sword' by no means meant avoiding involvement in public life.

Article VI of the Schleitheim Confession circles around three questions:

(a) May the Christian use the sword against the wicked for the protection and defence of the good; or for the sake of love:

(b) whether a Christian shall pass sentence in disputes and strife . . .

(c) whether the Christian should be a magistrate if he is chosen thereto . . .

Each time the answer is found not in a sentence from Jesus teaching as a rabbi, but in a decision made by Jesus as social actor in the Gospel narrative, surrounded by a Palestinian society which expected from him that he take some responsibility. The disciple's ethic is thus understood not as an especially rigorous application of certain key phrases or certain fundamental principles, but as having a share in the posture which Jesus took in the face of the challenges addressed to him by the messianic expectations of his time.

> As Christ our head is minded, so also must be minded the members of the body of Christ through Him, so that there be no division in the body.[32]

To constitute a visible community there has to be an answer to the problem of power.

9. Trustworthiness

It is hard for us to realize how important, in the culture of that time, was the moral support which the subjects' loyalty oath provided to a public order whose leaders were very aware of their fragility, but also trusting as to the power of the words of an oath.

The 'humanistic' or 'enlightened' argument against the use of the oath will accentuate the weakness of such pronouncements. Should one want to lie or break a promise, having spoken an oath will not prevent it. Demanding oaths in sober ceremonial settings amounts to conceding that in ordinary circumstances one may lie with impunity.

> Christ, who teaches the perfection of the law, forbids his followers all swearing . . . we cannot perform what is promised in swearing, for we are not able to change the smallest part of ourselves.

The argument of the Anabaptists (as of Jesus) rejects the oath for an opposite reason; namely because it claims to lay hold on God for one's own purposes. This may be to promise absolutely something one is not absolutely sure to be able to perform. Their concern is not that 'using the name of God' has no weight, but rather that the cultic presumptuousness of such an invocation constitutes an offence against divine sovereignty.

For there to be visible community, there must be an ethos of communication which is not dependent on sacral sanctions.

Epilogue

There would be more to say to explicate all of the intentions of the 'radical reformation', well beyond what clamoured for clarification in 1527, and still much more to sketch out its capacity for ecumenical confrontation and for adaptations to address other times and places. This should, however, suffice as a general description of a community capable of surviving, of making decisions, of propagating itself even on hostile terrain, and of creating an internal culture of moral and economic mutuality.

In a form befitting their century, and within the limits of their capacities and opportunities, the Anabaptists were able to rediscover and realize[33] a functional equivalent of the original messianic Jewish universalism, as of the original Jewish messianic pacifism, which had characterized the earliest churches, which had later been abandoned by both the anti-Judaic Catholicism of 'Christendom' and (to a lesser degree) the defensive Judaism of the Mishnaic codification.

Notes

1. This essay originated in a seminar presentation that John Howard Yoder gave at a seminar of Jewish and Christian theologians at José C. Paz on 18 November 1970. José C. Paz is one of the outer suburbs of Buenos Aires. At that time it was the site of the Lutheran Theological Faculty which was in the process of merging into the Instituto

Superior de Estudios Teologicos, of which Dr José Miguez Bonino was the outgoing rector. This was the second session of the tri-faith group to which I was asked to speak. (The first one had occurred on 16 September 1970.) I had no memory of this second session until I found my text in the files, June 1996. The following text is translated from the original Spanish typescript. It is added here despite some duplication as a testimony to the context of the original paper's setting, where 'radical reformation' and the loss of Jewishness were already interlocked.

2. The meeting of 16 September in the Seminario Rabinico of Belgrano, Buenos Aires, was the first presentation of the paper which later became 'It Did Not Have to Be' (see Chapter 1 above).

3. I.e. in living as a dissenting community within a hostile world.

4. I.e. claiming to be the only true Church.

5. It was quite possible to talk in Hellenistic terms without becoming either conceptually or socially anti-Jewish. There were for generations (in fact for centuries) other Christian groups which did not become anti-Jewish.

6. This theme is dealt with elsewhere in the present volume; cf. Chap 1, p. 49–51.

7. This is yet another notion of 'Fall', we note; but this time a pre-historic Fall nearly identical with creation.

8. My host Professor Miguez Bonino, the senior ecumenical Protestant churchman of Latin America for decades, is himself Methodist. The style of Methodism in South America's southern cone was closer to the aggressive evangelicalism of Wesley's age than to modern Methodism in North America. [Editors' Note: Yoder did not attempt to offer a full explication of his claim that early Methodism was 'possibilist', but had he done so he could have discussed John Wesley's notion of the 'covered promise' – whatever God commands, God will provide the grace necessary for the performance of the divine mandate. In sum, Wesley believed it was possible to obey all of God's commands, including those found in the Sermon on the Mount, which theologians in the Lutheran tradition tend to think of as impossible to fulfil.]

9. The textual basis in the NT would be the usage of the verbs *areskein, eudokein, arestos*.

10. Since the question was opened by reference to Augustine I should ward off a reference to Pelagius. The confidence that there can be human obedience is not (for the posture I here seek to characterize, as it seemed to be for Pelagius) a statement about the capacities of the human. It is a statement about Jesus and the Holy Spirit.

11. If there were time I should argue that this 'possibilist' perspective involves an understanding of human depravity which is more pessimistic than Augustine's.

12. First annotated English translation in my *The Legacy of Michael Sattler*, Scottdale, PA: Herald Press, 1973, 27ff.

13. At the request of Dr Miguez, on behalf of the regional association of theological schools, I was editing and translating at that time a Spanish collection of radical reformation texts, since published by *Editorial Aurora* as *Textos Escogidos de la Reforma Radical*, including the Schleitheim 'Brotherly Union'.

14. Donald Durnbaugh's *The Believers' Church* (New York: Macmillan, 1968/ Scottdale, PA: Herald Press, 1985) gathers a representative bouquet of such stories, but does not seek to be inclusive of all the movements that would fit the definition.

15. Called by that name only outside of the Netherlands. In the early generations they differed from the others in their view of the humanity of Christ.

16. They differed from the others in the practice of community of goods. They were also more intentionally structured than the others in the sending out of missionaries.

17. In some respects the groups can be further subdivided, but not in ways that matter for our purposes.

18. Cover letter to the Schleitheim articles, in *The Legacy of Michael Sattler*, 35f.

19. *Legacy*, 21ff.

20. This notion of 'love' was a common theme of the magisterial reformers; cf. its fuller expression by Zwingli in my *Taufertum und Reformation im Gespräch*, Zurich: Zwingli Verlag, 1968, 44–51.

21. 'Wir sind vereinigt worden.'

22. The proto-Protestant congregationalist epistemology is described on pp. 96–116 in my *Täufertum und Reformation in Gespräche*, Zurich: EVZ Verlag, 1968.

23. Schleitheim, *The Legacy of Michael Sattler*, art. 1, p. 36.

24. *Legacy*, art. 2, p. 37.

25. *Legacy*, art.3, p. 37.

26. *Legacy*, art. 4, pp. 37f.

27. It is not clear whether this means promises one does not expect to keep, or promises to do wrong deeds.

28. *Legacy*, art. 5, pp. 38f.

29. The word is of course etymologically identical to 'pastor' but that has not yet become a synonym of a professional role parallel to 'priest'.

30. *Legacy*, art 6, pp. 39f.

31. Pilgram Marpeck, the strongest leader of upper-Rhine Anabaptism in the second generation, worked for city governments all his life as what we would call a civil engineer.

32. *Legacy*, art 6, p. 41.

33. [Editors' Note: Here, the original text of Yoder's text included a subtlety not easily rendered in English.] In Spanish 'realize' means not 'become aware of' as in English, but 'achieve'.

Commentary

PETER OCHS

In 'The Forms of A Possible Obedience', Yoder continues the rapprochement he introduced in Chapter 4, describing the overlapping virtues of the free church and the exilic strand in Rabbinic Judaism. With the exception of a minor reappearance of Yoder's dogmatic tendency, this chapter offers only positive reinforcement for post-liberal Judaism and its Christian dialogue partners. It positively reinforces Jewish and free church observance of several virtues, of which four merit special note. The first is the virtue of concrete obedience, as manifested in Jewish law and in Free Church 'nomism' (pp. 122–5). Yoder offers a wonderful image of the capacity of Jews, Anabaptists and Wesleyans to 'affirm the possibility of obedience within history' (p. 122). Since Jewish 'legalism' is perhaps the most misunderstood feature of Rabbinic Judaism in both Christian and highly liberal Jewish circles, post-liberal Jews should celebrate Yoder's labelling this love of law 'possibilism': the world affirming recognition that we could possibly imitate God's life here in this physical world. For comparable affirmations, readers may want to consult David Hartman, *Joy and Responsibility: Israel, Modernity, and the Renewal of Judaism* (Anti-Defamation League, 1986) and David Novak, *Jewish–Christian Dialogue: A Jewish Justification* (Oxford, 1992). Stanley Hauerwas and Novak also have very constructive dialogue on the nomological dimensions of both Christianity and Judaism in their contributions to *Christianity in Jewish Terms*, ed. T. Frymer-Kensky et al. (Westview, 2000), 115–26 and 135–40.

The second virtue is that of community. For supportive presentations, readers may refer once again to the Hauerwas–Novak discussion and the epistemology of communal study of Scripture that is ubiquitous in Hauerwas' writings and that appears in such recent Jewish studies as Steven Kepnes, *The Text as Thou: Martin Buber's Dialogical Hermeneutics and Narrative Theology* (Indiana University, 1992); Emmanuel Levinas, 'The Temptation of Temptation', in *Nine Talmudic Readings by Emmanuel Levinas*, trans. Annette Aronowics (Indiana University, 1990) and Kepnes, Ochs, and Gibbs, *Reasoning after Revelation* (Westview, 1998).

A third virtue worthy of special note is that of non-conformity to the world: the proven capacity of both Jews and members of the free churches to live within, yet apart from western culture as witnesses to the life we must live in the world, yet guided by that which is not of the world. A final virtue worthy of note is what Yoder calls 'autochthonous leadership'. Here is a wonderful meeting place between the rabbis' and the radical reformers' fidelity to both the universality of God's directives and the locality through which, alone, those directives are heard and lived.

6

The Restitution of the Church:
An Alternative Perspective on Christian History[1]

A. Introducing Restitutionist Movements in Christian History

My task is to introduce and interpret – sympathetically – a group of Christian churches, and a body of distinctive convictions, which are only slightly known within the Orthodox and Catholic communions. I shall undertake this in the pedestrian form of a sketchy historical account.

1. Protestant – 'Official' and 'Radical'

The label 'Protestant', especially in European usage, usually refers to those movements whose right to exist over against Roman Catholicism was fought out on the political level in the sixteenth century: the Church of England, the Churches of the Confessor of Augsburg, and the several national Reformed Churches. These groups differed from one another significantly, but they had in common that all held socially, each in its province, to what could be retained of the pre-Reformation arrangement; the structure of the Church remained under the control of the civil authorities; the membership of the Church (except for the Jews) remained continuous with that of the civil society, unity expressed by the obligatory baptism of infants.[2]

The phrase 'radical Protestantism' takes its definition from the contrast with the 'official Protestantism' just described. The numerical identification of Church and society, i.e. the obligatory features of being 'Christian', and the ecclesiastical prerogatives of the civil rulers, have no basis in the New Testament. They came into being with and after Constantine. Therefore a more radical reformation will reject them.

Historians of the Reformation have always known about the dissenters on the left, who despite their very modest number seem to have threatened the Reformers more than the Catholics on the right. But these dissenters, usually called 'Schwaermer' or 'fanatics', were for a long time not studied for their own sake, but rather served as a foil to show how right the official Reformers were. Only the last century has seen the beginnings of a more objective historiography, of which the massive summary by Prof. George H. Williams of Harvard University is a first culmination.[3] I shall attempt to limit my summary to matters on which scholars agree.

The 'radical reformers' of the sixteenth century 'went beyond' the official Reformers in a simple biographical sense. Almost all of them were first followers of Martin Luther or of Calvin's predecessor Ulrich Zwingli. They 'went farther' because they became convinced that to leave the Church under the control of the state, and to keep church membership obligatory, would prevent the fundamental renewal which the return to Scripture as sole authority offered.

Yet it cannot be said simply what 'going beyond' these two reformers had to produce. By the nature of the case, there could be no firm central definition of single unified alternative 'church' form. There were some, whom the historians call 'Spiritualists', who rejected not only civil control but all visible social forms and rituals. A few others became far more notorious by seizing and reversing the former view of the state rather than abandoning it; they blessed violent revolution as an instrument of reform. A few others centred their 'radicality' upon dogmatic questions, challenging (on biblical grounds) the inherited formulations of the doctrine of the Trinity or of the 'two natures' of Christ.

More important numerically though less visible, more important for the future, were those whom we might call 'Free Churchmen' or 'ecclesial Anabaptists'. They replaced obligatory church structures with voluntary ones, able at least in some places to survive despite the persecution of both Catholic and Protestant governments. Three major strands survived beyond the sixteenth century and until our time; one in the upper Rhine valley, one in the Netherlands, migrating eastward along the Baltic and into Russia, and a third, the Hutterian Brethren, distinguished by the practice of the community of goods. Descendants of all three strands survive in North America.

It was fitting that one should first locate the 'radical reformation' in the same sixteenth century with the 'official Reformation'. The coincidences of time and personality illuminate both. But once we have clarified the 'model', we are equipped to identify parallel phenomena in other centuries as well. Thus it is that some historians accept an anachronistic use of the 'Anabaptist type' to designate this kind of church whenever it occurs. Differing in detail, these other groups still show the same marks, reflecting the same structural options.

2. Precursors of the Radical Reformation

In the twelfth century the shape of the struggle for church renewal was the preaching of evangelical poverty; vernacular retelling of the gospel story and mendicant itinerancy. The 'centre' of this movement became Franciscanism. Its left wing, almost identical in content but dealt with very differently by the hierarchy, became the Waldensian movement.

The first 'Reformation' in the sense of a regional-political break with Rome was the Czech Reform of the fifteenth century. Like the larger movement a century later, it had as well its lonely spiritualists and its violent visionaries. After successive disappointments in the national-official church, it too produced a 'free' or 'Anabaptist-type' fellowship, the *Unitas Fratrum*, formalized in 1467.

3. The English Reformation

Britain's major radical reformations came in the seventeenth century. On the left edge of Puritanism, leaning but only slightly on earlier continental Anabaptist models, we find both the Friends and the Baptists, the former a little more original, the latter a little less, than their continental precursors.

4. 'Free Church' Protestants

Pietism was in the late seventeenth and the eighteenth centuries predominantly a renewal ferment within official Protestantism. Yet it happened twice – once with Zinzendorf and the Moravians, and again with Wesley and his Methodist – that the inability of the official structures to contain the new patterns of mission and piety led to the formation of separate fellowships. Still less often did it occur, as in the case of the several 'Brethren' movements emigrating to Pennsylvania, that such groups would appropriate the Anabaptist/Quaker view of the State or anti-paedobaptism.

The impact of these several movements upon the Anglo-Saxon social order was to make increasing room for varieties of church forms. Even Lutherans and Catholics when they moved to America had to become 'free churches', competing on the free market. The resulting dividedness and debate soon became the source of a new spiritual concern, even a new sense of fallenness.

Thus in both Britain and North America the nineteenth century was marked by new beginnings seeking to overcome divisions by simply rejecting denominational structures and labels, regaining thereby the freedom to live directly from the 'New Testament Pattern'. 'Pattern' is the word, both for the 'Brethren' gathered in Plymouth and Bristol, and for the American 'Disciples' or 'Christians'.

The impact of these frontier movements, joined to the continuing mobility and growth of the Baptists, produced in America, especially in the south and west, the paradox of a kind of informal 'establishment', with the free church way becoming the numerically dominant form of Christianity. This could not fail to call forth new renewals, but they have tended to stay within the forms of the traditions they speak to revitalize; evangelism and believers' baptism, relative congregational autonomy, trusting the Bible in the hands of the laity, etc.

Thus the 'Bible churches' and Pentecostal communities which have shown the greatest growth during the last century are formally in the 'believers' church' family, even though their rapid expansion and their weak sense of history make the link somewhat tenuous.

I should offer one brief note about terminology before proceeding beyond this very rapid survey: I have intentionally used interchangeably, as designations of the same phenomenon the several current terms 'free church', 'radical', 'restitutionist', 'anabaptist,' and 'believers' church', quite aware that in a full treatment closer definition would be needed and that *in other contexts* some of these phrases have been used quite differently. Especially the phrase 'free church' in Anglo-Saxon usage is usually much broader, although Franklin Littell uses it in this sense. 'Believers' church' is the phrase of Max Weber, which seeks to be sociologically neutral, but can be misinterpreted as prejudicial.[4]

B. Observations about Common Features of the Believers' Church

Now that we have sketchily before us the outlines of this other stream of reformations, from clandestine Waldensians to the Pentecostal explosion, what do these people stand for?

1. *Congregationalism*

The first observation may not be the most important, but it must be noted first because it gets in the way of giving simple answers down the lines. The commonality of 'these people', 'these movements', is not first of all dogmatic or doctrinal. Some are children of Zwingli and retain his views on the sacraments. With regard to the doctrine of election, some are Calvinist and some Arminian. The commonality must be discerned inductively, within their variations, and biographically, within their coming-into-maturity as responsible movements.

Nor is the commonality organizational. What makes it possible for Lutheranism or Calvinism to have a unified body of doctrine is the coincidence of two requisitions; a leader of unchallenged authority, and hierarchy both ecclesiastical and civil to support him. The free church movements seldom had leaders of such pre-eminent weight, and they were opposed to hierarchy as a definition of the unity of the Church. With the early Zwingli and early Luther, they help that every local congregation, assembled around the Word of God and led by the Holy Spirit, is qualified to rule concerning faith, practice, and ministries. If there is but one Word of God and one Spirit, the local decisions, if reached validly – i.e. with freedom and order – will be in essential agreement all over the world, but there is no organ, and no need, for seeking full uniformity. Sometimes this congregationalism is radicalized in the *rejection* of all structures wider than the congregation. More after broader consultation and collaborations are affirmed through conventions and conferences yet without relinquishing the priority of the local assembly, and while seeking to make the other meeting 'congregational' rather than 'parliamentary' in quality.

2. *Voluntary Membership*

The voluntariness of adherence to the Christian community – as expressed by the rejection of infant baptism – is both a personal and a social statement. Stated negatively, it breaks the givenness of the social order into which the sacrament of birth incorporates every child. Positively it enables the creation of a visible counter-community, distinct from the structures of clan, city, and state. Later debates, especially after the individualizing impacts of Pietism and the Enlightenment, could argue as well that only believers' baptism as testimony to one's own, unique conversion experience, is compatible with modern western personalism.

3. *Religious Liberty*

But this voluntariness was not a change that could be achieved in a vacuum without opposition. Medieval religion and politics were inseparable. Voluntariness in religious community thus meant the rejection by a voluntary community of the control over its members claimed by both state and state church. The modern label for this theme is 'Church–State separation' but that designates the legal solution to the problem. Unfortunately when the independence of the believing community from civil control was at stake, 'separation' was not an option. Official Church and State were so united, that religious liberty was tantamount to civil insurrection, and was punished as such.

4. Non-violence

Behind religious liberty there lay yet another level of challenge to the authorities of Christendom. Not satisfied to deny to Caesar the authority to govern the Church, the radicals followed Jesus in rejecting the violence with which men claim the right to govern the world. For most of the 'radical reformers' this meant a non-violence or non-resistance of principle and conscientious objectives to military service. For a handful it flipped over in the vision of an apocalyptic 'end-time war'. For others, mainly the Baptists, thoroughgoing non-resistance was not affirmed, but a greater effort war invested in safeguards to keep the State's claims modest and the Church's freedoms clear.

Other dimensions of distinctiveness that characterize congregations in the 'believers' church tradition' include consensual decision-making, non-clerical ministry, reconciling discipline, communal economics, and love of enemy.[5]

C. Restitutionism: An Alternative Perspective on Christian History

In what sense can it be said that these movements represent 'an alternative perspective' on Christian history?[6]

1. Defectibility and Apostasy

The terms 'restitution' and 'restoration' were given currency in the nineteenth-century American debate, and have been used by historians since then. A contrast is intended with the softer term 'reformation'. To advocate 'reform', although one may be very critical of things as they are, still expects the needed change to be accessible in continuity with the present. A new direction can be taken from where we are. For the advocate of restitution, that trust is too optimistic. It trusts a sick organism to heal itself. The radical renew of the Church must be not a mid-course correction but a new beginning, to correct for a fundamental wrong turn in the past.

The key difference is how to understand the *defectibility* of the Church of the past. The 'mainstream' churches are affirmative about God in history, since they give him the credit (i.e. claim his authority) for their own existence and their positions, including the rightness of their respective ways of differing from Jesus (and from each other). But they do not take history *critically*. They do not consider it as seriously possible that God might have been abandoned by the people claiming to act in his name.

The backdrop for the concept of restitution is thus the reproach of apostasy. Fundamental unfaithfulness within history is not only hypothetically possible; it has happened, and it is we who have done it. Christendom does not merely need improvement around the edges; it has become disobedient at the heart. The unfaithfulness is at the same time ritual, dogmatic, moral, ecclesiastical, etc. No realm of divine–human concern is exempted. But it is most pointedly *exemplified* by the near-mythological figure of Constantine, symbol of the alliance of the cross and the sword. It was not the restitutionists who gave Constantine such symbolic importance.

That had been done by his friends, ever since Eusebius, who had made of

Constantine's 'conversion' the beginning of the millennium and of his pact with Pope Sylvester the ratification of the papacy's prerogatives. Nor was the verdict of apostasy an invention of 'restitutionists'. It had been pronounced before by monastic critics of the corrupt princes and clergy.

All that the reformation radicals did that was new was, freed by this analysis, to set out again according to an apostolic lifestyle. It was not that they first diagnosed apostasy and then prescribed as a cure itinerant evangelism and anti-paedobaptism. They rather set out preaching according to the New Testament and then needed the concept of apostasy to explain why churchmen and statesmen threatened their lives. *Then* it became evident that the reversal of the Church's role in the world, from suffering servant to Imperatrix, of which Constantine was the symbol (by no means the first or the only agent), was the key to the other abuses.

Later 'mainstream' Protestant historiography, like the majestic Lutheran 'Magdeburg Centuries' also used the concept of the 'Fall of the Church'. Yet for Lutherans and Calvinists the use of the concept was more delicate. They needed to retain the *consensus quinque-saecularis*, the common deposit of the first five Christian centuries, the Christian Empire and the Ecumenical Councils. After that it became rather difficult to denounce as a 'Fall' some smaller specific shift in the doctrine of the Eucharist, of justification or of the Papacy.

2. *Deepening the Thrust of* Sola Scriptura

[handwritten marginalia: ✳ Scripture critiques us,]

Any reformation, including that of Trent and that of Vatican II, like those of Luther and Zwingli, appeals to Scripture as an alternative perspective from whence critique and creativity may be brought to bear. Yet 'reform' (in the specific softer sense here contrasted with 'restitution') trusts the existing structures to set the rules for Scripture's pertinence. Radical reformation biblicism is different in kind, whatever be the logical puzzles or circularities involved in seeking to let a book interpret itself. Interpreted by the community which its very proclamation in the Spirit creates, the Scripture itself legitimates and empowers a new apostolicity, accredited as such not by juridical succession but by consonance of method and message.

'Back to the Bible' is a misleading though understandable slogan. It seems to suggest a retreat out of history, when in fact what 'restitution' calls for is the only way to go forward taking history with ultimate seriousness as under God's judgement and promise.[7] The event of 'restitution' is not a new start 'from scratch', going 'back to "GO"'. It takes place in the face of the specific forms of apostasy which must be discerned in one's own century, be it the twelfth, the fifteenth, the sixteenth, or the nineteenth. That denunciation and the new start it enables is a new event in God's history, a new formulation of God's good news. The words of the Puritan leader John Robinson as he saw a boatload of congregationalists off from Plymouth to America in the early seventeenth century were 'the Lord hath yet more Light and Truth to break forth from His Holy Word'. Biblical faithfulness is ahead of us, not behind us.

3. *The Seriousness of History*

In other ways as well, 'restitution' is serious about history. Some consider the restitutionist Pietist Gottfried Arnold to be the father of the history of doctrine, because it is only when the distance between dogma and Scripture becomes visible that history can be written. Traditions which trust ultimately to their own story to be the right one, the central one, can care about reading history, but they do not have to. Spiritualist traditions for whom all history is necessarily fallen may study it to prove their point, but they need not. Only if specific judgements on particular histories and specific infidelities are confronted by particular new beginnings does the historical crunch take on the kind of earnestness it has within the Bible itself. That is the shape of the radical Protestant claim.

It has been fitting that, since this 'perspective on history' is that of a specific group of churches, I should have introduced it in the setting of their particular origins. It will however be no less needful to ask how the same should and can apply in ongoing church life, or in inter-church conversation, where the crisis of being thrown out of the establishment does not obtain. Suffice it to suggest that some of the marks noted above (consensual decision making, non-clerical ministry, locality, voluntariness, reconciling discipline, enemy love, etc.) would make for wholesome changes of style and mood in such settings as well.

It is a disadvantage of the approach through history that we are no longer in the world of those beginnings. Catholics, Anglicans, and Lutherans in the 1970s will not easily identify with their forbears who forced out the 'separatists' of the sixteenth century. Nor do Mennonites or Baptists today feel quite like the confident iconoclasts it took to make the break back then. This difference however should facilitate, rather than hindering, our use of the classical typologies to illuminate our present search.

D. The Jewishness of this Perspective

In all of this narration I have consciously left in the shadow the pertinence of half of my title. What can all of this post-medieval, western, largely Protestant history have to do with the Jewishness of Jesus? I trust that the ground already covered may facilitate the answer.

1. *The Givenness of the Particularity of Jesus*

What is ultimately, formally at stake in the conflict among various views of the authority of the New Testament in the Church is the meaning of the incarnation. Classical Protestant/Catholic scholastic debate in the sixteenth and seventeenth centuries, ostensibly about the revelatory status of Scripture, or about whether the Bible had produced the Church or vice versa, only diverted attention from what was more profoundly at stake, namely whether the real Jesus of Nazareth is the norm for Christians. Evolutionary visions of the authority of continuing tradition claim grounds, reverently, to leave the earthly Jesus behind.[8] Constantinian triumphalism replaces him with a *Christus Rex* whose preferred instruments are princes and patriarchs. Official Protestantism called for reform, but trusted the princes to do the reforming, and stated the issues at stake primarily on the levels of doctrine.

It is after all a most Hebraic way to put the question, to say that what has come into being in the course of history (the 'fallenness' of the Church) has to be critiqued within history (in the dialogical events of restitution) on the grounds of criteria drawn from the same story.

2. *The Indispensable* Halakah

The radical critique is also 'Jewish' in that it posits a unity of *halakah* and *aggadah*. Restitutionism has been generally unoriginal on the dogmatic level. When it suggested alternative formulae on themes like the two natures of Christ or trinity or election, they often were not very informed, or very expert, or very important. They differed substantially about ethics and ecclesiology; i.e. about the way of a committed minority through a world they could not control.

This concern for ethos was often held against the Anabaptists, the Quakers, and the Wesleyans by other Protestants who accused them of a relapse into either Catholic or Jewish works religion. That is of course simply to rephrase the question we are identifying here, namely whether the call of Torah may legitimately be blunted by the concern for justification, or by religiousness, or by speculative theology.

3. *The Jewishness of Jesus'* Halakah

To complete the shift from the formal to the material: the critique of the radical reformers is Jewish in that the ethical guidance given by Jesus, as interpreter of Torah, is at the heart of their denunciation of triumphal Christendom as defined by Pope and Emperor. Centuries of bias have predisposed us to read Jesus as setting aside the Law when he said he was fulfilling it, and to read Paul as abandoning Judaism when he was the most effective interpreter of Moses and Abraham to the Gentiles. Thus we are not prepared to see how simply it is true that the ethic of Jesus, to which the radical Protestants reached back, the ethic of Peter Waldo and Peter of Cheltschitz, of George Fox and Dorothy Day, the ethic of truth-telling which needs no oath, of enemy love which needs no sword, of jubilee sharing which needs no treasures, *is a Jewish ethic*. There is nothing platonic, nothing gnostic, nothing Persian about it. The ethic of the Sermon on the Mount is nothing but Jewish.

4. *Fear and Trembling: Defectibility Abides*

Still deeper perhaps is the Jewishness of the very idea of apostasy. In contrast to the assurance of 'having it made', salvation being achieved not only in God, but already in history in the form of an indefectible institution, or that of an irresistible apologetic demonstration, I suggest – only as an hypothesis, but as a serious one – that it befits far more the Hebrew earnestness about the refractoriness of history to deny that God has given his people any such blank cheque. Indefectibility belongs then only to his promise, never becoming negotiable as our appropriation of it.

Mainstream western historiography in the style of Hegel or Harnack would tell us that by forsaking, even denouncing its Jewish roots in the second and third centuries Christianity finally broke through to ecumenicity, to the potential of a world religion. The radicals (like the Jews) respond that the Romanization of the Church with regard to hierarchical form and political loyalty, and her Hellenization with regard to cult and speculative theology, were a sell-out to Mediterranean provincialism; true enough, the largest provincialism available at the time, but a narrower world all the same – that of prophetic universalism or Jeremianic cosmopolitanism. When Paul barges into Athens in the encounter of Acts 17, which is really the wider world, that of the Acropolis or that of Sinai? Athens (as culture) or Rome (as politics) is not more universal than Jewishness. They are only bigger, and that only for a while.[9]

When then under the rubric of 'restitution' we place historical progress under the judgement and the promise of the Jewish Jesus, his humanness, his style, his vulnerability to historiography, we are not asking history to stand still or turn back, but are confessing which way is forward, in the only way Christians can if we really choose to stand with those first Jews who trusted that one day every tongue would confess as Lord the one whose servanthood has brought him to the cross.

E. Epilogue: The Modesty of This Perspective

1. The Objective Criterion

I am the first to be aware of the appearance of arrogance, which may be out of key with the urbane good manners of ecumenical pluralism. This impression is inevitable when one seeks to interpret the truth claim of a minority. Is not the language of 'apostasy' exaggerated, anachronistic, uncouth, in an age of mutual recognition and reconciliation? How can such a small handful of dissenters have claimed to be right over against the whole Christian world? An adequate response to this very fitting challenge would demand a broad survey of the limits and the mandate of ecumenical dialogue. Here however I must be content with little more than a set of slogans that speak to the question.

The judgement of apostasy which derives from the regretful application of an objective criterion, after the semantic form of the historically verifiable proposition, 'Jesus and Constantine exemplify mutually incompatible life styles', is less arrogant than judgements like 'an apostate is one who denies the primacy of the bishop of a certain city', or 'an apostate is one who denies the following doctrine'.

2. The Ethical Corrective

The arrogance of Empire, Crusade, and Inquisition includes the duty to destroy the apostate. The truth claim of the radical reformation, dependent as it is upon the rejection of all violence and upon the specific commitment to the dignity and the life of the adversary, can never inflict more harm than the denial of fellowship, and that only in the hope of future reconciliation.

3. The Roses among the Thorns

This judgement as to the fallenness of Christendom as hierarchical structure and triumphal ethos does not deny the good faith of the possible salvation by grace through faith of persons within Christendom who despite its intrinsic bias nonetheless live in Christ and in Christian fellowship. The radicals affirmed the persistence of saving truth despite apostasy, using in their sixteenth-century debates the image of the rose among thorns from the Song of Songs 2.2.

4. Inevitable Arrogance

But I do not have the right to explain away all the offence for which the radical reformers suffered. Continuing concern for the reality of 'dialogue' as designating something more than polite relativism will have to bring all Christians to admit that there is no faith claim, no truth claim, not even a pluralistic one, that can escape the reproach of the counter-question, 'Why should *we* accept what *you* think as the truth?' The corrective for that scandal is not to retract the claim, but to let the substance of the truth which is claimed dictate the form of its defence. We do not *have* the truth; we *confess* a truth which has taken possession of us through no merit of our own. That truth, being the revelation of God's own vulnerability on the cross, cannot be otherwise commended than in the vulnerability of open encounter with the neighbour.

Thus stated, to confess that God has acted, not only once in the first century but repeatedly before and since then, to redeem and restore his people despite their repeatedly forsaking his way, and then to develop from this confession a vision of the mission of the Church, would seem to be structurally less arrogant, and more hopeful, than the claim that there is one institution within history which by its nature is exempt from such judgement and from the purview of such a promise.

Notes

1. A lecture presented 12 February 1976 at the Ecumenical Institute for Advanced Theological Studies (Tantur) in Jerusalem. It was the first of a series of three presentations on 'The Jewish Jesus and Radical Protestantism'.

2. Other conservative traits concerning social ethics worship and ministry, which followed logically from their decisions, need not be listed here.

3. George Huntston Williams, *The Radical Reformation*, Philadelphia: Westminster Press, 1962.

4. For historical perspective, see Franklin Littell, *The Free Church*, Boston: Starr King, 1957. For a perspective on Max Weber's sociological claims about the 'free church' traditions, see Donald Durnbaugh, *The Believer's Church Tradition*, New York: Macmillan, 1968.

5. It may seem at first that while the first eight items are 'ecclesiological' this one is 'ethical'. That split is deceptive. The ecclesiological ones are all ethical, as I displayed in my 'Sacrament as Social Process' and *Body Politics: Five Practices of the Christian Community Before the Eyes of the Watching World*, Nashville, TN: Discipleship Resources, 1992; enemy love is also ecclesiological since it has to do with who counts as a brother [or sister].

6. From this point on, the text is transcribed from the February 1976 manuscript Yoder wrote for the lecture at Tantur Ecumenical Institute for Advanced Theological Studies.

7. Cf. the articles on 'The Authority of Tradition' and 'Anabaptism and History' in *The Priestly Kingdom,* 63ff. and 123ff., and the several references to how Scripture 'works' in my 'How to be Read by the Bible'. [Editors' Note: This collection of essays has subsequently been published under the title *To Hear the Word*, Eugene, OR: Wipf & Stock, 2001.]

8. Cf. 'The Authority of Tradition' in my *Priestly Kingdom*, 63–79.

9. I am not espousing a permanent ethnocentrism, in the style of Thorlief Boman, with Hebraic thought forms always sacred and safe and Greek always pagan. My objection is not to entering the Hellenistic world as a cultural arena. Jews had been doing that long before Jesus and Paul. Paul did it again, with no sacrifice of his Jewishness or his faithfulness to Jesus. What is to reject is the subsequent abandonment of Jewish substance, as the 'apologetes' succeeded the apostles and the goal of insight displaced that of obedience. [Editors' Note: Yoder's shorthand reference to Thorlief Boman is a gesture toward the latter's study *Hebrew Thought Compared with Greek*, Philadelphia: Westminster, 1960. Yoder provides a fairly nuanced discussion of the difference between his version of 'biblical realism' and Boman's position in *To Hear the Word*, 136–9.]

Commentary

PETER OCHS

In Chapters 4 and 5, Yoder first drew attention to the exilic theology within Rabbinic Judaism and then identified that theology with the theology of the free church. In Chapter 6, he identifies specific churches that anticipate or articulate the virtues of the radical reformation, concluding with some brief comments on the Jewishness of these virtues. I find that the way Yoder isolates and favours certain religious virtues may give us an insight into how and why his appeals to Judaism can be at once helpful and, at times, burdensome. On the positive side, he attends to free church virtues that post-liberal Rabbinic Jews would also want to nurture in their own religious lives: such as the importance of local congregation, of voluntary adherence to religious belief, of non-violence (albeit as a regulative ideal rather than a dogma), of an effort to 'restore' the place of scriptural study in our practices of knowing and to acknowledge and respond to our concrete place in history. On the negative side, Yoder tends to render some of these virtues conceptually pure in a way that would undermine post-liberal Judaism's affirmation of a scriptural hermeneutic that is irreducible to the overly rationalistic logics of modernity. One example is Yoder's Cartesian-like calls for a total 'renewal' of the Church, a 'new beginning' in the very 'heart' of the Church, empowering a wholly 'new apostolicity'. Such appeals summon reform energies in a way that should appeal to post-liberal Jews, but they also risk an indifference to history and tradition that may replay too much of the individualism and foundationalism that post-liberal Jews reject in modernity.

PART III

REFUSING MIS-LOCATED DUALISMS OF JUDAISM

7

Judaism as a Non-non-Christian Religion[1]

A. Historical Patterns of Christian Thinking about Judaism

1. Anti-Jewish Patterns

Since the second century CE mainstream Christianity has been resolutely anti-Jewish. The form in which this bias first appears is the supersession thesis, according to which Christians have replaced the Jews as the people holding the right understanding of the Abrahamic and Mosaic heritage and as the bearers of the salvation history. Already within the apostolic writings an argument is going on about how properly to understand the Hebrew Scriptures and the fulfilment of their promises. Yet when these documents were written, the debate was taking place within Judaism, according the rules for Jewish debate. Since the middle of the second Century, however, this context was no longer affirmed. Then the claim of Gentile Christians to be the valid bearers of the faith of Abraham was no longer part of the Jewish debate, as it had been in the first century, but rather became anti-Jewish.

Then in the fourth century, and ever since, this anti-Jewish bias was linked to political ostracism. Now that all the western world (i.e. the Roman Empire) has been declared Christian from the top down, there are no more real live pagans living free within the *oikumene* so that it is the remaining Jews within 'Christian society' who have to take over the role of the 'infidel'. Frequently the price of this is persecution or expulsion. When the rejection is milder, it forces the Jews into a ghetto culture. In still rarer circumstance it may offer special privileges to some of them, in compensation for their special loyalty to a ruler. Generally speaking, though, Jews were not dealt with [this way] by Christians as was later to be the case under Islam, after it had taken over much of the Mediterranean world a few centuries later.

Frequently the rejection was more than enclosure in the ghetto or banishment, moving to active persecution. In other less brutal times and places the means preferred was forced conversion, i.e. the end of their identity as Jews. Where Jews were tolerated, it was for special reasons, such as the financial services that some late medieval bankers rendered to the princely houses of Europe.

To undergird this anti-Jewish bias there developed a strong theology of the Jew as 'infidel'. The Jew was not, like any other non-Christian, an honest adherent of some other faith or no faith; he was properly the infidel; the negation of proper belief.

One of the ways to sharpen this attack was the formal reproach of 'deicide'. This bound together in a powerful way a number of claims:

(a) a specific historical reconstruction of the way the execution of Jesus took place in the Gospel account, with 'the Jews' acting as Jesus' accusers and in fact affirming their desire to be responsible for Jesus' death;

(b) a specific naïve understanding of the deity of Jesus Christ, so that it could be claimed that in letting the man Jesus go to his death, those who brought about that event were also killing God;

(c) a global claim that 'the Jews' who did that were representative of the entire Jewish people back then;

(d) the further questionable assumption that all members of an ethnic group centuries later can be declared guilty of the sins of their very distant forbears.

Behind this specific libel there was a further host of anti-Jewish dimensions of the wider culture: legends about the wandering Jew, the Jew as cheating merchant, usurer, Jews as a threat to the peace of society, etc.

When thanks to cultural modernity and theological objectivity these simple negations were less respected, more sophisticated arguments arose to shore up the same divisions. Jesus was seen as specifically opposing Jewish tradition in his attitude on the Law, on in specific moral teachings as on violence or divorce.

The apostle Paul was seen even more eminently as rejecting Judaism. He attacked the Law in a far more logical and sweeping way than Jesus had, and developed with regard to Jesus himself a 'high christology' which had to seem blasphemous to Jews, and for which Jesus' being himself a Jew was not essential but only accidental.

2. Philo-Judaism and Patterns of Ambiguity about Christian Mission to Jews

As a result of this generally negative vision of western Christianity toward Jewish identity, there has arisen an abiding ambiguity in the face of the question of 'mission' addressed to Jews. One strand of Protestantism has been preoccupied with a witness to Jews as more important than to other non-Christian people. This often led to deep concern for understanding Jewish life and culture. This stance was often derived from pietistic or chiliastic convictions that assign to the conversion of the Jews a special place in the End Time calendar. Sometimes it was linked to odd ideas about the British people being Israelite.

More often, however, the larger Christian bodies ignored Jewry as a possible particular target of their missionary message. 'Missions', being thought of prototypically as going overseas to 'foreign' cultures, would not apply to Jews who were at home among us. They are not really like 'pagans' elsewhere, to whom we ought to carry a message about the only true God. They know of the Christian message and have rejected it, so they are refractory, as if vaccinated, a less promising, less potentially responsive target audience than genuine pagans would be.

In this century new cultural currents have thrown a different light on our questions. The culture we called 'Enlightenment' boiled Christianity down to the truth value of its various statements about human nature, about the nature of the morally good, and about the arguments for God's existence. Particular details like the name of Jesus or the specific moral content of the Christian life could be thought of as merely one more expression, beside others equally valid, of those more general truths. Then it was easy to consider Jewish moral monotheism as one more religious variety, beside Protestantism and Catholicism, which also have to be boiled down to moral monotheism in order to pass inspection in the modern world. Especially in the case of those theologically more liberal traditions, where the classical formulations of (e.g. christological) confession were not considered important or perhaps even not (philosophically) credible, little stood in the way of treating Judaism as one more Christian denomination. Little stood in the way, that is, from the Christian side.[2] Orthodox and Traditional Jews had their own reasons for not wanting to accept this compliment, but some strands of Reform Jewry, especially before 1948, could feel relatively at home in being accepted as one more variant, in fact the oldest and quietest, of 'the Judaeo-Christian tradition'. The most prominent Protestant exponent of this view in his age was Reinhold Niebuhr, who explicitly argued that Christian faith has nothing to offer to the Jew.

An utterly different kind of philo-Judaic orientation is the eschatological tradition of John Nelson Darby, propagated in North America by the Scofield Bible.[3] For Scofield et al. the Jews have a permanent priority as the people possessing inalienably the promises of God, in no way superseded by Christianity. One of the gaps in the story of how the Huguenot village of Le Chambon-sur-Lignon saved a good number of Jews from capture by the Nazis, as that story has been recounted by Phillip Hallie and Pierre Sauvage, is the component of 'darbyste' philo-Semitism, resulting from the impact of the British revivalist John Nelson Darby among the conservative Protestants of central France generations before.[4] All of the promises made to Israel by the ancient Hebrew prophets are still to be fulfilled in favour of the Jews who live among us today, and who will be alive when the promises are fulfilled.

Contrary to the other view, Darby was strongly committed to evangelizing Jews, since their conversion has a key place in the divine timetable, quite distinct from mission to Gentiles. At a certain point the Church (i.e. the believing Gentiles) will be removed from the scene.[5] The Jewish people, having returned to their homeland, will then be won to faith in Jesus as their Messiah by the witness of the few believing Jews left over from the preceding dispensation. The throne of David will be restored and the promises of World Sovereignty, left over unfulfilled from the age before the Church, will be implemented, picking up the main line of theocratic history which had been interrupted in the first century when Jesus was not accepted as King.

This special vision of the place of Judaism correlates with the personal and social values of the small number of Jewish individuals who have been converted in response to such a message. These individuals tend to prefer to maintain some Jewish identity rather than be swallowed up in ordinary predominantly Gentile western churches. Therefore special missions to Jews, or 'Hebrew Christian' fellowship are more satisfactory to them.[6] They feel at home in a messianic Jewish fellowship in which modern Gentiles, while not excluded, would hardly be expected, thus bringing into being again 'from the other side' the kind of separation which was the object of Paul's explicit criticism in Galatians 2.

Still a third form of renewed respect for Judaism has arisen in European Protestantism as a result of the combination of neo-reformation theology (Karl Barth, Dietrich Bonhoeffer) and the experience of the Holocaust. Especially in the Netherlands, but significantly as well in France, Switzerland and Germany, to make a point of confessing the sin of Christendom against the Jews has been correlated with a renewal of theological respect for their distinctive mission in salvation history. From this new biblical perspective, as well as from the liberal one of Reinhold Niebuhr, some have come to reject the notion of any explicitly Christian proclamation to Jews.

This last-mentioned development is the most profound of the three. It arises from biblical and theological renewal, rather than from the mere dilution of Christian specificity or from an esoteric eschatology. The first thesis is that the election of Israel is irrevocable. Not even outright rebellion against the gracious call of God can withdraw the elect from that privilege. In fact, once the fulfilment of the meaning of the election of Israel has come in Christ, the ongoing existence of Jewry is only possible because of the refusal to accept that fulfilment (i.e. only in revolt against the meaning of its election). That revolt becomes the most dramatically paradoxical sign that the Grace of God persists, maintaining the rebel's identity despite the elect's rejecting it. That very survival in unbelief is a sigh of the grace in whose fulfilment Jews refuse to believe.

These theological statements about the identity of 'unbelieving Israel' – as a special sign of the grace of God – could not be made if it were not for the historical fact of the survival of Judaism in the West. Is this historical fact then theologically important? At least it prevents our forgetting or denying the priority of the calling of Israel, if it does not mean proof thereof. There is surely some mystery in the survival of Jewry, as no other people has done, without common territory, common political authorities, common language. There is also an evil mystery in the sense of scandal, in the way in which the various host cultures, amidst whom Jews have lived, have sought their destruction. The facticity of survival and of scandal reinforces the theological confession of election.

Several of these lines of thought have gained momentum in the last generation, especially since the 1960s when this lecture material was first developed. It finds vehicles within European Protestantism, within the World Council of Churches, in various Christian research agencies in Israel and the West, and in the writing of growing numbers of revisionist theologians. Some of these affirm that 'the Jews' are a sister communion within the biblical faith, and disavow any invitation to Jews to recognize Jesus as the Christ. Others, without drawing those conclusions, are so strongly concerned for Christian guilt, atonement, and for honouring the special suffering of Jewish minorities, that the idea of an evangelistic message seems extraneous.

These various philo-Judaic attitudes are still minority positions. Most of the rest of Christendom, whether Eastern Orthodox, Western Catholic or Protestant, whether or not explicitly anti-Jewish, would still pay no attention in their missionary concern to Jewish identity, thereby in effect neglecting the Jews as a people to be told about the Messiah, and thereby remaining unable to counter antisemitism with any effectiveness.

I have told this modern story in its own terms. I have thus granted tacitly the two erroneous assumptions that are usually made; namely that 'Judaism' is a stable and autonomous entity, identical with itself through the ages, and that the 'Christianity' which is trying to relate to 'Judaism' is that too. Those wrong assumptions cramp our thought in ways we are seldom aware of. Therefore I return to the old story to lift up the strands this account has missed.[7]

B. How Christianity Forfeited its Original Credibility as Witness to Jews

The radical reformation and the New Testament, as contrasted with most of the Christian thought reviewed just above, agreed that the reconciliation of people is essential in defining the nature of the Church and her reconciling message. This meant that the gospel proclamation could not be separated from reconciling Jew and Gentile. The truth of the claim that Jesus is Christ, or the Messiah has come, is inseparable from the functioning of a community in which the two kinds of people have become one.

The form that this same prophetic vision took in the sixteenth century, in the face of the apostasy of that time, was the rejection of coercion in matters of faith, the rejection of the governance of churches by civil rulers, and the rejection of obligatory religious uniformity in each province.

If we read back through the history of Jews and Gentiles, churches and states, with these priorities in mind, we see the 'standard picture' changing.

Jesus was not anti-Jewish. What he said he did with the Law was to fulfil it. He did not set it aside; he increased its wholeness, its binding-ness, its breadth and its depth. At some points he differed with other rabbis of that time or later, on just how some of the provisions of the law were to be obeyed, but his differing on those matters was well within the parameters of tolerable diversity which the Judaism of the time could support, and which Judaism today can support. The same is true of the non-violence or the non-resistance of Jesus. What his disciples saw to be 'filling the law full' or filling the role of the Suffering Servant, was the same as what others drew from the defeat of the Maccabees, or the position which Jochanan ben Zakkai was to oppose to the general, Menachem, a generation later. The newness which Matthew reports Jesus as proclaiming (Matt. 5) is fulfilment; it neither supersedes nor rejects Jesus' Jewishness.

Paul likewise was nothing if not fully Jewish. The reason he went to the Gentiles to proclaim the coming of the Messiah was that as a Jew he believed that this was what would happen in the Messianic age. Nobody but a Jew could believe that the Messiah had come. Any Jew with that belief would then believe that a new epoch was opening for the nations to know the name and the law of God. How Paul led, including his solutions to the detailed problems of building communities in Corinth facing dietary and calendar conflicts, was very similar to the solutions which had been found to the same problems during the previous two centuries of Jewish proselytism under the leadership of rabbis like the great Hillel. Paul's work in a Gentile city always took off from the synagogue. If that community was divided because some accepted and some rejected his message, the 'messianically believing' portion resulting from that division was still a synagogue.

In the above summary both 'Jesus' and 'Paul' are named as symbols. We cannot know all of the details of the thought or the ministry of either man. What we do know is their impact in the apostolic writings.

Not only was this affirmation of Jewish identity the centre of the mission of Jesus in the first generation and that of Paul in the second. The social fences remained down between church and synagogue for two or three more generations at least. The first Christian (i.e. messianic Jewish) communities remained basically Jewish in style and language even in the Hellenistic cities. It happened only well into the second century that some Gentile minorities started to take the Church away from the Jews, thereby moving one step toward the creation of a provincialized Christianity. Hellenistic culture at that time was spread all around the Mediterranean basin, and thought of itself as 'the whole world' (Luke 2.4), but in terms of world culture it was already a serious narrowing of the faith community when it came to be identified with that culture, its language and its wisdom.

So the 'fall of the Church' which Protestants, including Czech Brethren, Anabaptists and Baptists have been talking about since the late Middle Ages, and which they often located in the fourth century, because the sword of Constantine was so important, really began in the second century. The 'apologetes' like Justin Martyr, who re-conceived the Christian message so as to make it 'credible' to non-Jewish culture, whether to philosophers or religious people or practical or powerful people, detached the message of Jesus from its Jewish matrix and thereby transposed it into an a-historical moral monotheism with no particular peoplehood and no defences against acculturation. Along with its Jewish rootage, the Church lost:

(a) her vision of the whole globe as under God, with all nations (e.g. even beyond the Roman Empire) having their place and needing to hear the message;

(b) her sense that Torah is grace and privilege, not a basis for recompense or an entrance requirement to the world to come;

(c) readiness to live in the diaspora style of the Suffering Servant.

These very elements were the ones that the radical reformers reached back to retrieve. When the radical reformers, whether the Waldenses or the Czech Brethren or the Anabaptists, 'reached back', it was to find in the New Testament the definition of what the post-Jewish Church in her acculturation had lost. But that meant that they were also 'reaching sideways' by implicitly standing in the same posture as the Jews in their midst.[8]

I have retold this story of how 'Christians' lost their credibility as witnesses to Jews that the Jews' messiah had come, but I should not dodge the challenge of retelling the same story from the other side.

C. Rabbinic Judaism is a Post-Christian Phenomenon

The calling of Israel was always to be a mouthpiece for proclaiming the Lordship of JHWH. Beginning with the break-up of the state structures in the land of Israel, this had already begun to include inviting significant numbers of people of non-Jewish birth into the fellowship and the lifestyle of the covenant. What Jesus did was simply more of the same. The communities that confessed in him the coming of the Messianic age were simply more free and aggressive in doing in the Gentile cities what the synagogues had already been doing.

For something like eighty years after Pentecost the (non-messianic) synagogues were not closed to messianic believers, and the 'churches' (i.e. messianic synagogues) did not break communion with the rest of Jewry. When the year 70 sealed the abandonment of visions of national restoration, Jochanan ben Zakkai firmed up the non-violence of the remaining rabbinic leadership and their acceptance of diaspora as a base of Jewish identity. As far as ethical substance was concerned, this meant that non-messianic Jewish people would act in exactly the same way as the Christians of the same time. There are those who believe that one reason for the rejection of Christians by the synagogues was that the Christians had refused, out of pacifism following Jesus, to share in the defence of Jerusalem. But Jochanan also rejected the Zealot campaign and withdrew from it. Whenever it was that the further separation took place, the Jews *at that time* were not fighting for Jerusalem.

The only possible exception to this statement would be if we thought that most of the Jews were together with Bar Kochba 130–135; but most of them were not. It may be that Rabbi Akiba thought, or thought for a time, that Bar Kochba might be the (or a) messianic liberator, but this act is not clear, nor permanent, and not representative.

Thus the move of Judaism, whereby it became able to survive the loss of the Temple, and of such approximation to a Jewish 'state' structure, was a move toward, not away from, accepting diaspora as the setting for identity and mission. That is parallel to the Jesus move.

About a century later, the *Mishna* backed away from this continuing missionary openness. It became less missionary because the Christians were more so. What was cause and what was effect in this increasing estrangement is not easy to see. Once it is sure that inter-visitation between non-messianic and messianic Jews (whom one begins to call 'Jews' and 'Christians') is being discouraged by the Jewish authorities, as is recorded (though lightly) in the *Mishna*, then the parties can make moral sense of the distancing by building up further theological backgrounds. *Then* one will say that the reason for the rejection is that the Christians affirmed that 'Jesus was God' and that 'Jews' cannot say that. That is however a construction after the fact. It does not deal with the fact that all the 'high christological' statements made about Jesus in the New Testament were made by radically monotheistic Jews and were not, when made, seen to be in any sense polytheistic or idolatrous. Nor have we any record of Jews in the first centuries rejecting such formulations, whether made by messianic Jews or by anyone else. Whenever and whyever it happened, Judaism slowed down and stopped its missionary openness before the onset of serious persecution of Jews by Christians. Persecution of Jews by Gentiles was endemic. Christian reasons were not needed; yet once Christians had the chance to accumulate their anti-Jewish arguments with the power of the Empire that enabled a tragic escalation [of Jewish persecution].

A further level of adjustment arises when the pressure of Christians pushes the rabbis to argue in detail why Jesus could not have been the Messiah. That led to further narrowing and clarifying the definition of the role and person of the Messiah; a direct response to the impact of Jesus. That the Messiah could not fail, that the Messiah could not be crucified, is a polemic that would not have had the same pertinence before the debates about Jesus. Even the widespread acceptance of the notion that 'Jews expect a coming Messiah' probably would not have obtained without the Christians' pressure. Some modern Jews [9] argue that the notion of the coming Messiah is important but is and should remain an empty set; i.e. that the prophetic impact of the expectancy is not dependent on its ever being fulfilled.[10]

It may be that 'Christians' progressively differentiated themselves from Jews in order not to suffer that persecution, and thereby diverted the anger of Gentiles toward the non-messianic Jews. Yet this in itself would not explain Jews' abandoning their missionary openness. In fact it could well have had the opposite effect. Jews no less than 'Christians' could argue that they had no secrets, that their God was for everyone, that their law was reasonable, open to others, as their thinkers were doing at that time anyway.

In any case the outcome is that Judaism will be an ethnic enclave, less missionary than before, at some points in fact practically discouraging the accession of Gentiles to membership in the synagogue. This abandonment of missionary perspective on the part of Judaism is an adjustment not to the Gentile world but to Christianity.[11] Non-missionary Judaism is a part of, a product of, Christian history. For Jews to renounce mission means that they have been contextually 'Christianized'. They have accepted their limited slot within a context where telling the Gentiles about the God of Abraham is a function left to others and the Jews are willing to leave it that way.[12]

If the abandonment of openness to Gentiles was the first stage of Judaism's being influenced by Christianity, one of the latest is the acceptance by Jews of their assimilation into western pluralism. Protestants, Catholics and Jews are seen as the three equally legitimate forms of moral theism called 'the Judaeo-Christian heritage'. In some cases this has lead to a degree of theological assimilation, but the same tripartite division of labour within pluralism can also be appealed to by Jews (or Protestants) who are much more orthodox.

The culmination of the Christianization of Judaism is the development of Zionism. Zionism creates a secular democratic nation state after the model of the nation states of the West. It defines Jews, for the purpose of building the state, in such a way that it makes no difference if most of them are unbelieving and unobservant. In America the Jews are 'like a church' with a belief structure, lifestyle commitments, and community meetings; in Israel Judaism is a nation and the belief dimension no longer matters. To be born in the State of Israel makes one less a Jew, in the deep historical sense of the term, than to be born in a ghetto. This is of course exacerbated by the fact that the Zionist state has taken on the challenge of governing subject populations who are not even ethnically Jewish. Committed Judaism, i.e. people who visibly order their lives around the Torah, is a minority sect in Israel just as are the Christians.

The same observation could be made on the level of intellectual history if we had the time and the expertise. Jewish culture and philosophy have not only interacted with Christian and post-Christian models in the last centuries, but have borrowed extensively from them, and with no apology. The most adequate continuing advocacy of the moral philosophy of Immanuel Kant may very well be that of the Jewish philosopher Herman Cohen. That involved no sense of betrayal or acculturation. It was like Philo or Maimonides believing that everything true that the classical Greek thinkers taught they had received from Moses. Similarly, the best interpreter of the thought of Reinhold Niebuhr in mid-century America was Will Herberg.

It will take us some time and testing to get used to the awareness that Judaism as we now know it, i.e. Rabbinic Judaism, is younger than Christianity – and in part a reaction thereto – but this is an indispensable straightening out of our categories. The Christians first made the Hebrew Bible a canon in the technical sense. Their claim to fulfilment, their conviction that the way to make understandable the significance of Jesus was to see him as fulfilling all the promises of Scripture, constituted a used of the scriptural heritage which if not new in kind was at least very new in degree. Scriptures are now being appealed to by Christians to justify the evaluation of an event, and the structuring of a community around that event. Thus Scripture becomes a fulcrum to move the present as it had not been before. As Rabbi Petuchowski of Cincinnati said in a lecture, 'when the Gentiles thumped the Bible, the synagogue had to respond'.

I would differ from this phrasing by noting that the Bible was appealed to by Gentiles not in order to read Jews out of their messianic community (as did happen a century later) but to invite them in. Only when appealing to the Bible became recognizable as something Gentiles could do did it become functional for the non-messianic Jews to thump in response. Now they develop a counter-exegesis holding that there cannot be a Messiah, or that Jesus was not the Messiah, or that the age of prophecy has ceased, etc. These anti-messianic Jewish claims are only conceivable logically and historically only after the Christian presence and perhaps only after the Christian presence had become largely Gentile.

There are other characteristics of later Judaism that only could have arisen in this post-Gospel context. One is the notion of two roughly parallel paths to God, the Jews having the more burdensome path of the Mosaic Torah, the other nations having the more accessible but still morally demanding covenant of Noah. This could develop only after the renunciation of openness to the Gentiles, which in turn can only have made sense when Christians had gone overboard in identification with the Gentiles.

D. Reshaping Dialogue Within the Common Story

One of the marks of the difficulty of authentic conversation is the frequent recourse to typology. We seek to describe our conversation by making it a subset of something standard; an instance of wider categories. Frequently in the effort to be fair, and to step back from one's own biases, we try to re-describe our conversation in a wider frame of reference.

One such standard way to restate the contrast is to say that a person is born a Jew but must become a Christian. Jewish identity is ethnic by the nature of the case. When Christian identity comes to be defined ethnically that is the result of a long history, perhaps one of degeneration over time.

This description of the contrast is insufficient on both sides. It seeks to define ideal types rather than reading real history inductively.

Since Constantine, most Christianity is not voluntary. The sacramental practice of baptism, which originally meant voluntarily entering a new community, was retained, but its meaning was reversed. It came to be done to an infant who had no choice, and soon it was done at the behest of a government which gave the parents no choice. When it was challenged by reformation radicals, infant baptism was defended by the reformers on the grounds that it was the modern equivalent of Jewish circumcision; i.e. a ritual of birth, not choice.

On the other hand, to be Jewish after Jeremiah often included some element of freedom. Not only were Gentiles able to join the synagogue community; children of Jewish parents could also lose themselves in the crowd. Sometimes in fact the surrounding pressure exerted on Jews a positive pressure to abjure; thus Jewish identity persisted because it was voluntary. Persons who could have done otherwise took it on themselves wittingly and at some cost to reaffirm as adults the identity of their fathers. Such pressure to convert continued in the modern world unto this generation. Thus the Judaism with which we are able to converse has faced the freedom to apostasize no less directly than has Catholicism, and more so than has the principal current of mainstream Protestantism which in the western experiences is still heir to centuries of establishment even though the formal enforcement has been loosening for generations.

Thus the ideal typology which calls Christianity voluntary and Judaism ethnic dodges the issues involved in the earlier discussion, since the Christian faith of the first century was a Jewish stance that was voluntary.

E. Who Needs Whom?

Another of those illuminating but also misleading capsule characterizations is the claim:

> Christianity needs Judaism; Judaism does not need Christianity . . . Judaism has no special theological necessity for dialoguing with Christianity. Christianity, on the other hand, . . . has a deeply rooted theological necessity to dialogue with Judaism.[13]

As valuable as this capsule may be, to make Christians aware of our tendency to impose our agenda on others, and to push us to honour Jewish culture in its own integrity, this description skews the contrast by assuming that 'Judaism' is just one reality. It differs from classical Christian prejudice in wanting to honour that identity, but it shares the a-historical image (which the scholar would not want to apply to 'Christianity') of a Jewish reality untouched by its having given birth to the Christian movement. It is to correct this error that it is helpful to review the ways in which Judaism is also a non-non-Christian religion. Rabbinic Judaism has been marked by the measures taken to disavow the messianism that led into the Christian movement, and continued to be vulnerable to other messianisms that would arise later.

The Jewish history which matters to today's Jews is one of involvement in the history dominated by the two monotheisms which branched off from Israel, Christendom, then Islam, and then their secular progeny in the West. Jews have been active participants in the growth of secular nations, in the growth of economies, the growth of sciences, the growth of socialism, the growth of nations. There have been significant Jewish communities in China, in India, in Africa, yet their story is not the one we hear told. The Jewish story remains a part of the story of western civilization.

Notes

1. John Howard Yoder, unpublished, 1981. An extract from the course 'The Theology of the Christian World Mission', offered several times between 1964 and 1973, transcribed in 1981. In this course, it became important to distinguish between 'other religions', which have long been a topic of doctrinal concern, and those cultural phenomena which are derived from the impact of the Christian message on world culture, even when that derivation takes a negative posture.

When Anglo-Saxon charismatic missionaries work in Catholic Brazil, or when Mennonite missionaries work in Coptic Orthodox Ethiopia, it is a mistake to consider this as identical to a mission addressed to pagans. Under this heading the course dealt with Constantinian Catholicism and Orthodoxy, with Islam and with modern secularism and Marxism. It was noted that similar attitudes should also respect the challenge of modern syncretisms.

The following material proposing a particular respect for Judaism as part of the ongoing Christian story was discussed in that meeting. A course extract similar to what follows was mimeographed in 1981. It is added to the packet as indication of the practical difference that a different reading of history might make.

2. This became all the more congenial when European Jewry had their own equivalent of 'enlightenment', the *maskilim*, and when American Reform Judaism's patterns for synagogue life and rabbinic ministry increasingly resembled those of liberal Protestants.

3. [Editors' Note: Here Yoder has in view C. I. Scofield's version of dispensational premillennialism as found in the 'annotations' of the Scofield Bible. The seven 'dispensations' that order human existence according to Darby and Scofield are:

   1. Innocence – Creation of Adam, ending in the Fall
   2. Conscience – From the Fall to the Flood
   3. Human Government – From Noah
   4. Promise – from Abraham to Moses
   5. Law – from Moses to the Death of Christ
   6. Grace – from the Cross to the Second Coming
   7. Kingdom or Millennial Age – personal reign of Christ, which ends with 'Satan loosed a little season' but quickly defeated. After the Millennium, comes the New Heavens and the New Earth.

As Scofield's notations display, this makes a difference in the way you interpret a text like Matthew 5–7 in relation to Romans 12 and Romans 13. The command to 'love your enemies' is a command that is intended for the seventh dispensation, which in turn means that for those living in the sixth dispensation, obedience to the governing authorities as per Romans 13.1–7 defines Christian behaviour with respect to military service instead of the mandate of Romans 12.9–21, which specifies that Christians are not to use evil means to overcome evil.

For an excellent discussion of premillennial dispensationalist patterns of biblical interpretation, see George Marsden, *Fundamentalism and American Culture*, New York: Oxford University Press, 1981, especially 110–11. Marsden also provides a helpful explanation about how Darby's revision of millennialism resulted in a new way of interpreting the Bible (58–9)].

4. A missing element in the accounts of how the French Huguenot village of Le Chambon-sur-Lignon saved Jews from the Germans, as told by Phillip Hallie in his book *Lest Innocent Blood Be Shed: The Story of the Village of Le Chambon and How Goodness Happened There*, New York, NY: Harper Colophon, 1979, and Pierre Sauvage in his film 'Weapons of the Spirit'(1989), is the importance of the eschatological piety of many of the 'Brethren' who were heirs to Darby's missionary ministry in France.

5. Dispensational hope calls this event 'the rapture' and sees it as predicted in 1 Thess. 4.17f. ('we who are alive . . .will be caught up in the clouds . . . to meet the Lord in the air'); and Matt. 24.40 or Luke 17.34f. 'One will be taken and the other left.'

6. Many such 'Hebrew Christians' or 'Jews for Jesus' do not, however, accept the peculiar 'Darbyite' eschatology sketched above. [Editors' Note: The issue to which Yoder gestures in this note comes into focus with respect to the eschatological significance of Jewish 'conversions' to Christianity. For 'Christian Zionists', the conversion of Israel as the people of God is viewed as a penultimate step immediately prior to the second coming of Jesus. For more details about the tension between 'Christian Zionists' and 'Messianic Jews' in the State of Israel, see 'Appendix B' of this volume.]

7. The reader will recognize here thoughts expressed more fully in other texts in this collection. They differ in being connected here not to social ethics or community identity but to the theme of mission.

8. Legend has it that Han Denck, the Anabaptist who first translated the minor prophets of the Old Testament, got some language help from a rabbi friend.

9. See Chapter 4 above, p. 112.

10. If I understand correctly Steven S. Schwarzschild called himself 'messianic' because it is theologically important always to hold the place open for divine intervention, and that Jews should not presume upon messianic prerogatives, but there should be no concrete expectancy. *The Pursuit of the Ideal*, ed., Menachem Kellner, Buffalo, NY: SUNY Press, 1990, 15–28, 209–28.

11. From the 'radical reformation' perspective with which the rest of this collection of essays is concerned, it should be added that the Christianity of which this sentence speaks is *already* an apostate Christianity.

12. A further facet of this adjustment is the development of the notion that Gentiles can have a part in the world to come if they keep the covenant God made with the world in Noah. This makes it even more fitting to have no outreach. In rabbinic thought this conceptual adjustment came later. Cf. the brief treatment of the 'Noachides' in Chapter 3, n. 8.

13. Krister Stendahl, 'Saint Paul and the Jews' in *engage/social action*, 3/12, December 1976, 19–25.

Commentary

PETER OCHS

From Chapter 7 to the end of the book, Yoder displays the polemical telos of his entire thesis, thereby bringing both the wonders and the burdens of his project into complete view. Chapter 7 is a prime example, and if I focus more on the burdens than the wonders of this chapter, it is only because we have already examined most of the wonders in the previous chapters. Post-liberal Jews should be maximally grateful for Yoder's unflinching critique of Christian supersessionism. With his characteristic clarity and economy of argument, he displays the syllogism that leads from Constantinian Christianity's theological supersessionism to the ethnic and racial antisemitism of various types of modern Christianity and post-Christianity (pp. 147–8).

At the same time, Yoder's final outreach to the Jews will appear to most post-liberal Jews as yet another form of supersessionism. During our years of work among the co-editors of *Christianity in Jewish Terms*, David Novak often appealed to Jews and Christians to retain their separate truth claims while at the same time engaging in warm and mutually constructive dialogue. I would expect David Novak to affirm Yoder's loyalty to the traditional Christian mission to the Jews. I would expect him to argue that Yoder should respect the truth of his own tradition relative to any other, just as much as Novak should argue for the ultimate truth of Judaism against any competing Christian claims. Dialogue, he would argue, does not require our abandoning our differences. I do not believe, however, that Yoder would accept these conditions for his own claim. His strategy has been to delegitimate those features of both Christianity and Rabbinic Judaism that fall outside the boundary of what he considers Exilic Judaism. He then argues that Exilic Judaism is not merely compatible with 'messianic Judaism' (that is, the Nazarene tradition of Jewish messianism), but completed in it. Having argued this way, he could not also endorse Novak's premise for appropriate theological competition, since he (Yoder) rejects the assumption of theological boundaries between Judaism and Christianity.

Post-liberal Jews, more generally, could not endorse this aspect of Yoder's approach to theological dialogue. This is not merely because of some theological claim, but because of a disagreement in method. They would argue that, at some point, Yoder appears to have replaced the ongoing practice of scriptural reading with an effort to generalize the conclusions to which his reading has brought him. Were post-liberal Jews and radical reformers to share a fellowship of scriptural study, *would they already know, before the study began, what Scripture would say?* In Chapter 7, Yoder no longer appears to be drawing new and unpredictable conclusions from his reading of Scripture, but to be drawing Jews and non-Anabaptist Christians into a sphere of already completed interpretive conclusions. If radical reformers and exilic rabbinic thinkers are to share in a community of interpretation that *has not previously occurred and of which Yoder's words may be the harbinger*, then we cannot possibly know, before the fact, how that community of study will read Scripture and what voice will speak from out of their reading.

Book Eph.

God creates unity —

Volunteery Community

Movement involuntary (Christian)

ban = shunning
Anabaptist Way
Outsiders
• no Lord Supper
• excommunication
• social / psychological
  factor
ICor 5 + 2 Cor
(Lapses cont)

8

Earthly Jerusalem and Heavenly Jerusalem:
A Mis-located Dualism

A. Terrestrial Jerusalem and Celestial Jerusalem

The title of this chapter and the session of the conference at which it was initially presented[1] could be taken seriously in numerous ways.

1. It could be taken as a call to interpret that unique Talmudic text in which the juxtaposition of these two Hebrew phrases was the author's actual point, within the current usage of diaspora Jewish faith. Rabbi Cytron has done that.[2]

2. We could compare and contrast the above to what the Jewish *shaliach* Saul/Paul meant by referring to 'the Jerusalem above' in his letter to the Galatians (4.26), or to what the anonymous letter to the Hebrews meant by 'the city of the living God, the heavenly Jerusalem where the millions of angels have gathered for the festival' (10.22), or what the Seer John of Patmos meant by 'the Holy city, *new* Jerusalem, coming down from Heaven' (Rev. 21.2). But all of that comparative literary exercise could connect only very tenuously to anything we could work with. There is no reason to think that the three non-earthly Jerusalems being written about in these three apostolic texts are the same, or that if they were, they would appropriately be juxtaposed to what Rabbi Yochanan meant or what Jewish thought have done with the words since then.

3. Especially we must avoid the trap of thinking that the duality in the title could somehow be distributively correlated with the Jewish–Christian difference, as if Christians sought to *celestialize* Jerusalem and Jews to keep it earthly.[3] The phrase in our titles is, after all, in Hebrew. It is true that Augustine did organize his historic vision around two cities, one of them celestial: but that was because he was a Neo-Platonist, not because he was Christian. The earthly city which Augustine was concerned at the same time to relativize and to be on good pastoral terms with was not Jerusalem but Rome, not a holy city but an empire.[4] Philo and the Kabbalists could speculate about other levels of reality as well as Augustine. Nor was Augustine's problem the issue of urbanization, to which Rabbi Cytron's introduction pointed. It has been radical Protestants who have tried to found new earthly holy cities; Münster or Strasbourg in the 1530s, Zion on Lake Michigan or the Great Salt Lake in the 1800s, or the 'Jerusalem' of the 'Kimbanguist' independent church in Zaire today.

The poetic duality will therefore not properly serve to typologize Christians on one side and Jews on the other. It might tend rather to divide between *very* Zionist and *less* Zionist Jews, between fundamentalist and liberal Protestants, or between crusading and Augustinian Catholics.

Beyond denying that the celestial/terrestrial duality correlates with the Christian/

Jewish duality, I must further question the notion of a bilateral dialogue as such, in a meeting like this, if it should mean that there are only two postures in conversation. What I shall say here is no more 'Christian' than it is 'Jewish'. What I shall say here I have learned mostly from Jews. It is more critical of Christendom as a cultural mistake than it is of anything Jewish. It points to a debate that divides Christians from other Christians and Jews from other Jews. Our conversations can only be freed to honour the God who makes all things new if we refuse to let the Procrustes of past religious liberty struggles force every question into a bilateral shape.

4. The duality could be taken as a pointer to the tendencies existing in both Jewish and Christian thought, and probably also in Muslim thought, to make the ancient city a symbol of the age to come, of the ideal human community, or of a Platonic timeless and palace-less, temple-less eternity, or of the concept of Divine Sovereignty. Each of these usages would make the metaphor tributary to some specific non-biblical philosophy.

5. I am thus left to come to terms with a more modest conception of the point of the two phrases. To juxtapose them bespeaks the awareness that for all of the concerned parties, what is at stake in the controversies about the destiny of that city in the Middle East is more than its present populations, more than its cemeteries and holy sites, more than its economic and political structures.

It is not only that Jerusalem is more than a place.[5] That is also true of Rome or of Moscow, even of Washington or Wall Street. It is not only that it is a holy place; other faiths have places that are more holy. What matters is *why* Jerusalem matters as more than a place or a population. The answer to that question must be a statement not about the city but about the God who some three millennia ago chose it for a special function.

The initial version of that special vocation is represented by the historical origins of the city's metaphysical centrality. It was the last of David's conquests. For centuries, namely from Joshua's time to David's, the city of the Jebusites had remained impregnable. It could serve as David's capital, and then as site for the Tabernacle, and then for the Temple, precisely because, although encircled by Judah, it had belonged to none of the tribes. The Lord's choice of Jerusalem left behind their tribal judges' seats and their local holy places. Even on earth, extraterritoriality was part of his self-definition.[6]

The Davidic generation thus updated the symbolism, which the patriarchal account had already identified in the shadowy figure of Melchizedek, at once King of Salem and 'Priest of God Most High'. Something of this meaning continued in the ephemeral mobility of the Tabernacle from the age of Moses to that of David. The transcendence of the Most High God is represented not by a platonic denial or spiritualization of space, and not, after the pattern of the mystery religions, or the Hindus, by setting aside a special spooky space – even though the beneficiaries of his visitations tried to tie him down by setting up stones where they had seen him pass. The transcendence of the Most High is acted out in the fact that the place of his manifestation is not our own turf.[7]

God's choosing to pitch his tent in our midst is his mercy, not our merit or our property. That God chooses neutral ground (or foreign ground) as the way to be graciously in our midst points to a truth, which all three Abrahamic faiths have retained, though in different ways.[8] God is never our God in the sense of our possessing him. God's compassionate intentions always include the others, the outsiders, the nations, the sojourners. The fact that Jerusalem is spoken of by apostles and prophets as 'beyond', or as 'to come', as 'above' or 'holy' or 'heavenly', reflects the self-limiting modesty, which that transcendence demands of the believer. It would be wrong to philosophize any of these 'otherness' terms, i.e. to explain the otherness in terms of some metaphysical dualism. Suffice it that they all relativize the empirical, manipulable 'reality'. They relativize the given in favour of the gift.

The same self-limiting understanding takes other forms in the later history. In the Jewish experience it is represented by Jeremiah's acceptance of *galut* (exile) as mission, and by the much later development of the theory of the Noachic covenant, whose observance by the Gentiles may entitle them to share in the age to come. In the Christian experience it is the place of mission to the Gentiles as mark of the messianic age.

That the otherness of Jerusalem, as cipher for the otherness of God, points us away from possessiveness and toward the redefinition of providence so as to favour the outsider, is an easily forgotten truth. We all fall back easily into provincial self-definitions that reduce the Most High God to a graven image by reducing his causes to our own. Christians have done that the most culpably, especially since their alliance with Imperial Rome, but the other faith families enjoy no automatic exemption from the same temptation, and terrestrial Jerusalem has been one of the victims of their conflicts ever since.

One further phase in the prophetic defence of God's continuing to transcend his own chosen place is evoked when that place is thought of not as people and buildings alone, not only as sites for worship and burial, but in the implicitly Solomonic or messianic terms of dominion. Rabbi Cytron's quotation from S. Talmon refers to 'statehood' and 'nationhood'.[9] Both of these concepts have taken on special meanings in modern western experience, not all of which the Rabbi can have intended. To avoid anachronism, it makes more sense to speak here of 'kingship', and to recognize that the adoption by ancient Israel of models of kingship 'like the other nations' was seen quite ambivalently even at the time,[10] by the earliest historians,[11] and even more so by the prophets. Isaiah condemned his king's 'realistic' foreign alliances, Jeremiah accepted the loss of national sovereignty, and Ezra and Nehemiah restored the worshipping community without political sovereignty.[12] The efforts of the Maccabees, of Menachem in the years after 66 CE. and of Bar Kochba later are seen by the rabbis not as having been wrong because they failed but as having failed because they were wrong. As Steven Schwarzschild, the rabbi from whom I have learned the most once wrote me, 'The Maccabees are in the Christian canon, not in the Hebrew one.'[13]

When Jesus said to his disciples: 'The kings of the nations domineer over them, and have themselves called "benefactors", but it shall not be so for you' (Luke 22.25ff.), that was not a new idea nor an un-Jewish one. It was shared at the time by most of his people's teachers, except for the ruling Sadducean and Herodian elites off on one side and the Zealots off on the other. The line of the school of Yavneh, the only one that remained visible for the centuries following the final defeat of Bar Kochba, was not merely making the best of a bad deal.[14] It was the proper moral response to the lessons learned. Christian usage would say that to abandon kingship-like-that-of-the-Gentiles was not a pragmatic but a theological decision. It was a matter not merely of tactics but of integrity.

As Christians gradually forsook their bond with the other Jews, they also gradually turned their backs on that Jewish wisdom. They repeated the error of the age of Samuel, first with Constantine and then with the other Caesars in Byzantium, Aachen, Moscow, and Berlin. The resulting triumphalism was bad for the integrity of the Christian gospel, and often it was bad for the Jews.

Authentic reverence before divine sovereignty must accordingly mean a critical judgement upon nationhood/statehood in its modern as well as its medieval forms. Again this is not a distinctively Christian view. It is in fact held by only a minority of Christians, as by (today) only a minority of Jews.

As members of the several monotheistic faith communities we all have a stake, in different ways, in both the transcendent symbolism and the Realpolitik. A half-century after the founding of the Third Reich, a third of a century after the founding of the State of Israel,[15] we cannot avoid the issues of peace and justice, which are represented in the conflicts we must speak to. The issues of our common agenda are unity or partition, national integration or extraterritoriality, the choice of which UN resolutions, under which constructions, to honour, the safeguards for the rights of minorities, and whatever the Camp David agreements meant by 'autonomy'.

We all have a stake in seeing those conflicts be worked out with more flexibility, more modesty, more imagination, more readiness for risk, more restraint on the part of meddling superpowers, more repentance in the face of the evidently counter-productive impact of the self-righteous polarizing strategies used hitherto on both sides. We have a stake in the virtues assigned by the Bat Kol to the school of Hillel, namely the readiness to hear the other opinion before deciding. We have a stake – even the polar parties have a stake – in unlearning the tendency of the advocates in any tense struggle to demand that all third parties take sides. Yet beyond such broad and formal phrases it is not for me or for us to project. It is precisely the truth of those phrases about 'the other Jerusalem' that forbids that anyone, sitting in Bloomington, Indiana [16] in the absence of the major actors and their victims, should presume to prescribe or even to claim adequately to empathize.

What can we then contribute? We can state the common witness of all authentic monotheism to the transcendence of God's claims upon us in favour of the others, the outsiders. The Most High God (I use the name from Genesis because it helps to make the point), we saw, does not accentuate transcendence in the interest of Platonism or ritualism, but in the interest of relativizing our claims to locate him on our own turf and make him the enemy of our enemies.

The needfulness of accentuating that view of Jerusalem's being 'above' and beyond us, or 'to come', has only grown in our post-Constantinian, post-religious age. Since Machiavelli we have been confronted with explicitly, refined and intelligently argued advocacy of provincial presumptuousness, making one's own Prince (or, two centuries later, after Enlightenment had updated Renaissance, one's 'nation') morally sovereign, accountable to no one else. Since the great revolutions which focused their justice claims on the imperative of domestic political renewal through the seizure of power in the name of 'the people', the dignity of the outsider as also God's child, whose blood is just as red as ours, is even more in need of being defended by a quality of advocacy whose leverage must be greater than mere social contract utility. What could that leverage be, if not the transcendence of the Most High God, reflected in the denial of ultimacy even to that place where he has chosen to meet us?

Then both the local actors in the Middle Eastern struggles and we more distant concerned observers are under the judgement and the promise of God's extraterritoriality. How can the use which we make of the earthly city be subject to, or be renewed by the 'good news' that Zion's promised liberation is not only from but more fundamentally for the nations? How can short range politics be kept sober by the knowledge of the other, 'higher' or 'future' city of peace toward which today's is supposed to point us forward?

To conclude: I state it more formally. We have to do with two-and-a-half models of transcendence. One, in which the Neo-Platonist and the realist concur, is concerned primarily to keep the 'ideal' from impinging too directly on the 'real world'. The 'realists' want this in order to free themselves from criticism, to free their hands for effective action. The Neo-Platonists want it in order not to be sullied by the contact. The other, more Hebraic view considers transcendence much less purely. That which is not yet 'earthly' is not 'ethereal' but 'to come'. The dualism points toward new possibilities for this world, toward promises which both condemn and redeem.

Then there is a third mode, in which the language of transcendence is appropriated – the critic will say 'usurped' – for the purpose of stating the claims for one's own sovereignty and possessiveness. The basis for judging[17] whether such appropriation is a legitimate act of faith or an usurpation is not whether the claim to 'celestial' authority is 'literal' or not,[18] but whom it excludes or expels; whether our enemies are God's enemies or his children. Those who enter Jerusalem's gates sing that it is 'built to be a city where people come together in unity' (Ps. 122.3).[19] Those people are qualified to work at the building of the city who build it for others, who recognize it as not their own turf but God's. [20]

Notes

1. Paper presented at an 'Institute on Jewish–Christian Relations' convened at Bloomington, IN by the Anti-Defamation League of B'nai B'rith and the Lilly Foundation, 10–13 December 1984. The text, read 11 December, was never printed. Here it is transcribed from the original notes. The title 'Earthly Jerusalem and Heavenly Jerusalem' had been assigned to me by the planners of this event, without their giving me any instructions about what it meant, or why I had been the person asked to treat it. I was not fully informed, and did not seek to be, about the particular culture-political 'line' represented within American Jewry by the ADL, so I took the text straightforwardly, *pshat*, as it stood. In the course of the meeting it became more evident that the title did in fact represent a specific rationale. When I came across these notes over a decade later, in the course of preparing a possible text on the normativity of *galut* for Jewish and Christian identity, it occurred to me that reviewing the Bloomington conversation might be good homework. It is an occasion to test the applicability to real dialogue of the Jeremianic model interpreted in the earlier parts of this packet.

2. Barry Cytron was at that time serving the congregation Adath Jeshurun in Minneapolis. His contribution to the symposium, including some of the basic text/word study, had been circulated in advance. The 'one text' referred to is *Taanit* 53, where Rabbi Nachman cites Rabbi Yochanan, interpreting a text from Hosea in the light of Ps. 122. Cytron went on to show that the notation that there are two Jerusalems, one of them heavenly, is a misunderstanding even of that passage. I have no grounds to challenge either his interpretation or his report that this is the only such text. Shemaryahu

Talmon in 'The Biblical Concept of Jerusalem' in the *Journal of Ecumenical Studies*, 8, 1971, 300–16 refers (p. 309) to what he calls 'the ideological transfer of terrestrial Jerusalem to the celestial plane', but neither cites a source for that phrase nor explains his meaning.

3. The later course of the event at Bloomington in fact gave some grounds for thinking that some of the planners in the Anti-Defamation League had had this dichotomy in mind, as if assigning the heavenly city to the Christians would facilitate leaving the earthly one to the Jews.

4. Nor was his concern the problem of urbanization, to which Rabbi Cytron's introduction creatively pointed.

5. S. Talmon (cf. 'The Biblical Concept of Jerusalem', 305) suggests another dimension; the Abrahamic legend of Melchizedek, the king/priest of Salem, accentuates the allusion to 'Peace' in the very name of the place.

6. Talon ('The Biblical Concept of Jerusalem', 310f.) draws attention to this fact. He calls the city a 'melting pot', indicating that that was both a fact and a vision, an advantage.

7. Other dimensions of the tradition, not tied to the city, make a similar point. The concerns of the Torah for the *ger* who sojourns in the midst of Israel also relativize the tribes' natural ethnocentricity.

8. The cynic will add that all three faiths have also found their own ways to betray this insight.

9. By these terms Talmon meant the Davidic state, as contrasted with the pre-conquest nomadic culture. It would be a serious mistake to read into this change all of what 'nation' or 'state' means today. David was a warlord more than a Caesar or a Kaiser.

10. E.g. Jotham's fable in Judges 9.7ff.

11. 1 Samuel 8.6ff.

12. I do not seek to speak here to the historians' questions about how the narratives about Ezra and about Nehemiah relate to each other or to 'real history'.

13. See Chapter 2, n. 18 above.

14. Jochanan ben Zakkai seems to have left Jerusalem and made his overtures to Vespasian before the last onslaught on Jerusalem had begun.

15. The passage of another dozen years since this lecture was drafted have only strengthened the point.

16. I learned after the meeting at Bloomington began that some participants did believe that it was supposed to be about proximate political solutions in the Near East, and about whether to ratify or to relativize various parties' claims for access to holy places.

17. I say this as an interested outsider, but I think Martin Buber made it the touchstone too.

18. This was the thesis of Rabbi Cytron in his paper for the Bloomington event.

19. This is the text which Rabbi Nachman, speaking to Rabbi Isaac, citing Rabbi Yochanan, seemed to be alluding to in the oldest Talmudic passage about 'heavenly Jerusalem' interpreted by Rabbi Cytron in his background paper.

20. [Editors' Note: At the conclusion of the 1996 manuscript of this essay, Yoder offered the following 'Postscript' about what transpired 'after the event at Bloomington'.]

'Pre-conference correspondence had indicated that the papers would be published in the Anti-Defamation League publication *Face to Face*. As far as I know they were not. At least mine was not; at least I never received a copy. I was not informed why this did not happen. It may be because *Face to Face* is understood as an advocacy organ for a particular line, and the educational events which the Anti-Defamation League barn-storms around the country are intended rather to be educational than substantially original.

The Anti-Defamation League has (or had then, according to my limited understanding) a stake in a particular understanding of the shape of the discriminatory situation under which Jews suffer. It also has a stake in a particular 'liberal' conception of Jewish identity, such that Jews would not bring any discrimination upon themselves by their apartness or by their truth claims. The programme people who set the tone for such events are mostly those who fit that model, best represented by Roy Eckhardt, whose 'summing up' at the Bloomington conference rejected the challenge I had addressed to the bipolar model of the dialog, as well as the way my reading had (although only by tacit implication) relativized mainline Zionism. Eckhardt's reason for setting my argument aside did not need to be argued in the meeting. He was the founder-figure of the conference genre, whose 'summing up' had to be true to tradition. It would appear that the reason I was invited was not the intention that I should contribute something particular to the dialogue, but rather that I was an available Protestant in Indiana, and someone thought that a Lilly-sponsored event in the Midwest should not be staffed only with people from the East.'

Commentary

PETER OCHS

This is the one chapter that begins with an allusion to a Talmudic text. Since the text is not, however, reproduced or examined directly in the chapter, I will take this one opportunity to illustrate what a sampling of Talmudic reasoning looks like; in this case, the reasoning is not legal or *halakhic*, as is much of the Talmud, but homiletic, or *aggadic*. The text in question belongs to a tractate that examines the special fasts that the community takes upon itself in times of severe drought when not even extended prayer appears to save the community from this divine punishment. Our passage is placed within a literary context of what we might call anxious reflection on Israel's suffering: cases of drought that bring to mind even more severe calamities, such as the destruction of Jerusalem. The passage is as follows:

> Further, R. Nachman said to R. Isaac: What is the meaning of the scriptural verse, *The Holy One in your midst and I will not come into the city?* (Hosea 11.9) [Surely it cannot be] because the Holy One is in your midst that I shall not come into the city! He replied: Thus said R. Yochanan: The Holy One, blessed be He, said, 'I will not enter the heavenly Jerusalem until I can enter the earthly Jerusalem.' Is there then a heavenly Jerusalem? – Yes; for it is written, *Jerusalem, you art built as a city that is compact together* (Ps. 122.3). (TB *Taanit* 5a)

Let us first consider the plain sense of the two scriptural passages around which this homily, or *midrash*, revolves, and the gaps or mysteries or difficulties in that plain-sense that stimulates the rabbis to look deeper. The setting of Hosea 11 is a vision of Israel's terrible suffering under the Assyrian invasions. God sees this suffering – it is the sting of his own punishment – and is moved to compassion, for 'I fell in love with Israel when he was still a child, and I have called him my son ever since Egypt' (11.1). So, 'how can I give you up, O Ephraim?' (11.8). Therefore, 'I will not act on my wrath, will not turn to destroy Ephraim. For I am God, not man, the Holy One in your midst: I will not come in fury (*b'ir*, 'in fury'? or *ba'ir*, 'in the city'?)' (11.9). Traditional rabbinic commentators are puzzled by the last passage. Poetic parallelism would seem to suggest that God is assuring them that, unlike a human, he is holy and can overcome his anger; he will not approach them in his full fury. That reading seems best to fit the plain-sense, but it is still awkward in grammatical structure, so there is room for other hypotheses. One is suggested by the different ways that '*bir*' could be vocalized: the word itself might also mean 'in the city.' However awkward that might be in the plain sense of chapter 11 (working against both the poetic structure of the chapter and its situation in the north of Israel), it does bring to mind, particularly for rabbinic readers, the destructions of Jerusalem that are yet to come and, thus, yet another context for musing on God's capacity both to destroy and to forebear. Now, consider Psalm 122. It is a joyous 'Song of Ascents', a song sung by pilgrims as they ascend to Jerusalem: 'We are going to the House of the Lord. Our feet stood inside your gates O Jerusalem. Jerusalem built up (*b'nuya*, or 'rebuilt'), a city knit together (*sh'chuvrah*).' Why 'knit together'? The plain sense of the next verse seems to be clear: a city 'to which tribes would make pilgrimage', that is, a city in which the different tribes are knitted together in praise for God. Juxtaposed, however, to the passage from Hosea, the rabbinic interpreters suggest another meaning that could, at least theologically, apply to the context both of the Psalm and of Hosea. The passage could be read: 'Jerusalem built as a city that has a companion (*she* [*yesh lo*] *chavurah*)', that is, has a companion in heaven (!). The implication is that this 'earthly city' has a correlative city, or prototype, in heaven. The psalm would then read: we are going into your gates, O Jerusalem, which is a city here, on earth, that also embodies what is there, in heaven. The passage in Hosea can then be read this way: I will not enter the heavenly city but only the earthly one. One way to interpret the rabbis' homily (and there is always more than one way to interpret) is that God's mercy for us is displayed in his choosing to make the earthly Jerusalem his abode rather than withdrawing to the Heavenly one. This, I believe, is also consistent with the lovely reading that Yoder offers us in this chapter.

This time Yoder concludes, I am happy to say, with a three-part rather than a two-part distinction. Rather than suggest there are two ways to consider Jerusalem's transcendence, one to be accepted one rejected, Yoder suggests there are three models (or at least in his words, 'two-and-a-half'): a Neo-Platonic model of a city beyond this world; a Hebraic vision of the city that is to come (in the world to come); and an oppressive model that appropriates the status of the transcendent for some earthly polity. Post-liberal Jews may be encouraged by Yoder's three-part distinction, since it enables him to promote a third model that avoids not merely one but two extremes – here the extremes of otherworldliness and oppressive landedness. The holy is present within the earthly Jerusalem as the telos of its salvation history. We may note, with interest, that a proof text for this intermediate model appears later in Psalm 122: 'Pray for the well-being of Jerusalem; may those who love you be at peace' (122.9). Here is an intriguing correlate to Jeremiah's 'pray for the welfare of the city' (that is not Jerusalem but Babylonian!). Perhaps here, Yoder meets the rabbis in that middle place on which post-liberal Jews rest their hopes: the holy on earth.

9

On Not Being in Charge[1]

A. The Shape of the Question

If you begin thinking, as in our culture we usually do, with the assumption that it is our moral responsibility to administer the course of human events, then the position I have been asked to describe may be designated as 'quietism.'[2] If the assumptions are further specified to provide that we normally have a duty to enforce upon others, by military means, our conception of the desirable direction of events, then the position I describe may be called 'pacifism'. Yet both of these characterizations, which figure in our programme title, presuppose a framing of the moral question which is already tilted. Therefore the more functional or formal phrase in my title 'not being in charge', is more fitting.

The dominant frame of reference for the institutional and moral thought of our culture is the legacy of the transitions symbolized, and to some extent caused, by Constantine.[3] Since then the public order, especially the civil order or 'the state', is understood to be the primary bearer of the meaningful movement of history, so that social ethics is about how we would want those structures to move, and why. Despite the many structural changes in detail since the Middle Ages, including such major matters as royalty's yielding to democracy and the separation of Church and State, the basic logic in most people's minds, including the unselfconscious assumptions of those who do not examine the matter, has not changed.[4] We assume that we both can and should 'take responsibility' for the macro course of events, and then from that objective we derive the justification for the practical measures it takes to get there, such as getting elected to office, organizing and deploying military might, and whatever else it takes. That set of assumptions is so omnipresent that for many it is inconceivable that it might be doubted.

My task then is to make doubt at that point conceivable. In a prefatory way I shall remind you that doubting those assumptions might be justified on general logical and empirical grounds; but the substance of my assignment will be to narrate the experiences of some people from the underside of history, in order to concretize how reasonable the view from below can seem under certain circumstances, which in fact are not rare but typical.

B. The Limits of the Imperative to be Responsible

First by way of preface: logically and empirically it cannot be the case that 'Thou shalt take responsibility for governing the world' is a univocal moral obligation. In the quadrennial civil ritual the United States is experiencing in the fall of 1992, at least half of the persons offering to take on that responsibility as elected officials will not be chosen. Many of the voters are not offered a candidate representing their values, and thanks to low voter turnout the persons elected will probably have been

[handwritten: Luther (Soteriologist —) did not believe you contributed to your salvation / quietist]

chosen by a minority of the electorate. Most of those elected and believing themselves mandated to do something will find that pre-existing structures in both the
legislative and the executive agencies of state management will keep them from
doing what they believe in. This does not keep me from believing with Winston
Churchill that parliamentary democracy is the worst form of government, except
for all the others.[5] Yet this awareness should (and for a growing number of people
does) undercut the naïve notions of *vox populi* and 'responsibility to serve' which
dominate the public rhetoric. All civil government is oligarchy; all of it is a few
people (to use the language of Jesus) 'lording it' over the rest of us. The value of
democracy is the relatively greater capacity which victims and third parties nonetheless have to speak critically.[6] But then those persons, sometimes heroic individuals
and sometimes committed communities, who are committed to value systems which
have no chance of being elected, are not being 'sectarian' or 'withdrawing' when
they do not join the electoral fray as if their dignity depended on it.[7]

A second logical observation: some argue (and some take for granted as not even
needing argument) that the price of 'involvement' in public life and discourse is
that one must filter out, or reserve to the private realm, or 'compromise' the particular identifying value commitments of a faith community, in favour of
common-denominator moral language. Yet if in order to 'be involved' you commit
yourself to values less clear or less imperative than your own, which are more
acceptable because the 'public' out there already holds them, then your involvement
adds nothing to the mix but numbers. Joining the majority on grounds that others
already are committed to, in favour of policies which others already support, winds
up paradoxically having the same effect as abstention; it lets the values of the others
be decisive.

These two prefatory comments are not meant to be probative; they seek only to
open some space for the alternative narrative to which I now turn. I shall select
several episodes from a much broader history, speaking schematically and not in
chronological order.

C. The Social Criticism of the First Reformation

The movement which Czech Protestants call 'The First Reformation' faced its first
crisis when the perfidy of Emperor Sigismund and the Council of Constance made a
martyr of the nation's chief theologian, Jan Hus. The protest that resulted went off
in three directions. One of them, nationalistic and noble, which came to be called
'utraquist' or 'calixtine', because the issue of communion in both kinds became its
symbol, negotiated for a degree of ecclesiastical autonomy, with some success for a
while. Another, the apocalyptic 'Taborites', chose the path of revolutionary
violence, with some success for a much shorter while. The third path, guided intellectually, non-institutionally, by the lay theologian Peter Cheltschitsky, unfolded
the first deeply thought-through critique of the Constantinian synthesis.[8] Having no
military power base, Peter's movement grew slowly from below, thanks only to the
power of his ideas and the way the other two 'take-charge' strategies had failed. In
1467 his pupils formed the *Unitas Fratrum*, strictly speaking the first Protestant
church.

Retrieving the Gospel image of the Church as a net holding together 153 fish (John

21.11),[9] Cheltschitsky explained the sad shape of Christendom as being the result of two sea monsters which had broken the net, thereby making it impossible to discern the true Church. The two monsters[10] were the Emperor and the Pope, jointly responsible for the betrayal of the gospel.[11] Behind this metaphor Cheltschitsky was able to discern and denounce the Constantinian shift as a betrayal of gospel substance.[12] Peter was non-violent on both gospel and practical grounds. After both the noble Utraquists and the crazy Taborites had been beaten by the weapons they had chosen, namely militarily, non-violence was not a hard position to take. Perhaps more crucial was Peter's social doctrine, prefiguring the Levellers. The three-level stratification of society into Nobility, Clergy, and the rest of us is to be rejected by appealing to both Genesis and Jesus. The ordinary Christian life is to be restructured around the Sermon on the Mount, which as taught by Jesus has the same moral status as the decalogue and the Two Great Commandments.[13]

The implication of this revisionist reading of the fourth century is not that Constantine should not have become Christian, but that on becoming Christian, if he really had chosen to so,[14] the Emperor should have, like anyone else, taken on the Christian life, subject to the same repentance and disciplines as other converts. This undercuts the same notion I identified among modern 'pluralists', namely that in order to participate in the civil world one must forsake a specifically[15] Christian allegiance.

D. The Grounds of the Early Christian Attitude to Caesar: The Polity of the Dispersion

Peter's having identified the fourth century as historical hinge sends us back in time to our second specimen, whose specificity we may discern more easily now than if we had begun with it. It is the 'not in charge' stance of Jewry, from Jeremiah into the Middle Ages, of which the early Christians were a derivative and minor strand. As I said at the outset, this position may not inaccurately be called 'pacifist' or 'quietist', but both characterizations would be skewed.

It is one of the marks of our culture's anti-Judaic heritage that the pacifism of the early Christians is routinely understood as having taken off from scratch from a few words, or a few deeds, of Jesus,[16] when as a matter of fact it was a part of the common Jewish legacy which Jesus and the apostles shared with their non-messianic contemporaries like Jochanan ben Zakkai.

There were exceptions to the 'pacifism' of 'not being in charge' which marked Jewish experience since Jeremiah, but they were exceptions, and they failed. God did not prosper them. One set of exceptions were those people who concentrated on rebuilding and managing the Temple at Jerusalem, with the political and financial backing of the Empires, first of the East and then of Rome. From Ezra and Nehemiah to the Sanhedrin of the time of Jesus, this restorative elite, called 'Sadducees' in the Gospels, did the best it could to defend Jewish values, but ultimately it failed.

The other set of exceptions were the Maccabees and the so-called Zealots;[17] they too ultimately failed, but not before triggering the Roman Empire's devastating response. The 'Judaism' which survived after the last Zealot defeat in 135 assumed the same stance which Jewry everywhere else but in Palestine had already been taking since Jeremiah, namely 'seeking the peace of the city where they had been sent' (Jer. 29.4–7).

The Jewish settlers in Babylon (and in all the other cities to which they were scattered of which we know less) did not accept 'not being in charge' as a lesser-evil strategy of mere survival, nor as a mere tactic, but as their mission.[18] That experience created the culturally unique traits which define 'Judaism' and thereby Christianity in turn:

- the phenomenon of the synagogue; a decentralized, self-sustaining, non-sacerdotal community life form capable of operating on its own wherever there are ten households.
- the phenomenon of Torah; a text around the reading and exposition of which the community is defined. This text is at once narrative and legal.
- the phenomenon of the rabbinate; a non-sacerdotal, non-hierarchical, nonviolent leadership elite whose power is not civil but intellectual, validated by their identification with the Torah.

Each of these marks was sociologically innovative. Each was indispensable to define Jewish identity outside of Palestine and to make it viable. Each had its Palestinian counterparts, but the home of each was in the diaspora. Each of them guaranteed that while 'quietist' and 'pacifist' in the senses defined above, this community would be neither silent nor powerless. Cumulatively they made of Jewry an effective missionary people all across the Middle East, not ending their outreach completely even when the Christians, with the same ethos and polity, took over that role.[19]

There is wide recognition that the Christians of the first two centuries were pacifist, or at least that their most articulate teachers of whom we have record were. The historians debate about whether this was univocally the case, and ethicists debate about whether, if it was, it should be normative for later Christians. Yet in all of that voluminous debate, neither party takes account of the fact that the ethos of the early Christians was a direct prolongation and fulfilment of the ethos of Jewry.[20]

Both sides of the debate about the question: 'were the early Christians pacifist?' have tended to proceed legalistically, as if the Christian movement had taken off from scratch with only a few words of Jesus to guide them, so that a fine-grained debate about whether those few words had to mean just this or that would have been be the primary tool of moral discernment.

It is rather the case that Jesus' impact in the first century added more and deeper authentically Jewish reasons, or reinforced and further validated the already expressed Jewish reasons,[21] for the already established ethos of not being in charge and not considering any local state structure to be the primary bearer of the movement of history. To this same stance the second generation of witnesses after Jesus, the 'apostles', added another layer of further reasons, still utterly Jewish in form and substance, having to do with the Messiahship of Jesus, his Lordship, and the presence of the Holy Spirit.[22] Much later, some non-messianic Jews formally rejected these ideas about Jesus, or about the Spirit; nonetheless they were at the time unimpeachably Jewish ideas, and they made clear why a 'quietist' stance in the Roman/Mediterranean world made good sense. Until the messianity of Jesus was replaced by that of Constantine,[23] it was the only ethos that made sense.[24]

Thus when Cheltschitsky reached past the Constantinian shift to 'original

Christianity', what he found back there to stand on was not a simple moral rigour about not shedding blood,[25] but a robust alternative holistic social system, capable of surviving and prospering against the stream of the polytheistic culture-and-state-religions of the respective empires which the Jews and the Christians underwent and outlived. Not withdrawal for the sake of moral purity or immaterial spirituality, but resistance for the sake of justice and the honour of God, had set the tone for the nonconformity of the Jews after Jeremiah and the Christians before Constantine. It was when the Christians were still in a minority in the third century, benefiting from the respect of many of their neighbours, that their weight led some rulers to seek alliance with them and others to seek to destroy them. Both the phenomenon of occasional persecution and the event of its ultimately ending bear witness to the cultural and even political power of a morally committed minority.

When Jews in Babylonia 'sought the peace of that city to which God had sent them',[26] this did not mean merely that they hoped and prayed to be granted social tranquillity and saved from persecution. Jewish minorities, within a few generations of their arrival, almost everywhere they went, came to be valued as specialists in cross-cultural communication. Sometimes that meant leadership in trade, sometimes in literacy or language, sometimes in diplomacy. Sometimes they pioneered with schools, sometimes with medicine, sometimes with banking. The models of Joseph, Esther, and Daniel from the ancient story and legend found contemporary counterparts from Babylon to Salamanca to Worms. Not being in charge of the civil order is sometimes a more strategic way to be important for its survival or its flourishing than to fight over or for the throne. In dramatic and traumatic cases the Jews were murdered or banished; in more, quieter cases they were needed and appreciated despite (or thanks to) their nonconformity. This was the case in similar ways for the pre-Constantinian Christians.

E. Dissent in Early Modernity

Having noted in Cheltschitsky an early strong specimen of the post-medieval critique of the concept of Christendom, and having seen in Judaism and early Christianity its fulcrum, I should return now toward the present. I shall renounce any vision of stopping in every century along the way,[27] leaping first to the rise of the Puritan witness toward the end of the reign of Queen Elizabeth.[28] Once it had become clear that the most optimistic hope, namely that all of the Church of England would be reformed according to the Puritan vision, would be disappointed, the Puritans' attention turned to the conditions for the survival of the radically Protestant testimony under conditions of non-establishment. The *internal* vision of the Church as developed by congregationalism over the preceding generation had been derived from the convictions of those thinkers about the marks of the faithful community; but here we look at the *external* implications of that testimony.

The moral imperative of freedom for assembly, for speech including preaching, and for the press, is derived according to the Puritan witness from the sovereignty of God whose word, already accessible in the Scriptures, must be communicated in every time and place without let or hindrance. The demand that speech and assembly be freed thus becomes a claim upon the civil order, but its rootage is in divine revelation. John Milton, partly because of his other claims to fame, became the most noted spokesman of this demand for freedom, but the case had been worked out well before him. If the omnipotent and all-wise Creator determined that he could afford to give his creatures the freedom to sin – the theodicy which underlies Milton's *Paradise Lost*, transposed to the civil order in his *Aeropagitica* – then certainly the royalty of England could afford to let their loyal subjects read, gather, and preach freely.

At a second point as well, the inner integrity of dissent could extrapolate into a constructive witness *ad extram*. As is said most simply in Paul's epistle to the Corinthians, the right way for believers to hold a meeting in the power of the Holy Spirit is to authorize everyone to speak. Scripture guides the Church not primarily when its words are exposited by a linguist (and certainly not when their meaning is decreed by an absentee bishop) but rather when all believers gather and speak freely of its testimony.[29] Historians agree that in this reformation vision of the congregation as gathered and conversing freely we may find the model for the 'town meeting' in congregationalist America.[30] A culture that calls for dialogue rather than zero-sum conflict has its roots in a faith understanding of the Holy Spirit as active in the assembly.

The call for civil liberties and the consent of the governed is the way the anti-Constantinian critique took shape in England. What would it do in the greater openness of the New World? For that we advance two generations to another radical Puritan, William Penn, who founded four of the original American colonies in the light of the Quaker vision of history,[31] after Roger Williams had begun something similar in Rhode Island [32] (chartered in 1644). In these two men it is evident that the position which *usually* is not in a position to determine the shape of a society as a whole, because it does not have the power, would not be incapable of doing so in the odd case of its being entrusted the chance to lead.

Penn did not fight to acquire his land, either from the crown or from the Indians. He was not a very good manager, did not choose very wisely the people to whom he delegated the care of his affairs, and could not prevent following generations from forsaking the Quaker faith.[33] The 'experiment' could not succeed forever; yet the three generations from Penn's groundwork in 1681 to the Quakers' abandoning control of the Pennsylvania Assembly in 1756 are closer to a success story than most regimes, most dynasties can claim. Penn's establishment differed from the rest of the Colonies (except for Rhode Island) in fundamental ways:

- in dealing honestly with the original occupants of the land, paying an agreed price for the land, making un-coerced treaties with them and honouring those treaties as long as Quaker government lasted;
- in guaranteeing religious liberty, on theological and not merely pragmatic grounds, and encouraging free immigration of European dissenters;
- in humanizing civil justice and corrections;
- in moving more rapidly than other colonies toward one man/one vote democracy, including more rights for women than elsewhere;
- in creating the first public schools;
- in challenging slavery. Penn did not legally outlaw slavery, but when protest against slavery did arise, it was Friends and Mennonites who led it, on grounds dictated by their faith and not by their economic interest.

When Friends were outvoted by the non-pacifist Europeans with whom they had shared their commonwealth, during the build-up to the French and Indian war,

free church, they don't think their goal is to run the world / *Quietist (Not Being in Charge)*

their leadership in these realms did not cease; from then on they exercised it very effectively in the ordinary way, namely without being rulers.

My present concern is not to review the Pennsylvania experiment for its own sake, but only to take note of it as a probative specimen on the systematic question. Those whose ethic *ordinarily* would disqualify them from 'being in charge' of a civil society, *in the sense that* their ethic is expressly not designed after the Constantinian model with a view to enabling them to take charge violently, and *in the sense that* majorities would seldom elect them, and who could therefore be qualified as 'quietist', can nonetheless and do in fact discharge social responsibilities, when such are entrusted to them without demanding that they betray their truth-telling, non-violent ethos. There is nothing intrinsically otherworldly about that ethos. It is not *a priori* inapplicable in the real world.

F. Social Effectiveness from Below

More often, the way in which 'not in charge' minorities contribute to social process is backhanded. By denouncing the veneration of the national flag as idolatrous, the Jehovah's Witnesses in the US enlarged the notion of religious liberty. By conscientiously declaring themselves unavailable for military service, the 'objectors' widen the notion of religious liberty to include not only ideas but also behaviour, not only cultic but also political behaviour. By conscientiously claiming responsibility for their children's education the Old Order Amish break the stranglehold of homogeneous state education. Christian Scientists and charismatics who believe that God heals challenge the American Medical Association medical-care cartel. Non-co-operation, when empowered by a level of conviction that is willing to suffer, is a more powerful way to move a society than is the ballot box; it can be used defectively by minorities.

Thus far I have been directing your attention to the underside of history in a narrative mode. I have been demonstrating that people who are not in charge, and for whom therefore an ethic or an ethos of 'responsibility' would be wrong or incoherent, are nonetheless socially important. Underlying this account I next need to indicate that most people who are in that way practically in step with a different drumbeat also hold to a different cosmology. Their deviant behaviour reflects a deviant reading of reality.

G. The World-view of the Elect Underdogs

1. There is the paradox of the power of weakness. Sometimes this alternative vision of the shape of the world affirms that weakness is strong, that suffering is powerful, and that relinquishing control is the most responsible way to intervene in history. In very different ways this kind of argument has been represented by the apostle Paul,[34] by contemplatives over the centuries, by movers and shakers like Gandhi and Martin Luther King, and by intellectuals like H. Richard Niebuhr.[35] It can follow as logical entailment from the notion that there is one true God who is at once all good and the ultimate historical actor. One of its oldest forms, though still alive, as already noted, is the orthodox Jewish perspective of the *neturei karta*, which does

not acknowledge the State of Israel because it was not established by the Messiah, but by human initiative.

2. There is the power of promise. In some settings the alternative vision is articulated in terms of hope. Hope sets aside our pragmatic notions of managing rationally the consequences of our actions, i.e. of making our decisions on consequential grounds, by virtue of the promise that God will intervene to liberate and vindicate. The cultural mode and the literary genre which we call 'apocalyptic' were once simply set aside by our contemporaries as useless, meaningless or silly, whether they occurred in the Jewish and Christian Scriptures, or in historical and social thought. Now they are being given more attention, as offering a way to make important statements about God's transcendence,[36] or about human sinfulness, or about the finiteness of the human project. These are dimensions which more ambitious visions of human dignity as being 'in charge' of history by virtue of one's own control of the levers of power make people unable to perceive.[37]

3. Yet another mode of articulation echoes the way in which the apostle Paul spoke of the historical world as being the prey of 'principalities and powers'. These are creaturely structures, whose role should be to serve human flourishing and God's glory, but which in their rebelliousness become our oppressors.[38] The fallenness of the world is not just the fallenness of individual sinners; the world as structure is awry. Those of us who seek to 'take charge' of events by challenging the Powers at their own game, trying to manipulate events in terms of their own inherent dynamics, may be selling out morally and practically at the very point where they claim to be taking responsibility. By agreeing to play by their rules we grant their idolatrous claim to be in charge of history in JHWH's stead. Our refusal to play the game by the agreed rules may be morally more basic than our courageous wrestling with things as they are.[39] Jesus defeated the powers not by being better than they at their trade of domination, but by refusing to meet them on that terrain, at the cost of his life.

Each of the above three paragraphs points to a theme which has made its way through history, and which would reward further attention in its own right. For my present purposes, what matters is not what further argument might be made, or what examples recounted, for any one of them, or whether to these three a few more might be added.[40] What matters is what they have in common, namely that they testify to the possibility of a very intelligent, very realistic view of things, which makes good sense of living under God in a world which we do not control, and in which moral discourse is guided by other rules than those of generalizability and optimizing consequences.

Matthew's Jesus told his listeners not to worry about their material survival, not because he was summoning them to ascetic renunciation, but because their heavenly father knew their needs. 'Seek first the righteousness of the kingdom, and the rest will be thrown in', is a recipe not for poverty but for plenty. It may be similar when we ask how the value-laden sub-community goes about caring about justice in the wider society. It may be the case not only by happenstance but by a deep inner logic, if God is God, that the sub-community's fidelity to its own vocation will 'contribute to state policy' more strongly – and certainly more authentically – than if they worried about just how and why to go about compromising their principles in order to be effective.

Notes

1. Presented at Washington University, St Louis, 25 September 1992. Published 1996 in J. Patout Burns (ed.), *War and Its Discontents*, Washington: Georgetown University Press, 74–90. Yoder indicates that he did 'minor editing' to adjust this essay for use in this collection.

2. This term had been central in an earlier phrase of the conference planning. I had argued that it skews the question.

3. My fullest statement of the logic of this shift is in my essay 'The Constantinian Sources of Western Social Ethics' in *The Priestly Kingdom*, Notre Dame, IN: University of Notre Dame Press, 1984, 135ff.

4. I described this persistence of the Constantinian logic in ever new forms in my essay 'Christ, the Hope of the World', in *The Original Revolution*, Scottdale, PA: Herald Press, 1972, 141ff.

5. I have myself argued this point, on grounds which seem to me more valid than the usual ones, in my 'The Christian Case for Democracy' in *The Priestly Kingdom*, 151ff.

6. Cf. previous note.

7. I have commented elsewhere on the inappropriateness of the code word 'ghetto' to describe the moral consistency of minority communities. The ghetto in medieval and renaissance Europe was not a place to which Jews withdrew in order to keep kosher. It was a place where the 'catholic' 'Christians' penned them in, in order better to dominate them.

8. Cf. Peter Brock, *Political and Social Doctrines of the Unity of Czech Brethren*, The Hague, Netherlands: Mouton, 1957; Murray Wagner, *Petr Chelcicky*, Scottdale, PA: Herald Press, 1983. There had been less clear precursors of the same posture in the Waldensian movement, and among radical Franciscans. In important ways Vaclav Havel is the successor of the distinctiveness of the Czech Reformation. I use here the German orthography for Peter's name because it is phonetically more accessible to western readers.

9. In the Gospel account the abundant catch is neither a miracle nor a parable; yet preachers had long since made it the latter.

10. *Communio Viatorum XVXI* (1988), 127–44 on 'The Whale of Per Chelcicky'. Neither Jonah's big fish nor Job's Leviathan can be the source of the image of two sea monsters. The term Peter uses is found in Gen. 1. 21 and Ezekiel 29.3 and 32.2, Ezekiel apples the image to the King of Egypt.

11. The historiography of the time believed the account of the donation whereby the Emperor and the Pope had reciprocally confirmed one another's authority.

12. That the Constantinian shift was epoch-making was no new idea. Picking on Constantine as symbol of that tectonic shift was not something the radicals thought up. That had been done by Eusebius already in Constantine's lifetime. What the radicals did was to evaluate the change as a loss rather than as a gain. Cf. my review of the notion of apostasy in church history, in Richard Hughes (ed.), *The Primitive Church in the Modern World*, Urbana, IL: University of Illinois Press, 1995, and in my *The Priestly Kingdom*, 135ff.

13. Cf. Martin Lupá, *Probacio preceptorum minorum*, ed., Amedeo Molnar, *Communio Viatorum*, 1966, 55–62. The 'minor precepts' were the six '. . . but I say to you . . .' words of Jesus in Matt. 5: they stand beside the 'two great commandments' and the decalogue. We should remember that this discussion of what constitutes a binding commandment represents a time before the Lutheran polemic placed 'Law' in tension with 'Gospel'. Geoffrey Nuttall is right in using the phrase 'The Law of Christ' to

describe the spirituality of late medieval pacifism in his *Christian Pacifism in History*, Oxford: Blackwell 1958, reprinted Berkeley: World Without War Council, 1971, 15–31.

14. Constantine's postponing baptism to his deathbed testifies to a possible awareness on his point that authentic conversion would demand a different lifestyle.

15. 'Specific' means fitting one's species. To be specifically Christian need not be 'distinctive', since distinctiveness depends on the other parties in the comparison. A position that is specifically Christian might be specific to others as well, for their own reasons. Especially in the post-Christian West, there are very few humane ideas, even when of clearly Jewish and Christian origins, which will be held only by believers.

16. Cf. below n. 20.

17. This is a 'type' name, describing an attitude toward righteous violence, as the term is used in Luke; few of the people who took this stance used the name. Cf. my comments on its use in the revised edition of my *The Politics of Jesus* (1994), 56ff.

18. It would be inappropriate to designate their reasons as 'theological', only because that term as modern westerners use it is alien to the Jewish tradition. Nonetheless the reasons were of the principled kind that we would call 'theological'.

19. [Editors' Note: Seven paragraphs found in the original version of this essay have been deleted because their content overlapped directly with the argument of Chapter 10. See pages 190–1 below for the text in question.]

20. The neglect of attention to the Jewishness of Christianity is as striking in the pacifist-leaning works of Cadoux, Hornus, Bainton, and Brock, as it is in the non-pacifist readings of Helgeland, Cunningham, Ryan, Swift, Johnson etc. The literature has been most recently surveyed by David Hunter 'A Decade of Research . . .' *Religious Studies Review*, 18/2, April 1992, 87–94. The term 'research' is something of a misnomer. Most of what Hunter reviews here is revision of old and much-read material. Christians who are interested in learning from the dialogue with Judaism and the historians who follow the contested history of thought on the morality of war seem not to be doing their research in the same world.

21. Cf. my chapter 'The Moral Axioms of the Sermon on the Mount' in *The Original Revolution*, and my earlier projection of this part of the present paper's theme in a part of my Toronto paper 'War as a Moral Problem in the Early Church: Some Hermeneutical Assumptions' in Harvey Dyck and Peter Brock (eds.), *The Pacifist Impulse in Historical Perspective*, Toronto: University of Toronto Press, 1996.

22. Cf. my chapter 'If Christ is Truly Lord' in *The Original Revolution*, Scottdale, PA: Herald Press, 1972, 52ff. Some interpreters make much of the delay of the parousia as forcing on the Christians of the second or third generation a revision of their world-view. There is no evidence that such a change made any difference for their attitude toward violence. The Jewishness of their pacifism was not contingent on a particular apocalyptic perspective.

23. By the fourth century *christos* had become a proper name. Thus neither Constantine nor his biographer Eusebius would literally have used that title; yet functionally 'messianity' describes Eusebius' view of Constantine's place in salvation history. The *meschiach*, the 'Anointed', is the man who by special divine intervention ('unction') has been empowered to inaugurate the next phase of God's saving history. That is what Eusebius said about Constantine and his age.

24. When not long after the middle of the second century some Christians did in some way participate in the Roman army, as some clearly did (although we know about it only from the words of those who thought they should not), it was not because they had any theocratic visions of taking charge of history, or controlling the destiny of the Empire, or

implementing the kingdom of God by the exercise of social responsibility. They probably did it because (in peacetime) the work was easy and the rewards generous, without troubling themselves with much moral analysis.

25. This is the Tolstoyan and Niebuhrian oversimplification. Since the advocate of legitimate violence considers himself to be a realist, he must project on the other option an idealistic purism.

26. Jeremiah 29.7. Originally and prototypically this 'mission' applied to Babylon; but by implication it extended to all Jewry outside Palestine: in 'all the peoples and places where I have sent you' (29.14).

27. Donald Durnbaugh, *The Believers' Church*, New York: Macmillan, 1968, reprinted Scottdale: Herald, 1985, does that. Durnbaugh has also used the image of 'hop, skip, and jump' as a description of the way spiritual continuity occurs in non-established communities; this might well characterize my selective presentation here.

28. The account I summarize here is in no way original. Political thinkers like A. D. Lindsay, social historians like Christopher Hill, and church historians like Geoffrey Nuttall concur in its main outlines.

29. This view was held by the early Luther, by Zwingli, and by Martin Bucer, but most thoroughly carried out by the so-called 'Anabaptists'. All of them called this practice 'the Rule of Christ'. It was implemented still more thoroughly by Friends a generation after Milton. It had appeared much earlier, in the movement called 'conciliarism', the late medieval vision for renewal, for which the model was not only 1 Cor. 14 but also Acts 15. I sketch its import for Church and society today in my *Body Politics: Five Practices of the Christian Community before the Watching World*, Nashville, TN: Discipleship Resources Press, 1992, 1–13.

30. I have further illustrated the paradigmatic role of the Church's order in my booklet *Body Politics*. The link between 1 Cor. 14 and democracy is noted on pp. 67f.

31. Only Pennsylvania stayed in his hands and was named for him, but Penn was also involved in founding the colonies of North Jersey, South Jersey, and Delaware. In addition there were large Quaker settlements in Nantucket, Long Island, and North Carolina, where though involved in colony leadership they did not have charter status like Penn.

32. Williams received the charter for Rhode Island in 1644. His vision of the wrongness of religious persecution and his concern for humane relations with the Indians were like Penn's; but his Seeker style was less calculated to found a commonwealth.

33. The Penn heirs became Anglicans and thus could without embarrassment abandon the ethic of Friends. Other Friends continued to represent the same causes, no longer burdened with the status of Proprietors. They remained the strongest voices in the colony's Assembly for two more generations.

34. 'God's weakness is stronger than human strength' (1 Cor. 1.25); 'We have this treasure in earthen vessels, to make clear that this extraordinary power belongs to God' (2 Cor. 4.7); 'The weapons of our conflict are not fleshly but mighty' (2 Cor 10.4); 'My power is made perfect in weakness' (2 Cor. 12.9).

35. Cf. His 'The Grace of Doing Nothing', *Christian Century* (23 March 1932). 'Doing nothing' in fact mis-stated his point. He meant 'not being in a position to claim to take charge'.

36. The many writings of John Collins, concerning the heritage present in Jesus' world, and of Adela Yarbro Collins, as concerns early Christian thought, have provided leadership in the renewed interpretation of the apocalyptic genre.

37. I attempted to contribute to retrieving the apocalyptic mode as a part of moral

discourse in my 'Armaments and Eschatology', *Studies in Christian Ethics* 1/1, 1988, 43–61, and in 'Ethics and Eschatology', *Ex Auditu*, 6, 1980, 119–28.

38. The first popularly accessible sketch of this 'Pauline philosophy of history' was *Christ and the Powers* by H. Berkhof, ET by John Howard Yoder, Scottdale, PA: Herald Press, 1962, revised 1978. Since then it has been widely appropriated, most notably by William Stringfellow and Jacques Ellul. The textual basis of this vision in the New Testament has been thoroughly reworked by Walter Wink, beginning with *Naming the Powers*, Philadelphia: Fortress Press, 1984.

39. We become what we hate, if we let hatred enable the adversary to set the terms of the clash.

40. In my *Politics of Jesus* I attended to additional apostolic themes; imitation or participation (ch. 7), subordination (ch. 9), and justification (ch. 11).

Commentary

PETER OCHS

The rhetorical power of this penultimate chapter deepens our experience of both the wonders and the burdens of Yoder's vision. I believe post-liberal Jews will want to identify with most of the virtues of Exilic Judaism that Yoder calls Christians to adopt as their own. But these Jews will also need to resist Yoder's effort to collect these virtues into a few overarching principles of belief and practice. Among the virtues post-liberal Jews will be happy to call their own are these: the synagogue as a mark of 'decentralized, self-sustaining, religious-communal life'; the Torah, above all, as a text that sits at the centre of all study and all life; the rabbinate, as a leadership of study and of judicious judgement; the recognition that, ultimately, God alone is sovereign over history; and that we are to initiate the work of *tikkun olam*, repairing the world; but the Messiah alone, and God alone, will complete it. Yoder also notes several virtues of the radical reformers that post-liberal Jews will want either to add to this list or affirm as implications of it. Among these are several Yoder attributes to William Penn, such as dealing honestly with the original occupants of one's land; guaranteeing religious liberty; and humanizing civil justice.

At the same time, post-liberal Jews will prefer the rabbis' tendency to equalize the power and importance of dozens of virtues, rather than seeking, with Yoder, to capture the essence of obedience in such overarching principles as pacifism and 'not being in charge', in the explicit ways that he defines them. Post-liberal Jews would in no case argue against their Mennonite or Anabaptist friends' adopting these principles as their own. While celebrating significant overlaps among various disciples of the one God, post-liberal Jews would not expect different groups of practitioners – different Jewish groups as well as non-Jewish groups – to specialize in the same subsets of virtues. They would therefore not expect the radical reformers to bear the same responsibilities for landedness that Jews bear, just as much as they would not expect most Jews to bear the same responsibility for pacifism that the radical reformers bear. This is not a question of relativism; the virtues that each group practices must be true to the one God. It is a question, rather, of creatureliness. God, say the Rabbinic Jews, made each human, and also each human community, a finite creature: commanded to honour all the true virtues, but capable of mastering only some subset of them. Individual humans need community, and individual human communities need inter-communal dialogue, because no one of them can master the virtues that are made available when they all share in each other's powers and blessings. Yoder has made the holiness of the radical reformation visible to Jewish eyes, and this includes the holiness of the reformers' pacifism. But neither this pacifism nor, God forbid, its contrary, define the calling of post-liberal Judaism, nor of the Rabbinic Judaism it inherits. Post-liberal Jews should, indeed, be 'non-non-pacifists'. But there is a broad continuum of ways to do this, different ways in different situations, and the situations in which the God of history has put the Jews are not the same as the situations in which he has placed the radical reformers. Post-liberal Jews tend, for example, neither to affirm Zionism in the way Yoder fears, nor reject it in the way he advises. They would, above all, not reduce the broad spectrum of nineteenth- to twenty-first-century Jewish theo-political options under the rubrics of 'Zionism' and 'non-Zionism'. They know that the biblical record ties them to the land of Israel, whether they like it or not, in ways that Exilic Judaism never abrogated and in ways with which all disciples of the gospels are not burdened. But to be burdened with the land of Israel is not simply to apply a very modernist notion of national-political-ethnic sovereignty to that land. Nor is it to reduce all discussions of the land to the single issue of political governance. There are issues of home, of 'autochthonous religiosity' (to use one of Yoder's own terms), of the linguistic and historical traditions that bind members of this covenant to that land, of the physical survival of the bodies of the people Israel and of the place of land in that survival, of the unique burdens of Jewish life in nineteenth- and twentieth-century life in Europe, and much more. Post-liberal Jews cannot be encouraged by Yoder's failure to think of the question of Israel beyond the stark either/or that stands between 'anti-Zionism' and the particular Zionism of Israel's right-wing religious nationalists. But post-liberal Jews will also refrain from applying either/or judgements to Yoder's political position. There is an important place for Yoder's pacifism within discussions about Judaism's relation to politics, to land, to Israel, and to Palestine and Palestinians after the Shoah. Disciples of pacifist traditions would be beloved members of the study fellowships that address these issues in contemporary Judaism, but the fellowships would also include representatives of other theopolitical options. All participants who value the virtues of the one God would be welcome at the study-table, and Scripture alone would join them and lead them to conclusions that they could not have reached before they sat down at the table.

PART IV

CHRISTIANS AND JEWS SEEKING THE *SHALOM* OF THE CITY

10

'See How They Go with Their Face to the Sun'

I. Prologue and Prototype: *Galut* as Calling

The vision of things I have been invited to present in this special setting,[1] calls for several prefaces by way of orientation. It is at home in no one semantic world, in no one social world. My topic itself thereby fits our conference, in that it instantiates the cosmopolitan homelessness it describes.

I have drawn my title from a corpus of literature which fits our theme only in some ways, not in others. Stephan Zweig wrote his poem-drama Jeremiah during World War I, during his military service as a journalist and archivist in Vienna. While working on it he thought it was his most important work. It represents the last pre-holocaust generation of the German-speaking Jewish cultural elite, affirming both identities simultaneously, in the confidence that they could be reconciled. Zweig's own reaffirmation of his Jewishness took place in that setting. Zweig first made a confessional statement in a letter of October 1916 to Martin Buber; *Jeremiah* was finished the next spring. The ways in which that ambitious synthetic vision, as represented in the 1920s by Buber and his friends and the journal *Der Jude*, is irretrievably lost, need not be itemized here.[2] What does interest us here, and relates to our study, is that despite being obsolete in those ways, the dramatic poem *Jeremiah* affirmed the vision of *galut* or diaspora identity which accepted as normative God's negative judgement on the Davidic project, after the failures of four centuries.[3]

I am not concerned here to study where Zweig got the numerous new elements of the story of Jeremiah which go beyond what we find in the canonical prophetic book of Jeremiah or the last pages of 2 Kings and 2 Chronicles, in order to make a dramatic plot for a play that could be staged. Did he find some of that in rabbinic legend sources? Did he invent it from whole cloth as any playwright has the right to do?

Nor do I assume that the original Jeremiah, in any of the ways historical research or imagination can reconstruct, was as clearly a pacifist of the generation of *All Quiet on the Western Front* as Zweig makes him.[4] Settling those details is not necessary to enable us to see how Zweig's conclusion to the work affirms that dispersion is mission.

To be scattered is not a hiatus, after which normality will resume. From Jeremiah's time on, rather, according to the message of the play, dispersion shall be the calling of the Jewish faith community. That is our present concern. Zweig describes the procession of expellees from Judaea in a way which fully fits with the message of Jeremiah's later letter (chapter 29 in the prophetic book) to the people in Babylon, although he does not cite that letter. In that letter God instructed the people in Babylon to stay there, to renounce notions of an early return to Judaea, to

settle in, to buy land and plant gardens and vineyards, to marry off their children
and enjoy their grandchildren, and (especially) to

> Seek the welfare of the city where I have sent you, and pray to JHWH on its
> behalf, for in its welfare you will find your welfare.

Zweig sees the scattering of the Jews, in other words, not as a detour for only the
next seventy years after 586, but as the beginning of the mission of the next millennium and a half.[5] That is my present point. The move to Babylon was not a two-
generation parenthesis, after which the Davidic or Solomonic project was supposed
to take up again where it had left off. It was rather the beginning, under a firm fresh
prophetic mandate, of a new phase of the Mosaic project.[6]

Zweig's vision, like Jeremiah's letter, makes the hope of a return to Jerusalem
functional as postponed. The notion of return has its meaning not as something the
people in Babylon or elsewhere should be bringing about by their own strength, or
waiting around to see happen, or planning for. It is functional as metaphor for
God's renewing the life of faith anywhere. I shall cite only a few snatches from the
play:[7]

PEOPLE: Shall we ever see Jerusalem again?
          Schauen wir wieder Jerusalem?

JEREMIAS: Wo immer ihr euch in euch selber aufrichtet
           und feurig von Furcht und Fremdnis erhebt
           Da ist es aus Wunsch in die Welt gedichtet,
           Da ist der Traum unseres Heimwehs erlebt,
           an jedem Orte, wo euch Glaube inwohnet,
           Ueberwölbt euch hell seine mauernes Krone:
           Wer glüht, sieht ewig Jerusalem!

           Wanderers, sufferers, march in the name
           of Jacob your father, who erstwhile with God,
           Having wrestled the livelong night,
           Strove till dawn for a blessing . . .
           Wander your wanderings, watered with tears.
           O people of God, for wherever ye roam,
           Your road leads through the world to eternity, home.

Zweig's poem-drama culminates in five 'choruses of wanderers', which articulate
the Jewish sense of mission. The first three of these 'choruses' conclude with the
vision of an ultimate return to geographic Jerusalem; the last two do not. Here a few
lines from the fourth:

           (IV) Wir wandern durch Völker,
           wir wandern durch Zeiten,
            unendliche Strassen des Leidens entlang

           The tale of our suffering ever renewed;
           Aeon after aeon eternally vanquished . . .
           But the cities wither, and the nations

shoot into darkness like wandering stars.
The oppressors who scourged us with many whips
have become a hissing and byword among the generations
Whereas we march onward, march onward, march onward,
drawing strength from within, eternity from earth,
and God from pains and tribulations.

The prose which frames these concluding poems is a kind of chorus of men called 'Chaldaeans', i.e. the foot troops of the conquering empire. The Chaldaeans marvel at how the emigrants do not look defeated:

> We are the victors, they the defeated . . .
> an invisible force must sustain them
> What sustains them is their faith in the invisible God
>
> Siehe, siehe wie sie in die Sonne schreiten!
> Es ist ein Glanz auf diesem Volke.
>
> See how they are walking to meet the sun.
> His light shines on their foreheads,
> and they themselves
> shine with the strength of the sun.
> Mighty must their God be!

II. Diaspora as Normal Jewish Existence

The first way I sought to locate my point was in the poetic words of Stephan Zweig. The second will be to review the notion of what scholars call 'canonization', i.e. the process whereby a body of people come, over time, usually over a long time, to regard a particular body, not an unmanageably large body of literature, as the literature the reading of which defines who they are.

This phenomenon is misunderstood when it is taken, as it has been by the Protestant scholasticism of recent centuries, as calling for a debate about the miraculous way in which that literature came into being, or about the inerrant authority of its contents. It is also misunderstood when Catholics, responding to that Protestant critique, claim that it was the hierarchy which gave the canon that status.

What matters more is that we take stock of the setting in which that selection took place. The action of selecting is itself a testimony to the normative self-understanding of the community which did it.[8] The Hebrew scriptural canon was selected in the dispersion, and it is best understood as throwing light on the diaspora identity into which God's people have been sent.

Life in *galut* or diaspora[9] is not without its dimensions of profound and painful alienation. Psalm 137 has become for us the prototypical expression of that suffering:

> How can we sing Zion songs in a strange land?

Yet, painful as the question is, that is what the Jews learned to do, and do well. It may well have been in this age of *galut* that the Psalter began to form as a central identity resource, part of the canon, beside the Torah. The very possibility of the mocking challenge 'Sing us one of the songs of Zion!' (137.3 RSV) presupposes the awareness on the part of the 'captors' that despite having no temple, the Jews had an important worship life of their own.[10] Even that experience reinforces their identity.

Within this missionary vision, the role of 'seeking the welfare of that city' becomes quite concrete, both in real experience and in legends which reflect, interpret, and in turn further foster that experience. What we might call the 'Joseph paradigm' became a standard type,[11] In three different ages and places, the same experiences recur in the Hebrew story.[12] Joseph, Daniel and his three friends, and Esther all found themselves involuntarily at the heart of the idolatrous empire. Each ran the risk of faithfulness to their people and to the revealed will of the one true God, when their civil disobedience could have cost them their lives. Each was saved by divine intervention, with the result that the pagan tyrant was converted to the recognition of the one true God, vindicating them against their enemies, and giving Jews a role in running the empire.

Periodical pilgrimages back to Jerusalem were a part of diaspora identity. The pilgrim psalter, Ps. 120–134, one of the nuclei for the formation of our psalter, begins with the singer living 'among those who hate peace' (120.5f.). The places named, Meshech and Kedar, are neither in Mesopotamia nor in Palestine. One is in Arabia and the other in Anatolia; they testify to the resilience of Jewish identity all across the Ancient Near East. They remind us that although it was the deportation of 586 which became prototypical, and although with time Babylonian Jewry became culturally central, the phenomenon of dispersion always was much wider.

More than Christians are aware, Babylon itself very soon became the cultural centre of world Jewry, from the age of Jeremiah until the time we in the West call the Middle Ages. The people who re-colonized the 'Land of Israel', repeatedly, from the age of Jeremiah to that of Jochanan ben Zakkai, and again still later, were supported financially and educationally from Babylon, and in lesser ways from the rest of the diaspora. Our palestinocentric reading of the story is a mistake, though a very understandable one. It was imposed not only on Christians but also on many Jews because of the way the first-century events became legend.

What it meant to be Jewish on a world scale, from the age of Jeremiah to that of Theodore Hertzl, depended more on the Babylonian leadership, where living without a Temple was possible and was accepted as permanent, than on the Palestinian institutions, distracted as they were by the agenda of Maccabean rebellion and Herodian negotiation, and then by Roman destruction. In all the different ways represented by Sadducees, Pharisees, Maccabeans and Essenes, Jews in Palestine had no choice but to define their identity over against the dominant Gentiles, and to be divided from one another by their conflicting responses to that challenge. On the other hand, the synagogues and the rabbis in Babylon, and in the rest of the world where the Babylonian model was followed and the Babylonian teachers were consulted, were spared that self-defeating distraction, so as to enter creatively into the Jeremianic phase of creating something qualitatively new in the history of religions.

I leave the experts in the history of religions to determine which component of this innovation was the most original, which was more central or definitional than the others, and how to label them with the special kind of vocabulary of the guild.[13] In lay terms, living without a temple, while yet retaining the mythic memory of the Temple and the hope of the return in the messianic age, enabled the creation of a faith community with a globally new Gestalt, marked especially by the following:

- The primary vehicle of identity definition is a text which can be copied, and can be read anywhere. Decentralization and fidelity are therefore not alternatives, as they are with any religious forms which need a priesthood in a temple.
- The ground floor of 'worship' (if that is the word for it) is reading and singing the texts.
- A valid local cell of the world Jewish community, qualified to be in that place the concretion of the people of God, can exist wherever there are ten households. No priesthood, no hierarchy is needed. If they can afford a rabbi, his role is that of a scribe, rather than that of prophet, priest, or prince.
- The international unity of the people is sustained by intervisitation, by intermarriage, by commerce and by rabbinic consultation, needing no High Priest or Pope or King to hang together. When, some time later, a central senior Jewish spokesman, the resh *galut*, 'ethnarch' or 'exilarch', was called forth by the Babylonian power structure, he was intermediary, co-ordinator, culture broker, between the community and the Gentiles. He was not a Jewish emperor.[14]
- Although there is plenty of material, and plenty of freedom, with which thinkers over the centuries can develop Jewish philosophical systems (cosmological, mystical, linguistic, scientific), the ground floor of identity is the common life itself, the walk, *halakah*, and the shared remembering of the story behind it.

Nothing about the self-esteem of the bearers of this new lifestyle is dependent upon or drives toward cultural homogeneity, or toward political control, or toward autarchy. Jewish culture is comfortable and creative in dialogue with whatever Gentile world it lands in, as long as it is tolerated. The foundational narrative from the Davidic age and institutions is now placed in a wider frame where Abraham, then Joseph, then Shiphrah and Puah, then Moses, then Daniel and his three friends, then Esther and Mordecai live among the nations, confounding the Gentile seers and emperors with the superior wisdom and power of the one authentic God.[15]

This cultural *novum*[16] was capable of enormous flexibility, planting colonies of similar shape from Spain to China, from the North Sea to the upper Nile. Wherever they went they created new trades, new arts, new literatures, even new languages, without losing their connections to Moses, or to one another, or their hope of return.

III. The Ambivalence of the Davidic Project

It is of great significance that, however the traditions now grouped in the Hebrew canon were remembered and then redacted, these texts kept alive the memory of how the rise of the Davidic dynasty had been a disappointment not only to Samuel but to God. As we read the narrative of the book of Judges (9.7ff.), the oppressive nature of kingship 'like the other nations' was already discerned in Jotham's fable, in the face of Abimelech's false start. That awareness was still there when God and Samuel gave in to the demand of the elders in 1 Samuel 8, saying in effect to those who wanted a king like those of the Gentiles: 'You'll be sorry.'

The Northern Kingdom, subject to recurrent 'charismatic' usurpations resembling the rise and fall of the 'judges' from Joshua to Samuel, and like David's own takeover from Saul, fell first. Judah was dynastically stable and lasted longer, but God finally gave up on both of them. The historiography which scholars call 'deuteronomic' and 'deuteronomistic' retold the history, correlating the ups and downs of the royal houses with their rising and falling faithfulness to the Law, but when we remember that that retelling was done and committed to writing in the setting of diaspora, it constitutes a document of the acceptance of the Jeremianic turn; there is in the multiple strata and versions of the entire narrative no irridentism.

The story goes on from there in the same key. What the books of Ezra and Nehemiah recount, whatever be their historicity and their relation to each other, all that happens stays well within the constraints of submission to the Gentile empire. Nothing like 'kingship' or 'statehood' is advocated by any party as desirable for the honour of God or the dignity of the people. Thus the reorientation of identity by the Jeremianic shift even comes back to give a new quality to the part of the story which returns to *Eretz* Israel.

IV. Retrieving the Genesis Legend

Both by its argument and by its snappy title, Jeffrey Stout's *Ethics After Babel*[17] has become a landmark around which the discussion of the social setting of values is organized. His theme is a very contemporary, very methodologically sophisticated analysis of what it does to ethical discourse to have to be carried on in a setting of pluralism. Yet Stout claims depth (and attracts attention) for his topic by juxtaposing it to the ancient Hebrew legend.

In the following paragraphs I shall, like Stout, converse in an interlocking way both with the modern methodological challenge of how to converse about morals and how to converse with our Hebrew backgrounds. Yet it is not primarily with Stout that I seek to converse. I propose to reach beyond what Stout intended to do with those resources, to retrieve the heritage of the centuries during which the people of God discharged their mission without being in charge of the world.[18]

A. 'Babel' the Primeval Symbol

'Babel' in Stout's use, as in much of our literate culture, is used as the code word for the recognition, which Stout's generation of moral philosophers cannot overlook, in the 'post-modern' late twentieth century, that meaningful moral discourse is always located within a given community, so that there can never be just one right way to talk morally. Therefore we must face the fact of the multiplicity of communities of moral discourse. For Stout, 'Babel' stands for that multiplicity.[19]

This way of putting the question of validity would seem to assume the structural *a priori* of establishment. It posits as a desideratum, the loss of which has now put us at a disadvantage, a setting where there could be, would be (and, by implication where there once was) only one community whose shared meanings defined value language. The little word 'After' in Stout's title does make it seem that there was some earlier time, maybe not too awfully long ago, since we in modern times are just now struggling with its loss, some pre-Babel state of things, when this confusing pluralism did not bother people as it does us. 'Babel' before the divine intervention then becomes the mythic metaphor for that lost unity.

Yet as we shall soon see, what Stout 'after Babel' regrets losing is what JHWH in the Genesis story said his creatures should not have been trying to protect (and did not yet possess) in the first place. The first meaning of Babel in the Genesis legend is the effort of a human community to absolutize itself. The canonical setting[20] is the story of the spreading out of the immediate descendants of Noah around the narrator's entire known world.[21] Babel in the myth of Genesis places the multiplicity of cultures under the sign of the divine will. It was rebellious humankind, proud and perhaps fearful, who wanted to live all in one place, and thereby to replace their dependence on divine benevolence by reaching heaven on their own. The intention of the people at Babel was to resist the diversification which God had long before ordained and initiated, and to maintain a common discourse by building their own unprecedentedly centralized city.[22] They were the first foundationalists, seeking by purposive focusing of their own cultural power to overcome historically developing diversity.[23]

B. Dispersion as Grace

The second level of meaning of Babel is that God responded graciously to that defensive effort, namely by the divinely driven dispersal of the peoples, restoring the centripetal motion. It was JHWH who scattered them, for their own good. This scattering is still seen as benevolence in the missionary preaching of the Paul of Acts (14.16f.; 17.26f.). It is 'confusion' only when measured against the simplicity of imperially enforced uniformity. It is narrated as a gracious and creative intervention of God, reinforcing the process of dispersion and diversification which had already begun[24] and which God intended as a good thing. Thus the 'confusion of tongues' is not a punishment or a tragedy, but the gift of new beginnings, liberated from a blind alley.

Later readings, in ways which reach all the way down to the present,[25] have considered that first dispersion to have been a wrathful act of an offended God, punitive or defensive in intent and destructive in its effect.[26] That is not in the text.[27] The more we understand the general vision of God as Creator and Sovereign, the less reason there is to see this intervention as in any way petulant or punitive. Diversity was the original divine intent; if God is good and diversity is good, then each of the many diverse identities which resulted from the multiplying of languages and the resultant scattering is also good.[28]

C. *Galut* as Vocation

The third meaning of Babel is not just a metaphor or a legend. Here we begin to move beyond the purview of Stout's modern methodological agenda, rejoining the theme with which we began. Babylon was the actual imperial capital of the Ancient Near East when Jerusalem was captured in 587 and Jews were taken there as captives.[29] That transfer is of course understood as in some sense the earned chastisement for the sins of the people (or more properly of their ruling elites)[30] but that is not the primary point made by Jeremiah, when he interprets the event in the light of God's gracious sovereignty. It is the false prophets who promise that the captivity will soon be over, a mere detour along the triumphal path of the house of David.[31] The real mission of the scattered Jews, according to Jeremiah's message, we already saw, is to settle into Babylon, to make themselves at home (marry their children, buy land and eat its produce, build houses), and to

> seek the welfare of that city where I have sent you, and pray to the LORD on its behalf, for in its welfare you will find your welfare.[32]

Seldom does one see it pointed out that the development of the Genesis story as we have it constitutes a piece of evidence on what I was saying before about the age of canonization. It was the generations of Jewry living around Babylon who told the Babel story as the immediate background to the call of Abraham.

V. How the Jeremianic Model Prefigured the Christian Attitude to the Gentile World

Thus far I have been recounting the Jewish experience as it were for its own sake. Yet an important benefit of seeing this story more clearly, and the reason I do it now, is the way it illuminates Christian origins. I illustrate it here by lifting out only one representative dimension. There is a standard debate among the historians of Christian ethics, concerning whether (or rather how or why) Christians before Constantine were pacifists. People like Tolstoy said they were, on the basis of a simply rigorous reading of a few words of Jesus. Others said they were not, on the basis of the fact that Tertullian, a century and a half after Jesus, arguing that those of his fellow Christians who served in Caesar's armies should not be doing so, thereby proved that it was happening.

What has been completely absent in this scholarly debate [33] has been any recognition that Christian moral standards may have been largely derived from, and therefore could be fruitfully illuminated by, older Jewish models of how to relate to this world's powers.[34] The historians on both sides have quibbled about this or that legalistic reading of a few words of Jesus, ignoring both the sociological and the theological contexts within which first-century believers sustained their view of history under God.[35]

I first defined this 'Jewish quietism since Jeremiah'[36] in sociological terms; it is marked by the synagogue, the Torah, and the rabbinate. Of course I could have added *kashrut* and circumcision. Yet if you had asked those Jews (including the first

Christians) to explain themselves, and their attitude to pagan empires, whether the Mesopotamian ones before or Rome in the first century, their answers would have been theological.[37]

(a) They would have said that since God is sovereign over history, there is no need for them to seize (or subvert) political sovereignty in order for God's will to be done.[38] God's capacity to bring about the fulfilment of his righteous goals is not dependent upon us, and certainly not dependent on our needing to make exceptions to his Law in order to make events come out the way he wills them.

(b) They would have said that establishing the ultimate righteous social order among nations will be the mission of the *Meschiach* and should be left to him; to do his work for him would be presumptuous if not blasphemous. This is what the mainstream critics of Zionism said a century ago, and what the *neturei karta* community says of the State of Israel even today.

(c) They would have said that the efforts of the Maccabees, the Zealots, and Bar Kochba to restore a national kingship had not been blessed by God, and that three failures should have been enough to teach us that lesson.[39] The Maccabees and the Zealots have a larger place in the Christian memories of those centuries than they do in the thought of the rabbis.[40]

(d) They would have said that if an all-righteous God wanted to chastise us for our sins, which (at the very least) some prophets have said may sometime be God's purpose, our self-defence would interfere with that purpose. The notion that God's own people are especially subject to having their sins punished, by virtue of the special privileges of their election, may have become more weighty in the Jewish thought of a later age than it was in the canonical period, but it is already present in the prophets. As soon as that attitude toward one's own sufferings is possible, the injustices suffered by God's people take on a different meaning, and seeking to prevent them becomes impious.

(e) They would have said that the death of the righteous 'sanctifies the Name', i.e. makes a doxological contribution, on the moral scales of history, which our avoidance of suffering (even if unjust) would obviate. We cannot be clear that 'Your name be sanctified' in the 'Our Father' already meant that then, but clearly that phrase soon became the technical label for martyrdom as a positive human contribution to the achievement of God's purposes.

Each of these five explanatory sentences ought to be a chapter; yet even in this brevity, the Jewishness of the case against 'taking charge' of the course of history is evident. From Jeremiah until Theodore Hertzl this was the dominant Jewish vision.

There is wide recognition that the Christians of the first two centuries were pacifist, or at least that their most articulate teachers of whom we have record were. The historians debate about whether this was univocally the case, and ethicists debate about whether, if it was, it should be normative for later Christians. Yet in all of that voluminous debate, neither party takes account of the fact that the ethos of the early Christians was a direct prolongation and fulfilment of the ethos of Jewry.[41]

Both sides of the debate about the question: 'were the early Christians pacifist?' have as I said above[42] tended to proceed legalistically, as if the Christian movement had taken off from scratch with only a few words of Jesus to guide them, so that a fine-grained debate about whether those few words had to mean just this or just that would have been be the primary tool of moral discernment.

It is rather the case that Jesus' impact in the first century added more and deeper authentically Jewish reasons, and reinforced and further validated the already expressed Jewish reasons[43] for the already well established ethos of not being in charge and not considering any local state structure to be the primary bearer of the movement of history. To this same stance the second generation of witnesses after Jesus, the 'apostles', added another layer of further reasons, still utterly Jewish in form and substance, having to do with the Messiahship of Jesus, his Lordship, and the presence of the Spirit.[44] Much later, some non-messianic Jews formally rejected these ideas about Jesus, or about the Spirit; nonetheless they were at the time unimpeachably Jewish ideas, and they made clear why a 'quietist' stance in the Roman/Mediterranean world made good sense. Until the messianity of Jesus was replaced by that of Constantine,[45] it was the only ethos that made sense.[46]

VI. How the Jeremianic Model is Bigger Than Stout's *Fragestellung*

Leaping from the grand lines of the Hebrew story, here narrated from the record, to the post-modern agenda, as named and epitomized by Stout, with which we began to describe the contemporary encounter with relativity, we may now be able to note the ways in which the Jeremianic missionary vision, presupposing and moving beyond the world-historical vision of Genesis 11, transcends as well our modern problematic, stated prototypically by Stout, in ways that might have something to tell us. They might have something to tell both the dispersion communities[47] and those who would want to be the cultural establishment.

There is in the Jeremiah vision no counterpart for our regretting the loss of the univocality of the age, which in Christendom stretched roughly from Eusebius to Hegel (but lingers on in philosophical foundationalism), when European intellectual elites could claim to prescribe one unified meaning system for the world. Stout does not say he bemoans the loss, yet the way he shapes the story signals a kind of wistfulness, as if the exercise of his profession had been more rewarding, or at least simpler, before somebody moved the landmarks.

Jeremiah does not tell his refugee brothers and sisters to try to teach the Babylonians Hebrew. The concern to learn goes in the other direction. Jews will not only learn the local languages; they will in a few generations (and for a millennium and a half) be serving the entire Ancient Near Eastern world as expert translators, scribes, diplomats, sages, merchants, astronomers. They will make a virtue and a cultural advantage of their being resident aliens, not spending their substance in fighting over civil sovereignty. Their conviction that there is but one God, Creator, Sovereign, anikonic, historically active, able to speak, enhances their cultural creativity over against the polytheistic, superstitious, tribally structured, fertility-focused popular religions of their neighbours.

Somewhere, some time, in the Jeremianic setting, there arose what I claimed above was the most fundamental sociological innovation in the history of religions, namely the culture of the synagogue.[48] There is here no priest accredited by his qualification to administer cultic ceremonies. There is no high priest mandated by the Emperor. Precisely because the Jerusalem Temple is not portable and its functions not replaceable, what Jews gather around elsewhere will be not an altar but a scroll. The legitimacy of the local gathering depends on no central hierarchy, although its fidelity to the message of the scroll may be served by a rabbi trained in a school.[49] Any ten households qualify as a local cell of the world-wide people of God. Since what they do when they gather is to read together, a canon of scriptures must develop.[50] There will be no orally transmitted mysteries reserved to the initiated.[51]

When Jews in Babylon participated creatively, reliably, but not coercively in the welfare of that host culture, their contribution was more serious than 'bricolage'.[52] There was no problem of shared meanings, since they had accepted their host culture and become fluent in it. Their own loyalty to their own culture (*kashrut*, anikonic monotheism, honouring parents, truth-telling, work ethic, circumcision) was not dependent on whether the Babylonians accepted it, yet much of it was not only transparent but even attractive to Gentiles. Living in Babylon then, amidst the cultural phenomenon which Stout now calls 'Babel', namely the absence of univocality, was not a problem for them.[53] The surrounding Gentile culture had become their element. The polyglot Jews were more at home in any imperial capital, more creative and more needed, than were the monolingual native peasants and proletarians (and priests and princes) in that same city.

The one thing that never would have occurred to the Jews in Babylon was to try to bridge the distance between their language world and that of their hosts by a foundationalist mental or linguistic move, trying to rise to a higher level or dig to a deeper one, so that the difference could be engulfed in some *tertium quid*, which would convince the Babylonians of moral monotheism without making them Jews, and to which the Jews could yield without sacrificing their local colour. They did not look for or seek to construct common ground. Jews knew that there was no larger world than the one their Lord had made and their prophets knew the most about. Its compatibility with kinds of 'wisdom' that the Gentiles could understand[54] seemed to them to validate their holy history rather than to relativize it. When Hellenism penetrated their world, they did not hesitate to affirm that whatever truth there was in Plato or Aristotle was derived from Moses.

VII. Further Testing

To take thus seriously the Babylonian basis of continuing Jewish identity would call for further discussions, not provided in this text as of now, at some of the points where it goes beyond the limits of the standard account:

(a) The standard account sees the course of history moving back from Babylon to Jerusalem with Sheshbazzar and Zerubbabel, Ezra and Nehemiah, and the construction of the Second Temple.[55] The Maccabees are part of that story, i.e. of the effort to reinstate Palestinian kingship as the normative posture, and they too failed. A more consistently Jeremianic account will need to retell that story of the too-early returns to the land, attending both to the events and to their theological interpretation by prophets and by the several 'priestly' historians and redactors.

According to one way of disentangling the sources,[56] the books of Ezra and Nehemiah are not two faces of the same story, but alternatives. To take Jeremiah seriously, it would seem to me as a lay reader not versed in historic de- and re-construction, that both of them need to be seen as inappropriate deviations from the Jeremiah line, since each of them reconstituted a cult and a polity as a branch of the pagan imperial government.[57] Of course the Maccabees were even more a mistake, as was the Sadducean collaboration with the Roman Empire, in order to maintain the cult, the system which was in charge in Jesus' time.

(b) A more adequate account would need to make more of the anti-royal strand of the earlier history, only briefly noted above; Judges 9, 1 Sam. 8, Deut. 17.14ff. The later redactors of the historical books who left stand those anti-royal accounts at the front of their narrative certainly counted on their readers' memories to see later events in their light.

(c) The prophesied hope of return to Jerusalem, which would ultimately be implemented not by politicking elders but by messianic miracle, needs to be further interpreted. Whether that mythic return be 'next year' as in the Seder ritual,[58] or 'seventy years' as in Jeremiah's message, it is clear by now (whether 'now' be the first century of our era or the twentieth) that the adequate fulfilment of that promise was not in Ezra or Nehemiah, or in the Maccabees or Bar Kochba.[59] Most Christians do not say either that it was fulfilled without remainder in Jesus.

(d) If the Babel event of Genesis does not denote a divine judgement but a positive mission, what then becomes of the standard Christian vision of Pentecost as the miracle of interlinguistic reconciliation? I am confident that a fair reading of the account of Luke in Acts 2 will be compatible with the best reading of Genesis, but I shall not argue that now.

VIII. The Polyglot Advantage in Matters of Language: The Limits of a Metaphor

I already noted that there is something odd, perhaps paradigmatically odd, about Jeffrey Stout's use of the French term *bricolage* to describe how one goes on working toward cross-community communication after abandoning hope for univocality. The overtones of the verb *bricoler* in ordinary colloquial French include:

(a) that one is amateur, not expert, not credentialled, and not needing to be;

(b) that there is no reason to have to do it right, perhaps no firm definition of what it would mean to do it right;

(c) that one does it irregularly rather than routinely and reliably;

(d) that every trial is tentative, 'trying this on for size', with no great stake in any one effort; flippant self-spoofing and mockery of others protects against too much investment. There is nothing in *bricolage* worth dying for.

When we hold this list of overtones up against the life of Jews in Babylon from 580 BCE for a millennium (or for that matter the life of Jews in Spain before 1492, or Jews in Vienna or Vilna until this century), watching how they talked Babylonian well enough to be scribes, translators, diplomats, and merchants, we would have to say that 'none of the above' characteristics of *bricolage* apply, except for the wholesome presence of a little Jewish humour (d above) around the edges. They not only kept their subculture alive; Jews in fact contributed mightily to making the Gentile world viable.[60]

This enormous flexibility and creativity force us to return to the question; is there anything non-negotiable in the dispersed minority's witness? Anything untranslatable? Of course there is; it is that there is no other God. The rejection not only of pagan cult but also of every way of putting their own JHWH/LORD in the same frame of reference with pagan deities, even not speaking the divine NAME as others would, was tied for the Jews in Babylon with the proclamation of his sovereignty over creation and history. There is no setting into which that deconstructing, disenchanting proclamation cannot be translated, none which can encompass it.

That anti-idolatry message is not bad but good news. It can free its hearers from slavery to the powers that crush their lives.[61] Many Gentiles watching the Jewish culture saw it that way, so that long before Christian beginnings, standard ways had been found to welcome 'god-fearers' on the edge or even in the middle of the synagogue.

IX. The Setting of Suffering

Beyond the above three meanings of Babel there is another, less clearly located than those three in time and place, and less broadly present in the record. In Scripture and tradition, the name 'Babylon' came to be used as metaphor for any and every great idolatrous and oppressive empire. Christians recognize this usage, perhaps even give it priority, because the Apocalypse of John used the name 'Babylon' (although not very often) as a cipher for Rome (whereas the rabbis had used an earlier metaphor, calling the Romans 'Hittites'). Assyria in the age of Isaiah, Babylon in that of Jeremiah, Nineveh in that of Jonah, and then Rome in that of the New Testament apocalypse, are in one sense all the same thing: the great world city, oppressive, drunk on power, worshipping idols, claiming to be the centre of the world, persecuting the saints, and doomed to destruction.

Yet it will not be the saints who will destroy Babylon. Their suffering at its hand is part of 'sanctifying the name of JHWH'. There is no thought (when this meaning of 'Babylon' is used) of the saints' escaping that fate by emigrating to the earthly land of Israel, any more than by assassinating the tyrant.

X. Is This a Way Other Subject Peoples Might See Themselves?

I close by declaring my complete lack of authority to answer this next question. Is there something about this Jewish vision of the dignity and ministry of the scattered people of God which might be echoed or replicated by other migrant peoples, like the expatriate Chinese around the edge of Asia or the Indians in East and South Africa? Might it give hope to other refugees, like the Armenians who were scattered in the 1920s? To other victims of imperial displacement, like African-Americans?[62] To the victims of the most recent horrors of Rwanda or the Balkans?

Might there even be something helpful in this memory which would speak by a more distant analogy to the condition of peoples overwhelmed by imperial immigration, like the original Americans or Australians, or the Ainu or the Maori? *At least* this juxtaposition may serve to challenge the assumption of the imperial immigrants that they ought to interpret their racist triumphalism (as we know some of their predecessors did) as analogous to the conquest of Canaan.

Notes

1. This essay was first presented at Loyola Marymount University, Los Angeles, 23 September 1995, as opening address of a colloquium on 'Communities in Exile' convened by the University's Institute on Faith, Culture and the Arts. [Editors' Note: This essay was first published in Yoder's book *For the Nations: Essays Public and Evangelical*, Grand Rapids, MI: Eerdmans, 1997, 51–78. Reprinted here by permission of Eerdmans Publishing Company.]

2. This short-lived but enormously creative world is evoked well by the introductory materials in Arthur A. Cohen's *The Jew: Essays from Martin Buber's Journal* Der Jude, University of Alabama Press, 1980. It is also well characterized by Leon Botstein's introduction to the 1987 edition of Zweig's *Jewish Legends*, New York: Markus Wiener.

3. Zweig himself wrote:

It is the tragedy and the hymn of the Jewish people, of the elect; yet not in the sense of prosperity, but of endless suffering, endless collapse, endless rising again, and the power unfolded through that destiny. The conclusion proclaims simultaneously the exodus from Jerusalem to the endlessly rebuilt Jerusalem. The war opened this tragedy up to me, who love suffering as power, yet feel it with chills as fact. Should my intent ever be efficacious, this will be the time.

Letter of 8 May 1916 to Martin Buber, *Gesammelte Werke*, Vol. 4, Frankfurt: S. Vischer, 1982, 347f.

4. Nor do I need for present purposes to unravel the small differences between the German version in the 1982 *Gesammelte Werke* and the 1922 English version by Eden and Cedar Paul 'from the author's Revised German text'. I shall take the liberty of citing either version.

5. 'I love the diaspora, and affirm it as the meaning of [Judaism's] idealism, as its cosmopolitan general human vocation. I would wish for no other union than in the Spirit, in our own only real element, never in one language, one people . . . I find the present condition the most magnificent in humanity; to be unified without a language, without obligation, without homeland, only through the fluidity of being . . . Every narrower, more real togetherness would appear to me as a diminution of this incomparable condition. All we need to strengthen is to appreciate this condition, as I do, not [see it] as humiliation.' Letter to Martin Buber, 24 January 1917, *Gesammelte Werke*, Vol. 4, 349f.

6. I don't think that a careful reading of Ezra and Nehemiah denies this, but that argument is not my present concern. That is a subject concerning which Daniel Smith-Christopher of this University knows more than I ever intend to. Jeremiah, Ezekiel, the prophet of the servant songs, Ezra, and Nehemiah, all have distinctive slants. I am not convinced that 'Second Isaiah' is an exception to this, as was suggested by someone at the Loyola Marymount University event. See *A Biblical Theology of Exile*, Minneapolis: Augsburg Fortress, 2002.

7. Stephan Zweig, *Jeremiah: A Drama in Nine Scenes*, *Gesammelte Werke*, Vol. 4, Frankfurt: S. Fischer, 1983; translated from an author's revised text by Eden and Cedar Paul, New York, Seltzer, 1922.

8. It is important to say that at bottom it was done by the community. More often people will credit 'the rabbis' or 'the priests', but there were also scribes and sages, each with necessary roles. Yet the role of each made sense only thanks to the viability and the integrity of the community as a whole.

9. Etymologically these terms, one Hebrew and one Greek, both mean simply 'scattering'. Those with a view of the past as ideal will give them the negative overtones of 'exile' or 'banishment'. For Jeremiah it is mission. (The Greek form includes the sense of broadcasting seed.) The Jews were sent there to identify their own welfare with that of that place, to bloom where they were sown.

10. We might compare this to the way in which white Americans' awareness of the power of the spirituals and of blues have contributed to both the viability and the self-respect of African-Americans.

11. Cf. Lance M. Wills, *The Jew in the Court of the Pagan King: Ancient Jewish Court Legends*, Minneapolis: Fortress, 1990. Wills unfortunately limits his analysis to the literary level. He does not ask what community life these legends testify to or contributed to, what concept of God or of history, and so forth.

12. As with the Babel story itself, my present interest is not in testing the historicity of these accounts. Our concern is their portrayal of the stance of fidelity under pressure, as it contributes to a community's self-understanding. The less these stories of Hebrew heroes in pagan courts are historical in the modern sense of attestation in the face of doubt as having 'really happened', the more valid they are as testimonies to the world-view and lived experience of the people of the Jeremianic mission. Part of the Tobit story fits the same pattern.

13. Jonathan Z. Smith uses the conceptual grid of 'local/alocal'; see Smith, *Map Is Not Territory: Studies in the History of Religions*, Leiden: Brill, 1978. Other religions, whether tribal and traditional or imperial, locate God. Jews can serve their Lord any-where. We might debate what is cause and what is effect about that observation; there can be no debate about the shift's being definitional,

14. The same is true of the central role of the *Gaon*, a sort of senior rabbi. His authority was great but it was earned, in a setting devoid of central sacral authority or imperial appointment.

15. Cf. above notes 11ff. The 'historicity' question we need to pursue in these stories is not about whether there ever was really an Esther, or when was Daniel, but about the life setting in which rereading these stories in the synagogues made sense of peoples' lives in the diaspora. Nor were such experiences limited to the courts of kings; there were also Tobit and Susanna.

16. Jacob Neusner in *Method and Meaning in Ancient Judaism*, Missoula: Scholars Press, 1979, 151, cites Jonathan Z. Smith in describing this atopical as the inner mental structure of the *Mishna*. It would however be an historical error to think that it first arose in the second and third centuries of our era. It arose in the age of Jeremiah. What happened after Bar Kochba was that the alternatives fell away, and the Jeremian vision expanded to fill in the available space.

17. Jeffrey Stout, *Ethics After Babel*, Boston: Beacon Press, 1988. Cf. The 'Review Symposium' in *Theology Today*, 46/1, April 1990, 55–73.

18. Cf. Chapter 9 'On Not Being In Charge' above. Cf. also another aspect of the conversation with Jeffrey Stout in my 'Beyond Babble' in the April 1996 *Journal of Religious Ethics*.

19. It is never quite clear whether for Stout the challenge he means 'Babel' to symbolize is the *modern* loss of a common discourse or a trait of the human condition every since prehistory. Most of the time the former seems to be intended, but Stout is not

interested in analysing whether community-dependent pluralism was a problem before modernity.

20. 'Canonical' as a method code term means that if we want to know what a term means over the long run, we do best to read first the text as received by those who preserved it. This involves no disrespect for the several other hermeneutic or historical sub-disciplines which seek to discern or project more detailed understandings of how the text came to have its present form, or of 'what really happened' behind the legends.

21. Although chapter 10 of Genesis lays out a confusing spread of names and places, it accounts for only three generations. Verses 5, 20, and 31 had anticipated the Babel account by already describing a multiplicity of languages and nations. Claus Westermann (*Genesis 1–11*, Minneapolis: Augsburg, 1984, 531ff.) catalogues how all of the components of the Babel account are prefigured by other legendary material in ancient Asia; aetiology for the name 'Babel', aetiology for the diversity of languages, aetiology for the placing of the nations, aetiology for the ruins of a tower. Brueggemann (*Genesis*, Atlanta: John Knox, 1982, 97ff.) agrees that adding up such components does not exhaust the text's message.

22. Later interpreters and archaeologists, taking the *ziggurat* to be a kind of temple, have seen here an account of the origins of some specifically pagan cult. The story does not say that. That the building was supposed to reach the sky is compatible with the vision of the one true God as ruling from heaven which prevailed in the previous ten chapters and which was present in the Ancient Near Eastern legends. The metaphor is monotheistic. Some readers make the point that while bricks and bitumen are fine for ordinary buildings you need stone for skyscrapers. I doubt that the ancient bards also wanted to make that point.

23. The Akkadian/Babylonian root *babili* is taken to mean 'Gate of God', although linguists can doubt that. In any case the Hebrew etymology assumed in Genesis 11.9 from *balal* (to confuse) misleads the reader. What the tower builders wanted was unity. Diversity, which is only 'confusion' if you posit uniformity as desideratum, was God's prior purpose and was the product of God's corrective intervention.

24. In the light of the dispersion already mandated and completed in chapter 10, the Babel project is explicitly narrated as conservative, defensive, restoring God's original intention. The people who had gone to Shinar were the children of Nimrod (the first 'mighty man', whatever that means), son of Cush (whose other descendants went mostly to Africa), son of Ham. This passage 11.1ff. relates to chapter 10 as 2.4ff. relates to 1.1–2.3; it reaches back into the earlier broader narrative to retell one fragment of the story.

25. William Schweiker's use of Babel in his paper 'Power and the Agency of God' in *Theology Today*, 52/2, July 1995, 215, exemplifies the temptation of American intellectuals to appeal to biblical material as prototypical for whatever one is interested in, leap frogging over the historical and linguistic disciplines.

Several of the features of the text stand out for the purpose of our present inquiry....The parallel between Genesis 11 and the contemporary world-view as I have specified it is perhaps too obvious to elaborate.

Yet very little of what Schweiker finds 'standing out' or 'obvious' needs the Babel story to make sense, or relates to scattering. In his confidence that the Bible is a mine of symbolic connections for anyone to exposit, Schweiker is typical of our age's confidence that antiquity is an open book. Another specimen of this confidence is Reinhold Niebuhr, *Beyond Tragedy*, New York: Scribners, 1937, 27–46.

26. Some of this notion of petty punitive anger on God's part is affirmed in Westermann's account. One of the places where this tilt surfaces most easily is in Christian interpretations read into the Lucan account of Pentecost. But its omnipresence in history is also represented by Stephan Zweig's 1916 essay on the Babel story 'Der Turm zu Babel', *Gesammelte Werke; Die schlaflose Welt*, 1983, 68ff.).

27. The later dispersion to Babylon (in the age of Jeremiah) may have been seen as a punishment by some Hebrew historians, but nothing in the text says this about the first dispersion from Babel.

28. Cf. Bernard Anderson, 'The Babel Story: Paradigm of Human Unity and Diversity' in *Ethnicity, Concilium*, ed., Andrew Greeley and Gregory Baum, New York, Seabury/Crossroad, 1977. One set of thinkers of the first generation who have had a stake in retrieving this affirmative vision of multicultural diversity were the conservative Protestant theorists of 'Church Growth'. Brueggemann's commentary supports this view.

29. There is room for considerable historical refinement and debate concerning how many of the inhabitants of the then territory of Judah were in fact carried off, and what kind of vestigial Jewish life remained possible in the land of Israel. What matters for our purposes is that the story line moves to Babylon, even though not all of the people did.

30. The general understanding, held by scholars today, of the editorial slant of the 'deuteronomic historian(s)', is that those narrators' reason for retelling the whole history of royal Israel was to show who was to blame for the exile. But the fact that there was unfaithfulness along the way does not make the mission to Babylon any less a mission. It merely intensifies what we have already seen about the moral ambivalence of kingship.

31. The false prophets are Hananiah in chapter 28: Ahab and Zedekiah in 29.15 and 21; Shemaiah in 28.24f., 31ff. Shemaiah is described as rejecting Jeremiah's message after it had been delivered.

32. Jeremiah 29.7. Cf. my earlier description of this vision in my essay 'Exodus and Exile: Two Faces of Liberation', *Crosscurrents*, Fall 1973, 297–309. Recently it has been creatively restated in the work of Daniel Boyarin.

33. Recent summaries confirm no real change in the field for a century. David G. Hunter's 'The Christian Church and the Roman Army in the First Three Centuries' in Marlin E. Miller and Barbara Nelson Gingerich (eds.), *The Church's Peace Witness*, Grand Rapids: Eerdmans, 1994, 161–81 reviewed the literature, as he had done before in 'A Decade of Research . . . ,' *Religious Studies Review*, 18/2, 1992, 87–94. That title wrongly suggests that there has been scholarly progress. Even if Turner had drawn on the fuller bibliographies of Peter Brock (*The Military Question in the Early Church: A Selected Bibliography of a Century's Scholarship: 1888–1987* Toronto, copyright P. Brock, 1988) and David Scholer (*Early Christian Attitudes to War and Military Service: A Selective Bibliography*, Theological Students' Fellowship *Bulletin*, September/October 1984, 23f.), there would have been no new wisdom to report. Since Thomas Clarkson published *An Essay on the Doctrines and Practice of the Early Christians as They Relate to War*, London: Hamilton, Adams and Co., 1832, no new sources have been found.

34. The next few paragraphs parallel and expand upon the argument of Chapter 9 above 'On Not Being in Charge'.

35. Cf. note 41 below.

36. The term 'quietism' was inserted in the study by the conference planning process at Washington University [at which Chapter 9 'On Not Being in Charge' was originally presented.] I accepted the term as aptly pointing toward an issue, but I challenge the adequacy of this characterization. It is not the case that the only alternative to violently taking charge of society as a whole is to be 'quiet'.

37. This adjective is not the one either the Jews or the Christians of the first century would have used. Yet something like it is needed to undercut the claim, made (about Jews) in a paper by M. Broyde in the St Louis symposium, and (about Christians) by numerous historians (cf. above Scholer, Hunter), that the early Christian renunciation of violence was *merely* tactical, a pragmatic survival technique, with no roots in spirituality or in an understanding of how God works in history.

38. This is the obverse of the Constantinian assumption, which would have been unthinkable in the first century, that only the Christian king can move history as God wants.

39. It is not only that the Maccabees and the Zealots did not ultimately triumph. Their first successes led them to become oppressive and to fall out among themselves. Not because they were weak but because they were strong and 'succeeded', they fell prey to what they claimed to defeat.

40. One need only note that the Maccabees are not in the Hebrew canon, a point first made to me by Rabbi Steven S. Schwarzschild.

41. The neglect of attention to the Jewishness of Christianity is no less striking in the pacifist-leaning works of Cadoux, Hornus, Bainton, and Brock, than it is in the non-pacifist readings of Helgeland, Cunningham, Ryan, Swift, Johnson, etc. Cf. note 33 above. David Hunter's term 'research' in the title cited above is something of a misnomer. Most of what Hunter reviews is old and much-reread material. Christians who are interested in learning from the dialogue with Judaism, and the historians who follow the contested history of thought on the morality of war, seem not to be doing their research in the same world.

42. Cf. above note 33. My 1991 statement of the same point has been published in 'War as a Moral Problem in the Early Church', in *The Pacifist Impulse in Historical Perspective*, ed., Harvey Dyck, Toronto: University of Toronto Press, 1996, 90–110.

43. Cf. 'The Moral Axioms of the Sermon on the Mount' in John H. Yoder, *The Original Revolution*, Scottdale, PA: Herald Press, 1972, as well as my earlier summary of this part of the present paper's theme in the paper cited in note 42.

44. Cf. my chapter 'If Christ is Truly Lord' in *The Original Revolution*, 52ff., now retitled as 'Peace Without Eschatology?' in my *The Royal Priesthood: Essays Ecclesiological and Ecumenical*, ed., Michael G. Cartwright, Grand Rapids: Eerdmans, 1994, 143ff. Some interpreters make much of the delay of the parousia as forcing on the Christians of the second or third generation a revision of their world-view. There is no evidence that such a change made any difference for their attitude toward violence. The Jewishness of their pacifism was not contingent on a particular apocalyptic perspective; and in any case an apocalyptic perspective is not contingent on confirmation or falsification through events.

45. By the fourth century *christos* had become a proper name. Thus neither Constantine nor his biographer Eusebius would literally have used that title for him; yet functionally 'messianity' describes Eusebius' view of Constantine's place in salvation history. The *meschiach*, the 'Anointed', is the man who by special divine intervention (unction) has been empowered to inaugurate the next phase of God's saving history. That is what Eusebius said about Constantine and his age.

46. When not long after the middle of the second century some Christians did in some way participate in the Roman army, as some clearly did (although we know about it only from the words of those who thought they should not, and there is no way to know how many there were, or what their roles were), it was not because they had any responsible theocratic visions of taking charge of history, or controlling the destiny of the Empire. They probably did it because (in peacetime, which prevailed in most of the Empire most

of the time) the work was easy and the rewards generous, without troubling themselves with much moral analysis.

47. That the faith community should properly be expected to be a minority in a wider world is said in very diverse ways by Karl Rahner, Juan-Luis Segundo, George Lindbeck, Stanley Hauerwas, and others.

48. 'Synagogue' is here a code word for the set of social changes already described formally above. Messianic Judaism in the first century, which we now call 'Christianity', went on from here with no basic change as far as social structure and world-view is concerned. 'Christians' (most accurately described for the first generations as 'messianic Jews') modified the synagogue pattern but only slightly by their openness to non-Jews, and by their love feast; the lay, book-centred, locally managed format of the synagogue remained. When the synagogue polity came later to be overshadowed among Christians by sacerdotalism and episcopacy, that represented a fall back into the pre-Jeremian patterns of Hellenistic paganism.

49. The intellectual capital of world Jewry remained in Babylon for a millennium, despite the recurrent efforts to reconstitute a centre in Judaea or (later) in Galilee. Rabbis, including the great Hillel, were sent from Babylon to set up schools there.

50. The very notion of canon is/was one component of the originality of the syna-gogue. All major religions have Scriptures; but something more is going on when the set of texts which are worthy of being copied, read ceremonially, and exposited reverently is limited by a decision which one records, and is thereby made usable for the community as identity marker. It is fascinating that in the recent renewal (in academic scholarly milieus) of the notion of 'canon', there is more attention given to the importance of reading the scriptural texts side-by-side than to the diaspora situation in which they came to be chosen for canonical status. The notion of 'canon' is not itself present in the texts which are the canon. That notion is defined by the social setting in which those texts begin to function to formulate identity. It other words; the meaning of 'canon' is not in how the texts come to be (so as to make us study authorship and accuracy) but in how (and in what setting) the disciples came to be guided by them (so we should study the diaspora). This insight is assumed but not exploited in Joseph Blenkinsopp, *Prophecy and Canon*, Notre Dame, IN: University of Notre Dame Press, 1977.

51. Later the notion of a second, privileged oral tradition, beside and besides the written text, was to surface both in Rabbinic Judaism and in Roman Catholicism. When it does arise, its role is paradoxical; although it claims orality as a further mode of revelation (to bypass the fact that it is not authorized by the first test), that claim serves to validate a second body of writings, called (in the Jewish case) 'the oral Torah' but in fact also written down, and (in the Roman case) 'oral tradition'. This 'other canon' must validate as well an institutional magisterium claiming the monopoly of interpreting (in writing) what (it claims but need not – and in fact cannot – prove) had been handed down orally.

52. This was the term Stout pressed into service (borrowed from Levi Strauss) to signal his modesty about the scale and strength of trans-community conversation. I shall make more of it later.

53. Jews in fact enjoy linguistic diversity so much that they keep on developing their own further variants. The Ashkenazim of Eastern Europe used, and carried with them to America and Israel, their own form of German. The Shephardim scattered around the Mediterranean world carried with them their own variant of early Spanish. But Yiddish and Ladino/Judesmo are only the best-known examples of a large variety. The many ways and places in which Jews interacted with host culture languages are reviewed in Herbert H. Paper, (ed.), *Jewish Languages: Themes and Variations*, Cambridge: Association for Jewish Studies, 1978 (brought to my attention by colleague Michael

Signer). Like the hermit crab, Jewish culture positively enjoys being at home carrying around someone else's shell.

54. 'Wisdom' is the literary critics' term for a kind of literature which is cross culturally understandable and does not refer much to holy history. For some moderns, the existence of 'Wisdom' material in the Hebrew canon is taken as relativizing the particular identity of the JHWH, the 'God who acts', of the stories of Abraham and Moses. For the Jews living the experience, however, the opposite was the case. They made Gentile proverbs their own. It was they who brought Egyptian and Mesopotamian proverbs to Asia Minor and to Rome.

55. Sheshbazzar is mentioned only in Ezra 1 and 5; Zerubbabel is in Ezra, Nehemiah, Haggai, and Zechariah. James D. Newsome, Jr., *By the Waters of Babylon* (Atlanta: John Knox, 1979), is one of several attempts to construct a continuous story around these four names. Yet his conclusion is that there is no story to tell; there is no narrative that goes on from there. Newsome's mistake is thinking that 'the History and Theology of the Exile' should conclude in three generations with the return to Judaea, rather than recognizing that the dispersion has continued, properly, faithfully, for two and a half millennia. Similarly Ralph Klein, *Israel in Exile* (Philadelphia: Fortress, 1979), while very creative in reading some of the texts written (or redacted) after 587, is completely blind to the way those texts gave a long-term identity to the permanent diaspora. Klein reads the material, oddly, counterfactually, as if the 'exile' was supposed actually to end in three generations, and did.

56. Scholars have always had trouble connecting these two accounts. They tell significantly different stories about more or less the same time, places, issues, and people. The perspective cited here is that of Prof. Daniel Smith Christopher, one of the planners of the conference at Loyola Marymount and a student of the literature of the 'Exile'.

57. Most of the text of Ezra is about the politicking for imperial authorization to rebuild the temple. In 7.12 Ezra is called 'the scribe of the law of the king of heaven'. To Artaxerexes these words meant 'secretary for Jewish affairs'. It was the title for a cabinet role in the pagan empire.

58. That phrase 'next year in Jerusalem' has been in the Seder a long time (in Gentile terms) but not more than a thousand years, according to L. Hoffman. For the first millennium of the diaspora Jews did not conclude their Passover with those words. But with or without the words, the worshippers did not expect literal fulfilment.

59. Jews whom I respect have the right to say, and some do say, that it was not fulfilled either in David Ben Gurion, Golda Meir, or Menachem Begin.

60. 'Seek the peace of the city' is too weak a translation for Jeremiah's command. It should be translated 'seek the salvation of the culture to which God has sent you'. Joseph's answer to Egypt's famine problem, or Daniel's role in Darius' reorganizing the Persian Empire into manageable satrapies, represent prototypically a Jewish role in contributing to secular well-being which is far more than mere minority survival. As a twentieth-century observer, I have the impression that Jews are too hesitant to avow the importance of their contribution to the viability and the quality of many societies, perhaps out of fear of provoking more antisemitic mythmaking.

61. This is the parcel of truth in the movement which a generation ago characterized biblical faith as 'secular'; cf. Harvey Cox, Ronald Gregor Smyth, and a few lines from Dietrich Bonhoeffer. Authentic monotheism disenchants an otherwise spooky and ironclad cosmos.

62. We have long been aware of how the ancient Hebrew message was preached and sung by African slaves in American and their descendants. Other forms of the question, as experienced by other peoples, were of course part of the conference at Loyola Marymount for which this paper was commissioned.

Commentary

PETER OCHS

Yoder completes his book with a rhetorical flourish: a stylistically powerful reading of the Jewish writer Stephan Zweig's poem/drama *Jeremiah*, composed during World War I. Since the chapter replays most of the themes we have discussed previously, I will comment only on Yoder's loving, but nonetheless mildly troubling, treatment of two Jewish figures: the poet Zweig and the prophet Jeremiah.

The sad, tragic prophet Jeremiah dominates Yoder's book in the end. Is it because one chapter of Jeremiah's prophecy offers a proof text for Yoder's whole thesis? Or is Yoder also drawn to Jeremiah's awkwardness on this earth as a fitting image of his own mission? We can say this much for sure: for this concluding chapter, the image of Jeremiah joins our Mennonite theologian to the German Jewish intellectual Zweig as well as to the one Yoder calls 'his rabbi', the German Jewish philosopher Schwarzschild. In that sense, Jeremiah is the one who links Yoder to the two Jews with whom he may identify most closely. For both Zweig and Yoder, chapter 29 of Jeremiah's prophecy offers a scriptural warrant for their desires to join the fate of the people Israel directly to the universal goal of redeeming humanity and, thereby, to avoid the embarrassment, burden, and unreasonable complexity of Israel's landedness. For both Zweig and Yoder, there is no middle between Israel's exilic separation from the land and the Maccabean strategy for remaining in it: that is, between an ancient foreshadowing of modern nationalist sovereignty in that land and Israel's forced separation from it in this world. There is, therefore, no middle that mediates Israel's two roles as embodied Word to the nations (for what is light but a trope for the Divine Word?) and as a prototypical sample of the recalcitrance of human nature. The tragic appearance of this unmediated tension may correspond, for both Zweig and Yoder, to the tragic image we have of the face of Jeremiah.

For post-liberal Jews, life is no longer defined by these stark alternatives. Those alternatives, and the dichotomous modern logic that accompanied them, defined the reality of Jewish life in late-modern Europe. But that life ended, literally and metaphorically, in the Shoah. Post-liberal Judaism emerges as an early phase of Judaism's rebirth after the Shoah. As in previous rebirths – after both *Chorbanot* (destructions of the ancient temples), after the Expulsion from Spain, and after comparable disasters in Jewish history – we may expect that this one will also bring with it a transformation of the religion of Israel. After the traumas of previous disasters, Israel eventually recovered its trust in the body of its Covenant, which is nothing other than the written Word of Torah. But that body was filled, each time, with the spirit of a new reception of Torah, a new *Midrash* or way of reliving the tradition of being Jewish in a new historical setting.

The periods that precede and follow these terrible interludes in Israel's history appear to display the kind of inner tension that defines late modern Jewish life and that defines Zweig's and Yoder's (and perhaps also Schwarzschild's) strategies for coping with the reality of Israel. Israel's body and spirit no longer fit together, we might say. For post-liberal Jews, however, this lack of fit is not a perennial feature of Israel's history, but only of its periodic epochs of transformation, when one religion of Israel seems to give way to a new one, the way biblical Israel gave way to Rabbinic Israel during those fateful first centuries of what we call the 'Christian era'.

In its present composition, the state of Israel remains a product of that period of late-modern discomfiture. But Zweig's German humanism remains a product of that discomfiture as well. This means that political Zionism as it is embodied in the conservative

elements of Israel's Jewish government is most likely not the form that Israel's landedness will take when the next religion of Israel emerges from the disasters of the twentieth
century. If it were the only form of landedness, then we would have reason to be sympathetic to both Zweig's and Yoder's efforts to prophesy against it. But the image they have
of Jeremiah is not Jeremiah's own. It is an ethically moving yet still late-modern effort to
over-generalize one chapter of Jeremiah's long prophecy, as if it were the only prophetic
alternative to what remains Israel's late-modern practice of landedness.

The stark separation that both Yoder *and* conservative Zionists assert between exile
and land is a lingering mark of this immediately past and present period of transformation. It is, however, not a mark of our near future, and it is, in that sense, not prophetic.
The voice of prophecy begins by observing the separation that Israel is about to suffer
between its body and spirit, but it ends, each time, with the vision of that historically
specific new heaven/new earth that will be realized in the religion that is immediately to
come. This is the religion in which Israel's body and spirit will be reintegrated once again,
albeit, we fear, not forever, since the cycles of Israel's history do not appear to be over.

For post-liberal Jews, the emerging religion of Israel will draw both exilic and landed
life into a relationship that we cannot yet define. The story of the Jews on the land of
Israel, alongside or with the Palestinians on the soil of Palestine, is no morality play nor
theo-drama but a fact offered us by the unhappy turmoils of modern western civilization
and its colonialism and antisemitism (meaning both anti-Jewishness and anti-Arabism);
and also offered us by those who removed Israel from its home and for two thousand
years reinforced that removal. Those who, in Yoder's terms, respect God's sovereignty
must also have the imagination to foresee that western nationalism may not remain the
only political model for life in the Middle East, or in Europe, for that matter. The question and status and manner of Jewish life on the soil of Israel, as well as on the soils of
all other lands, may not be defined for so long by the extremes of nationalist sovereignty
versus landlessness. Just as Yoder has encouraged us to imagine the past in new ways, so
must we post-liberal Jews ask our newfound Anabaptist friends to imagine with us new
ways for Israel's future in a post-modern world. This means, as well, new ways for
western economics and politics, rather than just new forms of the old western dichotomy
between the ways of power and the ways of powerlessness.

It is not helpful, therefore, for Jews who have escaped from the limits of German-
Jewish humanism to be shown again the old model of Zweig's humanism. The Shoah has
brought us beyond that, and post-liberalism inhabits this beyond. It is helpful for us to
be reminded of Jeremiah's patience and openness to seek the welfare of the city, so long
as we are reminded, as well, of his own desire and plan to return to, and seek the welfare
of, the city of Jerusalem. Yoder has made a beautiful monument of one chapter of
Jeremiah's ministry. But there are many chapters, and the post-liberal Jewish voice is one
that says, with Franz Rosenzweig (that German Jewish humanist who also anticipated a
life after humanism), 'both/and,' rather than 'either/or'. How the 'both/and' can be
achieved can never be clear before it is attempted, and the attempt must be made with
both God and human, your community and ours joined together at the table of study
and dialogue. We do not yet know how Judaism's exilic and landed lives will be
integrated into a renewed religion. But we trust that God's directives for that integration
will emerge only out of our renewed study of his Torah. And we expect that, this time,
the study table will have seats around it for Yoder's students as well as Rozenweig's, for
Palestinian as well as Jewish scholars. And there is no way for us to know, beforehand,
the Word that will be heard through this study.

Afterword: 'If Abraham is Our Father . . .'

The Problem of Christian Supersessionism
after Yoder

MICHAEL G. CARTWRIGHT

Whatever else one might say of John Howard Yoder's essays on *The Jewish–Christian Schism Revisited*, they surely comprise a Christian theology of history, namely 'an account of the process whereby the eternal mystery of God . . . brings "near" to him and to each other those who were once "far off" . . .'.[1] Inasmuch as Yoder advocated 'evangelical revisionism'[2] in writing history, he offered a witness to the one 'who came preaching peace' (Ephesians 2.15) – as discussed earlier in my contribution to the Editors' Introduction. How students of Yoder's work ultimately register the significance of this theology of history for contemporary Christian identity – not to mention for Jewish–Christian dialogue – is an important question because it has implications for *where we think we are* with respect to the problem of Christian supersessionism.

As Nicholas Lash deftly explains in his provocative collection of essays, *Theology on the Way to Emmaus*, theologies of history attempt (among other things) to answer the query, 'How do we know where we are?' Lash's own approach in these matters has been to adopt the perspective of 'the middle-distance.'[3] Adapting the counsel of John Henry Cardinal Newman, Lash observes, 'when we have "lost our way", we would be ill-advised to plunge into the nearest thicket to take our bearings'.[4] For Lash, this disposition is not merely applicable to the world of literary criticism of fictional narratives; it is also a matter of ethical prescription in registering the interaction of memory and hope in our theologies of history.[5] In this latter sense, for Christians, 'setting our gaze on the middle-distance' means that we do not pretend that we are in a position to take a perspective that 'stands above human history'. Nor will we succumb to the despair that would leave us stuck with 'the view from the parish pump'. I would like to suggest that Christian theologians should attempt to adopt such a perspective as we investigate the problem of Christian supersessionism 'after Yoder'. This vantage point is necessary, if we are to appreciate both the ambition of Yoder's project and the limits of what he was able to achieve.

I believe that we also need a middle-distance perspective in taking the measure of Yoder's essays. It would be myopic for contemporary Christian theologians not to appreciate what Peter Ochs has described felicitously as the 'wonders'[6] of John Howard Yoder's reconsideration of the Jewish–Christian schism. As Ochs's appended *responsa* to Yoder's ten essays display so admirably, there is much in these essays that post-liberal Jews can appreciate. And the same should be true of contemporary Christians, particularly those of us who regard ourselves as 'post-liberal' in our theological sensibilities. At the same time, if we are not able to recognize the inadequacies of Yoder's proposed resolution of the Jewish–Christian schism, it would be tantamount to holding on to an astigmatic vision of reality in the face of the opportunity to correct our sight. In this respect, I believe that learning to see the problem of Christian supersessionism for what it has been and continues to be in Christian ecclesiology will require that students of Yoder also be able to accept what Ochs aptly calls the 'burdens',[7] of Yoder's theology of history.

To that end, I invite readers of Yoder's essays – including but not limited to those theologians who have been strongly influenced by Yoder's conception of Christian peoplehood – to join me in attempting to take the measure of the ecclesiological problem of Christian supersessionism as it can now be seen with Yoder's essays in full view. This will involve three steps, each of which constitutes a set of questions for further exploration. First, I ask whether we may need to revisit Yoder's own conception of 'the children of Abraham' by exploring the ways Yoder's moral history of Judaism shapes his views of Jewish and Christian peoplehood. Second, I invite readers to take the measure of the supersessionist *effects* of Yoder's argumentation that may diverge from his own stated intent. Third, I suggest that we should *extend* the conversation that Yoder initiated about the historical character of revelation by revisiting Yoder's reading of Ezra, Nehemiah and other post-exilic writings in relation to contemporary Jewish conversations about this same problem.

The cumulative effect of these three investigations will be to re-engage a fourth topic that Yoder largely avoided – the matter of God's covenant with the Jewish people, the election of Israel to be God's 'chosen one' for the nations. In the process, I attempt to shed some light on the ways that supersessionism continues to be re-structured in the context of our ongoing theological efforts to foster a renewed sense of Christian identity.

Because of limits of space, I will be able to develop only one set of these questions in any comprehensive sense. In the remaining cases, I will have to be content to state the issue as well as I can. Readers who are intrigued by this discussion, may want to follow up by reading a related essay – 'Misplaced Icons of Christian Peoplehood: The Problem of Christian Supersessionism Revisited', http://www.pages.uindy.edu/~mcartwright/icons where I address these same concerns with more fully developed arguments that engage the substance of Yoder's essays.

I. Hermeneutics and History: Yoder's Engagement with Christian Supersessionism

As Stanley Hauerwas and Alex Sider have rightly observed, the principal motivating factor that led Yoder to *rethink* the Jewish–Christian schism was not the Shoah, but rather 'that one of the reasons Christians had lost their ability to read the Scriptures was due to the attempt to make Christianity intelligible without Israel'.[8] Yoder approached the problem of interpretation from a disposition formed by his own historiographical perspective about the significance of the radical reformation. More specifically, he contended that the Anabaptists of the sixteenth century 'were alone among the reformers in their insistence that the New Testament be read as a continuation of and development of the Old. This meant that the Anabaptists alone understood that revelation is historical'.[9] Although the logic is not immediately obvious to first-time readers of these two assertions, Yoder was drawing a theological correlation between the doctrine of peoplehood and the doctrine of divine revelation. This move was clearly intended to enable Yoder to disengage from the centuries-old patterns of Christian supersessionism. The question to be re-engaged, I believe, is whether it succeeded.

A. Learning to Recognize the Shapes of the Problem

Judging the adequacy of Yoder's resistance of Christian supersessionism, requires that we place Yoder's work in the wider context of the history of Christian supersessionism. In the context of his own theological exploration of what it might mean to offer an 'Israelogical' account of Christian peoplehood, George Lindbeck has identified two distinct historical patterns of Christian supersessionism: (1) the Church replaces Israel; (2) the emphasis on the Church as Israel disappears. The former involved straightforward expropriation. The latter erasure of Israel as a marker of Christian identity is more complex precisely because it also involves the *eclipse* of Christian peoplehood *as well as* Jewish peoplehood, thereby eliminating *the iconic structure* within which the social embodiment of Christianity had been understood.

Initially, Christians used Judaism as a means for making Christianity intelligible *to themselves* understood as the Church. This 'expropriation' of Jewish peoplehood was the predominant pattern of Christian self-understanding until roughly the time of the Protestant Reformation. During and after the Reformation, Christians attempted to make Christianity intelligible in the context of debates about the Church and modernity. The modern pattern of 'supersession without Israelhood' arose in the context of 'sixteenth-century controversies over how and when the Church was founded'. As Lindbeck astutely observes, one of the *unintended* consequence of these debates was that the resultant pictures of the Church were marked by discontinuity rather than continuity with Israel.

As a consequence of the Enlightenment, attention shifted from the Church and Israel as bodies of people to Judaism and Christianity conceived of 'as religions that individuals believed in and/or practiced. In time, these shifts of attention brought on by the Reformation and the Enlightenment gave way to the now prevailing theo-logies of replacement, which do more than neglect the church as Israel: they discard it . . . The notion of fulfilment continues to be realistically affirmed, but with a radically different meaning. Fulfilment is no longer conceptualized in terms of the biblical narratives of God keeping and confirming promises and prophecies to persons and groups, but in terms of the impersonal patterns of evolutionary progress according to which one religion provides the conditions for the emergence of a better and higher one. Fulfilment now applies to religions, not peoples.'[10]

Lindbeck's historical sketch is useful for several reasons, not the least of which is to provide a historical framework for registering the distinctiveness of Yoder's argument at the same time as we begin to see how Yoder's argumentation has its roots in the dynamics of Reformation critiques of the Fall of the Church. Yoder not only recognized most aspects of these two forms of supersessionism, but also tried to avoid such errors. Clearly, he had no intention of repeating the *modern* error that results in nineteenth-century Protestant liberalism any more than he wanted to re-introduce the *pre-modern* practice of seeing the Church as having superseded Israel. Yoder sought to draw our attention back to what it means for Christians to be an *Abrahamic* people (again).

The first chapter of *The Original Revolution*, Yoder's book of essays on Christian pacifism, provides an explicit example of this trajectory of argument. There Yoder explicates the 'political options' of Jesus with reference to the biblical story of Abraham. Yoder invites his readers to consider the 'options' that Jesus confronted, and he identifies the challenge Jesus faced with the challenges faced by his 1970s-era readers.

> To answer our question . . . we must go back to what God had been doing or trying to do for a long, long, time. The Bible story really begins with Abraham, the father of those who believe. Abraham was called to get up and leave Chaldea . . . He could not know when or whether or how he could again have a home, a land of his own. And yet as he rose to follow this inscrutable promise, he was told that it was through him that the nations of the world would be blessed. In response Abraham promised his God that he would lead a different kind of life: a life different from the cultured and religious peoples, whether urban or nomadic, among whom he was to make his pilgrim way. . . . Yet in that apartness how present!
>
> This is the original revolution. The creation of a distinct community with its own deviant set of values and its coherent way of articulating them.[11]

On Yoder's reading of the biblical witness, then, Abraham is the 'father' of the 'believer's church tradition' and as such embodies what it means to convert from worldliness to participation in God's revolution for the world. Yoder's discussion also addressed the *failures* of 'the children of Abraham' to live up to the challenge of embodying the original revolution that God has intended to be their vocation. Nevertheless, God 'remained steadfast in his loyalty' to the children of Abraham:

> His promises of righteousness to be brought to the nations through His servant Israel were from year to year reiterated, reinforced, clarified, even though the likelihood that the Israelites would become the instrument of their fulfillment seemed less and less evident. These were the promises, Christians believe, Jesus came to keep.
>
> Jesus did again what God had done in calling Abraham or Moses or Gideon or Samuel: He gathered His people around His word and His will. Jesus created around Himself a society like no other society mankind had ever seen:
>
> 1. This was a voluntary society: you could not be born into it . . .
>
> 2. It was a society which, counter to all precedent, was mixed in its composition. It was mixed racially with both Jews and Gentiles . . . mixed religiously . . . mixed economically, with members both rich and poor.
>
> 3. When He called His society together Jesus gave its members a new way of life to live. . . . He gave them a new way . . . by forgiving them . . . by suffering . . . by

sharing [money] . . . by drawing upon the gift of every member, even the most humble . . . by building a new order, not smashing the old.

At the heart of all this novelty . . . is what Jesus did about the fundamental human temptation: power.[12]

Yoder argues that this 'new peoplehood, the being-together with one another and the being different in style of life' is what Jesus' disciples 'freely promised to do' in response to God's renewal of 'the promise [that] through them the world should be blessed and turned rightside up'.[13]

Accordingly, Yoder contends that when Christians are *most faithful* as disciples of Jesus they are carrying out the mandate of what God willed for the children of Abraham: Christians and Jews share the same vocation, Christians constitute a new peoplehood, but it is most meaningfully understood in continuity with the Abrahamic trajectory of obedience to God's call to leave one's homeland in faithful response to God's will. Or, as Yoder *stated even more explicitly* in the concluding paragraphs of that same essay, 'Jesus did not bring to faithful Israel any corrected ritual or any new theories about the being of God. He brought them a new people-hood and a new way of living together. The very existence of such a group is itself a deep social change. . . . If it lives faithfully, it is also the most powerful tool of social change.'[14]

I believe that this particular sequence of reasoning in *The Original Revolution* is noteworthy because the way John Howard Yoder tells the story of the 'children of Abraham' in this instance *does not vary* in any significant way from the more complex set of historical and theological explorations that comprise the essays of *The Jewish–Christian Schism Revisited* that he completed revising more than a quarter of a century later. In both cases, Yoder is narrating a kind of 'moral history' framed by the *unfaithfulness* of the Israelites, and the challenge presented by Jesus for those who would follow him to be God's *faithful* people.

The parallels in logic of argumentation between the two sets of essays are not limited to the conception of peoplehood. In a later essay in *The Original Revolution*, Yoder elaborates on *a related* issue of biblical interpretation that Christian pacifists confront with respect to the Old Testament canon. In the essay 'If Abraham Is Our Father', Yoder confronts a 'basic problem of interpretation, which cannot be avoided by Christians whose commitment to non-resistance or pacifism is oriented around loyalty to Jesus Christ . . .'[15] The issue in question is the impression that readers of the Old Testament get that violence is 'not merely tolerated but fostered and glorified'.[16] After explaining four ways in which this problem is manifested in the books of the Old Testament, Yoder reviews the four explanations that had been offered to resolve the tension between the words and deeds of Jesus and the Old Testament texts.

Yoder finds none of these explanations to be adequate. He discards the 'dispen-sational' interpretation not only because Jesus 'does not say He is setting aside the Old Testament', but also because of what this interpretation seems to be saying about God. 'It is all very well to appeal to an unaccountable sovereignty with which God has a right to prescribe a law to his creatures and to change that law; but it is quite another matter for the creature to make such distinctions and to attribute changed purposes to God when He has not clearly said so.'[17] Yoder finds the 'concession' to Israelite disobedience interpretation to be lacking not only because the analogy to divorce does not apply, but also because 'the concept of concession is foreign to the [biblical] material' about holy war.[18] He also finds the condescension of the 'pedagogical concession' interpretation to be unwarranted, and he also takes exception to the 'cavalier attitude' of the 'evolutionist liberal theological perspective' that looks down on the ancient Hebrews with modernist moral superiority.[19] And the fourth (Lutheran) interpretation that distinguishes realms of divine action he faults because it appears to 'recognize no movement at all in the course of holy history'.[20]

Instead, Yoder offers his own *revisionist* explanation – 'The Concrete Historical Anthropological Meaning' – which stands in contrast with the four preceding views in so far as it *reverses* the direction of interpretation. He begins by explaining that the holy war of Israel 'is the concrete experience of not needing any other crutches for one's identity and community as a people than trust in Yahweh as king . . . .'. With Yahweh as their God, Israel does not need to have earthly kings like other nations around them. With this in view, Yoder believes it is possible to make sense of the remainder of the canonical narrative.

> From the ancient Hebrews through the later prophets up to Jesus there was real historical movement, real 'progress'; but the focus of this progress was not a changing of ethical codes but rather an increasingly precise definition of the nature of peoplehood. . . . Once all men are seen as potential partakers of the covenant, then the outsider can no longer be perceived as less than human or as an object of sacrificing. Once one's own national existence is no longer seen as a guarantee of Yahweh's favor, then to save this national existence by a holy war is no longer a purpose for which miracles would be expected. Thus the dismantling of the applicability of the concept of holy war takes place not by promulgation of a new ethical demand but by a restructuring of the Israelite perception of community under God.[21]

Yoder's language here is precise and purposeful: What Jesus has done is to *restructure* Israelite peoplehood. It is noteworthy that it is also in this context that Yoder explains what he thinks John the Baptist meant when he said to his contemporaries, 'Do not claim that you are sons of Abraham; God can raise up sons of Abraham out of stones' (Luke 3.8). Yoder's definition of Abrahamic peoplehood is worth quoting in its entirety.

> To be a son of Abraham means to share the faith of Abraham. Thus the relativizing of the given ethnic-political peoplehood is completed in both directions. There is no one in any nation who is not a potential son of Abraham since that sonship is a miraculous gift which God can open up to the Gentiles. On the other hand, there is no given peoplehood which can defend itself against others as bearers of the Abrahamic covenant, since those who were born into that unity can and in fact already did jeopardize this claim to it by their unbelief. Thus the very willingness to trust God for the security and identity of one's peoplehood, which was the original concrete moral meaning of the sacrament of holy warfare, is now translated to become the willingness or readiness to renounce those definitions of one's own people and of the enemy which gave to the original sacrament its meaning.[22]

I have taken the time and space to unfold these two strands of argument from *The Original Revolution* in order to call attention to two important aspects of Yoder's engagement with the problem of Christian supersessionism. The first is to observe that Yoder's definition of what it means to be a 'child of Abraham' actually turns out to converge with the modernist pattern of Christian supersessionism inasmuch as the emphasis on 'faith' functions to detach Abrahamic identity from its historical embodiment in the people of Israel. As Michael Wyschogrod and other post-liberal Jews have argued, this understanding of faith is problematic for a variety of reasons, not least of which is that it removes Jews from human history.[23] Here, therefore, we encounter a vestige of modernist hermeneutics that Yoder could not see.

Second, Yoder's 'concrete historical anthropological interpretation' also functions to *bypass* the conception of the 'election' of Israel. Notice that *at no point* in this discussion does Yoder ever refer to Romans 9–11. For all practical purposes, this is also true of his discussion in The *Jewish–Christian Schism Revisited* essays where Yoder tends to shift discussion of 'covenant' and 'election' toward a conception of Jewish missionary vocation in exile. The question still to be addressed is, how shall we understand this (apparently deliberate) omission from Yoder's theological dialogue with Judaism?

In his book *Paul Among the Theologians*, Canadian theologian Douglas Harink persuasively argues that Yoder has 'occluded' the doctrine of the election of Israel in favour of offering a 'moral history' of Israel's obedience through his reading of the Jewish diaspora history since the exile.[24] Although he rightly notes that Yoder *does not misread* Paul's Letter to the Romans in the way that New Testament scholar N. T. Wright does, Harink contends that Yoder's *lack of focused attention to Romans 9–11 contributes* to the problem. A close reading of the text of these three chapters, Harink contends, reveals a single consistently argued Pauline thesis: '*God may harden and show mercy, now toward the nations, now toward a portion of Israel, as he wills, each in its season and for a purpose (the revelation of God's glory), but God will never reject his chosen fleshly people, nor allow them to fail in the race of salvation.*'[25] In both of these respects, then, Yoder's argument turns out to share more with 'modernist' readings of the Pauline writings than it might first appear.

B. Accepting the Burdens of Christian Supersessionism

To read Yoder in the context of the modernist erasure of Judaism is to recognize those respects in which his particular attempt to 're-Judaize' Christianity may have fallen short. If we inquire further into Yoder's struggle with the problem of Christian supersession, we may discover that at certain levels his own argument, while not intending to be so, nevertheless has resulted in what we might regard as a new variant of – '*neo*' or '*neo-neo*'– Christian supersessionism. To read Yoder in the context of the wider history of Christian supersessionism, I believe, is to *extend the project that Yoder began*, and arguably provide additional reasons why the Jewish–Christian schism continues to be the case in our own time. In particular, those who would aspire to re-engage this ecclesiological problem will need to inquire about how Christian identity might be narrated 'in Jewish terms'.

To that end, I suggest that students of Yoder may find it useful to re-examine how

Yoder's project paralleled other twentieth-century Jewish and Christian (Protestant as well as Catholic proposals) initiatives. Arguably, the effort to re-think Christianity *in Jewish terms* might be said to have its *most clearly Christian* origin in the writings of German Lutheran theologian Dietrich Bonhoeffer. *During* the period that the National Socialists were carrying out the Holocaust, he dared to think about what it might mean to 're-Judaize' Christianity. As he writes in *Letters and Papers from Prison*:

> The transcendence of epistemological theory has nothing to do with the transcendence of God. God is beyond in the midst of our life. The church stands, not in the boundaries where human powers give out, but in the middle of the village. *That is how it is in the Old Testament, and in this sense we still read the New Testament far too little in light of the Old.* How this religionless Christianity looks, what form it takes, is something I'm thinking about a great deal, and I shall be writing to you again about it soon.[26]

However fragmentary and elliptical these remarks may be, their ecclesiological significance cannot be ignored.

Clearly, Bonhoeffer (like Yoder) intends to resist the modernist paradigm of reading the Bible, which converged in so many ways with Christian supersessionist reading practices. But what is most significant for my purposes is the way Bonhoeffer attempts to do so. As David Ford perceptively observes, at the very end of his life, Bonhoeffer's reflections on the topic of Christian holiness led him to reflect theologically about 'the polyphony of daily life' in ways that are convergent with revisionist accounts of Christianity 'in Jewish terms'.[27] The broader outlines of his emergent conception of a 're-Judaized' Christianity are displayed in at least three ways: (1) While in prison, Bonhoeffer constantly read the Old Testament; (2) in his prayers throughout the day, he immersed himself in the Psalms, which he regarded as holding the key to reading Scripture over against ourselves; (3) he continually insisted on 'the this-worldliness of Christianity' in a context in which he *actually shared* the 'view from below' that the German Jewish community *had no choice* but to have in the context of the Nazi regime.[28]

Bonhoeffer's rejection of the kind of religion understood as 'inwardness' was very much of a piece with the emergent conception of *the self* that simultaneously exists in 'double-orientation' to God and others, as displayed in *Letters and Papers from Prison*.[29] (In certain respects, the perspective of 'double-orientation' appears to have some affinities with the notion of the middle-distance perspective.) As Ford notes: 'Because of its complete immersion in God and the world it can gain no overview of itself. Its selfhood is therefore something like the overall impression of a polyphonic piece in which there has been continual improvisation of the counterpoints. That impression cannot be had by the improvising musicians. In Bonhoeffer's polyphony it is only had by God.'[30] Bonhoeffer's proposals for a Christianity that takes seriously the fact that it can have 'no overview of itself' converge in remarkable ways with the Jewish tradition's strictures against idolatrous efforts to attain the kinds of knowledge and control that would dare to claim to have mastered divinity and human psychology.

Although Yoder was fully aware of Bonhoeffer's elliptical remarks about what it would mean to 're-Judaize' Christianity, he did not see his own project as convergent with Bonhoeffer's effort to rethink the Jewish–Christian relationship. It is not clear to what extent Yoder considered Bonhoeffer's proposals. The option that Yoder chose stands in contrast to Bonhoeffer's precisely at the point at which Yoder provides an account that presumes that it is *still possible* to offer an overview of Christian identity and peoplehood without engaging in idolatry. In this respect, Yoder's work aspires to something more than a middle-distance perspective in the way he goes about articulating a theology of history.

Given the notable increase in scholarly interest in Yoder's *The Jewish–Christian Schism Revisited*, [31] I believe that it is time for students of Yoder's ecclesiology to give more attention to the residual effects of a lingering modernism in Yoder's argumentation and the ways that may have shaped his analysis of the depth of the problem of Christian supersessionism. Recent essays by Alain Epp Weaver and Gerald Schlabach, among others, suggest to me that the kind of further inquiry that I am calling for may have already begun.

Alain Epp Weaver's paper on 'Constantinianism, Zionism, Diaspora: Towards a Political Theology of Exile and Return' is the first study that I am aware of that attempts to take the measure of Yoder's argument in relation to the legacy of Christian supersessionism. In that essay, Weaver draws upon Yoder's essays to articulate 'a non-supersessionist "orthodox" theological critique of Zionism' from an Anabaptist perspective.[32] Weaver argues that Zionism must be critiqued 'as an abandonment of Judaism's mission' and draws on *The Jewish–Christian Schism Revisited* essays to show how Yoder regarded the emergence of Zionism as 'the culmination of the Christianization of Judaism'. Weaver takes the argument an additional step when he contends: 'What Yoder did not say, but could have, was that Zionism was also a fall away from whatever remained of the nonviolent style of the Jeremianic vision into the violent politics of a colonialist nation-state.'[33]

In the context of his broader constructive argument, Weaver draws on Kendall Soulen's typology in *The God of Israel and Christian Theology* (1996) for the purpose of locating the senses in which Yoder's project is non-supersessionist. To that end, he identifies three different types of supersessionism, the first two of which are more precise descriptions of the patterns already noted by Lindbeck's historical overview. *Economic supersessionism* asserts that 'the people of God have become obsolete in God's salvific plans for the world, obsolete because supplanted by Jesus, and by extension the church'. As Soulen observes, while the first claim has been made recurrently throughout Christian history, there is a second 'more virulent form of the claim'. *Punitive supersessionsim* views God as having broken God's covenant with Israel in response to Israel's rejection of Christ and the gospel.

The third type, *Structural supersessionism,* is embodied in 'the standard canonical narrative' that informs the reading of Scripture. This narrative is structurally supersessionist 'because it unifies the Christian canon in a manner that renders the Christian scriptures largely indecisive for shaping conclusions about how God's purposes engage creation in universal and enduring ways'. The narrative 'skips from creation and the Fall to God's incarnation in Jesus: the patriarchal/matriarchal narratives, the dramas of exodus and exile, the struggle with kingship and prophecy play no role in the narrative'.[34] Unlike Soulen, who clearly marks this third form of supersessionism as a widespread problem in contemporary Christian theology, Weaver proceeds as if structural supersessionism *has not* shaped Yoder's own position. In fact, one of the stipulations of Weaver's original argument presumes that there is no sense in which Yoder's position is supersessionist: 'If one can be non-supersessionist while affirming traditional theological claims, then the burden of proof will be on revisionist theological positions.'[35] However, Weaver makes this move after sidestepping Soulen's own stated concerns about the problem of structural supersessionism associated with canonical readings of Scripture.[36]

Other students of Yoder are less sure that Yoder and the Anabaptist tradition can escape the charge of supersessionism so easily. Gerald Schlabach has called attention to yet another kind of supersessionism, which in my judgement has a bearing on Yoder's argumentation in *The Jewish–Christian Schism Revisited*.[37] Schlabach observes that even if the other issues can be resolved, the way Anabaptists have tended to assert their own identity vis-à-vis the Church catholic could be regarded as supersessionist. He identifies two such examples: the Anabaptist 'Fall of the Church historiography' and the consequent delegitimation of 1,200–1,300 years of Church history. Consideration of these narrative patterns leads Schlabach to ask, 'How shall we critique the practices of Christendom vis-à-vis the Jews, without succumbing to the same pattern of saying . . . (a) You aren't who you think you are. [and] (b) We are who you think you are.'[38]

Schlabach's admonition that Anabaptist theologians be self-critical about the possibility of engaging in supersessionist argumentation is by no means merely rhetorical. Rather, he acknowledges that this issue cannot be engaged without also exploring *the ecclesiological issues* of continuity and discontinuity that are embedded in Anabaptist historiography and identity. While Schlabach is fully aware of the complex character of Anabaptist 'expropriation' and 'appropriation' of Catholic practices, he also understands that the (anti-Constantinian) Anabaptist narrative of the 'Fall of the Church' unfolds *in precisely the same narrative context* as the 'erasure' of Israel's peoplehood that (George Lindbeck contends) *began to occur* in the context of Reformation debates about the nature of the Church.

This discussion – between two perceptive students of Yoder's work – about the problem of Christian supersessionism highlights the wonder and the burden of Yoder's ambitious attempt to narrate an Abrahamic identity for contemporary Christians in the context of his theological dialogue with Judaism. On the one hand, as Weaver contends, Yoder's work provides a way of engaging problems internal to the Jewish tradition. On the other hand, as Schlabach insightfully observes, Anabaptist accounts of 'Christian peoplehood' are themselves constituted in supersessionist ways. Their respective investigations also call attention to the discrepancy between Yoder's intent and *the effects* of Yoder's argumentation in *The Jewish–Christian Schism Revisited*. Accounting for this kind of separation requires, I believe, that students of Yoder's work closely re-examine his own 'hermeneutic of peace'.

II. John Howard Yoder's 'Hermeneutic of Peace' *Revisited*

Some issues of interpretation that arise in Yoder's essays on the Jewish–Christian schism can be straightforwardly stated. For example, as Stanley Hauerwas and Alex Sider have noted elsewhere, Yoder employs an over-simple understanding of the difference between Hebrew and Greek thought and practice.[39] This conceptual problem appears to have led Yoder himself to read 'priestly' practices as Greek or pagan even where they are arguably grounded in the biblical text. Other problems of interpretation that the reader encounters in Yoder's argumentation are more more intricate and therefore more difficult to state succinctly.

A. Learning to Recognize the Shapes of the Problem

'Polyphony' *would not* be a word that aptly describes Yoder's hermeneutic. However peaceable his pedagogical approach may have been in the way he engaged just-war theorists, the way Yoder goes about establishing the linkage between the Christian and Jewish 'vocations' to peacemaking is to create a new set of dichotomies to replace the Constantinian assumptions that he seeks to supplant.[40] While Yoder is determined to break through the typology of 'ethnic' Judaism and 'voluntary' Christianity, he does so at the price of (for all practical purposes) *dismissing* the moral casuistry of Rabbinic Judaism as a 'reaction' to Constantinian Christianity. In this respect, Yoder's own modes of argument betray a kind of Cartesian 'either-or' logic that requires *the rhetorical displacement and/or the elimination* of that which is opposed. This kind of binary logic does not comport well, I would argue, with Yoder's own best intentions as a practitioner of a hermeneutic of peace.

In this latter sense, Yoder's arguments display both how Christians ought and *ought not* to understand themselves in a post-Shoah world. Christians should be wary of arguments that would seek to authorize forms of violence as well as to explore what it can mean to be 'for the nations' and thereby think as carefully as possible about what it means to bring and/or embody 'good news'. In each of these respects, Yoder's arguments in *The Jewish–Christian Schism Revisited* are important. Moreover, as Stanley Hauerwas has observed, Yoder's emphasis on the importance of the *embodiment* of Christian witness by the Church *as a distinct people* can be said to constitute a major shift in the way Christians should think about the theological task in a post-Christendom world.[41] Unfortunately, in the essays contained in this volume, Yoder's account of Christian witness also appears to involve an 'erasure' of the *Jewish* witness as found in the institutions and practices of post-biblical Judaism, and therefore appears to be constructed upon a supersessionist – albeit 'non-Constantinian' – understanding of the Church.

For this reason, I urge students of Yoder to inquire further about the adequacy of Yoder's own reconstruction of the history of Jewish pacifism. Arguably, the material that comprises Chapter 9, 'On Not Being in Charge',[42] provides Yoder's own *most fully developed narrative* of the history of Jewish pacifism. This story unfolds within his identification of three 'culturally unique traits' that define Judaism – the phenomena of synagogue, Torah, and the phenomenon of the rabbinate, which Yoder describes as 'a non-sacerdotal, non-hierarchical, non-violent leadership elite whose power is not civil but intellectual, validated by their identification with the Torah'.[43] Yoder's 'sociology of Jewish experience' is interesting as much as for what it does not include as for what it describes. Notice that there is no reference to 'land' in this definition – synagogues can take shape 'wherever' the requisite minimum of households come together.

In this same context, Yoder also comments on the 'two sets of exceptions' to what he thought of as the 'dominant Jewish vision' of a 'pacifism of "not being in charge" that marked Jewish experience' between Jeremiah and Theodore Hertzl.[44] 'One set of exceptions were those people who concentrated on rebuilding and managing the Temple at Jerusalem, with the political and financial backing of the Empires, first of the East and then of Rome. From Ezra to Nehemiah to the Sanhedrin of the time of Jesus, this restorative elite, called "Sadducees" in the Gospels, did the best it could to defend Jewish values, but ultimately it failed.'[45] 'The other set of exceptions were the Maccabees and the so-called Zealots; they too ultimately failed, but not before triggering the Roman Empire's devastating response. The "Judaism" which survived after the Zealot defeat in 135 assumed the same stance which Jewry everywhere else but Palestine had already been taking since Jeremiah, namely "seeking the peace of the city where they had been sent" (Jeremiah 29.4–7).'[46] Elsewhere, Yoder goes so far as to say 'For two and a half millennia, from Josiah to Ben Gurion, Jewry represents the longest and strongest experience of religious-cultural-moral continuity in known history, defended without the sword.'[47]

To put it mildly, this is a sweeping narrative leading to a judgement about the moral history of the 'peoplehoods' of both Christianity and Judaism. Notice that the story Yoder tells functions both *to justify* Yoder's own contention of the normativity of 'the Jeremianic turn' (see discussion in the Editors' Introduction) and *to exclude* and/or marginalize historical examples and/or evidence that do not fit Yoder's narrative scheme. For example, later, in discussing the exceptions to the historical perspective that he offers, Yoder refers to the 'orthodox Jewish perspective' of the *neturei karta*'s rejection of the state of Israel 'because it was not established by the Messiah, but by human initiative'.[48] This example is used at several points in *The Jewish–Christian Schism Revisited*, in each case with the implication that non-secular or 'religious' Jewish self-understanding *cannot* be Zionist. Yet, however much the *neturei karta* may serve as a good indicator of the resistance among *haredim* (ultra-orthodox Jews) in Israel, they hardly constitute the majority position of the 'orthodox Jews' in Israel. Yoder appears to have no place for this view in his dialogue with Judaism.

As the preceding discussion hints at, Yoder's 'free-church' reading of the history of Jewish pacifism *overlaps* with his understanding of the role of the rabbi in the context of Jewish community and life. Not coincidentally, his account of 'the phenomenon of the rabbinate' in *The Jewish–Christian Schism Revisited* closely parallels the interpretative roles that he describes for 'Agents of Memory' in the Christian community as 'scribes of the kingdom'. Citing Matthew 13.52 – 'Every scribe who becomes a disciple of the kingdom of heaven is like a householder who brings out from his storeroom things both new and old.' – Yoder provides the following explanation of this role:

> The scribe as practical moral reasoner does not judge or decide anything, but he (or she) remembers expertly, charismatically the store of memorable, identity confirming acts of faithfulness praised and of failure repented. As we in the age after Auschwitz reread the New Testament with concern to unlearn our anti-Judaic biases, we may take it less for granted that the pejorative Gospel references to 'scribes' describes what most of the people in that leadership group in occupied Judea were actually doing then. We may then be able to recover our respect for the needfulness of the positive scribal task.[49]

While there are other roles to be played in Yoder's conception of the 'Hermeneutics of Peoplehood', the role played by such 'scribes of the kingdom' is critical. Significantly, Yoder also locates the function of worship within this role: 'Neither in the New Testament documents nor in radical Protestantism is there a discretely identifiable function called "priesthood" or a specific activity called "worship". The function which created the synagogue in central diaspora Judaism was the scribal one of reading the holy writings.'[50]

As these comments hint at, Yoder was ambivalent about the role and authority of the rabbinical (teaching) office. On the one hand, he recognized the necessity of having 'agents of memory' yet the way that he describes the 'positive scribal task' in *The Priestly Kingdom* and elsewhere is sharply circumscribed in such a way as to *rule out* most aspects of Talmud learning and many forms of Torah study.[51] In this respect, Yoder's portrayal of what it would mean to be a 'scribe of the kingdom', while envisioning an ongoing conversation within a 'priesthood of believers', is strangely abstracted from the kinds of joy, wonder, passion and playfulness that arguably can be associated with conversation about Torah that is enacted by rabbinical scholars as well as in the context of the Jewish *chevruta* or table study.

In sum: reading the holy writings of the Old Testament for Yoder is *not* a multi-faceted exercise; it is about obedience and faithfulness, disobedience (apostasy) and amendment of life. (I will have more to say about Yoder's hermeneutics of obedience in Part IV of this Afterword.) In this respect, Yoder's ever-present vigilance against the spectre of the biblical text becoming a 'wax nose' tended to foster a monological hermeneutic that sought to *limit* the range of possible meanings of the text of Scripture (when registered within the Jewish tradition). While Yoder's intent is clearly motivated by a peaceable concern, it is accomplished at the cost of eliminating the sense of delight and 'play' that Jewish readers associate with reading and keeping Torah.

B. Accepting the Lingering Burdens of Christian Supersessionism

While Yoder's essays clearly were written in the shadow of the Holocaust (see for example, p. 111 above) and in some sense this collection invites Christians to rethink their own self-understanding in the wake of the Shoah, Yoder appears to have been blind to the supersessionist *effects* of his own argument. In this respect, students of Yoder's ecclesiology need to revisit Yoder's portrayal of the problem of 'Constantinianism', which turns out not to be as complete as we might have thought.

One of the consequences of locating the 'fall of the Church in the second century' and the subsequent 'abandonment of missionary perspective on the part of Judaism'[52] – as a reaction to Christianity – is that Yoder's narrative *dislocates* the *Mishnah* from Jewish existence by characterizing it as largely defensive and there-fore implying that (for the most part) Rabbinical Judaism constitutes a mistake. Here also, Yoder appears not to have noticed the ways the 'Constantinian' legacy *may have marked his own perspective of what is central* to Judaism. For example, the practice of forcing Jews to separate Talmudic commentary from the reading of the Torah *began* in 553 CE when the emperor Justinian made an edict that prohibited Jews from reading rabbinical *midrash*. The rationale Justinian offered is worth pausing to consider: 'for it is not part of the sacred books nor is it handed down by divine inspiration through the prophets, but the handiwork of men, speaking only of earthly things and having nothing of the divine in it'.[53]

The hermeneutical logic here closely parallels Ulrich Zwingli's rejection of all 'human traditions' based on his reading of Matthew 15.3, where Jesus rebukes the Pharisees for the ways they use 'human traditions' to break God's commandments. As previously noted, Yoder's account of the 'The Authority of Tradition'[54] while far more sophisticated and cosmopolitan than that of Zwingli, nevertheless reduplicates that aspect of Zwingli's understanding of Jewish tradition. What Yoder describes as 'the form of Judaism with which we are able to converse' turns out, then, to be more of a construction than Yoder realized.[55] Sadly, Yoder's essays in *The Jewish–Christian Schism Revisited* do not display the kind of 'hermeneutics of peace' that there is good reason to believe that he displayed elsewhere in his teaching and writing.

With this problem in view, one of the issues that Christian theologians after Yoder must revisit is the extent to which the history of Christian theology and consequently the history of Christian de-legitimations of rabbinical exegesis can be told as a history of supersessionist accounts of Christian identity. A helpful first step in this regard would be to offer a critical assessment of the negative portrayals of the Talmud in particular Christian traditions, beginning with one's own. One good place for students of Yoder to begin this inquiry would be to re-examine specific features of anti-Jewish and/or supersessionist theology that arose in the context of the radical reformation. Given the polygenesis of radical reformation groups, these should not be lumped together without making necessary distinctions – as if all radical reformers were supersessionist in the same way or to the same degree. Nevertheless, some discussion of the ways early Anabaptists thought theologically about Jewish existence is needed if Yoder's account of Judaism and the 'free church vision' is going to have any continuing plausibility.[56]

The problem, then, with Yoder's argument in *The Jewish–Christian Schism Revisited* is that the hermeneutical logic that he deploys contradicts his own goal of fostering Jewish–Christian dialogue. This problem is most notable in Chapter 10 where he gives short shrift to the prospect of any kind of Jewish 'return from exile' in favour of his own view that the best narrative framework to account for Jewish existence is to be found in *galut* as the proper form of 'missionary' vocation of the Jewish people. Yoder believes that the move from Zion to Babylon 'was not a two-generation parenthesis, after which the Davidic and Solomonic project was supposed to take up again where he had left off. It was rather the beginning, under a fresh prophetic mandate, of a new phase of the Mosaic project.'[57]

According to Yoder, not only does the 'Jeremianic turn' constitute the perspective from which the 'deuteronomistic history' comes to be retold, but it also cannot be contradicted by the literature of the post-exilic context. 'What the books of Ezra and Nehemiah recount, whatever be their historicity and their relation to each other, all that happens stays well within the constraints of submission to the Gentile empire. Nothing like "kingship" or "statehood" is advocated by any party as desirable for the honour of God or the dignity of the people. Thus the reorientation of identity by the Jeremianic shift even comes back to give a new quality to the part of the story that returns to *Eretz Israel*.'[58] As this statement makes explicit, the logic of Yoder's position requires him to locate *any attempt* to include responsibility for the land of Israel within the framework of the 'Davidic Project' *not* the 'Mosaic project'.

Yoder also understands that in order for his argument to be persuasive he has to show that the books of Ezra and Nehemiah have *no real bearing* on this argument. He attempts to show that this is the case in two separate contexts in Chapter 10. Initially, he does so in a footnote to the lecture that he originally gave at Loyola Marymount University. In that context Yoder laconically stated: 'I don't think a careful reading of Ezra and Nehemiah precludes this, but that is not my present concern.'[59] What Yoder does *instead* is to gesture to the work of the early twentieth-century German playwright Stephan Zweig, whose vision of the return is metaphorical only. 'The notion of the return has its meaning not as something the people in Babylon or elsewhere should be bringing about by their own strength, or waiting around to see happen, or planning for. It is functional as metaphor for God's renewing the life of faith anywhere.'[60] Unfortunately, Yoder consistently renders Zweig's metaphor *monologically*, thereby ignoring other ways in which the metaphor of *galut* registers in the texts of the Hebrew Bible.

Later, in the section on 'Further Testing',[61] he returns to the question of what it would mean to take 'seriously the Babylonian basis of continuing Jewish identity'. Significantly, his principal agenda throughout this section is to attempt to *de-legitimate* the significance of the role of Ezra and Nehemiah in the canon of the Old Testament. After reviewing the historical critical efforts to construct linkages between historical personages mentioned in the post-exilic books of Ezra, Nehemiah, Haggai and Zechariah, Yoder concludes his survey with the following pronouncement: 'there is no story to tell; there is no narrative that goes from there to here.'[62] Here, Yoder's typology is not only over-determined but also fails to take into account not only the significant linkages that existed between the prophetic orientation of Jeremiah and the priestly vocation of Israel, but also the canonical shaping of the Hebrew Bible which ends with 2 Chronicles, 'Let him go up.'

This omission is particularly notable because Stephan Zweig's drama about Jeremiah not only provides the title for Yoder's piece but to a great extent serves as the inspirational text and narrative guide for his interpretation of the vocation of *galut* as well. As Yoder points out, the chorus that is sung in Zweig's *Jeremiah* has no 'vision of an ultimate return to geographic Jerusalem'. [63] From Yoder's point of view, then, Jewish existence after Jeremiah should be understood *solely* within the context of the people's dialogue with the Torah; the promise of land has been re-oriented in the context of Yoder's reconstructed account of Jewish peoplehood as the 'vocation' of *galut*.

By breaking *the triad* – Torah, land, and people – in this way, Yoder has constructed a conception of Jewish peoplehood that gathers around the reading and interpretation of a text 'which can be copied and read anywhere' and thereby 'enter creatively into the Jeremianic phase of creating something qualitatively new in the history of religions'.[64] By making the 'return to Zion' mythic, Yoder effectively disengages from the deeply rooted complex of Jewish theological claims that see the land of *eretz yisrael* as the locus of the sacred and thereby displaces the theological unity of election, covenant, and God's promise of redemption from exile. In effect, Yoder's conception of Judaism displaces land and/or Zion in the course of accentuating the possibilities for a *diaspora* peoplehood.

Those dealing with the problem of Christian supersessionism 'after Yoder' will need to confront the fact that Yoder's reading of the texts in question *ignores* the intricate ways in which Jewish peoplehood is narrated with the *promise of land* in view in the Talmudic conversations of the rabbinic tradition. Whereas there is abundant textual evidence for Christian peoplehood that locates what it might mean to be a 'a priestly kingdom, a royal priesthood, and a chosen nation' (1 Peter 2.9–10) in the missional context of a 'landless diaspora', those same Hebraic images register within a different range of meanings in the book of Exodus, where the promise of land is tied in integral ways to the divine instructions for how to exercise responsibility for the land of *eretz yisrael* (Exodus 19.5). Indeed some Jewish commentators on these texts have argued that responsibility for the land must be exercised in socially *transformative* ways that may entail personal suffering in the course of bringing about peace.

How do we account for Yoder's misreading of the texts in this regard? From the perspective of the Israeli scholar and peace activist Yehezkel Landau – who knew Yoder personally and greatly admires *The Politics of Jesus* – Yoder 'magnifies the prophetic dimension of Jewish vocation' and in so doing *displaces* the integral relationship of the prophetic vocation to the priestly role. From Landau's perspective, the priestly/prophetic vocation of the people of Israel 'has everything to do with sabbath, but does not make *galut* a normative existence'.[65] Landau's criticism highlights a feature of Yoder's argumentation that can be seen throughout the wider corpus of his theological writings: Yoder's way of describing the 'priestly role' of the people of God involves limits that he does not place on the roles of 'prophet', 'royal servant' and 'sage'.[66]

Christian critics have also raised questions about Yoder's tendency to regard 'priestly' practices as versions of paganism. Canadian Mennonite theologian James Reimer detects an implicit 'foundationalist rationality'[67] in Yoder's work that drives such dichotomous distinctions. Reimer questions Yoder's contention that the synagogue displaced the Temple. Contrary to Yoder, Reimer reads the Old Testament writings as providing the basis for 'a continuing hope for the restoration of the temple . . .'.[68] In this respect, Reimer believes that Yoder's thesis in *The Jewish–Christian Schism Revisited* does not adequately address theological issues that are already embedded in the New Testament witness itself (antisemitism in Acts of the Apostles, etc.). Reimer's critique leads him to raise a series of questions about Yoder's understanding of the relationship between Constantinianism and the emergence of 'theological orthodoxy' during the first five centuries of Church history.

From yet another theological perspective, Gerald Schlabach has suggested an amendment to Yoder's critique of Constantiniasm that would re-frame the constellation of issues (including questions of land) in terms of 'an even more basic problem', the Deuteronomic challenge (registered in Deut. 6–9) 'of how to receive and celebrate the blessing, the *shalom*, the good, or "the land" that God desires to give, yet to do so without defensively and violently hoarding God's blessing'.[69] On Schlabach's reading, the question at the heart of Christian identity is not unlike the problem that lies as the heart of Jewish peoplehood. 'God's very gift . . . brought with it the highest danger. For the day in which they seemed most fully to have entered the land and appropriated God's gift was actually the moment when they had proven most likely to forget the Lord, to trust and credit their own power, or to use their selective memory of God's gracious deliverance as irrevocable validation for them to possess the land in any way they chose.'[70] Schlabach's thesis opens up new ways for Yoder's students to engage the issues that Yoder was grappling with in the essays that comprise *The Jewish–Christian Schism Revisited*.

For example, in contrast to Yoder's argument in the last three chapters of this volume, Schlabach adopts a 'modified Augustinian perspective', contending that there can be no ultimate separations between the 'heavenly Jerusalem' and the 'earthy Jerusalem' precisely because 'the relationship between figurative "land", actual land, and the shalom God promises is precisely what requires discernment'.[71] Thus, for Christians *neither* the possibility of diaspora *nor* the challenge of landed-ness can be eliminated (as Yoder does). The logic of Schlabach's position enables him to raise serious questions about the Israeli government's occupation of the land of the Palestinian people without jettisoning the 'promise' of the land for Jews.

Similarly, Schlabach would encourage Christians to take seriously the important tensions that surround issues of 'liberation and responsibility', 'peaceableness and policing', 'discipline and hospitality' all of which are to be engaged dialogically.[72] In these ways, Schlabach encourages Christians to *engage* the moral challenges that they must live with and act upon. At the same time, Schlabach takes seriously that particular Christian communities will need to act within the limits of their history as they 'converse hospitably with new strangers amid life situations no community or tradition can fully anticipate'.[73] In this respect, Schlabach's approach is moving in a direction that approximates Bonhoeffer's conception of a 're-Judaized Christianity' while in its own way approximating the perspective of 'middle dis-tance' that Nicholas Lash advocates for theologies of history.

Having laid out the methodological challenges that such a 'Deuteronomic' approach would pose, Schlabach reminds his readers that the task of 'normative ecclesiology' nevertheless does – and likely will continue to – remain 'unfinished'. Deliberately using the Troeltschian 'church-sect' categories which Yoder's Constantinian thesis sought to resist, Schlabach summarizes his position this way: 'Thus the Christian community must be *kirche*-like in its inclination to enjoy and celebrate God's gift together, yet *sect*-like insofar as it understands that gift to be qualitatively different social existence. It must be *kirche*-like in its disposition to make its life available as "a people that 'enters the land,'" yet *sect*-like in its refusal to protect its gains by erecting violent military defenses.'[74] By refusing to relax the tension surrounding questions of 'land' in relation to Christian peoplehood, Schlabach succeeds in putting Christians from 'mainline' Protestant and Catholic traditions and those from radical reformation communities of faith *in the same context* of moral challenge with one another. In the process, I believe that Schlabach points us to a 'hermeneutic of peace' that is polyphonic precisely because it registers the ongoing problem of how to constitute Christian identity in relation to Jewish peoplehood within the tension between 'exile' and 'return'.

III. Post-Critical Accounts of Divine Revelation in the History of Israel and the Church

With the aforementioned problems with Yoder's argument in the essays of *The Jewish–Christian Schism Revisited* in view, it may be helpful to consider the recent work of Daniel Weiss Halivni in his book *Revelation Restored: Divine Writ and Critical Responses* (1997).[75] The comparison of Yoder's perspective with Rabbi Halivni's work is in order for several reasons. First, both Yoder and Halivni are committed to accounting for the character of Jewish disobedience prior to the exile to Babylon in reconstructing the circumstances of exilic and post-exilic Judaism. Second, both inquire after the criteria for hermeneutical judgements that have implications for how one is to regard the canon of texts that are to be authoritative. Both are also committed to seeking the 'original intent' of Torah for Jewish life and ethics, and *neither* of them would be content with arguments that attempt to resolve inconsistencies by blaming God instead of the people of God. Finally, both scholars understand the revelation of God to be *historical* and not timeless.

A. Recognizing the Shapes of the Problem

For these very reasons, Halivni's work can be very helpful in registering the vestiges of Christian supersessionism embedded in Yoder's argument. Several methodological differences should also be noted – without distorting their significance by ignoring the aforementioned similarities. First, there is a sense in which Yoder's argumentation, in effect – although it is not clear how intentionally – 'freezes' Jewish existence with the prophecy of Jeremiah, and *does not recognize* Ezra as a prophet or for that matter the canonical shape of the *Tanakh* or Old Testament as formed by the texts of the the books of Ezra, Nehemiah and 1 and 2 Chronicles. By contrast, Halivni describes the prophetic role played by Ezra in ways that make it clear that the hermeneutical trajectory of reading and the appropriation of God's revelation by the people of Israel *goes beyond* the Babylonian exile to encompass the return to the land.

> Ezra was not only the final biblical prophet; he also was the prophet in whose time the people of Israel, at long last, embraced the Torah. Moses by tradition, was the prophet of the original revelation, the medium through which God's will came to his people. But the people of Moses' time, also according to tradition were unfit and unprepared to hear the word of God. The people 'stood at a distance' as the Torah was revealed. Only in Ezra's day did the nation gather around, willing and eager to receive the written word. In this sense, the work of Ezra completes the work of Moses.[76]

Whereas Yoder contends that the post-exilic return and promulgation of the Torah by Ezra and Nehemiah *did not alter* the narrative that was established with the 'Jeremianic turn', Halivni argues (paradoxically) that to regard 'Ezra's activity as a project that he himself saw as a restoration of a pre-existing holy text enables us to account for the existence of persistent maculations [textual defects] in the holy scriptures'.[77]

With this line of argument in view, David Halivni ultimately concludes that divine revelation 'was indeed a single, unique event, endowed with unique power and authority. The Torah of the Sinai is the product of this revelation; and the Torah as canonized by Ezra . . . is not only the closest possible approximation of this original Torah, after centuries of idolatry, but is also the canon endorsed by prophetic authority. This Torah serves as the basis and inspiration of all subsequent decisions of law, and disputes arise, not because of continuous revelation of any kind, but because of the imperfection of human understanding and the lacunae of tradition.'[78] Clearly, Halivni is taking a position that is strikingly at odds with Yoder's view of the books in question. Where Yoder largely avoids discussing Ezra and Nehemiah, Halivni *builds* his argument around these books of the Hebrew Bible.

Halivni, then, provides a way of making sense of what it might mean to have a conception of Jewish peoplehood that is rendered by an ongoing conversation with an imperfect text, namely the maculate Torah. Halivni also provides a way of making sense of the 'return to the Temple' that is *more than* a mythic construction and does not preclude the possibility that there might someday be a 'return' to the temple in Jerusalem.[79] More to the point, Halivni's argument does not ignore the development of Talmud or suggest that it can be jettisoned as Yoder does. Rather it offers a way of engaging interpretive problems in the *Mishna* that face up to textual imperfections that various rabbinical authorities have struggled with over the centuries.

As the Editors' Introduction to *The Jewish–Christian Schism Revisited* explains, Yoder appeals to the canonical shape of the text to support his contentions that the 'palestinocentric reading of the story is a mistake'.[80] Given the larger framework of the Christian canon, Yoder's argument does appear to make sense within a hermeneutical horizon limited to readings of the Gospels and the Epistles of Paul, each of which appeal to the Jeremiah prophecy. Yoder's reading, however, largely ignores post-exilic literature (Ezra and Nehemiah) and flattens out the significance of Moses (by dislocating all 'priestly endeavours' as evidence for the 'Davidic project'). To borrow a phrase from Jon Levinson, Yoder does not accept the 'pluriform character' of the relationship between the covenant at Sinai and the covenant at Zion. 'In the Talmud and the Midrash, as well as in the Hebrew Bible, no single statement of the relationship suffices.'[81] On the other hand, it would appear that Yoder has chosen *not to discuss* the senses in which 'the Davidic covenant can be said to have "displaced" the Sinaitic covenant in the New Testament writings'.[82] Here is where Levinson's point about the ways in which the Christian canon 'flattens historical differences'[83] may arguably be said to apply to Yoder's own argumentation.

By contrast, Halivni's refusal to accept the rabbinical assumption of the 'contiguity of voices' in the context of midrashic reflection on Torah texts has the effect of *reintroducing* the *diachronic* element into the discussion of covenantal fidelity, an argument that in certain respects is convergent with Yoder's own understanding of the historical character of revelation. This historical-critical assessment of the sources, which as Halivni freely acknowledges does involve offering a kind of 'transcendent history', proceeds from taking seriously that 'the giving and receiving of the Torah, according to the Bible itself, were not one and the same event'.[84] This claim, in effect, *re-positions* the argument about the relationship of Jewish people-hood to the Torah within the context of human history.

The implications of Halivni's argument are congenial to some aspects of Yoder's argument even if they run counter to other theses that Yoder advocates. Halivni's work clearly has affinities with a 'hermeneutics of peace' (see section II above). Equally clearly, his work reflects a very chastened perspective about Zionism. Halivni offers a series of cautions about the *moral implications* of having inherited a text that contains errors. For example, he contends that this kind of moral awareness 'instills a sense of humility . . . Yet we cannot live without these words, and thus are doubly humbled by the knowledge that we have a history of having substituted our voice for the divine voice.' Such awareness, Halivni is careful to observe, calls for 'greater tolerance of the deviant' thereby dictating that we 'may not condemn others, or hate others or persecute them'.[85] While Halivni does not go out of his way to spell out what this might entail for Jews living in Israel, the value of his moral counsel to Israelis – in the context of their conflict with the Palestinians – should not be underestimated.

The care with which Halivni sets forth his 'double-humility' thesis is striking when juxtaposed alongside Yoder's argument. Halivni takes seriously the ever-present possibility that the people of God will (intentionally or not) seek to substitute their voice for the Word of God. As such then, the canonical narrative of Ezra and Nehemiah is not read as offering an 'end in itself' but rather it exists in a *double-voiced tension* as both witness to the eschatological ingathering as well as a warning of prematurely identifying any given word that the people of God hear with the Word of God as such. In my judgement, Halivni's argument converges at several points with the 'Deuteronomic' argument put forward by Gerald Schlabach (see above) even as it images the eschatological ingathering in ways that are different from the Augustinian 'city of God' imaged by Schlabach.

In sum, Halivni is able to account for key instances of Jewish disobedience and infidelity described in the biblical history while also displaying the constitutive power of the restoration of the Torah in the context of the *re-covenanting* of Israel brought about by Ezra and Nehemiah, which in turn enabled Israel to continue as a people. By contrast, Yoder wants to account for the former *to the exclusion* of the latter. One reason why Christian theologians should pay more attention to arguments like that of David Halivni is that it reminds us of the logical possibilities already available in the history of Talmudic debate that can be drawn upon for internal critique of Jewish peoplehood *without discarding the triadic unity* of covenant, people, and land. It might also serve as a reminder that Christians have our own contradictory history with respect to our reception of God's self-offering to us in the life, ministry, death and resurrection of Jesus Christ.

One might also say that Halivni's argument highlights the importance of 'table fellowship' (*chevruta*) as a practice, by clarifying the difference between 'reception' and revelation and thereby also situating the hermeneutic significance of rabbinical commentary for different segments of the canon of Hebrew Scripture. Interpretive decisions may have a 'pragmatic value' by fostering unity, but Halivni argues that they 'add no new divine dimension to the views they expound'.[86] The net result of Halivni's hermeneutical meditations about the complex interrelationship of written and oral Torah in the context of Jewish reading practices is to put forward an evolutionary theory of rabbinic text interpretation that accounts for the conflict between the original or plain sense (*peshat*) of Torah and the rabbinic commentary (*derash*).

Halivni's account of what it means to *read* Torah is not at all what Yoder has in mind when he describes the reading of Scripture in community. In this respect, however, it is also important to notice that Halivni's 'two-tiered theory of truth'[87] also provides for the existence of minority readings of Torah that *may stand outside* of whatever the contemporary Talmudic consensus might be, and yet enable Jewish readers to have access to the *plain sense* of the Torah. At the same time, Halivni's argument also provides a way of accounting for the *apostasy* of Israel as the people of God, and how it is nevertheless possible – in the midst of such transgressions – to retrieve the revealed truth of the Torah. In this respect, Halivni's hermeneutic might be said to be 'peaceable' in so far as he *does not attempt to eliminate readings* or otherwise stop the ongoing conversation with the text of Scripture.

B. Accepting the Burdens of Christian Supersessionism

As Peter Ochs points out, Halivni's account of what it means to read Torah can be read as an *extension and reformulation* of Yoder's approach to scriptural reading in a highly significant way. 'Halivni offers a depth-history of Second Temple and early rabbinic Judaism that complements the depth-history that Yoder offers' in his seminal essay 'Tertium Datur'.[88] That is, Halivni narrates

> a history that moves beyond the limits of the plain-sense evidence to re-imagine what we, today, are supposed to learn from the scriptural and salvation history of the people Israel. Halivni learns that the voice of God to the Jews today is displayed in the very 'maculations' that our Bible scholars believe they see in the texts of Torah as Ezra may have received them. These maculations may be received as signs to . . . contemporary Jewish readers, where a particular text or verse needs to be read more deeply, beneath the plain sense, so that, through our depth-reading, or *midrash*, we may hear in new ways what God wants of us today. What we hear will be part of God's speech to us, today, with respect to the particularity of our situation. This hearing is of God, but it is different than the 'hearing' that is offered in the written word of Torah. The written word is forever, but our hearing is for us, now. It is not, therefore, to be generalized beyond the immediate context of our reading today. 'God daily renews the words of creation' (from the rabbinic morning prayer service) and those places of maculation may deliver new words to us each day. Yoder's re-imagining of Jewish–Christian relations appears to represent such a re-hearing of God's voice through the maculations of our texts and text traditions. Halivni's caution to us may be this: to hear Yoder's call, but not freeze it. We should, in other words, hear the divine voice in Yoder's voice as it was displayed through the specific context of his hearing. We should therefore be prepared to renew our understanding of how what Yoder heard should be heard anew, and in ever-new ways, in our own contexts today and tomorrow. [89]

Halivni's hermeneutical insights also point in a different direction for how one might think about the issues of election, covenant, and promises of redemption and/or land. Indeed, the concluding paragraphs of Halivni's *Revelation Restored* calls for 'tolerance' and a sense of human fallibility that suggests that he is haunted not only by the spectre of the Holocaust but also by the possibility that Israel could *once again* engage in idolatry in the name of power and security. Halivni's ambivalent – yet committed – disposition toward the land of Israel signals the necessity of re-engaging some of the very elements that Yoder's argument occludes.

At the same time, Halivni's argument about the *theological significance* of the return to Zion (for the reception of the covenant given at Mt Sinai) and what transpired there highlights the difficulty of having a theology of the land and/or of

'Zion' that excludes 'the people of the land' (i.e., Palestinians) in such a way as to replicate some of the very evils that have been inflicted upon the people of Israel over the past twenty centuries.[90] By no means can it be said that David Halivni's argument provides unqualified support for Zionist arguments for the existence of the nation-state of Israel. Indeed, Halivni's reading arguably provides some of the very resources that would be necessary to offering powerful criticism of Zionism based on theological claims about the relationship of 'Zion' (the land) to people to Torah.

Halivni's argument in *Revelation Restored* displays a kind of non-Cartesian confidence that the Jewish tradition has resources that can be used to retrieve and/or reconstruct the textual basis for Jewish peoplehood. George Lindbeck, a post-critical theologian who also has a keen interest in the relationship of Jewish and Christian 'peoplehoods,' has noted the potential fruitfulness of this kind of 'triadic' approach to hermeneutical questions for Christian theology. In Lindbeck's judgement, David Halivni's book *Revelation Restored* 'gives Christians surprising suggestions for their own struggle with problems analogous to the Jewish ones with which David Halivni deals'.[91] One wishes that Lindbeck might have specified to which problems he judges Halivni's proposals to be most fruitfully applicable, but to date he has not published his judgements in this regard.

Among other things that Lindbeck may have in mind in this endorsement of Halivni's book are the host of hermeneutical problems that Protestant and Catholic Christians face as they emerge from the hegemony of Enlightenment and Constantinian paradigms, each of which has contributed to Christian supersession with its attendant erasure of the 'peoplehood' of Israel. Of these, the question of how we are to understand the Church as a 'people of God' is increasingly central. Lindbeck, like Yoder, grasps the importance of the analogies that exist between the 'peoplehoods' of Judaism and Christianity. However, as Lindbeck shows in *The Church in a Postliberal Age*, even if there are *ecclesiological* advantages to thinking through Christian existence 'Israelogically',[92] *the peoplehood of the one cannot be collapsed into the other*. The distinctiveness of their respective vocations and narratives of peoplehood must be preserved as these children of Abraham attempt faithfully to live out their theological understandings of covenant.

More recently, Lindbeck has commended Scott Bader-Saye's book *Church and Israel After Christendom* for 'setting the agenda for the next stage of what promises to become a major program of cooperative research . . . into the possibilities and implications of affirming without supersessionist traditionalism or reductionist progressivism that the church and Israel are one people of God'.[93] As this comment indicates, post-critical theologians like George Lindbeck share some of Yoder's interests and concerns about 'revisiting' the Jewish-Christian schism, – but they would move beyond the bifurcations that remain in Yoder's project. They would also move beyond Yoder's (Cartesian) tendency to historical foundationalism, or overstating our ability to recapture the 'essence' of Christianity in its founding years.

IV. The Politics of Election: Can Christians and Jews Share One Covenant?

With all of these concerns in view it is not unreasonable for Christians to be groping for their bearings. 'How do we know where we are – or who we are?' To recall Nicholas Lash's answer, to set our gaze on 'the middle-distance' (which he felicitously describes as doing theology 'on the way to Emmaus'), involves *resisting* disjunctive reasoning.[94] This does not mean that we disacknowledge those features of the tradition that have been corrupted, but it also does not mean that we treat all features of the tradition as *equally* corrupt. As an English-speaking Catholic, Lash is by no means unaware of the ways in which the tradition of the Church has been distorted (in Britain and elsewhere) by Protestants and Catholics alike, but he also knows that it is a grave illusion for any generation to act as if its thoughts have *not been* 'shaped by the tradition which precedes and constitutes it'.[95] While confident, Lash's approach is appropriately modest. If he dares to affirm the *possibility* of historical understanding, he also cautions that the understanding that we have is at one and the same time *provisional* and *unstable*.[96]

With respect to the problem of Christian supersessionism, I believe that this entails that we re-think how the doctrine of peoplehood and the doctrine of revelation are to be correlated. We dare not claim that we have fully comprehended God's self-revelation, and this begins with the very idea of fulfilment (*pleroma*) in the New Testament letters.[97] Rather, we must take seriously that in the context of our unfaithfulness, we have not heard all that God has to say to us about what it means to be 'a people in the world'. And we must also take seriously that we have much that we can learn from contemporary Jews about how to hear the polyphony of voices in the texts of the Jewish and Christian Scriptures. These are not courses of action that Yoder appears to have thought were necessary to take, and the reason turns out to have everything to do with the significance that Yoder assigned to a single text of the New Testament: Romans 9–11.

A. Learning to Recognize the Shapes of the Problem of Christian Supersessionism

Indeed, one of the most striking features of Yoder's essays on *The Jewish–Christian Schism Revisited* is *how little* a role Romans 9–11 plays in his argument. In fact, Yoder's primary interest in these chapters of the Letter to the Romans is to *refute* what he regards to be anti-Jewish readings of Paul's Letters.

> Neither the ancient claim of institutional and legal supersessionism stretching from the apologetic fathers through medieval Catholicism nor the specific Lutheran way of seeing Christ as the 'end of the law' is fair to what is really being said in Galatians and Romans. What Paul sees happening in Christ and the Christian Church, like what Jesus had said in Matthew, is the fulfilment and not the abolition of the meaning of Torah as covenant of grace. 'Fulfilment' is a permanently open border between what came before and what comes next. Whenever a Jew says that the Messianic age has not yet come, he or she is saying

as well that it might come. That means that such a Jew can never say *a priori* that anyone's statement that the Messianic age has come is unthinkable, but only that it has not yet been demonstrated.

Fulfilment must also be an open border from 'this side'. Christians must continue to be claiming as Paul did that Jesus whom they follow is to be interpreted to Jews as the one to whom they still look forward. Christians gave up their messianic claim in its most authentic and original form not when they adjusted to the postponement of the Second Coming (a development which had already begun in apostolic times) but when they renounced their claims regarding the first coming and the Jews: i.e., when they granted to the non-messianic synagogue that it had the right to exclude them, and then went on to give further occasion for the rebuilding of other barriers by forsaking the dietary compromises that had originally been accepted, and by sliding culturally into an increasing Romanization and Hellenization.[98]

This passage, which appears near the end of Chapter 3, 'Paul the Judaizer', might very well be said to be the heart of Yoder's argument in *The Jewish–Christian Schism Revisited*.

Here, Yoder comes closer than ever to saying that there is a *single* covenant shared by Jews and Christians, but it is also clear that the significance of Torah is being re-described in a way that also re-shapes what the covenant with Israel is understood to be. The notion of fulfilment that he puts forward (based on his reading of Ephesians 2), which he imaged as a *'permanently open border between what came before and what came next'*, conveys the strong sense of 'voluntariness' that he ascribes to Jews and Christians alike. At the same time, *the way Yoder deploys the term* 'fulfilment' (in opposition to abolition of the law) also functions to delimit the identity of authentic or 'true' Judaism. Simultaneously, then, Yoder is opening 'the border' between Christianity and Judaism even as he *re-locates* the centre of identity for Jews (in effect re-describing membership in synagogues as 'voluntary') in a way that frames the conversation as 'messianic' by definition. Here, I believe, Yoder's *neo-neo-supersessionism* is most evident.

It is precisely this (re-)description of Judaism that informs Yoder's argumentation in Chapter 8. There Yoder re-locates 'Jerusalem' within the context of a 'transcendence that is appropriated to state the claims for one's own sovereignty and possessiveness'.[99] Here again we recognize another example of the ways Yoder attempted to resolve a dualism of the celestial and terrestial 'Jerusalem' by *ruling out one set of meanings* in favour of another possibility that he introduces. While this reading is utterly consistent with his understanding of how the 'children of Abraham' are constituted (as he argued in *The Original Revolution*), the way Yoder ultimately resolves this conundrum is to invoke the hermeneutic principle of obedience. In sum, the criterion of judgement for whether the 'appropriation is a legitimate act of faith or an usurpation is not whether the claim to "celestial authority" is "literal" or not' but whom it excludes or expels: whether our enemies are God's enemies or God's children.[100]

What Yoder is doing is not unlike the way sixteenth-century Anabaptists went about interpreting the Bible. Indeed, like Hans Denck and other early Anabaptist leaders, Yoder concludes his discussion of the 'mislocated' dualism by correlating *obedience* with *knowledge*. 'Those people are qualified to work at the building of the city who build it for others, who recognize it as not their own turf but God's.'[101] Indeed, the way Yoder resolves this question has the same logical structure as the Anabaptist principle of interpretation that he himself identified nearly four decades before in his seminal article on 'Anabaptist Hermeneutics': 'Only he who is committed to the direction of obedience can read the truth so as to interpret it in line with the direction of God's purposes.'[102]

In other words, according to Yoder, those Jews and Christians who have voluntarily *committed* themselves to reconciling with their enemies (arising out of a vocational sense of who God has called them to be as a people in the world) are in the best position to know the true meaning of texts such as Galatians 4.26 or Jeremiah 29.7. When this kind of position is taken within the horizon of a doctrine of the perspicuity of Scripture (to which Yoder as an heir of the Anabaptist tradition subscribes), it results in the kind of dichotomized reading of texts that ultimately is not peaceable precisely because it eliminates ambiguities in the text at the cost of the very identity of the ones to whom the text ostensibly refers.[103]

Further, the way that Yoder goes about affirming the 'Abrahamic model' as constitutive for Jews and Christians alike involves narrating the history of Jewish peace witness in a way that is determined by the Anabaptist tradition. As a result, the very coherence of the vocation of the Jewish people turns out to be reliant upon 'the free church vision'. The immodesty of Yoder's narrative can be measured by the fact that he virtually ignores the biblical vision of Israel as the elect people of God affirmed in the Scriptures of the Old Testament and reaffirmed in Romans 9–11 by the apostle Paul. Here, Lash's counsel about the *provisionality* and *instability* of the 'middle-distance' perspective is useful to bring into view again. According to Lash, it is precisely when we forget that our very categories have been 'shaped by the tradition that precedes us' that we are most likely to err in our attempt to offer theologies of history. Yoder's apparent failure to take the measure of the limitations of the Anabaptist tradition of hermeneutics leads him to be blind to the displacing effects of those same categories of reasoning.

This way of explaining the problem accounts, in part, for what turns out to be the *neo-neo-supersessionism* of Yoder's project. In no sense, does Yoder seek to replace Judaism with Christianity in the punitive sense of classical Christian supersessionism. Neither does he engage in the kind of displacement and erasure of Judaism that modernist Protestant theologians sought in what in retrospect appears to be a form of *neo-supersessionism*. But in seeking a way for Jews and Christians to share a common witness for peace, Yoder slips into a form of *neo*-neo-supersessionism that, in effect, *erases* the covenantal basis of Jewish peoplehood even as it attempts to *redescribe* Jewish identity within the framework of the 'new covenant' of Jesus.

B. Accepting the Burdens of the Problem of Christian Supersessionism

Is it possible for Protestant Christians to do Christian ecclesiology from the 'middle-distance' perspective advocated by Catholics and Anglicans? I believe it is, and to some extent, I would argue that this is already being done. For example, in his aforementioned book, Scott Bader-Saye offers a very promising 'post-Christendom' account of the relation of Israel and the Church that looks to 'Abraham' as an alternative to the conception of the Church as a *polis*. Although Bader-Saye cites

Yoder's work only in a few places, his emphasis on the 'peoplehoods' of Israel and the Church is certainly consonant with Yoder's argument in so far as God is to be known *in relation* to (not apart from) 'the particularity of God's chosen ones,' namely Israel, Christ, and Church.[104]

Unlike Yoder, however, Bader-Saye pays careful attention to Jewish theological views about election, covenant and promised redemption to support his 'post-Christendom' ecclesiology.[105] In fact, he explicitly endorses Yoder's view that 'the call to "deconstantinize" [the Church] must be paired with a call to "re-Judaize"' Christianity.[106] Contrary to Yoder's position, however, Bader-Saye argues: 'By returning to its roots in the people of Israel, the church can recover a doctrine of election that is not mere information . . . but rather formation, or better yet, conformation to the ways of the triune God.'[107] Bader-Saye's argument promises to provide a more fruitful way for Jews and Christians to engage one another's respective 'peoplehoods' with the awareness of what they share while retaining a healthy awareness of the provisionality and instability of the middle-distance perspective.

To clear the way for this 'post-Christendom' narration of Christian peoplehood, Bader-Saye offers a revisionist reading of the Christian tradition that highlights the significance of the Reformed tradition of John Calvin and Karl Barth, both of whom are noteworthy for their refusal to accept the Constantinian 'repudiation of Israel'.[108] His assessment of the legacies of supersessionist Christian theology and modernity leads Bader-Saye to call for renewed attention to Israel as 'God's politics'. This includes a renunciation of the 'idolatry of voluntarism' – an overemphasis on the 'unbounded' freedom of the individual in Christian theological ethics that makes freedom the content of the moral life. Overcoming the distortions of freedom in Christianity after Christendom, Bader-Saye argues, will entail that Christians 'listen again to Israel's witness' and thereby revisit the 'de-Judaization of Christianity' that resulted in polarization of the free sovereignty of God and the free will of humankind.[109] Here, we see an example of what it would mean to seriously re-engage the tradition in a way that can help Protestants remove the blinders that have kept us from reclaiming the relationship of the doctrine of peoplehood and the doctrine of revelation.

According to Bayer-Saye, then, 'Abraham' gestures toward Israel as the paradigm example of 'a people whose very existence constitutes the reign of God'.[110] He argues that the Pauline language of the 'new covenant' should not be seen as a 'replacement or a parallel covenant but as a living covenant that embraces two peoples in a relationship of tense reciprocity'.[111] Here, the tension between Jewish and Christian conceptions of covenant is embraced, not collapsed, despite the important disagreements that surround how the 'visibility' of redemption is to be displayed in human history. Bader-Saye concludes: 'The calling of the church today, post-Christendom and post-Holocaust, is to embody again the politics of the redeemed people of God, a politics of peace and plenty, of fellowship between Jew and Gentile.'[112] In order for Christians to live out this vocation, we must practise a politics that not only recognizes the ongoing existence of Jews as part of our theology of history, but also accepts the burdens of learning *from Jews* some of what it might mean to be the people of God, if – as we want to continue to claim – Abraham is our father.

Conclusion

Yoder was not unaware of the 'burdens' associated with re-reading history theologically. Indeed, such recognition prompted him to argue that historians should discipline their readings of the past with a 'mandatory axiomatic nonviolence'.[113] I would like to think that the 'middle-distance' counsels that I have offered students of Yoder's work in this essay are convergent with the aspiration to have a disciplined approach to our attempts to offer a Christian theology of history, but there is no question that the investigative trajectories that I have traced in this essay go well beyond what Yoder would have done. The question of how we understand the character of the problem of Christian supersessionism accounts for the difference.

As the foregoing discussion suggests, I believe it is a mistake to think that the ecclesiological problem of Christian supersessionism can be viewed as a past-tense monolithic structure of thought that can be safely isolated from the present – or the future. Indeed, 'the claim that the church has replaced Israel as God's people chosen for the salvation and blessing of the world'[114] must be recognized as having had *multiple effects* throughout Christian history, only some of which have been discerned at any given point in time. In this respect, I argue that Christians must come to grips with the multifaceted character of Christian supersessionism, understood *as a pluriform structure of memory*, which in turn has fostered a peculiar kind of Christian imagination across the centuries about *what it does and does not mean* to be the Church, and *what it does and does not mean* to be a Christian.

In offering this assessment of Yoder's *The Jewish–Christian Schism Revisited*, I join other contemporary theologians – Anabaptist and/or 'baptist' as well as various 'evangelical catholics' with Anabaptist sympathies – who are paying tribute to Yoder's lifework by *extending* the conversation that he broached during his lifetime.[115] Such initiatives, I believe, are fully in keeping with John Howard Yoder's own disciplined practice as a historical theologian. Yoder's contention that the Jewish–Christian schism 'did not have to be' constitutes a thesis that Christians *must continue to test* in our own circumstance if we are going to engage the problem of supersessionism.

To that end, students of Yoder's ecclesiology need to investigate the ways in which the problem of Christian supersessionism – like the problem of Constantianization, which Yoder himself taught us can take shape within a *variety* of different socio-historical configurations[116] – should be seen as embedded within a variety of Christian reading practices, rhetorical strategies, and ethical behaviours that can be (re-)configured in new patterns in diverse historical and ecclesial contexts. By analogy, therefore, the 'disavowal' of Christian supersessionism will continue to be an ongoing struggle for Christians and Jews alike.

In that sense, I do not believe that it is possible for Christian theologians to escape the problem of Christian supersessionism.[117] I do believe, however, that we do not have to succumb to despair in this matter. Like Nicholas Lash et al., I trust that we are not left with only two options in this matter: we can also do our theology of history from the perspective of 'the middle-distance'. While we are not able to transcend supersessionism once and for all, neither do we have to resign ourselves to wallowing in the problem. So what can we do?

1. We can re-engage the problem by making better hermeneutical distinctions

about what we are doing in construing the writings of Hebrew Scriptures for Christian self-understanding, and in doing so we can learn better ways to identify the Church with Israel. One of those Christian theologians whose work has been helpful in this regard is George Lindbeck. In his response to the essays of *Christianity in Jewish Terms*, Lindbeck offers a helpful distinction between 'expropriation' and 'appropriation' that points the way forward for Christian self-understanding. Believing that 'The church's effort to identify itself with Israel need not lead to supersessionism,' [118] Lindbeck challenges contemporary Christians to reappropriate the Jewish heritage of Christianity. But Lindbeck is fully aware of the fact that if 'reappropriation without expropriation' is going to take place, it will require that Christians grasp the full significance of the challenge that 'pluralistic consumerism' poses for Christians and Jews alike.[119] By way of illustration, Lindbeck identifies some of the rabbinical hermeneutic strategies as valuable for post-Christendom churches: 'Consider, for example, the talmudic practice of juxtaposing contrary opinions as authoritative instead of blandly harmonizing or brutally rejecting one or the other as Christians have usually done.'[120]

2. Expanding on Lindbeck's suggestive remarks, I also suggest that Christian theologians *after* Yoder adopt the kind of 'hermeneutic of peace' that is fostered by learning to read Scripture polyphonically, a practice that in itself might do much to enable Christians to learn to think 'in Jewish terms' about what it means to be disciples of Jesus Christ. These two issues alone constitute a significant set of challenges for Christian theologians of all varieties. Indeed, there are no *a priori* answers that we can give to resolve these two sets of conundrums. Both require that we critically evaluate the reading practices that have informed our ecclesiological modes of reflection. Both invite us to explore what it might mean to engage in the kind of 'scriptural reasoning' that continues to be practised within the context of the Jewish tradition, and thereby to rethink how we have thought about Christian identity in the context of notions of 'fulfilment'. Both provide the opportunity to *extend* Yoder's project while taking into account those aspects of his ecclesiology that limited his own best efforts to *disavow* the complex and conflicted legacy of supersessionism in the history of Christianity, East and West.

3. This set of challenges also requires a different account of the 'authority of tradition' than Yoder provided in his book *The Priestly Kingdom* and elsewhere. This is a concern that brings us back to the issue of distance and proximity that I broached at the outset of this essay in the context of discussing Yoder's theology of history in *The Jewish–Christian Schism Revisited*. If my reading of the way the Anabaptist tradition shaped Yoder's perspective is accurate, then more was going on in Yoder's argument than he realized. The historical overview that he offers of the Jewish–Christian schism accounts for too much at the same time that it pays too little attention to the everyday world of contemporary Jewish–Christian engagement.

By contrast, the wisdom of Lash's 'middle-distance' perspective is not to be found in some kind of artificial constructed *via media*. Rather, it derives from paying close attention to the ways the eternal mystery of God is 'temporally transcribed in particular events . . .'. Or as Lash also puts it, it involves taking into consideration 'the entire exceedingly complex range of factors and conditions that constitute the problem of "distance" and "proximity", of "absence" and "presence", in historical and social existence'.[121] Paying close attention to 'the shape of living' (to borrow a

phrase from David F. Ford's book by the same title), requires that we simultaneously attend to the patterns of social interaction in everyday life while remembering
God's active presence in the midst of human history. This requires hope as well as
humility.

4. Finally, those of us doing Christian theology 'after Yoder' will need to face
squarely the implications of what it means to claim that Christians share in the
covenant of God to whom the Jewish people bear witness. This challenge is by no
means straightforward. Indeed, in some sense, it will no doubt involve a kind of
'double-orientation' not unlike what Dietrich Bonhoeffer was attempting to
describe in his *Letters and Papers from Prison*. To Jewish ears, the Christian claim
that we share the covenant of Israel with God makes little sense without reference
to specific practices (Sabbath observance, etc.). For the most part, then, what it
might mean for Christians to share particular practices with Jews while also living
as Christian disciples is something still to be discerned. One promising place where
we can begin is in *chevrutot* or 'table studies' where practising Christians and Jews
(and Muslims) gather to read Scripture texts together in the context of what has
come to be called the practice of 'scriptural reasoning'. However provisional and
unstable such 'tents of meeting' may be, such encounters are none the less possible
as we attempt to discern – in the 'middle-distance' – a renewed fellowship between
those peoples who recognize 'Abraham' as their 'father' albeit in different ways for
different reasons that are even expressed in diverse languages.

Such gatherings will also serve, I believe, as a continuing reminder to those of us
who are Christians that another ongoing challenge is for us to provide accounts of
Christian peoplehood that *avoid* using *misplaced icons* of Christian identity (see
Appendix B) that have the effect of eviscerating the theological bases of Jewish
identity and peoplehood. To continue to offer explicitly Christian theologies of
history while taking seriously the difficulty of using icons of Jewish peoplehood will
require that we learn to recognize new shapes of the problem of Christian supersession. For students of Yoder's work, this is part of what we need to accept as the
burdens and discipline of offering 'evangelical revisionist' readings of history. To
invoke Yoder's own words from another context, 'the only way to see how this will
work will be to see how this will work'.[122] It remains to be seen whether those who
dare to claim to be 'the children of Abraham' want the ancient schism to continue.[123]

Notes

1. Nicholas Lash, *Theology on the Way to Emmaus*, London: SCM Press, 1986, 71.
2. That Yoder saw a deep connection between his 'evangelical revisionist' approach
to history and his thesis that the Jewish–Christian schism did not have to be is demonstrated by his discussion of that issue in his essay, 'The Burden and Discipline of
Evangelical Revisionism' in *Nonviolent America: History Through the Eyes of Peace*,
ed., Louise Hawkey and James C. Juhnke, Cornelius H. Wedel Historical Series 5, North
Newton, KS: Bethel College, 1993, 27–8.
3. The notion of what it might mean to adopt the perspective of 'the middle-
distance' on any given social reality appears to have been originally developed by the
philosopher J. P. Stern, *On Realism*, London: Routledge & Kegan Paul, 1973, 120ff. I
have found David F. Ford's work to offer the best definition of this concept for

theological purposes. As Ford puts it: 'The middle distance is the focus which best does justice to the ordinary social world of people in interaction. It portrays them acting, talking, suffering, thinking and involved in institutions, societies and networks of relationships over time; in general, this perspective renders . . . the detail of how things are.' The perspective and the content are together. 'If one moves too close and allows the dominant perspective to become, for example, one person's inner world or stream of consciousness, then the middle distance has been supplanted. Likewise, if one takes too broad an overview and subsumes the particular people, words and interactions into a generalization, trend, or a theory, the middle distance loses its own integrity and becomes, at best, evidence or supportive illustration. . . [I]t is a matter of primacy and balance, which writers as diverse as the Evangelists, Iris Murdoch, and Thomas Mann all observe in various ways.' David Ford, *Self and Salvation: BeingTransformed*, New York: Cambridge University Press, 1999, 116, n. 9. Ford is quoting his own defnition of middle distance from his earlier article, 'System, Story, Performance: A Proposal about the Role of Narrative in Christian Systematic Theology' in *Why Narrative? Readings in Narrative and Theology*, ed., Stanley Hauerwas and L. Gregory Jones, Grand Rapids, MI: Eerdmans, 1989, 195.

4. Lash, *Theology on the Way to Emmaus*, 64. Lash is referring to two different letters that John Henry Cardinal Newman wrote. The first was written in response to a query from a reader of his *Essay on the Development of Doctrine* (1845) as found in *The Diaries and Letters of John Henry Cardinal Newman* XI, ed., C. S. Dessain, Thomas Nelson and Sons, 1961, 69. The second letter was written two decades later, but it uses the same imagery of the middle-distance perspective. For the latter correspondence, see *The Letters and Diaries of John Henry Cardinal Newman XXIII* , Oxford: Clarendon Press, 1973, 227.

5. Lash, *Theology on the Way to Emmaus*, 219, n. 14. In this respect, Lash's use of the notion of the 'middle-distance' is *not the same* as J. P. Stern's usage. As he observes in a note: 'My use of the metaphor is ethical, prescriptive, in a way that I take Stern's not to be. Nevertheless the two uses are not, perhaps, quite alien to each other. It could be that "realism" (in Stern's sense) in our telling the story of Jesus the Christ is an important factor in enabling Christians to sustain that "middle distance" (in my sense) hold on memory and expectation that I am advocating.' Elsewhere in that same volume, Lash notes that taking this kind of ethical perspective means that we refuse the 'stark options' we find ourselves presented: 'either unwarranted metaphysical assertion or unrestrained relativism; either 'absolute knowledge' or 'mere belief' (65).

6. See Peter Ochs' commentary on 'wonders' at the end of Yoder's preface and first chapter, above pp. 38–9, 67.

7. See Peter's Ochs' commentary on 'burdens' at the end of Yoder's preface and first chapter, above pp. 39–40 and 67–8.

8. Stanley Hauerwas and Alex Sider, *Introduction to Preface to Theology: Christology and Theological Method*, Grand Rapids, MI: Brazos Press, 2002, 20.

9. One of Yoder's fullest explorations of this question is his essay 'The Hermeneutics of the Anabaptists' in *Mennonite Quarterly Review* 41, 1967, 306–7. See also Sider and Hauerwas introductory essay for their commentary about the significance of Yoder's reading practices.

10. Lindbeck, 'What of the Future? A Christian Response' in *Christianity in Jewish Terms*, ed., Tikva Frymer-Kensky, David Novak, Peter Ochs, David Fox Sandmel and Michael A. Signer, Denver, CO: Westview Press, 2000, 360.

11. John Howard Yoder, *The Original Revolution: Essays on Christian Pacifism*, Scottdale, PA: Herald Press, 1971, 27–8.

12. *The Original Revolution*, 28–9.

13. *The Original Revolution*, 28–9.

14. *The Original Revolution*, 27–31. Here Yoder offers a précis of an argument that he later expanded into *The Politics of Jesus* in the chapter on 'The Possibility of a Messianic Ethic'.

15. *The Original Revolution*, 85–104. This essay was drawn from class lectures in his course on 'Christian attitudes to War, Peace and Revolution' taught at Associated Mennonite Biblical Seminaries in Elkhart, IN.

16. *The Original Revolution*, 85.

17. *The Original Revolution*, 88.

18. *The Original Revolution*, 89–90.

19. *The Original Revolution*, 91.

20. *The Original Revolution*, 93.

21. *The Original Revolution*, 101.

22. *The Original Revolution*, 103–4.

23. I am indebted to Stanley Hauerwas for helping me to make this point more clearly. The objection to the disembodiment of Jewish identity and the counterargument to the 'spiritual criterion' of faith put forward by liberal theologians has been articulated most forcefully in Michael Wyschogrod's study, *The Body of Faith: God in the People Israel*, New York: Harper & Row, 1983, xv.

24. Douglas Harink, See chapter 4, 'Israel: Who Will Bring Charge Against God's Elect', of the forthcoming book *Paul Among the Theologians: Pauline Theology Beyond Christendom and Modernity*, Brazos Press, 2003, pp. 201–2.

25. Harink, *Paul Among the Theologians*, p. 174.

26. Dietrich Bonhoeffer, *Letters and Papers from Prison* enlarged edition, New York: Collier Books and London: SCM Press, 1972, 282. Cited in Soulen, *The God of Israel and Christian Theology*, Minneapolis: Augsburg/Fortress, 1996, 18. Soulen adds the emphasis in the sentence in italics.

27. I am indebted for much, if not all, of this construal of Bonhoeffer's life in terms of 'polyphonic living' to the remarkable and penetrating study by David F. Ford, *Self and Salvation: Being Transformed*, particularly chapter 10, 241–65.

28. *Self and Salvation*, 262.

29. Ford's commentary at this point is entirely focused on the letter Bonhoeffer wrote to Eberhard Bethge on 21 July 1944.

30. *Self and Salvation*, 260–61.

31. I make no claims to providing an exhaustive listing of the theologians who have engaged Yoder's argument, but I will mention five that I think are particularly noteworthy. James Reimer's essay 'Theological Orthodoxy and Jewish Christianity' published in the *Wisdom of the Cross* collection of essays in honour of John Howard Yoder (430–48) was one of the first studies that I know of to contend with Yoder's theses in *The Jewish-Christian Schism Revisited* essays.

In *Witness* the third volume of James William McClendon's Systematic Theology, Nashville, TN: Abingdon, 2000, McClendon leans heavily on Yoder's *Revisited* theses at several points, including in Chapter Nine where he offers his 'Theology of Witness,' (see 46–7, 373–83), to articulate what it means for Christians to be a 'people of God' along with eschatological Israel.

At least four papers presented at the March 2002 Conference on 'The Theological Legacy of John Howard Yoder' focused on Yoder's essays on *The Jewish–Christian Schism Revisited*: David Burrell, 'An Ecumenical and Interfaith Reading of the Theology of John Howard Yoder'; Duane K. Friesen, 'Yoder and the Jews: Cosmopolitan

Homelessness as Ecclesial Model'; Alain Epp Weaver, 'On Exile: Yoder, Said, and a Theology of Land and Return'; and Doug Harink, 'The Anabaptist and the Apostle: John Howard Yoder as a Pauline Theologian'. These four papers are to be published in the forthcoming proceedings of the conference.

32. Alain Epp Weaver, 'Constantinianism, Zionism, Diaspora: Towards a Political Theology of Exile and Return', *Mennonite Central Committee Occasional Paper* 28 (I will be citing from the text available in the on-line version of Weaver's published essay.). This paper was originally presented at the October 2001 Mennonite Central Committee Conference on Peace Theology held in Winnipeg, Canada, 1–24.

33. Weaver, 'Constantinianism, Zionism, Diaspora', 12. As Weaver calls attention to later in his paper, at least one American Jewish theologian has publically drawn parallels between Constantinianism and Zionism in describing what he calls 'Constantinian Judaism'. 'Like Christianity in its Constantinian phase, Constantinian Judaism orients its texts and memory, and with that its religious rituals and intellectual endeavors, to serving the state, legitimating power, arguing in moral terms for policies that displace and disorient others, and silencing dissent.' Marc Ellis, 'On the Future of Judaism and Jewish Life', unpublished paper presented at the conference 'Judaism, Christianity, and Islam: The Next Fifty Years', sponsored by the Department of Theology and the Center for American and Jewish Studies, Baylor University, held in Birmingham, England, 11 Dec. 2000. Cited in Weaver, 'Constantinianism, Zionism, Diaspora', n. 76.

34. 'Constantinianism, Zionism, Diaspora', 3.

35. 'Constantinianism, Zionism, Diaspora', ms. p. 9. Cf. p. 5 for a slightly different wording.

36. 'Constantinianism, Zionism, Diaspora', 18, see n. 31.

37. See the outline of Gerald Schlabach's comments in response to Alain Epp Weaver's paper given at the Peace Theology conference in October 2001.

38. I am grateful to Prof. Schlabach for sharing a copy of his outline of a response to Alain Epp Weaver's paper with me and for his permission for to quote it for the purposes of my argument in this paper.

39. Hauerwas and Sider, 'Introduction' to *Preface to Theology*, 23–4.

40. Dyadic juxtapositions proliferate throughout these essays: Constantinian vs. Free-Church forms of Christianity, the Davidic Project vs. the Jeremianic turn, the 'palestinocentric reading' of Jewish history that highlights the return to Zion versus the exilic historiography that produces the story of the Tower of Babel as an exemplar of what it means to live in *galut*.

41. Stanley Hauerwas, *With the Grain of the Universe*, Grand Rapids, MI: Brazos Press, 2001. Hauerwas broaches this argument at the end of he first chapter (37–41) but develops it fully in the eighth chapter (205–41) of his Gifford Lectures for 2001.

42. Yoder presented this paper at Washington University in 1992, a conference to which Yoder may have been invited in part because of his relationship with Schwarzschild.

43. See Ch. 9 in this volume, p. 171.

44. Ch. 9, p. 170.

45. Ch. 9, p. 170.

46. Ch. 9, pp. 170–1.

47. John Howard Yoder, *Nevertheless: Varieties of Religious Pacifism*, revised and expanded edn., Scottdale, PA: Herald Press, 1992, 125.

48. See Ch. 9 in this volume, pp. 174–5.

49. Yoder, 'The Hermeneutics of Peoplehood' in *The Priestly Kingdom*, 30.

50. *The Priestly Kingdom*, 31.

51. Here I am reminded of a passage in Vanessa Ochs's book *Words On Fire: One Woman's Journey into the Sacred*, Boulder, CO: Westview Press, 1999, 336–7. Ochs uses a metaphor not unlike the one Yoder deploys when she describes her own ongoing struggle as a Jewish woman (with feminist convictions and concerns) with reading Torah. She describes the contents of the bottom drawer of her jewellery box where she 'stores the curious assortment of items I call the 'flat treasures'.

> Although the flat treasures don't tell the whole story or even key parts of it, they do tell something. I still go through them, sometimes discovering critical clues they contain. Sometimes meanings get belatedly unraveled. . . . Sometimes the meanings shift.
>
> This, in part explains why I keep going back to the difficult texts in Torah: *leyning* (chanting) them, studying them, teaching them. I understand the meaning of one's treasures is not always clear or even partially apparent. Still, I understand that if there was a meaning to them once and a rationale for being cherished, important meanings could return. (337)

Ochs does not intend to over-generalize her account of what it means for her as a Jewish woman to read Scripture. Rather, she simply describes this as a 'keeping on confronting it' approach.

52. See Ch. 7 in this volume, p. 152.

53. Nahum M. Sarna, 'The Authority and Interpretation of Scripture in Jewish Tradition' in *Understanding Scripture: Explorations of Jewish and Christian Traditions of Interpretation*, ed., Clemens Thoma and Michael Wyschogrod, Mahwah, NJ: Paulist Press, 1987, 11.

54. Yoder, *The Priestly Kingdom*, 69.

55. See Ch. 7 in this volume, p. 155.

56. As it is, he makes but one passing comment about the 'more profound' form of philo-semitic neo-reformation theology that regards the election of the Jews to remain in effect (Ch. 7, p. 149), but even there he goes out of his way to make sure that he regards this view as also having been shaped by the Constantinianization of Christianity. In particular, Yoder could have discussed the conversations associated with Pilgram Marpeck who (with the Apostles' Creed in view) theorized that the reason that Jesus had to descend to the dead was because Abraham and his descendents (i.e., Jews) of the Old Covenant had to be given an opportunity to hear the gospel that they had anticipated. This Anabaptist need to account (synchronically) for how God made it possible for Jesus to 'preach' to those captives arguably has certain analogies to Yoder's own 'presentist' conception of Jewish–Christian witness and/or dialogue. Had Yoder focused attention to this aspect of the radical reformation tradition, he might also have found it necessary to give more of an account of the relationship between the 'old' and 'new' covenants which in turn would have forced him to confront other omissions from his argument.

57. See Ch. 10 in this volume, p. 184.

58. Ch. 10, p. 188.

59. Ch. 10, p. 196, n. 6. Yoder avoids offering his own reasoned argument for this claim by alluding to the work of Daniel Smith Christopher (a student and associate of his friend Steven S. Schwarzschild, who was one of the hosts of the Loyola Conference at which Yoder's paper was originally presented), but this does not suffice as an answer.

60. See Ch. 10 in this volume, p. 184.

61. Ch. 10, see argument on p. 193–4.

62. Ch. 10, p. 202, n. 55.

63. Ch. 10, pp. 184–5.

64. Ch. 10, p. 187.

65. See conversation with the author following Yehezkel Landau's lecture on 'Exile and Homecoming' at Tantur Ecumenical Institute for Advanced Theological Studies, Jerusalem, 26 June 2001.

66. Here it is useful to note that Yoder consistently downplays the priestly nature of Christian and Jewish peoplehoods. For a particularly visible example of this compare the treatment that Yoder gives to prophecy, discernment, and servanthood as opposed to the 'priestly role' in his account of peoplehood in *A Declaration on Peace: In God's People the World's Renewal Has Begun* the book he co-authored with Douglass Gwynn, Eugene Roop and George Hunsinger, Scottdale, PA: Herald Press, 1991, especially 21–5.

67. James Reimer, 'Theological Orthodoxy and Jewish Christianity' in *The Wisdom of the Cross: Essays in Honor of John Howard Yoder*, Grand Rapids, MI: Eerdmans, 1999, 432.

68. Reimer, 'Theological Orthodoxy and Jewish Christianity', 446. Reimer also cites John W. Miller who regards Yoder's 'pejorative brushing asides of the whole second temple period portrayed in Ezra and Nehemiah' to be 'mind-boggling' (444–5).

69. Gerald Schlabach, 'Deuteronomic or Constantinian: What is the Most Basic Problem for Christian Social Ethics?' in *The Wisdom of the Cross*, 451.

70. Schlabach, 'Deuteronomic or Constantinian', 451.

71. 'Deuteronomic or Constantinian', 463. Here I use the language of Yoder's title for Chapter 8 for illustrative purposes. I do not mean to imply that Schlabach explicitly invoked this terminological distinction. Nevertheless, I do think that the position that he argues is consistent with the point that I am making.

72. 'Deuteronomic or Constantinian', 463–8.

73. 'Deuteronomic or Constantinian', 468, n. 32.

74. 'Deuteronomic or Constantinian', 470–71.

75. Daniel Weiss Halivni, *Revelation Restored: Divine Writ and Critical Responses*, Boulder, CO: Westview Press,1997. Interested readers will want to consult Peter Ochs's introductory essay to Halivni's book, 'Foreword: Revelation Restored *as Post-Critical Theology*', xi–xviii. There, they will discover a post-critical Jewish use of Halivni's work in ways that would support but also extend Yoder's project to foster a non-supersessionist Christian theology of the people of God.

Other introductionss to Halivni's writings that might help readers include: David Halivni, 'Prayer in the Shoah', trans. from the Hebrew by P. Ochs, *Judaism* 199 50/3, Summer, 2001, 268–91; Peter Ochs, 'Preface to David Halivni's Prayer in the Shoah' in *Judaism* 199 50/3, Summer, 2001, 259–67; Peter Ochs, 'Talmudic Scholarship as Textual Reasoning: Halivni's Pragmatic Historiography', in *Textual Reasonings*, ed., P. Ochs and N. Levene, London: SCM Press, 2002.

76. *Textual Reasonings*, 3–4.

77. *Textual Reasonings*, 19.

78. *Textual Reasonings*, 89.

79. While some readers might regard this aspect of Halivni's work to be ominous, I do not detect in Halivni's work any kind of intent to smuggle a Zionist agenda into his argument.

80. See Ch. 10 in this volume, p. 186.

81. Jon Levinson, *Sinai and Zion: An Entry into the Hebrew Bible*, Minneapolis, MN: Winston Press, 1985, 217.

82. *Sinai and Zion*, 218.

83. *Sinai and Zion*, 1.

84. *Sinai and Zion*, 84.

85. *Sinai and Zion*, 89. Although it is poignant to put it this way, in the face of Yoder's argument that 'Jews need Christians' in order to clarify their own mission and vocation, Halivni's hermeneutic provides a way of including Yoder's voice at the table of Torah study whereas it appears that Yoder's own argumentation would by necessity exclude Halivni's rabbinic approach.

86. *Sinai and Zion*, 89.

87. For a very helpful explication of Halivni's 'two-tiered standard of exegetical truth' in relation to his theory of 'the sins of Israel' which rendered Ezra's role in the revelatory process necessary, see Peter Ochs' lucid commentary on Halivni's body of work in *The Return of Scripture in Judaism and Christianity: Essays in Postcritical Scripture Interpretation*, Mahwah, NJ: Paulist Press, 1993, 131–3.

88. Peter Ochs, personal communication with the author, 16 June 2002. Personal archives.

89. Ochs, 16 June 2002. Personal archives.

90. Naim Stifan Ateek, *Justice and Only Justice: A Palestinian Theology of Liberation*, New York, NY: Orbis Books, 1990. Ateek is the executive director of Sabeel.

91. George Lindbeck offers this judgement in his jacket endorsement of *Revelation Restored* (see n. 75 above).

92. George Lindbeck, *The Church in a Postliberal Age*, London: SCM Press, 2002; see Lindbeck's essay 'Confession and Community: An Israel-like View of the Church', pp. 1–9. There, he deploys the category of 'Israelology' for the purpose of articulating the case for an ecumenical Christian peoplehood in the wake of the collapse of 'Christendom'.

93. George Lindbeck's review of Scott Bader-Saye's book *Church and Israel After Christendom: The Politics of Election* in *Theology Today*, April 2001, 120.

94. Nicholas Lash, *Theology on the Way to Emmaus*, 65.

95. *Theology on the Way to Emmaus*, 65.

96. *Theology on the Way to Emmaus*, 71–3.

97. For an excellent example of this kind of post-critical reassessment of the apostolic use of the term *pleroma* in the context of a particular epistle (with the theme of peace fully in view), see David Ford, 'He is our peace': The Letter to the Ephesians and the Theology of Fulfillment – A Dialogue with Peter Ochs' in the (on-line) *Journal of the Society of Scriptural Reasoning*, Vol. I, No.1. See section 2: The Problem, p. 3.

98. See Ch. 3 of this volume, pp. 97–8.

99. See Ch. 8 of this volume, p. 164.

100. Ch. 8, p. 164.

101. Ch. 8, p. 164.

102. Yoder, 'The Hermeneutics of the Anabaptists', 307.

103. Here, then, we see an instance in which Yoder elects to eliminate the 'darkness' of a particular set of biblical texts in favour of a reading that provides clarity, albeit at the cost of excluding other possible readings of the texts in question. Interestingly enough, in this particular context, what is bypassed by this conception is the very set of canonical and/or covenantal contexts that could provide the organic link to Rabbinical Judaism. In chapter eight, perhaps more than anywhere else in *The Jewish–Christian Schism Revisited*, Yoder's ambitious attempt to transcend what he regarded to be 'mis-located dualisms' of Jewish peoplehood turns out to reveal the limits of his own hermeneutic of peace. This interpretive matrix consists in the particular reading that Yoder gives to Paul's Letters to the Romans and the Galatians as well as the determina-

tive weight that he ascribes to Ephesians 2–3, which ultimately serves as the interpretive horizon within which his understanding of 'fulfilment' is oriented (as displayed in passage quoted earlier).

104. Scott Bader-Saye, *Church and Israel After Christendom: The Politics of Election*, Boulder, CO: Westview Press, 1999, 26–7.

105. While Scott Bader-Saye does not cite Yoder's work extensively, it is clear that Yoder's perspective has informed Bader-Saye's understanding of Constantinianism as well as the ecclesiological problems and possibilities of Karl Barth's work. See Bader-Saye, *Church and Israel After Christendom*, 69, 87, 170, n.14.

106. *Church and Israel After Christendom*, 69.

107. *Church and Israel After Christendom*, 69.

108. *Church and Israel After Christendom*, p. 70. *Please note:* By ignoring the Reformed conception of covenant, which registers the 'continuity' between the Old and New Testaments typologically with respect to baptism and circumcision, Yoder magnified the distinctiveness of the Anabaptist hermeneutic with respect to the continuity between the Old and New Testaments.

109. *Church and Israel After Christendom*, 122–3.

110. *Church and Israel After Christendom*, 94.

111. *Church and Israel After Christendom*, 100.

112. *Church and Israel After Christendom*, 110.

113. Yoder, 'The Burden and Discipline of Evangelical Revisionism', 28.

114. Here I invoke the definition developed by Scott Bader-Saye in *Church and Israel After Christendom*, 149, n. 1.

115. Sider and Hauerwas, *Introduction to Preface to Theology* (see n. 8 above), 26.

116. For a concise summary of Yoder's analysis of the shifting problem of 'Constantinianism Old and New' see 'Christ, the Hope of the World' in *The Royal Priesthood: Essays Ecclesiological and Ecumenical*, ed., Michael G. Cartwright, Grand Rapids, MI: Eerdmans, 1994, 195–7. In delineating the differences between various forms of 'neo' and 'neo–neo' Constantinianism, Cartwright summarizes: 'Yoder argues that these "new phases" or "new kinds of unity between church and world" are ultimately not so different from one another, despite the fact that each refutes the preceding marriage of church and world: 'Each says that it is right to identify God's cause with a human power structure. . . . They differ only in that the generation before made the wrong choice of which authority to bless. . . .' (192).

117. John David Dawson's study of *Christian Figural Reading and the Fashioning of Identity* (Berkeley, CA: University of California Press, 2002) offers persuasive reasons why this is the case.

118. Lindbeck, 'What of the Future?', 362.

119. 'What of the Future?', 365.

120. 'What of the Future?', 365.

121. Lash, *Theology on the Way to Emmaus*, 71.

122. This statement is the final line of Yoder's essay on 'The Hermenuetics of Peoplehood' in *The Priestly Kingdom*, 45.

123. I am grateful to Mary Wilder Cartwright, Douglas Harink, Stanley Hauerwas, Martha Yoder Maust, Tom Yoder Neufeld, Peter Ochs, Gerald Schlabach, Calvin and Marie Shenk, Kendall R. Soulen and Alain Epp Weaver for conversations, comments and criticisms in response to two earlier drafts of this essay. While some of these readers dissent from my judgements at various points, they were all very generous with their time and interest in this project. Their contributions have resulted in whatever strengths there may be in this 'afterword.' All remaining problems or errors are my responsibility alone.

Appendix A

Salvation is of the Jews[1]

JOHN HOWARD YODER

Now, when Jesus learned that the Pharisees had heard, 'Jesus is making and baptizing more disciples than John' – although it was not Jesus himself but his disciples who baptized – he left Judaea and started back to Galilee. But he had to go through Samaria. So he came to a Samaritan city called Sychar, near the plot of ground that Jacob had given to his son Joseph. Jacob's well was there, and Jesus, tired out by his journey, was sitting by the well. It was about noon. A Samaritan woman came to draw water, and Jesus said to her, 'Give me drink.' (His disciples had gone to the city to buy food.) The Samaritan woman said to him, 'How is it that you, a Jew, ask a drink of me, a woman of Samaria? (Jews do not share things in common with Samaritans.) Jesus answered her, 'If you knew the gift of God, and who it is that is saying to you, "Give me a drink," you would have asked him, and he would have given you living water.' The woman said to him, 'Sir, you have no bucket and the well is deep. Where do you get that living water? Are you greater than our ancestor Jacob, who gave us the well, and with his sons and his flocks drank from it?' Jesus said to her, 'Everyone who drinks of this water will be thirsty again, but those who drink of the water that I will give them will never be thirsty. The water that I will give will become in them a spring of water gushing up to eternal life.' The woman said to him, 'Sir, give me this water, so that I may never be thirsty or have to keep coming here to draw water.'

Jesus said to her, 'Go, call your husband, and come back.' The woman answered him, 'I have no husband.' Jesus said to her, 'You are right in saying, "I have no husband"; for you have had five husbands, and the one you have now is not your husband. What you have said is true!' The woman said to him, 'Sir, I see that you are a prophet. Our ancestors worshipped on this mountain, but you say that the place where we must worship is in Jerusalem.' Jesus said to her, 'Woman, believe me, the hour is coming when you will worship the Father neither on this mountain or in Jerusalem. You worship what you do not know; we worship what we know, for salvation is from the Jews. But the hour is coming, and is now here, when the true worshippers will worship in spirit and in truth, for the Father seeks such as these to worship him. God is spirit, and those who worship him must worship in spirit and truth.' The woman said to him, 'I know the Messiah is coming' (who is called Christ). 'When he comes, he will proclaim all things to us.' Jesus said to her, 'I am he, the one who is speaking to you.'

Just then his disciples came. They were astonished that he was speaking with a woman, but no one said, 'What do you want?' or, 'Why are you speaking with her?' Then the woman left her water jar and went back to the city. She said to her people, 'Come and see a man who told me everything I have ever done! He cannot be the Messiah, can he?' They left the city and were on their way to him. (John 4.1–30 NRSV)

The point of our reading this morning is not to exposit with care this particular sentence, spoken by the Samaritan woman in the Gospel according to John (4.22), but rather to be reminded by it that this Gospel is not in any way antisemitic. John, or Jesus as described by John, is critical of the Judaean establishment,[2] but not of the Jewish race or people as such. Our concern here is rather to take account of the fact that what Jesus here said is a historically ineluctable truth, and at the same time an abiding puzzle to Gentile Christians, particularly since the Protestant Reformation.

That Abraham is our father is a general formula in the New Testament to express what it is from the Hebrew heritage that others as well can receive. It was said by John the Baptist:

Do not presume to tell yourselves,
'We have Abraham for our father',
because, I tell you,
God can raise children for Abraham from these stones. (Matt. 3.9f.; Luke 3.8f.)

Jesus himself used the same contrast:

If you were Abraham's children,
you would do as Abraham did.
Your father Abraham rejoiced
to think that he would see my day;
he saw it and was glad. (John 8.39f.)

Paul used the same argument when writing to the Galatians:

Don't you see that it is those who rely on faith
who are the sons of Abraham?
Those therefore who rely on faith
receive the same blessing as Abraham,
the man of faith. (Gal.3.7–9)

Even more fully, the letter to the Hebrews makes of Abraham's example the theme of a whole chapter, beginning with the patriarch's believing that God is one who rewards those who believe him. What is meant here by 'believing' is not a merely intellectual operation of assent to some strange idea, as one might be able to understand from a phrase like 'one must believe that God is'.

The word we usually translate 'belief' should better be rendered 'faithfulness'. It means following the command of one who calls us into an uncertain future. It means being willing to obey not on the grounds of the promise of some kind of reward, but solely because of the authority of the one who calls. The meaning of such 'faithfulness' is obviously evident in a different kind of human behaviour: but more deeply it means we are talking about a different kind of God.

From the most simple traditional religion of an African or an Amerindian tribal culture – what we call 'primitive' in terms of western culture – to the most complex speculative construction of professional academics whether Christian or post-Christian, not to exclude along the way the majestic syntheses of urban and imperial culture from ancient Mesopotamia to Tsarist Russia, the name 'God' has been identified with human prosperity and security. Cultures dependent on agricultural productivity have identified God with the rain and the fields. Cultures dependent on navigation across desert or water saw the clearest divine identity in the heavenly luminaries. Is the culture based on herding or hunting? The divine power correlates with the health of the animal world.

Such a 'God' is dependent upon the culture of his/her worshippers. Anthropologists call her/him a 'culture God'. He/she needs to be fed and housed by them: sometimes to be appeased or cajoled. The power of God or the gods so understood is ultimately not distinguishable from the course of human events. 'God wills' is the functional equivalent of the way things actually go. One says 'God has prospered us' when things go well, and 'God has chastised us' when they do not. To worship (which in some languages is the same verb as 'to cultivate') such a god or God is costly. It may call for some sacrifice, but ultimately it is in one's own interest, both for the individual and for the community. Especially it is in the interest of the ruling persons and classes within the culture, any culture. In tribal culture the shaman is usually a blood relative of the chief: in ancient Babylon or Thebes, in imperial Rome or Moscow the royal and sacerdotal classes interlock.

The regular celebrations of such a religion pay attention especially to the cyclical dimensions of life:

– of the individual human life: puberty, childbirth, marriage, ageing, death;
– of agrarian life: solstice, spring, midsummer, harvest, winter;
– of the irregular drama: earthquake, famine, avalanches, shipwreck, chemical catastrophes.

Insurance companies call these 'acts of God'. I propose to call this attitude the 'religious' view of religion.

What begins in Abraham, and crests in Jesus, is not merely a different set of ideas about the world or about morality; it is a new definition of God. A God enters into relations with people who does not fit into the designs of human communities and their rulers. He is a God who saves, but not by reinforcing the selfishness and living up to the appetites of his people: who may save other people, other peoples as well, and who may even ask his people to love their enemies. Such a God affirms a given people's tribal identity and posterity as a good thing, but not as over against their enemies and adversaries. The purposes into which he calls them will involve sacrifice, but not in order to obtain his grace.

Let us let Joseph in Egypt serve as representative of this understanding of God, as he has served through the centuries of Jews' reading his story. Joseph found in his faith in God the resources for disobeying the commands of his superiors and thereby being willing to accept suffering as the price of his obedience. Secondly, when he had taken the risk, after that readiness to disobey had been tested and found solid, he was vindicated, and the pagan rulers honoured Joseph's God. Then Joseph was used by God to save the very same pagan nation which first of all had been punishing him.

The founder figures are people who leave behind the security and the at-homeness with which religion would normally be concerned, to go off elsewhere.

Abraham left Chaldea, Moses left Egypt, Jeremiah left Jerusalem. Of all these, Jeremiah is perhaps the most important: for it is only when they have left their homeland and maintained an identity elsewhere that the 'Judaeans' (named for their tribal background or their homeland) became 'the Jews'.

The worthy successors of those founders are heroes of costly obedience: Joseph (described above), Daniel refusing to stop praying, the three young men refusing to bow down before the great Image:

> If our God, the one we serve,
> is able to save us from the burning fiery furnace
> and from your power, O King, He will save us;
> and even if he does not, then you must know, O King,
> that we will not serve your God
> or worship the statue you have erected.(Dan. 3.17f.)

Esther continues the pattern. She disobeys the king's rules, risking her life for the sake of her people's survival.

It would be superficial to see these accounts as merely demonstrative of individual virtue. They define a distinctive understanding of the nature of God. A distinctive understanding of the nature of obedience as disobeying the authorities defines God as sovereign above and if need be against the kings of this world, rather than as the 'religious' undergirder of things as they are.

Since this is the case, it should be no surprise that on down through history, people who know that about God would be different from their neighbours, and would make problems for their rulers. Thus being out of place or out of phase will then be one of the marks of their identity. This is what has been going on in Jewish life, for now nigh on twenty six hundred years.

We who gather this day [at Bethel College] in North Newton, Kansas, have been taught to think that Mennonite history, with its account of migrations, sufferings and survival since the sixteenth century, is worthy of special honour, expressed in the building of historical libraries and the researching of the beginning generations. How much more should we honour the story in which the same kind of thing has been going on for six times that long, in many more places, with the numbers of victims being greater by far, the expulsions more sweeping, the persecution more brutal.

The paths of Mennonites and of Jews have crossed once in a while. The sixteenth-century Anabaptist leader Hans Denck is reported to have sought advice from Jewish rabbis to improve his first translation of the Hebrew Prophets into German. The Jewish philosopher Spinoza enjoyed Mennonite hospitality in the Netherlands. Russian Mennonite preacher P. M. Friesen got up from his sickbed to quell an Anti-Jewish riot in the Ukraine. Mennonites enjoy the Broadway musical 'Fiddler on the Roof'; both our subcultures have carried German dialects with them around the world. Both have been grateful for the hospitality of the United States and Canada. Yet what matters far more is that we see, behind the superficial folkloric peculiarities and the fortuitous coincidences, something having to do with the identity of the God we are called to serve. It does say more about God than about the virtues of the people serving him, that a nation with no land, no king, no constitution, no army, no pope, should be able to survive both persecution and prosperity with such tough fidelity, and should be present at the major hinges of history, such as (for instance, in our own generation) Auschwitz and the formation of the State of Israel.

We have recently been watching a series of debates among theologians about whether Christians should give a special place to Israel. On the far out fringe there is the 'British Israel' movement, renewed in a strange way by the Sabbatarian Pentecostal Herbert W. Armstrong, according to which Anglo-Saxon Christians are the descendants of the 'Ten Lost Tribes'. On the moderately far right, dispensationalist fundamentalism in the wake of John Nelson Darby sees in the State of Israel the beginning of the fulfilment of a detailed schedule, fixed by the interlocking of some texts from Ezekiel and some others from the Apocalypse of John, each interpreted according to an odd mixture of literalism and typology.

One step farther toward the centre, there is mainline ecumenical Protestantism in Western Europe, in the wake of Dietrich Bonhoeffer and Karl Barth, drawing theological lessons from the disaster of 'Auschwitz'. Still farther along the scale, Reinhold Niebuhr, followed by Roy Eckhardt and some statements of the National Council of Churches, say there should be *no* Christian message at all to Jews.

My present question is not to answer this question: I note for now only that for it to be a question at all one must assume the profound uniqueness which sets Jews apart from everyone else as a theological challenge to Christian thought. These alternatives are ways out of the question raised for us by the assumption that Jews, like all non-Christians, are outside the salvation story, in such a way that we must adjudicate among the several different available views of how or whether to bring them the gospel of Jesus Christ. But if as the woman at the well said, 'salvation is of the Jews', that might be the wrong question.

Notes

1. [Editors' Note: This is a condensed version of a Sunday morning sermon that John H. Yoder preached at College Church, Bethel College, Newton, Kansas in November 1992.]

2. As is indicated above, sometimes in the Fourth Gospel the term *ioudaioi* should be translated 'the authorities'.

Appendix B

Mennonite Missions in Israel and the Peacemaking of Mennonite Central Committee Palestine (1949–2002): Two Contexts for Locating John Howard Yoder's Theological Dialogue with Judaism

MICHAEL G. CARTWRIGHT

During the second half of Yoder's sabbatical (1975–76) at the Ecumenical Institute for Advanced Theological Studies at Tantur/Jerusalem, he was also serving an assignment for Mennonite Central Committee (MCC)[1] in Palestine. Yoder's principal responsibility was to give theology lectures at various places in the Occupied Territories including at Tantur.[2] It is not clear how many lectures Yoder gave beyond the two public lectures that were presented at Tantur, but we do know that he spoke at a workshop for Palestinian pastors organized with Revd Naim Ateek, a Palestinian Anglican clergyman who went on to become Canon of St George's Cathedral and later would serve as the founder and director of the Sabeel Ecumenical Liberation Theology Center.[3] While the academic year that Yoder spent at Tantur was Yoder's only occasion to visit Israel and Palestine for an extended time, by no means was it the only time that he made a contribution to the work of MCC-Palestine or Mennonite Board of Missions (MBM) endeavours in Israel. Indeed, these involvements provide two significant contexts within which to register Yoder's theological dialogue with Judaism as displayed in the essays that comprise this volume.

While it is far from clear how much or how little Mennonite missional experience in Israel and MCC peacemaking efforts in Palestine from 1950 to 2000 may have informed Yoder's arguments in *The Jewish–Christian Schism Revisited*, what is clear is that Yoder saw the mid-to-late twentieth-century social milieux of Israel and Palestine as *one set of contexts* within which Mennonites (and others) had the opportunity to 're-shape the dialogue within the story'[4] of Jewish–Christian relations. Having earlier exercised leadership in the Mennonite Board of Missions, before he ever set foot on Middle Eastern soil, Yoder was *already* well aware of the issues facing Mennonite missions endeavours in the West Bank and Israel. By registering the convergence between Yoder's writings and the work of Mennonite Board of Missions in Israel and the Mennonite Central Committee in Palestine, I want to highlight for readers the ways in which Yoder's theological explorations *correspond* with MBM and MCC activities and projects that have social and political implications even today.

Despite significant areas of overlap, because of the separate origins and different trajectories of the development of Mennonite Board of Missions initiatives and the programmes sponsored and/or co-ordinated by the Mennonite Central Committee in the Middle East, this narrative will treat them separately. In addition – in conjunction with discussing the work of MCC in the 1990s – I will also provide some perspectives about the peacemaking endeavours of the Christian Peacemaker Teams, a collaborative effort of Mennonites, Church of the Brethren congregations and Friends meetings, that has been working in the Occupied Territories in and around the city of Hebron since 1994. In the concluding section, I will draw attention to common threads that can be identified in the midst of the differences in relation to Yoder's theological dialogue with Judaism.

One final prefatory word: those parties in a position to make comparative judgements about the historical record of Mennonite missionary activities in Israel and Mennonite peacemaking efforts in Palestine would concur that what Mennonites have been doing across the span of the past half century is nothing less than remarkable. Oftentimes, the impact of Mennonite witness has been disproportionate to the numbers of persons involved and the quantity of money invested. The critical perspectives offered at points in the pages to follow are offered with admiration and respect, not in any sense out of the desire to indict the integrity of Mennonite witness – in the most inclusive sense of the term. Indeed, here I want to go on record as stating that it is the very candour and humble confidence of those leaders representing MBM in Israel and MCC Palestine – in conversation, correspondence, and publications – that would even make possible this kind of study in the first place.

I trust that those Mennonites who read this text will be able to add their own perspectives to what I regard to be a complex and fascinating history. I take it for granted some of these same readers will disagree with my judgement of Yoder's work as 'in the end supersessionist – despite his own best intentions'. Those same readers also may doubt the accuracy of my contention that Mennonite missions and peacemaking reflect this same set of tensions and problems. I trust that such readers will also note that I have gone to great lengths to try to offer a fairminded account of the issues in question. Those who believe that I have misrepresented matters or misunderstood the history in question are invited to engage me in further conversation.

I. Mennonite Central Committee Peacemaking in Palestine:
1949–2002

The peacemaking endeavours of MCC-Palestine have come into existence as an outgrowth of MCC's relief and development work among and with Palestinians. As Alain Epp Weaver and Sonia K. Weaver carefully explain in their book *Salt and Sign: Mennonite Central Committee in Palestine, 1949–1999*, the plight of the Palestinian refugees, victims of the *al-Nakbah* (Arabic for 'the Catastrophe' of 1948 in which hundreds of thousands of Palestinians became homeless), is what prompted MCC to begin providing relief in the refugee camps on the West Bank of the Jordan.[5] Initially, then, Mennonite volunteers with MCC tried to provide relief in the form of food and clothing to the displaced families of refugees. The needs of desperate and overwhelmed refugees, however, placed Mennonite volunteers in difficult situations where they found that they had to 'manhandle' unruly crowds in order to bring about order.[6]

Later, as the immediate needs for food, clothing, and shelter appeared to be met, Mennonite volunteers began to set up economic development opportunities. Needlework programmes, vocational schools, and small-business training were among the strategies used by MCC personnel to meet the long-term needs of the refugee population. At a few points, Mennonites also experienced the rage of Palestinian refugees as in 1955 when the MCC house and storage facility in Jericho was set afire by a group of rioting Palestinians angry at American political interference with Jordan.[7] After 1967 and the Israeli occupation of the West Bank, MCC leaders and volunteers discovered the depths of the Palestinian struggle as they witnessed the harassment of students and staff of the Mennonite school that they had founded in the village of Beit Jala and later turned over to indigenous leadership.[8]

In the wake of the 1967 Israeli triumph over Jordan, Syria, and Egypt in the Six Day War, MCC worked in co-operation with the United Nations and other voluntary agencies on Jordan's East Bank to offer emergency assistance in camps that the United Nations set up for displaced persons and refugees. Meanwhile on the West Bank, now under Israeli military occupation, MCC discovered that 'finding ways to work for peace proved challenging'.[9]

After 1973, as Arab nationalism grew, MCC began to work with Palestinians in new ways by encouraging co-operative endeavours such as the needlework programme. This latter initiative provided Palestinian women with the opportunity to gain valuable experience in business as well as to become more assertive in the context of their families. During the 1980s MCC started more child development education initiatives and worked diligently to open lines of credit for Palestinians wanting to start small businesses. But in a context of blatant injustice, MCC workers found that development was not enough.[10]

In the process of fostering collaboration with local Palestinian communities, MCC leaders also found themselves in conflict with the Israeli government for a variety of reasons ranging from their efforts to promote non-violent forms of Palestinian resistance to their public questioning of Israeli policies of settlement expansion and the abuse of human rights in the occupied territories.[11] 'MCC's legal status in the West Bank was called into question. Some MCC projects were threatened with closure.'[12] At least one MCC worker found it difficult to get a visa because he was perceived to be 'part of the PLO's "propaganda effort"',[13] and more generally, MCC leaders found themselves faced with quandaries about how to deal with Israeli inquiries into the 'clandestine activities' of MCC workers. The question of how upfront MCC could be about its support of non-violent resistance to the Israeli occupation became an increasingly pressing question during the last two decades of the twentieth century.

During the Palestinian *intifada* (1987–1993), MCC workers found themselves living in the midst of a political environment in which 'hundreds of Palestinians were martyred and thousands were injured' as the Israeli government answered the largely non-violent 'uprising' with force. This brought about changes in the way MCC deployed its resources as its leadership 'came to understand [MCC's] development role as that of supporting local Palestinian institutions, which were seen as the developing organs of a state in the making, rather than implementing its own projects'.[14] This was also the context in which MCC-Palestine leaders increased their 'efforts to promote a just peace'.[15]

After the Oslo accords (1993), it became possible for the first time for the Palestinian Authority to set up its own governance structures in Gaza and Jericho. The interim agreement divided the West Bank into Areas A, B, and C, with each of these areas having different arrangements for security, policing, and civil governance. While this arrangement held the promise of a future autonomy for the West Bank, it also created new constraints for MCC projects. In this circumstance, MCC workers struggled with their Palestinian partners in such projects as the Hope School in Beit Jala to negotiate the barriers posed by the location of the school in Area C, which was controlled by the Israelis with most of the employees and students living in Area A. In this circumstance and others, MCC-Palestine found itself facing conditions in which it was almost impossible to continue the ventures that they had started without appearing to skirt the legal restrictions imposed by the Israelis.[16]

How to understand peacemaking proved a difficult question under occupation, with some MCC workers in the 1970s questioning the seemingly 'bland "neutrality"' of an MCC country representative such as LeRoy Friesen. MCC workers, including Friesen, began to question whether peacemakers could be neutral in a situation marked by injustice and an imbalance of power.[17] Throughout this period, MCC leaders yearned to invest their efforts in 'something that will count' rather than to allow themselves to have their time be taken up by 'peripheral activities'.[18] In the 1990s, MCC expanded its work by creating new collaborations in the Gaza Strip. This brought about new opportunities to engage the largely Muslim population.[19]

With the beginning of the *Al Aqsa intifada* at the end of September 2000, MCC workers once again faced a new set of challenges. In the wake of the Israeli reoccupation of Palestinian cities in the spring of 2002, MCC has found itself once again providing relief to families of refugees who lost their homes when the Israelis reasserted control over areas previously under the Palestinian Authority. Even as MCC renewed relief activities, it continued to work through Palestinian non-governmental organizations to provide economic development opportunities for the Palestinian population of the West Bank and Gaza, although such projects became increasingly difficult to implement given the restrictions on movement within the occupied territories.[20]

From 1967 through the end of the twentieth century, the consistent concern of MCC-Palestine was 'to embody Jesus's way of peace in the midst of a violent conflict, coupled with the commitment to speaking the truth to power about the injustices and oppression faced by the Palestinians . . .'.[21] Humbly describing MCC as a 'work in progress', Weaver and Weaver note that this emphasis on peacemaking 'took concrete shape in multiple and changing ways'.[22] At the end of the twentieth century, Weaver and Weaver reported that there was a 'tacit consensus' that MCC-Palestine 'should maintain its presence among Palestinians until a just peace has been secured' but 'what that presence should look like is an open question'.[23] Conscious of the small-scale nature of their group's efforts, Weaver and Weaver ultimately chose to narrate MCC-Palestine as having played a 'small, yet at times significant' role in Palestine.

This is also a story of Mennonite volunteers who 'worked with changing models of what it meant to be an incarnational presence for peace and reconciliation'[24] in

Palestine. In summarizing what had been learned over the course of the fifty-plus-year history of MCC-Palestine, Weaver and Weaver identified several areas of discovery. First, they discovered that 'what constituted peace work was a vague and ambiguous affair'.[25] Not everything that MCC volunteers had done could fairly be said to be peacemaking, and in retrospect, MCC leaders had sometimes been guilty of overextending the use of the word 'peace'. Second, in the context of their aspiration to do 'something that will count', MCC volunteers discovered that they had to 'keep "being" and "doing" in balance, both embodying the peace of Christ and actively working for peaceful resolution of conflict'.[26] Finally, the volunteers from North America who worked with MCC-Palestine had to learn to struggle with the temptation to cynicism that resides in seemingly hopeless situations. 'Volunteers looked to minister in the light of the resurrection but regularly found themselves toiling in the shadow of the cross.'[27] *Weaver + Weaver*

At the end of the twentieth century, MCC's work in Palestine consisted of five 'priority areas' that correspond to MCC's broader efforts located throughout the Middle East: (1) peacemaking, (2) support for the local church in the West Bank and Gaza, (3) work with the marginalized population, (4) dialogue with Muslims, and (5) education of the North American constituency.[28] The latter task also proved to be fraught with tension and misunderstanding as MCC personnel sometimes found themselves having a different sense of what needed to be done 'on the ground' than did their largely Mennonite constituency.[29]

As the next section explains, the fivefold set of MCC work priorities overlaps at several points with the work of Mennonite Mission in Israel. For that reason, I will explain the work that has been done by the Mennonite Board of Missions over the past half-century before narrating the emergence of the Christian Peacemaker Teams as a new initiative that has brought more Mennonite volunteers to Palestine with the tacit support of MCC-Palestine.

II. Mennonite Missions in Israel

Mennonite missionary efforts in Israel have their own kind of complexity independent of the issues that Mennonite peacemakers found themselves facing in the West Bank and Jordan. Indeed, in order to describe Mennonite missions in Israel accurately requires careful attention to several different sets of issues, each of which exists in subtle relationship to tensions that inhere in the Mennonite witness. First, from the perspective of MBM leaders, the missional endeavours of 'dialogue' and 'evangelism' are not regarded as mutually exclusive. Neither are dialogue and evangelism to be regarded as exclusive of the Mennonite peace witness. In fact, reconciliation is regarded as an evidence of the reality of the Christian gospel.

With these factors in view it is perhaps not so surprising to read Marie Shenk's historical overview of Mennonite missions in Israel, 'There are no Mennonite monuments in Israel today, no firmly established programs or long-standing institutions. Yet, Mennonites have sustained a reconciling presence in the country for now almost 50 years.'[30] While perhaps a bit understated in its assessment of the work of the Mennonite Board of Missions in Israel, this statement does indicate one of the central contrasts between MBM and MCC. In the latter case, as Alain Epp Weaver has noted, 'MCC has established institutions and played instrumental roles

in the formation of Palestinian organizations which continue [to be in] operation
. . . .'.[31]

Although it can accurately be said that Mennonite experience in the Middle East extends back to the late nineteenth century, with a few notable exceptions, organized efforts to send North American Mennonite missionaries to Israel took place after the constitution of the State of Israel in 1948. Early on, those church leaders who helped establish the initial policy for Mennonite Board of Missions determined that Mennonites should not set up distinctly Mennonite programmes, but rather should 'make our denominational presence felt by being a positive, cohesive, cooperative unit in the developing evangelistic program'.[32] Thus, from the beginning, Mennonite missions in Israel were constituted within ecumenical partnerships. By 1960, Mennonite Associates had made its initial application for membership in the United Christian Council of Israel (UCCI).[33] That application was initially denied because of the fact that the Mennonite Church had not established *Mennonite* congregations in Israel, but later the Mennonite body would be accepted for membership and over the years would give leadership to that body in several different ways.

During the first two decades of MBM's activities in Israel, a variety of initiatives were explored. During the early years, the efforts were modest – ranging from establishing bookstores to sell Bibles to teaching in an orphanage for Arab children. By the 1960s, more ambitious efforts were launched in partnership with other ecclesial bodies in the UCCI. One of the most notable – and controversial – projects that MBM helped sponsor was the effort by a group of Messianic believers who envisioned a 'Jewish-believer *moshav* (cooperative)'. MBM field representatives expressed reservations about the wisdom of such an initiative. For example, Roy Krieder 'questioned whether the New Testament concept of church would encourage such a "ghetto of Jewish believers." He recommended that some Arab Christians be included as part of such a community, demonstrating reconciliation – Arabs and Jews able to live and work together in the project.'[34] Despite Krieder's intervention, Mennonite Board of Mission personnel were unable to persuade key people involved with the project to proceed with that expansive vision.

Ultimately, an international board developed a plan to form a Christian *moshav* – agricultural co-operative – that would be given the name 'Nes Ammim' from Isaiah 11.10 – 'a sign to the peoples'. In the journal *The Covenant Companion*, the philosophical framework for this project was stated this way:

Though the wall between Christian and Jew is high, it may be bridged by Christians seeking to identify themselves with the Jews of Israel and their land, thus making possible the dialogue through which we may find one another. The new state of Israel provides a unique opportunity to establish such a dialogue. The Jewish people are busy with nation-building and developing their country. If a group of representative Christians is willing to share the difficulties and hardships of pioneering a community similar to the kibbutzim the Jews have pioneered, their demonstration of love and goodwill may prepare the way for communication on the deeper levels of life. [35]

As this initiative indicated, Mennonites believed that it mattered *what kind* of 'sign to the peoples' was being displayed in their missionary initiatives. When 'divisions and dissension grew to intolerable proportions' in 1967, the Mennonites ultimately withdrew from this project.[36] However, at a later point, they were actively involved in another initiative by assisting an indigenous congregation of Messianic Jews known as *Beit Immanuel*. At one point Mennonite missionaries served as pastors of this messianic congregation, where evangelism was the principal mission, not Jewish–Christian dialogue, as such.

In the context of their earliest encounters with Judaism in Israel, Mennonite missionaries came to believe that Jews would 'take a second look' at Christianity if they saw the message of Jesus Christ being lived out in socially embodied ways. Thus, during the early 1970s, Mennonites sought 'new opportunities, new directions, and new beginnings' for their missionary encounters with Judaism.[37] In sum, John Howard Yoder would have come to Tantur in the mid-1970s at a time of experimentation and openness being experienced not only by Mennonites but by other Christian groups as well.

This receptive atmosphere would prove to be short-lived, however. Less than two years after Yoder returned to the United States, the Israeli *Knesset* passed a bill ruling that as of 1 April 1978, it would be illegal to offer or give money or other material benefits to induce someone to change their religion. And it would be against the law to receive money or benefits for changing one's religion. This bill came to be regarded by MBM leaders as the 'first real anti-missionary legislation'. In response, Mennonite Board of Missions leaders worked with the UCCI to engage this legislation and where the opportunity presented itself they disseminated information in the USA and elsewhere 'to alert church leaders and responsible statesmen to the dangers facing believers in Israel'. [38] After many negotiations, an acceptable resolution to the problem was reached. 'The Attorney General gave assurance that he personally would see to it that all legitimate rights of the churches would be safeguarded.' Unfortunately, this struggle took its toll in a variety of ways. Interfaith relationships were also strained in the process.

While new mission personnel replaced these leaders and new roles emerged for MBM leaders in Israel, the Krieders' involvement with the Messianic Jewish community *continued* throughout this period. Also, Garry Denlinger has served on the Israeli Messianic Jewish alliance.[39] In fact, MBM support for and active participation in fostering Messianic Jewish congregations in Israel would appear to have been one of the areas where Mennonite missionary efforts were most effective.

By the mid-1980s, Mennonites in MBM and MCC began to recognize that it was time to reassess where their various efforts had taken them in their mission to and in the Middle East. In 1986, Mennonite Board of Missions proposed a joint study to be conducted with Mennonite Central Committee and Eastern Mennonite Missions to 'identify countries, issues and opportunities where a visible Mennonite presence is possible and where Mennonites have the capacity to respond'. Four goals for this study were identified:

1. How the agencies should related to the Messianic movement within Israel.
2. The relationship of a 'Christ-ward movement' in Israel with the Messianic movement and how Mennonites should be supportive.
3. Possibilities for deeper Mennonite involvement in Jewish–Christian dialogue.
4. How Mennonite agencies were viewed by adherents of Judaism.[40]

In light of Yoder's study, the proposed focus of the interagency Mennonite study is particularly significant. Here, it would appear that initial MBM interest in 'Jewish–

Christian dialogue' later took a backseat to engagements with the Messianic community.

LeRoy Friesen, who had earlier served as country representative for Mennonite Central Committee, was given the task of conducting the study, which took place in June–August 1988. Friesen's project report was subsequently presented to Mennonite interagency leaders in the Middle East as well as in North America, and it was subsequently published in 1992 as a MBM resource (and later re-issued in a new edition in 2006). With regard to the cluster of issues for Jewish–Christian dialogue, Friesen came to the conclusion that although prosyletizing and non-prosyletizing initiatives had *coexisted* in the 1970s, 'such a balance no longer existed among Mennonite personnel in Israel'. Friesen expressed the hope that Mennonites would 'find their way somewhere between those advocating "vigorous proselytizing of all Jews" and those "who contend that it is not the task of Mennonite Christians to seek to proselytize Jewish persons". He recommended further study on 'how the Mennonite body views the Jews.'[41] As Marie Shenk's chronicle makes clear, there was by no means unanimity among Mennonites about how to engage Jews in the context of missionary endeavour. Friesen's final recommendation stands as an invitation to further exploration.

Among the resolutions that grew out of the Friesen report was a recommendation that the same three agencies which commissioned the study likewise co-operate in developing 'a sensitive presence'[42] among the religions of the area. Several different persons would be assigned the task of engaging Islam, Judaism, and eastern Christianity. Ultimately, Mennonite Board of Missions elected to appoint Calvin and Marie Shenk to engage in 'a dialogue role in Jerusalem'. They were being sent with the understanding of 'interfaith exchange as an incarnational stance, a genuine Christian presence – being among and in conversation with adherents of Judaism'.[43] Arguably, in doing so, the Mennonites 'were returning to the position that had informed their earliest mission strategy: interfaith dialogue with Judaism – alongside evangelism in which Mennonites were already involved'.[44]

Calvin and Marie Shenk would carry this portfolio for three missionary sending agencies from January 1994 until June 2001, when they relinquished this assignment in preparation for Calvin's retirement from Eastern Mennonite University in Harrisonburg, Virginia. Significantly, Marie Shenk's summary assessment of this missionary endeavour identifies continuity of the vision of 'reconciling presence' and points to the 'living and giving that Mennonites have incarnated in their encounter with Judaism and within the Messianic fellowship' as a 'unique offering of incarnational presence'.[45]

While it would be overstated and erroneous to tie these developments in the work of the Mennonite Board of Mission to John Howard Yoder's influence at all points, it would also be wrong to view Yoder's conception of Jewish–Christian dialogue as completely detached from these Mennonite efforts. In fact, Yoder's influence on Mennonite missions is demonstrable both at the level of missiological conception of Jewish–Christian dialogue and the level of mission deployment policies. Published books and articles by the two principal Mennonite missiologists who have written about their experience in the Middle East, LeRoy Friesen and Calvin Shenk, reveal Yoder's influence at key points.

For example, Calvin Shenk's book *Who Do You Say That I Am? Christians Encounter Other Religions* (1997) cites Yoder's 'The Disavowal of Constantine' essay (originally presented at Tantur in 1976) at several points[46] in the course of explaining to readers what it means to engage in 'dialogue' with other religions. Significantly, Shenk also sets up this aspect of his book by attempting to disentangle Jesus from the western ethnocentric 'story'. Like Yoder, Shenk assumes that where Mennonites and other Christians can bear witness to a 'different' Jesus than the one communicated in Constantinian garb, then the dialogical witness to Jews and other non-Christians can proceed in humility without coercion.

Throughout Shenk's discussion of 'dialogue' in mission, 'voluntaryness' is ascribed – implicitly and explicitly – to would-be Jewish and Muslim interlocutors in the expectation that if they are persuaded by the witness to Christ that they encounter, then they will become followers of Jesus. In the case of Judaism, the existence of 'Messianic' fellowships constitutes the example of what can result from a successful 'dialogue' where the 'surprising grace' of God coincides with a witness offered in humility.

> Witness is not an imposition. We do not trample on another. Embracing truth with confidence should not lead to conceit or dogmatism; the gospel cannot be communicated with condescension. We entreat people on behalf of Christ to be reconciled to God (2 Cor. 5:20), and we commend the gospel (2 Cor. 4:2). Truth is not merely asserted but must be recognized. Truth stands at the door and knocks. There must be consent from within; too much pressure keeps one from opening the door.[47]

In this same context, Shenk recalls a particular instance of Jewish–Christian dialogue that he witnessed:

> In a Jewish–Christian conversation in Jerusalem concerning Jewish understandings of Messiah, a Christian student, shaking his finger, insisted that he could prove from Hebrew Scriptures that Jesus was Messiah. But conviction stated forcefully is not always convincing. When one enters the Church of the Nativity in Bethlehem, one has to bend low because the door is small. This is a fitting symbol for the mystery of the incarnation and a model for Christian witness.[48]

This emphasis on 'humility' in witness is not merely rhetorical. Friesen's book provides testimony from Muslims in the West Bank that the Mennonite witness is indeed humble and authentic. It should also be noted that those Jews who have had the opportunity to engage Marie and Calvin Shenk have offered similar attestations to the authenticity of these two Mennonite representatives appointed to be in dialogue with Jews in Israel.

But as the April 2002 flight into the Church of the Nativity by a mixture of Palestinian radicals who were joined by priests, Palestinian civilians, and international peace activists reminds us, just because one enters through the 'door of humility' *does not mean* that ambiguity about the content of the Christian witness has been eliminated. Indeed, as LeRoy Friesen's own study makes abundantly clear, one of the principal foci of Mennonite missions in Israel – the congregations of Messianic Jews in Tel Aviv, Tiberias, Jerusalem, and elsewhere – display patterns of instability (personal and communal) that have everything to do with their ambiguous identity. This circumstance deserves more careful examination than Mennonites appear to have given it to date.

Yet the most consistent focus of MBM efforts throughout the half-century of missionary activity in Israel has in fact been the Messianic congregations, an emphasis with which it appears Yoder may have been in concurrence. In fact, on at least one occasion that can be documented, Yoder 'weighed in' on decisions that were to shape the Mennonite Church's missionary strategy in Israel and Palestine. According to Marie Shenk's chronicle, John Howard Yoder played a role in the Mennonite Board of Mission's policy for Israel. In 1967, Wilbert Shenk proposed that the Mennonites change their policy, which had been to engage in co-operative endeavours with other missionary agencies and denominations in support of indigenous congregations, and begin founding Mennonite congregations in Israel. Yoder, acting as a consultant to the Mennonite Board of Missions, argued against Shenk's proposal, taking the position that if the Mennonite Church should make this change after nearly fifteen years of missionary activity, it would be inconsistent with their own vision of what it means to offer a 'reconciling presence'.[49] He also believed that such a change would have an adverse impact on the work of MCC in Palestine.

As the historical events recounted above display and as the logic of Yoder's own position makes clear, Yoder and more generally the Mennonite Church did experience tension in trying to hold interfaith dialogue and evangelism alongside one another. The rhetoric of 'incarnational presence' that Marie Shenk uses in her historical narrative about the work of MBM – both to describe the original vision of the mission of MBM in Palestine and to describe the nature of the assignment that she and her husband Calvin carried out from 1994–2001 – appears to have succeeded in preserving the integrity of the church's witness in the midst of the tensions that would surround Christians and Jews during the 1990s and which would become even greater in the context of the *Al Aqsa intifada* after October 2000.

Given the fact that Yoder can be shown to have had influence on Mennonite missions at both the bureaucratic level and the level of the theory of mission dialogue with Jews, it may also be helpful to consider the possible impact of Yoder's teaching about the 'theology of world missions' on the Mennonite Church's own mission in Israel and Palestine and vice versa. As Chapter 7 of *The Jewish–Christian Schism* indicates, Yoder taught a course on 'The Theology of the Christian World Mission' several times during the decade between 1964 to 1973. In that context, he reports that 'it became important to distinguish between "other religions", which have long been the topic of doctrinal concern, and those cultural phenomena which are derived from the impact of the Christian message on world culture, even when that derivation takes a negative posture'.[50] Yoder contended that it is a mistake to consider missionary efforts in Coptic Orthodox Ethiopia or Catholic Brazil as 'identical to a mission addressed to pagans'. Yoder reports that in this course he discussed Christian world mission to Judaism as a 'non-non-Christian religion' in the same context as Constantinian Catholicism, Orthodoxy, Islam, modern secularism and Marxism, thereby 'proposing a particular respect for Judaism as part of the ongoing Christian story'.[51]

Although he does not spell out all the ways in which he thought that this is the case, Yoder believed that reading history this way can make a 'practical difference' in the way a church conducts its mission to Jews. Following his logic, the difference that it makes might be summarized this way: (1) The mission would not be constituted within a supersessionist thesis, therefore Jews are not to be treated as 'infidels'. (2) Once this 'negative vision' of Jewish identity has been dispelled, then Christians can *re-engage* Jews in a new way, thereby avoiding the pattern of profound neglect of missions to Jews on the one hand and the pattern of preoccupation that came about as a result of the errors of various forms of 'philo-Judaism' including: (a) 'Darbyite premillenial dispensationalism' (in which Jews play a special role in the final dispensation) with its own Christian Zionism; (b) special missions to Jews that seek to establish 'Hebrew Christian' fellowships for messianic Jews; (c) renewed respect for Jews that arises from the combination of European Neo-Reformation theology and response to the Holocaust, which in some cases has resulted in the rejection of the notion that there should be any explicitly Christian proclamation to Jews.[52]

According to Yoder, *re-thinking* Christian mission to Jews also requires that we reconsider the 'erroneous assumptions' that both Christianity and Judaism are best understood as 'stable and autonomous' entities that retain identity across time. When we do so, he argues, then we are in a position to begin reading the history inductively, which produces the awareness that Jesus did not reject Judaism as such, and Paul, far from being anti-Jewish constitutes the paradigm example of what it can mean for a Jew to register the reality of Jesus as the Messiah. Thus, the sociology of the 'first Christian (i.e.messianic Jewish) communities' was such that Jewish language and conceptual style was retained 'even in the hellenistic cities' for 'two or three more generations'[53] until apologetes like Justin Martyr 'reconceived the Christian message to make it credible to non-Jewish culture. This – according to Yoder – constitutes the site of the 'fall of the Church' which coincides with the loss of its 'Jewish rootage'. This state of affairs persisted until radical reformers 'reached back to retrieve' these very elements of Jewish witness. Significantly, Yoder also claims that 'by implicitly standing in the same posture as the Jews in their midst', the radical reformers were also 'reaching sideways'.[54]

Yoder's historical account of how the 'theology of Christian world mission' has impacted the churches' mission to Jews is structured in such a way as to *resolve* the 'abiding ambiguity'[55] that contemporary Christians experience as they struggle to enact the Great Commission in an apostolic manner 'to the Jew first, and also to the Greek'. Yoder wants to help Mennonites avoid the two extremes that he sees floating through the history of western civilization: the pattern of ignoring Jews 'as a possible target of their missionary message' and the pattern of engaging Jews as if they are already constituted as a people of God in some unitary sense. Instead, he urges his Mennonite students to consider the possibility that inasmuch as Jewish identity has been constituted by the Constantinian story, then Jews need Christians in ways that they themselves do not understand. From Yoder's persective, Mennonites, as bearers of the 'free church vision' of the good news that 'it did not have to be' are, therefore, in a good position to engage Jews with the opportunity to recover their Jewish roots, which simultaneously involves the invitation to recognize Jesus as the Jewish Messiah.

Yoder's discussion of 'Hebrew Christians' in the context of the Constantinianization of western Christianity is interesting to consider here, however sketchy it may be. To the extent that messianic Jewish fellowships exist in part because Jewish converts to Christianity 'prefer to maintain some Jewish identity rather than be swallowed up in ordinary predominately Gentile western churches', Yoder recognized that they may end up 'bringing into being "from the other side" the kind of separation which was the object of Paul's explicit criticism in Galatians 2'.[56] On the other hand, given that Yoder sees Zionism as 'the culmination of the Christianization of Judaism', the contemporary nation-state of Israel has created a new circumstance: 'Committed Judaism, i.e., people who visibly order their lives around the Torah, is a minority sect in Israel just as are the Christians.'[57]

Stressing the voluntariness of Jewish identity, Yoder then appeals (repeatedly) to the pluralism of Jewish identity throughout human history as a way of *redrawing* the boundaries of the Jewish–Christian conversation. Mennonites should not accept the typology of Jewish–Christian identity that places them in a category outside or opposite Jews. Rather, Jews and Christians can exercise their choice to live as an alternative to the Constantinianism of *both* Christendom and Zionism. In doing so, Mennonites and Jews (understood as a 'non-non-Christian religion') can live out their common vocation as God's missionary people living in exile (*galut*).

In sum, Yoder wants North American Mennonites (and presumably in Israel and Palestine as well) to see themselves as existing in the same kind of sociological situation that Jews exist in Israel, and he wants Jews and Christians to see that the reconciliation of people is 'essential' to their respective vocations as missionary peoples of God. Here is where Yoder's reading of the New Testament and his conception of the content of the radical reformation witness coincide: 'The truth of the claim that Jesus is Christ, or that the Messiah has come, is inseparable from the functioning of a community in which the two kinds of people have become one.'[58]

Given this rather unnuanced claim, it is also useful to apply Yoder's definition to the existence of Messianic congregations in Israel, which as noted above has been a primary focus of MBM activities over the past half-century. While it is clear enough why Yoder would not automatically regard 'messianic Jewish fellowships' as such to exemplify this radical witness, under this definition it would appear that a congregation largely composed of messianics with a critical mass of non-Messianics (Palestinian Christians, North American Mennonites, etc.) would fit this description. And in fact, such congregations did exist at the time Yoder lived at Tantur, and more than a few existed throughout the last three decades of the twentieth century.

Yoder's definition of the basis of 'messianic community' also lends itself to the development of the kind of missiology that is contextual. In fact, LeRoy Friesen has actually attempted to develop a contextual approach to mission that I judge to be consonant with Yoder's emphases, and – not surprisingly – displays many of the same tensions and problems that I have described. This approach is centred on what Friesen calls the *theologia mysterion* or 'that which, while formerly closed and unknowable, has now been laid bare for all to see'.[59] Discussed in the exegetical context of Ephesians 1.19–23 and Ephesians 3.9–10, this notion is presented as 'the theme around which the entire letter is written'.[60] Repeatedly Friesen (following Yoder) describes this mystery as 'laid bare'. In particular, it is manifest in the 'new humanity' of those who are formerly Gentile and Jew. Friesen explicitly associates the theological *mysterion* of Ephesians with the *missio Dei*, which he defines as 'the intent, the grand design, the mission of God to draw up everything into a transforming and healing unity of Christ everything that is'.[61]

It is this notion which makes it possible for the church to articulate its mission in the world. Friesen makes it clear that the church has no message of its own.

Its mission most expansively understood is, rather, to witness to the mysterion of

God, whether in the radical alternativeness of its common life (presence), in its internal life of love spilling over and impacting those around it (deed), or in its proclamation that in Jesus Christ both the meaning and *telos* of the universe has been laid open (word).[62]

Throughout his book, Friesen candidly indicates the struggle that Mennonites working in MBM and MCC have experienced in seeking to have presence, deed, and word converge. Interestingly, Friesen adopts the viewpoint of the veteran missionary Roy Krieder, who opines 'We were healthiest when we were cultivating the widest range of mission, both evangelism and dialogue.'[63] On the other hand, Friesen also reports that Krieder *withdrew* from some of the ongoing dialogues because he judged them to have become excessively academic or politicized.[64]

It should be noted that there are also Arab-speaking fellowships in Israel that constitute more complex examples that appear to fit Yoder's missiological model. For instance, the *Musalaha* Ministry of Reconciliation attempts to bring Palestinian Christians and Messianic Jews together in the context of the Ephesian vision of a reconciled 'new humanity'. Given that in an Israeli context both Palestinian Christians and 'Hebrew Christians' are, sociologically speaking, minorities Yoder might see this group as a step closer to the Ephesian vision. However, to the extent that both groups remain creations of western Christianity, he would see *Musalaha*'s ministry as still operating from Constantinian assumptions. Nonetheless, I suspect that Yoder would draw a strong distinction between the reconciliation efforts of *Musalaha* and the peacemaking efforts that take place in the venture known as 'Open House' in the city of Ramleh, an outgrowth of the efforts of a particular Israeli family to begin to reconcile with the Palestianian family who had lived in the house prior to being driven out by the Israelis in 1948. Simply put, the latter is not 'in Christ' but given Yoder's sociological description of Jews, Muslims, and Constantinian Christians, it is not clear how he would understand this particular peacemaking effort except perhaps as a parable.[65]

Even if the aforementioned conundrums did not exist, it is not at all clear what could serve as the constitutive practices to bind such groups as *Musalaha* into 'one body'. Given that their practices of reading Scripture are embedded in different sets of traditions and practices, even the appeal to Scripture is problematic, particularly given the fact that these Christian groups in Israel operate with divergent hermeneutics, especially when it comes to discussing the theological significance of the Land, *eretz yisrael*. Although it is not well known, some messianic Jews in Israel as well as elsewhere in the world 'advocate a use of traditional rabbinic approaches to hermeneutics and exposition' of Scripture. While 'there is no consensus among messianic Jews regarding the use of rabbinic sources and interpretation',[66] the fact that such exploration coexists with a strong Christocentric identification of being part of the 'new man' points to the tensions and/or instability of this kind of hermeneutic.

These problems aside, it is striking to note that in the judgement of the person designated to carry out the Mennonite Church's efforts to foster Jewish–Christian dialogue from 1994 to 2001, the reconciliation ministries and projects offered by *Musalaha* constitute 'one of the most significant set of Jewish–Christian dialogues to take place in Israel during the last decade of the twentieth century'.[67] This judgement may or may not be indicative of the lingering ambiguity in the Mennonite

Church about how to constitute its 'witness' to Jewish people in Israel, but it does suggest that however much John Howard Yoder may have wished to clarify the muddles that surround Christian world mission to Jews, in practice, the ambiguity remains.

In fact, at the dawn of the twenty-first century, significant doubts exist about whether the Mennonite Board of Missions will be able to continue to provide a 'reconciling presence' in Israel.[68] Recalling LeRoy Friesen's 1992 report that called for 'further study about how the Mennonite body views the Jews', which was embraced as an open-ended task not limited to Jewish–Christian dialogue in Israel, it may be that Yoder's *Jewish–Christian Schism Revisited* may also have value for the Mennonite Church in the future. In any event the tensions in Yoder's account can also be said to be displayed in the ongoing missionary endeavours of the MBM and MCC peacemaking efforts. In both cases, the vexing question lingers as to what constitutes a *fully embodied* ministry of 'reconciling presence' in contemporary Israel given that Israeli Jews and Palestinian Christians remain unreconciled. Mennonite leaders like Friesen and the Shenks are to be credited for lingering with such a vexing question. At the same time, it is not clear whether Friesen and company have come to grips with the compartmentalizing effects of their missionary and peacemaking efforts.

III. Christian Peacemaker Teams in Hebron: 1994–2001

As Weaver and Weaver indicate in *Salt and Sign*, from the beginning of MCC Palestine's efforts, 'Working for peace in the Palestinian-Israeli context . . . meant for Mennonites not only supporting the Palestinians in their nonviolent resistance to Israeli occupation, but also incarnating a peaceful way of life.'[69] Mennonites have been quite candid with themselves about the challenges posed by this latter objective. Weaver and Weaver report that while some of the Palestinians with whom they have worked over the years indicate admiration for the peace efforts of MCC volunteers, they have also been disappointed to see the humanity of these broken vessels: 'MCC workers unable to work together and forgive each other; marital discord among volunteers leading to divorce', etc.[70] This reception of their witness poses both 'a missiological challenge' for the work of MCC Palestine at the same time that it pushes Mennonites to be more creative and purposeful in their peace witness.

The work of the Christian Peacemaker Teams (CPT) in the city of Hebron has been one of the ways that Mennonites have engaged this twofold challenge in a way that goes beyond what MCC had been able to do, while also constituting the kind of peacemaking endeavour for which MCC can provide liaison support. Conceived 'in the mid 1980s when peace church people were seeking new ways to express their faith',[71] CPT emerges at a time when both the Mennonite missionary endeavours and the work of MCC-Palestine are being reassessed. According to Leo Driedger and Donald B. Kraybill, the 'newer, more assertive mode of peacemaking' displayed by Christian Peacemaker Teams is a good example of the shift 'from quietism to activism' that took place in Mennonite peacemaking during the second half of the twentieth century. [72]

The idea for this kind of Christian Peacemaking Teams originated in Ron Sider's memorable address to the Mennonite World Conference in Strasbourg, France in 1984.

> Over the past 450 years of martyrdom, immigration and missionary proclamation, the God of *shalom* has been preparing us Anabaptists for a late twentieth-century rendezvous with history. The next twenty years will be the most dangerous – and perhaps the most vicious and violent – in human history. If we are ready to embrace the cross, God's reconciling people will profoundly impact the course of world history . . . Now is the time to risk everything for our belief that Jesus is the way to peace. If we still believe it, now is the time to live what we have spoken.[73]

After reminding those gathered of the millions of people who have died because they believed 'in peace through the sword', Sider challenged his fellow Mennonites to 'take up our cross and follow Jesus to Golgotha. We must be willing to die by the thousands.'

> Unless we . . . are ready to start to die by the thousands in dramatic vigorous new exploits for peace and justice, we should sadly confess that we never really meant what we said, and we dare never whisper another word about pacifism to our sisters and brothers in those desperate lands filled with injustice. Unless we are willing to die developing new nonviolent attempts to reduce conflict, we should confess that we never really meant that the cross was an alternative to the sword.[74]

Sider's dramatic call for Mennonites to take up the cross in faithful witness to Jesus Christ could be described as a call to vocational clarification and recommitment in the face of a cultural climate of what some observers were describing as 'practical atheism'. Sider's call for Mennonites to embody their witness with their very lives was presented in the context of challenging them to 'risk everything' for their belief in 'the God of shalom'. According to Gene Stoltzfus, Sider's call resulted in renewed conversations in Anabaptist congregations throughout North America. A group of 100 persons gathered in Chicago in 1986 issued a call for persons to form Christian Peacemaker Teams (CPT). Initially composed of Mennonites and the Church of the Brethren, the newly formed Christian Peacemaker Teams later included Quakers as well.

By 1994, CPT had sent its first team (a team consists of 6 to 8 persons) of peacemakers into Hebron, which according to Jewish and Islamic traditions is regarded as the burial place of the Hebrew patriarchs – Abraham, Isaac, and Jacob – and was the site of increasing tension due to a group of several hundred Jewish settlers who had moved into this city of 120,000 Palestinians, the majority of whom are Muslims. The saga of CPT in Hebron is a story of courage disproportionate to the small numbers of the 6 to 8 person teams who rotate in and out of this intensely conflictual site of Palestinian–Israeli conflict.[75] In many ways, CPT can be seen as the logical unfolding of what it means for a small group of people to live according to the 'politics' of Jesus. Indeed, one might imagine CPT as a specific kind of embodiment of what Yoder described (used the Quaker idiom) as 'the war of the Lamb'.[76]

In fact, connections between Yoder and CPT are extensive and explicit. The

Director of CPT, Gene Stoltzfus, readily acknowledges the influence of John Howard Yoder's work on CPT. Yoder's nephew, Rich Meyer, is one of the leaders of this initiative, and various other members of the Yoder family are strongly supportive of CPT's efforts to 'get in the way' of the conflicting parties. Although I am not aware of Yoder having commented on CPT's work in any of his books or essays, I strongly suspect that Shalom Communications – the not-for-profit foundation that Yoder founded – contributed funds to this venture.

CPT's objectives are straightforward:

- To advance the cause of lasting peace by giving skilled, courageous support to peacemakers working locally in situations of conflict.
- To inspire people and governments to discard violence in favour of non-violent action as a means of settling differences.
- To provide home communities with first-hand information and resources for responding to world-wide situations of conflict, and to urge their active involvement.
- To interpret a non-violent perspective to the media.[77]

Given this agenda for action and response, it is not surprising to discover that CPT and MCC-Palestine have collaborated at various points since 1994.

The Christian Peacemaker teams that have served in Hebron are well known in both Israel and Palestine for the ways they have gone about achieving these objectives. In some cases, members of CPT have been arrested as a consequence of their peace actions. In addition to taking photographs and making other forms of documentation of human rights abuses, team members have shielded Palestinians from Israeli violence. Team members have sometimes been successful in using creativity to disrupt violence. CPT use of computer technology has also proven to be inventive. Team members use websites and e-mail to post information to their supporters as well as to co-ordinate peacemaking activities on the West Bank. As North American citizens, CPT members also have greater freedom to move around within the West Bank, and when necessary can go and come to Jerusalem, Tel Aviv, and elsewhere in Israel.

In addition to its advocacy and witness for peace in and around the city of Hebron, CPT has been very active in convening various *ad hoc* and regular conversations with Jewish and Muslim peacemakers at neutral sites such as the Tantur Ecumenical Institute located on West Bank land annexed to 'Greater Jerusalem' by the Israeli authorities. For example, CPT has been instrumental in fostering conversation in the 'Circle for Sanity' – a loose-knit gathering of Jewish, Christian, and Muslim peace activists in Israel – as well as some non-religious activists – who in the wake of the *Al Aqsa intifadah* came together in an attempt to find ways to seek peace together. CPT's role in these weekly conversations held at the Tantur Ecumenical Institute has been straightforward – if admittedly complex – ranging from offering encouragement to confrontation, from offering hospitality to those who struggle to continue seeking peace to offering documentation of human rights abuses to those who doubt that the Israeli government has engaged in any kind of wrongdoing. Because the membership of the Hebron team changes throughout the year, the persons representing the CPT perspective at one point in the year more likely than not will not be the persons representing the peacemakers later in that same year. That having been said, the 'culture' of CPT is fairly consistent, and they do not pretend to be neutral. Indeed, they believe that it is *necessary* to 'take sides' where human beings are being abused.

While CPT may be seen by some Mennonites as an embodiment of the vocation of Anabaptist peoplehood (as per Ronald Sider's 1984 manifesto), and in that sense could be said to have ecclesiological implications, members of these teams do not regard themselves as attempting to 'be the church' in Hebron. Certainly, there is no desire for them to be tightly linked with the Mennonite Church as such, although individual Mennonite congregations support CPT, and MCC-Palestine's peace development worker provides liaison and communications support in several ways. In fact, most teams are 'more than Mennonite' in the ecumenical sense. While numerous participants have been Mennonites, recent teams have been made up of persons from Church of the Brethren, Quaker, United Methodist. In addition, at least one Catholic priest and a member of a Catholic women's religious order have participated in recent years. CPT members typically gather with one of the English-speaking congregations in Jerusalem or Bethlehem or worship with one of the Arab-speaking Christian congregations in the West Bank or Gaza.

While it is clear that CPT's objectives are not those of MBM, that does not mean that there is no interest in dialogue-in-mission. Some CPT members have displayed a strong interest in dialogue with Jews. For example, Kathy Kern's book *We Are the Pharisees*[78] is a careful attempt to unmask antisemitic habits of mind that exist among American Protestants. Her book has been well received in Mennonite congregations where it has been used in Sunday School classes. Interestingly, Kern's study converges with Yoder's *The Jewish–Christian Schism Revisited* at several points although Kern does not cite Yoder's essays at any point.[79] At least some of the folks associated with CPT have seen it as providing a vital link between 'the spirit of activism' and the non-violent legacy of the sixteenth-century Anabaptists. For example, in *The Anabaptists Are Back*, Duane Ruth Heffelbower contends that in CPT, 'Mennonites are rediscovering the original Anabaptist vision in which non-resistance was a dramatic force for social transformation.'[80]

Clearly, the saga of CPT's work in Hebron has proven to be a new kind of catalyst for North American Mennonite involvement in the struggle to make peace between the Israelis and the Palestinians. CPT has also 'contributed to MCC reflection on the question of prudence and compromise.'[81] Indeed, Weaver and Weaver speculate that 'CPT's presence in Hebron likely will continue to spur MCC's deliberations about how to work for a just peace in Palestine'.[82] What remains unclear, from my point of view, is whether the 'original Anabaptist vision' that many Mennonites are now associating with the heroic activism of CPT will prove to be an adequate vision of the church for Mennonite missions in Israel and peacemaking efforts in Palestine in a context in which many lay claim to being among the 'children of Abraham'.

IV. The Kenosis of 'Incarnate Presence' Amid 'Lost Icons' of Mennonite Peoplehood

If there is a common thread to be identified between the initiatives discussed in the three preceding sections of this paper it is that in one way or another they seek to offer a witness of 'incarnate presence'. One of the texts that virtually all parties invoke in one way or another is Ephesians 2.1–21, and 14–15 in particular. This is the same text that I have identified (see Editors' Introduction) as being the key texts that informs Yoder's own image of Jewish–Christian reconciliation. As the foregoing discussion makes clear, Yoder's conception of Jewish–Christian dialogue converges in several significant ways with the issues, programmes, and projects associated with MCC, MBM, and CPT. Such images may be more or less useful depending on the context of application, so we should not be surprised if the same text is invoked for different purposes. We should ignore neither the differences nor the underlying commonality of reference.

In a written response to an earlier draft of the text of this Appendix, Alain Epp Weaver has suggested that there are 'two different models of Christian–Jewish reconciliation' operative in the midst of the various ministries and projects of MBM in Israel, MCC-Palestine, and CPT in Hebron: 'one model focuses on reconciliation within the body of Christ, the church, another which focuses on Jewish–Christian solidarity against injustice.'[83] Weaver understands the latter to stand in a kind of parabolic relationship to the ecclesial embodiment of peace, which he would also argue is consistent with Yoder's own understanding.

I am inclined to agree with Weaver's judgement in both cases. Indeed, we dare not eliminate the sense of mystery of how the Reign of God is enacted through the Church from our ecclesiological reflections. How we think about that mystery, however, makes all the difference. As the *Afterword* to this volume explains, Yoder's understanding of 'mystery' in the context of the Letter to the Ephesians is presented in the context of an analogy to 'a military battle plan which is previously hidden from the public eye, although it was present in the mind of the strategist, but is now visible for all to see because the acting out of what was planned is itself its revelation'.[84] The perspicuity of this understanding of mystery is very striking in relation to the three examples of Mennonite witness in Israel and Palestine.

First, with Weaver's distinction in view, it is interesting to reflect on the difference between the kind of witness 'incarnated' in CPT and the Nes Ammim *moshav*, and the 'processing station' model discussed in Friesen's study. As described above, for a variety of reasons, the idea of establishing a Christian *moshav* in Israel in the 1960s proved not to be feasible. One wonders if – in addition to the various social and political factors that have already been noted – part of the issue ultimately did not come down to the ways in which such a project would involve Mennonites in 'landedness' in ways that would require more or less permanent involvement with the nascent State of Israel. If so, such hesitance would have intensified after the Israeli occupation of the West Bank in 1967.

In the case of CPT, by contrast, the witness offered is clearly temporary, and in that way, unambiguously an 'exilic' witness. Unlike the *moshav* model, CPT is not implicated in the Zionist ideology in which 'landedness' and secularity are so intertwined in the context of the contemporary nation state of Israel. Precisely because

CPT is engaged in active protests against Israeli settlements in and around Hebron, it is important that the witness of CPT *not be compromised* by commitments to the land of Israel and Palestine. By contrast, the MBM model of the congregation as a 'processing station' would appear to be unable to disentangle itself from the nation state given that the very context for the meaningfulness of this analogy depends on the ongoing 'return' of Jewish refugees to Israel.

This (third) example of the 'processing station' model is also intriguing precisely because it represents the desire of Mennonite missions personnel to be contextual in its missionary witness without giving up its countercultural intent. Employing an Israeli image that is derived from the Israeli experience of welcoming Jewish refugees from around the world and helping them to become citizens of the Israeli nation state, Friesen contends that 'the church must be an "absorption center" for the comprehensive re-socialization of immigrants and strangers.'[85] The question is what are the implications of having this kind of vision of the mission of the Church? That it reflects a continuing yearning to embody the reconciliation described in Ephesians 2 is reasonably clear, but is the original purpose of the 'comprehensive re-socialization' of Jewish returnees to Israel in the context of the Zionist dream of a homeland for Jews to be entirely ignored?

While Friesen does discuss some of the implications of the 'processing station' image of the Church, he appears to be unconcerned about the ways in which this model might be misunderstood or seen to be unduly reliant on the nation state of Israel. Unfortunately, the only narrative example that Friesen provides to illustrate what it might mean for the Church to be an 'absorption center' is that of *Peniel* Messianic congregation in Tiberias. 'Named after the Jordan Valley site Peniel (Gen. 32.24–32), this congregation began in Tiberias, one of Israel's "religious cities" (together with Jerusalem, Hebron, and Safad), in 1977 with prayer meetings involving eight people.'[86]

By 1988, Peniel had grown to a membership of 100, nearly two-thirds of them of Jewish origin. Clearly Messianic in ambiance, the body has nevertheless become a home for people of non-Jewish origin as well, including several Bedouin. Earlier in its history, the Jewish members had decided to worship separately, but this experiment had ended after a short time. Non-rabbinical and not locked into any one worship pattern, participation in their leadership with a strong eldership rather than a centralized pastor, and emphasizing a strong life of koinonia, the Peniel congregation has reached out to a diverse spectrum of neighbors. Its various health ministries in both Christian and Moslem villages in Galilee, in some instances the result of Arab invitations, now include two evangelism elders. In addition, Peniel has initiated cooperative efforts with other Galilean Messianic bodies as well as secular Jewish settlements. Their most difficult relationships have been with fellow citizens of Tiberias.[87]

Indeed, the congregation has experienced so much harassment from the local population of predominately Orthodox Jews that it no longer has access to a building where it can worship. In recent years, the congregation has gathered for worship in various open air sites associated with the life and ministry of Jesus around the northern edge of the Sea of Galilee.

Friesen commends the 'nomadic pattern' of worship-in-exile of the Peniel congregation as a kind of parable for the Mennonite Mission Board as it 'rediscovers' the existence of ecclesial 'siblings in the Anointed One' in the Middle East. Friesen states: 'We Western Christians coming to the Levant must do so assuming that the church there contextualized is the given in relation to which we contribute. Beyond that, it is only that indigenous church that can continue to identify the particularity there of the unfolding of God's saving mission today.'[88] From Friesen's perspective, the life together of Peniel Messianic fellowship has definite implications for the Mennonite Board of Missions (and all parties that participate in its missionary endeavours), for it holds the prospect of a kind of transformation en route to dissolution of MBM:

> For a Western mission body to contemplate seriously the surrender of its own name, polity, denominational pride, envisioned achievement, and institutional continuity so as to immerse itself in the indigenous faith community in a manner that will be acknowledged and remembered by only a few, is itself nothing less than a kind of death. It is a recapitulating of the means of the God of the mysterion. The succumbing of Jesus to the temptation to engage in empire-building was blocked by the cross, and it is really no different for ourselves as Westerners working in the Middle East.[89]

For Friesen, then, the model of 'incarnate presence' to be embraced by Mennonite missions (and MCC alike?) is that of a church-in-diaspora living in the midst of 'the *kenotic* mystery' of the cross. Friesen's account is admirable in its attempt to embrace the unknown of what such a course of action could mean for the Mennonite mission in Israel (as well as its parent bodies), but it appears to me to stand in tension with the belief that the *missio Dei* has been 'laid bare' in ways that are visible in the 'new humanity' of Ephesians 2. The perspicuity of the latter tends to overshadow the mysterious darkness of the former. In this respect, Friesen's missiology for the Middle East clearly converges with Yoder's missiological commentary in *The Jewish–Christian Schism Revisited*. (Not surprisingly, Friesen's text also displays ambivalence about the doctrine of election of the Jews as God's covenant people.[90])

However much this tension may be in view, the circumstance described by Friesen and Shenk nonetheless involves serious change – most notably for North American Mennonites. Still, I have the sense that the 'peace' being enacted has some elements of surrogacy to it. For all of the *kenosis* that is described, it remains premised upon *Jewish conversion* to Jesus or Messiah (MBM leaders prefer not to say 'conversion to Christianity), a transition that is not entirely symmetrical with the 'conversion' of Euro-American Mennonites to the social realities of Levantine culture. For all of Friesen's extensive discussion of 'contextualization', it is by no means clear how this example involves 're-Judaizing' the Mennonite Church. On the contrary, the Israeli context is regarded in much the same way as other Middle Eastern countries.

It is also rather disconcerting to notice that the exemplar of what Mennonite missionary contextualization should be like in the future is a 'Messianic' congregation that remains *unreconciled* with the local Jewish community in which it exists. It would be unfair to Friesen and to the Messianic congregation in question, I believe, to ascribe any kind of metonymic significance to the scenario in Tiberias, but nonetheless I find it rather troubling to consider the degree to which Friesen's example appears to verge on endorsing a kind of compartmentalization between the kind of Jewish–Christian reconciliation in Peniel that is being presented as an embodiment of Ephesians 2 and the kind of 'non-ecclesial' Jewish-Christian reconciliation efforts that are being fostered by MCC and CPT. That having been said, there is no question that the wider Israeli perception of Messianics as 'apostates' from Judaism makes local reconciliation with Israeli Jews a very difficult question.

This example also raises several related concerns that I find to be deeply poignant. First, given the documented evidence of the 'identity crises' that individual Messianics experience in the context of Israeli society, I find it odd that Mennonite missiologists have not probed this aspect of the matter more carefully. It is precisely here that Yoder's consistently held assumptions about the 'voluntariness' of Jewish identity runs into conflict with the thickly woven practices of Jewish communities, including but not limited to the rabbinical conversations about observance of (*halakhic* and *haggadic*) Torah. To the degree that Messianic Jews in Israel regard themselves as 'completed Jews', they place themselves within an eschatological horizon of self-understanding that stands at variance with their daily experience of life in Israel. Given the thick set of 'biblical' resonances that surround them in both the Christian and Jewish traditions, they experience the deep tensions of both heritages while also bearing the burden of having to display the resolution of those tensions (individually and communally) in their own lives. As such, I believe that the image of Messianic congregations that include Arab Christians in terms of the 'proleptic reconciliation' of Ephesians 2 constitutes a kind of misplaced 'icon' (in Rowan Williams' sense of the term) for Mennonites of their own peoplehood.

To his credit, LeRoy Friesen describes the tensions being experienced by the congregation of 'Beth Immanuel' in Jaffa, a Messianic congregation that during a five-year period in the 1980s went from having 'three Messianics to each non-Messianic' to precisely the opposite proportionality of membership.[91] During that same time, 'the principal corporate language of the congregation had changed from English to Hebrew' and the worship services were marked by the kinds of joyful ebullience as evidenced in the practices of singing and dancing that are characteristic of native Israeli Jews.[92] Friesen candidly discusses the ways in which the Beth Immanuel congregation displays 'the outgrowth of selective commitment to contextualization'.[93]

> The understandable inability of the congregation to hold Arabs within an increasingly strong Hebraic fabric raises the question whether its trajectory is compatible with being an interethnic community of reconciliation. In addition . . . there was little indication that members viewed the reaction of the Israeli Defence Forces to the Intifada in the territories, and their own possible complicity in that response, as a part of their context being addressed by the emerging reign inaugurated by Yeshua. Beth Immanuel raises difficult questions for Messianics in Israel: is the principal party in interaction with which its life unfolds that of Judaism in quest of a more authentically Hebraic faith, or Arab Christians in quest of Israeli-Palestinian reconciliation? Can it be both? And to what extent can it be only or primarily one before accommodation and co-optation set in?[94]

Such candid reflection about an obviously troubled Messianic congregation that reflects the wider conflictedness of its social context in Israeli society would seem to me to have import at other levels than that of the particular Messianic congregation, but Friesen does not explore such additional possibilities for perplexity for Mennonites or non-Mennonite missions in Israel. Arguably, however, these questions could be posed to those who participate in and lead the MCC in Palestine and MBM in Israel given that this kind of *de facto* compartmentalization of mission-evangelism and peacemaking has been a feature of Mennonite existence in Israel and Palestine for better than a half century.

Second, despite the efforts of Friesen and other Mennonite leaders, to date MCC and MBM have not been able to find a way to collaborate within a unified missiological mandate. To some extent, these two 'sibling' agencies (Friesen's usage) are operating with different kinds of missiological assumptions, and yet they both can be traced back to John Howard Yoder's own theological dialogue with Judaism. I am inclined to think that Alain Epp Weaver may be correct when he speculates that the inter-Mennonite agency decision not to start Mennonite churches in the Middle East, including in Israel (a decision that Yoder helped to make), contributed to MCC developing its own missiological purpose, one which has 'valued being a reconciling presence and supporting local initiatives over planting churches'.[95]

Third, the question of the basis of Christian identity is admittedly very tricky – for Friesen or anyone else involved with MBM in Israel or MCC in Palestine – to broach in the context of the end of Christendom (see introduction to *Afterword*), much less at a time when Mennonites in North America found themselves in the process of discussing possible ways to merge. Ultimately, after a decade long process of conversation, in 2001 the General Conference Mennonite Church merged with the Mennonite Church to form the Mennonite Church USA. This circumstance no doubt made it even more difficult to sustain missiological conversations in the last decade of the twentieth century in the context of MCC and MBM. No matter how one looks at it, then, LeRoy Friesen displayed considerable courage in calling for the kind of 'sibling' ecumenism in which Mennonites would risk *losing* their hard-won sense of Anabaptist identity as a people of God in the context of rediscovering Christianity in Israel where the kinds of American denominational ties and Western European divisions are not as constitutive as they are in the USA.

On the other hand, precisely because Friesen's primary audience in his book was the North American Mennonite constituency, questions can legitimately be raised about what is going on when North American Mennonites are invited to think about the church through the icon of a Messianic fellowship that in turn is regarded as being analogous to an Israeli 'processing station'. This question is particularly important to ask when one considers the underlying similarities between the 'life together' of the North American Mennonite congregations of Friesen's audience and the Messianic fellowships that he has depicted. In fact, given the description of the worship practices of the Peniel congregation, it is striking to observe how closely this 'indigenous' congregation resembles an American Mennonite congregation. In each case, there is a feature of traditional Jewish identity that has been excluded as a means of registering the kinship of Messianics and Mennonites.

Would North American Mennonites be able to discern the parabolic significance of this congregation if they were 'rabbinical' and if they had celebrated some modified version of the Jewish liturgical cycle of festivals? Would North American

Mennonites find such a congregation intelligible if they had been liturgical – and not 'free church' – in their worship practices?[96] However much these questions or queries like them may have been broached in other Anabaptist contexts, these are questions that appear to have been *occluded* from the published studies of MCC and MBM. In this respect, the contexts of MBM's missionary activities in Israel and MCC-Palestine's peacemaking activities in Palestine appear to me to display some of the same kinds of ecclesiological problems that I have identified in Yoder's essays.

It remains to be seen whether the publication of *The Jewish–Christian Schism Revisited* will assist North American Mennonites (in MCC and MBM among others) to engage the question that LeRoy Friesen first posed a decade ago. *How do Mennonites think about Jews [given who Mennonites believe God has called them to be as 'a people in the world']?* That is a possible conversation for 'Mennonite scholars and friends' to have in the future. In the meantime, I hope that this Appendix helps interested readers to locate the significance of Yoder's essays in relation to the history of Mennonite missionary endeavours in Israel and the peacemaking activities of the Mennonite Central Committee-Palestine and more recently the Christian Peacemaker Teams.[97]

Notes

1. During the time period that is the focus of this study, the Mennonite Central Committee (MCC) was the relief and development agency of the Mennonite Church (MC), the General Conference Mennonite Church (GCMC), the Brethren in Christ (BIC) and several other Mennonite groups. In 2001, the Mennonite Church and the GCMC merged to form the Mennonite Church USA. MCC began work in the Middle East in 1949. I am grateful to Mr. Alain Epp Weaver for our exchange of correspondence. As the principal historiographer of MCC's relief and development work in Israel and Palestine, Weaver has been very helpful in clarifying issues. Alain Epp Weaver does not necessarily agree with my assessment of these matters, but his perceptive remarks in response to a first draft of Appendix B have saved me from making obvious errors and caused me to do additional reading and research as I completed work on this document.

2. Alain Epp Weaver and Sonia K. Weaver, *Salt and Sign: Mennonite Central Committee in Palestine, 1949–1999*, Akron, PA: Mennonite Central Committee, 1999, 138.

3. I am grateful to Alain Epp Weaver for confirming this detail. Weaver serves as the Country Representative of the Mennonite Central Committee Palestine office in East Jerusalem.

4. For a summary, see the Editors' Introduction to *The Jewish–Christian Schism Revisited*, pp. 22–4 above.

5. Weaver and Weaver, *Salt and Sign*, 2.

6. *Salt and Sign*, 26.

7. *Salt and Sign*, 24.

8. *Salt and Sign*, 6.

9. *Salt and Sign*, 6.

10. *Salt and Sign*, 6–8.

11. *Salt and Sign*, 104.

12. *Salt and Sign*, 8.

13. *Salt and Sign*, 8.

14. *Salt and Sign*, 9.

15. *Salt and Sign*, 9.

16. *Salt and Sign*, 10, 108–10.

17. *Salt and Sign*, 92.

18. *Salt and Sign*, 83.

19. *Salt and Sign*, 11.

20. This observation is based on the daily updates sent from MCC-Palestine in April–May 2002.

21. *Salt and Sign*, 13–14.

22. *Salt and Sign*, 13.

23. *Salt and Sign*, 133.

24. *Salt and Sign*, 133.

25. *Salt and Sign*, 132.

26. *Salt and Sign*, 132.

27. *Salt and Sign*, 133.

28. *Salt and Sign*, 11–13. The book *Salt and Sign* is itself a clear example of how MCC-Palestine has worked diligently to educate its North American Mennonite constituency about the nature of its work in Palestine over the past half century.

29. *Salt and Sign*, 125–8.

30. Marie Shenk, *Mennonite Encounter with Judaism in Israel: An MBM Story of Creative Presence Spanning Four Decades, 1953–93*, Elkhart, IN: Mennonite Board of Missions, 2000, 1.

31. Alain Epp Weaver, personal correspondence with MGC, 'comments on Appendix B', p. 3.

32. Marie Shenk., *Mennonite Encounter*, 7. Shenk is here citing the initial recommendation of Paul and Bertha Swarr and Roy and Florence Krieder.

33. *Mennonite Encounter*, 8.

34. *Mennonite Encounter*, 8.

35. *Mennonite Encounter*, 8–9.

36. *Mennonite Encounter*, 9–10.

37. *Mennonite Encounter*, 13–17. Marie Shenk reports that among the new initiatives were 'various forms of hospitality and interaction. Jewish persons were invited to special events such as concerts of recorded classical music. Faith-oriented films were selected for public showing. Musicians and songwriters performed . . . in an informal atmosphere' (17).

38. *Mennonite Encounter*, 18.

39. *Mennonite Encounter*, 19.

40. *Mennonite Encounter*, 19.

41. *Mennonite Encounter*, 20.

42. *Mennonite Encounter*, 20.

43. *Mennonite Encounter*, 21.

44. *Mennonite Encounter*, 21.

45. *Mennonite Encounter*, 21.

46. Calvin Shenk, *Who Do You Say That I Am? Christians Encounter Other Religions*, Scottdale, PA: Herald Press, 1997, 240, 257 and 259. More recently, Shenk has published a study of key theological differences between Palestinian Christians and Messianic Jews based on his observations and conversations with both groups while serving with MBM in Israel. See Calvin Shenk, 'The Middle Eastern Jesus: Messianic Jewish and Palestinian Christian Understandings', in *Missiology: An International Review*, XXIX/ 4, October 2001, 404–16.

47. Shenk, *Who Do You Say That I Am?*, 259.

48. *Who Do You Say That I Am?*, 259–60.

49. In part, it appears that Yoder was concerned about the consistency of the Mennonite witness, but it may be that other factors also informed his decision. What we do know is that he argued that it would be unfair to MBM personnel, who had articulated a particular vision of mission and had been supported in that vision for over ten years to simply announce and impose a change of direction (I am indebted to Mrs. Marie Shenk for clarifying this matter (conversation on 25 June 2001)). Second, as Alain Epp Weaver explains, to start Mennonite churches in Israel at that particular juncture would have an impact on MCC's work. I am also indebted to Alain Epp Weaver for locating a copy of Yoder's letter to Wilbert Shenk.

50. See above, Ch. 7, p. 156, n.1.

51. Ch. 7, p. 156, n.1.

52. Ch. 7, p. 148–9.

53. Ch. 7, p. 151–2.

54. Ch. 7, p. 152.

55. Ch. 7, p. 148.

56. Ch. 7, p. 149.

57. Ch. 7, p. 154.

58. Ch. 7, p. 151.

59. LeRoy Friesen, *Mennonite Witness in the Middle East*, Elkhart, IN: Mennonite Board of Missions, 1992; rev. edn, 2000, 95.

60. *Mennonite Witness*, 95.

61. *Mennonite Witness*, 100.

62. *Mennonite Witness*, 100.

63. *Mennonite Witness*, 115.

64. *Mennonite Witness*, 116.

65. For a different perspective on the way Yoder understood analogies, see Alain Epp Weaver's essay 'Parables of the Kingdom and Religious Plurality: With Barth and Yoder toward a Nonresistant Public Theology' in *Mennonite Quarterly Review*, July 1997. Weaver would argue that the reconciliation outside the Church can serve as a parable of our reconciliation with God and therefore by analogy can be 'in Christ'.

66. Lisa Loden, 'Knowing Where We Start: Assessing the Various Hermeneutical Approaches', in *The Bible and the Land: An Encounter – Different Views: Christian Arab Palestinian, Israeli Messianic Jew, Western Christian*, ed., Lisa Loden, Peter Walker and Michael Wood, Jerusalem: *Musalaha*, 2000, 23. Given that only recently has the Messianic Jewish community begun to reflect on the hermeneutical questions associated with their theological convictions, Loden's summary of the 'patterns' of interpretation that are creating more 'challenges' for the Palestinian Christian and the Messianic Jew in their efforts to be reconciled *with one another* about the status of *eretz yisrael* are worth listing here:

> The theological focus of each group tends to be particular to the needs and life situation of their respective communities. For the Palestinian, issues of justice and righteousness prevail and for the Messianic Jew, promise and prophecy are ascendant. The Palestinian Christian sees in Jesus the one who universalized the story of the chosen people in the chosen land from the particular reference of localized Israel to the wider community of the world and all her peoples, whereas the Messianic Jew sees continuation and fulfillment of the story and destiny of Israel once again in her ancient, promised land.
>
> When it comes to issues of the Land and promise, the theology of the Arab church

is largely drawn from the New Testament whereas the Messianic Jew, on the same issues, situates himself almost totally within the context of the Old Testament. For the Arab Christian, particularly the Palestinian, the person and teachings of Jesus are the key to understanding and interpreting scripture. This has resulted in a serious neglect of the Old Testament. The Messianic Jew on the other hand, draws theological buttressing for his view of the Land from the Old Testament promises and prophecies. Israel (as the eternal people of God, the remnant) has become a hermeneutical key for many. For the concerned observer, this difference is both striking and alarming. Challenges exist for all; Palestinian, Jew and Christian, separately and together.

Loden, of course, does not speak for Palestinian Christians, who struggle with the ways the Old Testament has been used to legitimize the disappropriation of their land by the Israeli authorities. In his book *Justice and Only Justice: A Palestinian Theology of Liberation*, Maryknoll, NY: Orbis Books, 1989, the Palestinian liberation theologian Naim Ateek tries to recover the Old Testament for the use of Palestinian Christians.

67. I am indebted to Calvin Shenk for our conversations in June 2001 when both of us were living at Tantur Ecumenical Institute.

68. In the wake of the *Al Aqsa intifada* that began in October 2000, relationships between Christians and Jews in Israel and Palestine became much more strained. It was in the wake of these events that Calvin and Marie Shenk's work came to a conclusion.

69. Weaver and Weaver, *Salt and Sign,* 98.

70. *Salt and Sign*, 99.

71. Stoltzfus, 'History of CPT', 1 <www.prairienet.org.cpt/history.php>.

72. Leo Driedger and Donald B. Kraybill, *Mennonite Peacemaking: From Quietism to Activism*, Scottdale, PA: Herald Press, 1994, 51. Weaver and Weaver also use these categories in their history of Mennonite Central Committee-Palestine, 95–6.

73. Stoltzfus, 'History of CPT', 1.

74. 'History of CPT', p. 1

75. In addition to the various e-mail reports that are sent out by the team, some of the narratives have been collected in a book by Arthur Gish, *Hebron Journal: Stories of Nonviolent Peacemaking*, Scottdale, PA: Herald Press, 2001.

76. John Howard Yoder, *The Politics of Jesus*, Grand Rapids, MI: Eerdmans, 1972, 233–50.

77. Stoltzfus, 'Christian Peacemaker Corps' <www.prairienet.org/cpt/corps/phil>

78. Kathleen Kern, *We Are the Pharisees*, Scottdale, PA: Herald Press, 1995.

79. Despite several attempts to contact Kathleen Kern, to date I have not been able to clarify whether Kern's work has been influenced by Yoder in any respect.

80. Driedger and Kraybill, *Mennonite Peacemaking*, 157.

81. Weaver and Weaver, *Salt and Sign*, 96.

82. *Salt and Sign*, 96.

83. Epp Weaver, 20 March 2002, p. 2.

84. John Howard Yoder, *He Came Preaching Peace*, Scottdale, PA: Herald Press, 1985, 109.

85. Friesen, *Mennonite Witness in the Middle East*,163.

86. *Mennonite Witness in the Middle East*, 166.

87. *Mennonite Witness in the Middle East*, 166–7.

88. *Mennonite Witness in the Middle East*, 169.

89. *Mennonite Witness in the Middle East*, 170–71.

90. On the one hand, Friesen confesses: 'Few of us even began to understand the significance of the Jewish people for us as believers: painful embodiment of election as

"the servant of Yahweh"; fierce custodian of the link between divine transcendance and human responsibility; ambivalent parent of the faith traditions inaugurated by Jesus and Mohammed; incarnated reminder above all else, that God is the central reality with which humanity has to do.' (74). On the other hand, Friesen's discussion of 'messianic Jews' does not display any puzzlement.

91. *Mennonite Witness in the Middle East*, 126.

92. *Mennonite Witness in the Middle East*, 126–7.

93. *Mennonite Witness in the Middle East*, 127.

94. *Mennonite Witness in the Middle East*, 127.

95. Weaver, comments on Appendix B, 20 March 2002.

96. Elsewhere in his book, Friesen does discuss the significance of Mennonite discovery of liturgy, but it is worth asking the question: In the context of learning to appreciate the Christian liturgy in Jerusalem, should Mennonites come to understand that *not all* aspects of the liturgical tradition are marked by Constantinianization, does that not have consequences for how Mennonites engage western Christians – inside and outside of Israel – who have retained aspects of the liturgical tradition that Anabaptists have tended to leave behind? In other words, if in the course of rediscovering the ecumenism of indigenous congregations in Israel, Mennonites should continue to discover that Christian worship is actually formative for Christian discipleship, would they not also have to *re-think* the ways in which they have constituted their mission to Jews in Israel and their ministries of relief, development and peacemaking in Palestine?

97. I am grateful to Alain Epp Weaver, and Calvin and Marie Shenk for their comments on an earlier draft of this Appendix.

Glossary

This glossary presents brief, and therefore general, definitions of key terms that appear throughout the essays of this book. For more information, and for terms not included here, the reader should consult one or more of the following references: the *Encyclopedia Judaica*, the *Anchor Bible Dictionary*, the *Encyclopedia of Religion* and the *Mennonite Encyclopedia*. Another useful resource is the glossary initiated by Robert Kraft (expanded and refined by others) for the University of Pennsylvania course 'Religions of the West'; it can be found on the World Wide Web at http://ccat.sas.upenn.edu/-rs2/glossopt.html

Aggadah Literally 'the telling' or 'narration' (Hebrew): this refers in Rabbinic Judaism to the homiletical or theological interpretations of Judaism (or the Bible, specifically), as distinguished from the legal or ethical interpretations (*halakhah*). The related term *Haggadah* refers to the narrative of Passover.

Am Ha Aretz Literally 'people of the land' (Hebrew): a rabbinic term for uneducated Jews.

Amidah (also spelled **amida**) The 'silent prayer' or 'eighteen blessings' (Hebrew: literally, *Shmoneh Esrei*) that are the central and holiest part of the rabbinic morning, afternoon, and evening prayers.

Apostasy From Greek for 'falling away': this term is used by Christians to refer to those 'apostates' who forsake the path of Christian discipleship. In Yoder's usage, this is closely associated with the problem of Constantinianism and the so-called 'fall' of the Church.

B'nai B'rith Literally 'children of the covenant' (Hebrew): name of a major Jewish organization, primarily in the USA, but also including an international programme. This is primarily a charitable organization, previously the major source of funding for Jewish student organizations on campuses, currently addressing more general social and cultural services.

Birkhat Ha-Minim Literally 'blessing concerning sectarians' (Hebrew): the label given to what is actually the 'nineteenth' of the 'eighteen blessings' of the Amidah (see above) – nineteenth, since it was added after the original eighteen were established. This blessing asks: 'May slanderers have no hope; may all wickedness perish instantly . . . Blessed are you, O Lord, who breaks the enemies and humbles the arrogant.' Some historians have conjectured that the rabbinic sages added this maledictive blessing against the entry of Christian sectarians into the synagogue. Others suggest that the blessing was added to protect against informants among the

Jewish people who, in Roman and again in medieval times, would betray their people to curry favour with foreign rulers.

Chevruta/Chevrutot (plural) (also spelled *Chabourah/chabouroth, chavurah/chavurot*) Literally 'fellowship' (Hebrew): commonly used to name Jewish study fellowship, or more recently, informal Jewish gatherings for worship and study fellowship.

Constantinianism This word is used frequently in Yoder's ecclesiological essays to refer to the shift in the public status of Christianity that occurred in the Roman Empire between the second and fourth centuries CE. While Yoder does not regard this transformation of the church to have taken place literally in 312 CE, he does regard the Emperor Constantine to be a primary symbol of the shift that profoundly distorted Christian existence. *Before* Constantine, according to Yoder, Christianity was 'visibly distinct from the world, even from the Church's point of view, as the unity of the church and the world were presupposed under the lordship of Jesus Christ'. *After* Constantine's 'conversion' to Christianity, 'these two visible realities, Church and world, were fused'. In Yoder's own usage, Constantinianism has existed in different sociological configurations in different historical epochs. Thus, he regarded the Protestant Church–State alliances that emerged after the end of the Wars of Religion (1648) as 'neo-Constantinianism'; similarly, those circumstances where the Church blesses its society without any formal identification with it (as in the USA), Yoder regarded as 'neo-neo-Constantinianism'.

Diaspora – *see* Galut.

Dispensational Premillennialism This evangelical Protestant framework of interpretation is noted for the way it distinguishes seven 'dispensations' or orderings of divine providence in human history: (1) *Innocence* – Creation of Adam, ending in the Fall; (2) *Conscience* – from the fall of humanity to the Flood; (3) *Human government* – from Noah onward; (4) *Promise* – from Abraham to Moses; (5) *Law* – from Moses to the death of Christ; (6) Grace – from the cross to the second coming of Jesus, and (7) *Kingdom* or the *'millennial age'* which is believed to involve the personal reign of Christ, which ends with Satan temporarily set loose but quickly defeated. After the Millennium comes 'the new heaven and the new earth' described in the Book of Revelation. This pattern of biblical interpretation is closely associated with the 'annotations' to the Bible written by the American biblical scholar C. I. Scofield. The 'Scofield Bible' is closely associated with Fundamentalism in American culture. Yoder uses this pattern of interpretation as an example of one way that Christians have attempted to reconcile the Old and New Testaments while maintaining the view that the Bible's commands are not contradictory.

Eretz Yisrael (Hebrew) The land of Israel: this term is used in some contexts to refer to the State of Israel, but Yoder's use of the term is restricted to its biblical contexts.

Essenes Sect of Jews in the Second Temple period who retreated to the caves of Qumran where they obeyed rules of separation and purity and where their leaders preached about the coming of a Teacher of Righteousness who would overthrow wicked rulers and bring Israel's messianic time.

Free church This is one of the sociological terms that Yoder uses to refer to those Christians who seek to live out their faith independent of state sponsorship or control. Those persons who would choose to be part of a 'free church' congregation of Mennonites or Church of the Brethren, etc., would do so in a context in which persons are free to join or not join, but those who do join are committing themselves to live a disciplined life as judged by the respective 'order' or 'discipline' of the congregation. Yoder's 'free church' narration of Judaism constitutes his attempt to narrate an identity for Jews and Christians outside the framework of Constantinian Christianity. The related term 'believers' church' is used in an overlapping way to refer to those communities of faith that accept the challenge of living out the demands of Christian discipleship, such as mutual aid and non-violence. *See also* Radical Reformation.

Galut (Hebrew): The situation of living in 'exile', for example, the Jewish diaspora. In Yoder's usage, the term is also used to designate the common vocation of Christians and Jews to live a landless missionary existence as envoys of God's messianic reign.

Gentile – *see* Goyim.

Ger Toshab Literally 'resident alien' (Hebrew): in rabbinic teaching, the Noachide laws were employed in governing the ways Gentiles were accepted as 'aliens' living among the chosen people of God. An analogous term also shows up in the *koine* Greek of the New Testament where the notion of the resident alien is used by Pauline authors to refer to Christians living in kingdoms other than the 'kingdom of God', but who live in fidelity to that reign of Christ.

Goyim Literally '[the] nations' (Hebrew): in the *Tanakh*, or Hebrew Bible, the term refers to all nations of the world including *goy kadosh*, or the 'Holy Nation' of Israel. In the rabbinic period, the term tends to refer only to the *other* nations of the world, that is, non-Jews.

Gush Emunim Literally 'the block of the faithful' (Hebrew): this Israeli coalition emerged after 1967 and adopted its formal name after the Yom Kippur War. It is a movement of ultra-orthodoox and ultra-nationalist Jews who believe that the Bible promised Jews secure life in a Holy Land whose borders include the territories of Judaea and Samaria (the West Bank) and that they were thus commanded now to settle and defend all the land within those borders. While relatively small in number, members of the Gush Emunim have been the strongest lobby in Israel for Jewish settlements on the West Bank. They have also been the most energetic and extreme religious apologists and activists on behalf of these settlements.

Haggadah (Hebrew) – *see* Aggadah.

Halakhah (also spelled **halakah**) Literally 'the way' (Hebrew, from *halakh*, to walk or go): this refers in Rabbinic Judaism to the legal or ethical interpretations of Judaism (or spefically, the Bible) as distinguisged from homiletical or theological interpretations (*aggadah*).

Holocaust – *see* Shoah

Jabneh – *see* Yavneh

Kashrut / kosher The biblical and rabbinic rules for making everyday practices holy by separating certain permitted practices from certain non-permissible practices.

The best-known examples are the rules of permissible eating, set down in the Torah (for example Leviticus 11), articulated and expanded in the Mishnah and Talmud and often called the rules of 'keeping kosher' by contemporary Jews.

Maccabees The followers of Judah the Maccabee (or 'hammer') who led a guerilla war against Seleucid Greek rulers of the third century BCE who forbade the observance of Jewish religious practices. The Maccabean victories led to the Temple cleansing that is celebrated as Hanukah (literally, 'rededication') and to the Hasmonean period of nationalist and zealous Jewish government that was later derided (and, on some occasions, also praised) in the rabbinic literature.

Magisterial Reformation (also known as 'Official' Reformation) The sixteenth-century reform movement in Europe associated with 'Protestant' leaders such as Martin Luther, John Calvin, Ulrich Zwingli, et al. These leaders utilized the official power of the princes, magistrates, city councils, etc. to enforce their respective reforms of the Catholic Church. This term has been used by Reformation historians to distinguish the 'mainstream' reformers from the 'radical' Protestants such as Menno Simons, Pilgram Marpeck, and Michael Sattler. In Yoder's usage, it designates an example of 'neo-Constantinian' Christianity that shies away from the radical reforms of the church. See also Radical reformation, Free church.

Maskilim (Hebrew) *maskil* refers to an 'Enlightened one' (which in turn stems from the related Jewish notion of 'enlightenment' = *Haskalah*) or any Jews of the period of the European Enlightenment and after, who first opened themselves to University learning (plural *maskilim*). The term was often used critically by various orthodox critics of this 'secularization'; it was used positively, of course, by the Jews who sought this opening.

Messianic Jews Yoder used this term to refer to those Israelis and American Jews who regard themselves as followers of Jesus or 'Yeshua' as they would prefer to refer to the one they regard as the Messiah of God. As such, these messianic fellowships constitute a possible instance of a non-Constantinian form of Christian discipleship, the authenticity of which is all the more intriguing where it occurs in the precincts of present-day Israel. Contemporary Jews use the term, however, to refer primarily to members of 'Jews for Jesus' or related movements who claim to affirm both Jewish tradition and a Christian witness to Christ. Most contemporary Jews understand these movements to represent disguised methods of converting Jews away from their traditional faith. For this reason, Yoder's use of the term may not convey the spirit or content of what he intended.

Minim Hebrew word used to refer to 'sectarians'; as the schism developed between those Jews who regarded themselves as disciples of Jesus and those Jews who did not regard Jesus as the Messiah, this word came to be applied to the former group.

Midrash (Hebrew, 'interpretation') A general term for rabbinic interpretation of Scripture, as well as for specific collections of rabbinic literature.

Mishnah (also spelled **Mishna**, Hebrew, 'teaching') An authorized compilation of rabbinic laws, promulgated *c.* 210 CE by Rabbi Judah Ha-Nasi. *See also* Talmud.

Neturei Karta Hebrew phrase that refers to the Israeli coalition of ultra-orthodox Jews who live under the authority of the State of Israel but deny its Jewish legitimacy as a state, believing that secular Zionism has usurped the role of God. Yoder uses this group's objections as an example in making his case for a Jewish peoplehood that would be marked by its embrace of its diaspora missionary role.

Noachic Covenant (also referred to as **Noahide**) In contrast to the Mosaic covenant, which God gave to the children of Israel, the covenant with Noah is regarded in Jewish tradition as applying to Gentiles as well as the Jewish people. According to rabbinic interpretation, seven laws were given to Noah (see Genesis 9) and were binding on all humankind. A Gentile who followed the 'Noahide laws' was considered righteous (see Sanh. 105a).

Notae Ecclesiae Latin phrase, the classical 'marks' of the Church – unity, holiness, apostolicity, catholicity – associated with Chalcedonian Christianity as displayed in the Nicene and Apostles' creeds. In Yoder's usage, the marks of the Church are not exhausted by the traditional list of 'one, holy, apostolic, and universal', but includes such radical characteristics as non-violent peacemaking, voluntary membership, mutual accountability, etc.

Nozrim (Hebrew, 'the consecrated ones') This term came to be used by Jewish synagogue leaders to refer to those Jews who were followers of Jesus ['Nazirites'] who they rejected from synagogue life on moral grounds (violations of *kashrut*) as well as because of the concern that these dedicated followers of Jesus were idolatrous.

Radical reformation (as opposed to the 'magisterial' Reformation) Refers to those leaders of the Protestant reformation *who did not rely* on city councils, princes, or magistrates for the purpose of enacting their reformation. Instead, they initiated a more radical kind of reform located in the renewed integrity of congregational life brought about by the restitution of practices that were regarded as more biblical, such as 'believer's baptism', the priesthood of all believers understood in a communal sense, and the 'giving and receiving counsel'. Yoder uses this term in combination with the phrase 'the free church' and 'the believers' church' to refer to the spectrum of Christian groups that are associated with the Anabaptists, the Church of the Brethren, and the Religious Society of Friends, or Quakers.

Restorationism This aspect of Protestantism has marked a variety of nineteenth-century Christian non-denominational groups ranging from the Disciples of Christ to the Churches of Christ and the Reorganized Church of Jesus Christ of the Latter-Day Saints (recently renamed 'Community of Christ') all of which attempted to restore early Christian practices. Yoder's use of the term refers more broadly to the aspiration to 'restore' the Church from its *fallen* or corrupted state, and in this latter sense, the term designates a *non-Constantinian* vision of Christian identity and peoplehood. Thus, groups like the followers of Peter Chelchitzsky known as the *Unitas Fratrum* and the Anabaptists can also be regarded within this company. *See also* Restitutionism.

Restitutionism A recurrent theme in Protestant Christianity, this current of thought envisions the Church of the first century as being the model for Christian identity and peoplehood. This focus on the 'primitive church' of the first century presumes that it is possible to identify practices and doctrines that are not soiled by the Christian traditions associated with the majoritarian churches of western Christianity. *See also* Restorationism and Constantinianism.

Seboumenoi Greek term used by first-century Jewish leaders refer to those uncircumcised proselytes who worshiped YHWH like those Jews who obeyed the Mosaic covenant. These 'God-fearers' were welcomed, therefore, within certain limits, into synagogue life. For Yoder, this was a significant example of the capacity of Jews in the first and second century to integrate 'non-Jews' into their synagogal fellowships.

Shoah (Hebrew, 'destruction') The term used for the destruction of European Jewry by the Nazis during World War II. The English term 'holocaust' comes from the Greek meaning 'wholly burnt', which is itself a translation of a Hebrew word, olah, found in the Tanakh, referring to a sacrifice that was completely burnt. When applying the word 'holocaust' to the Nazi destruction of European Jewry, the images of sacrifice and of being wholly burnt are troubling to Jews, who are increasingly using the term 'Shoah', as are Christians who are sensitive to these same concerns.

Supersessionism The theological claim that the Church has replaced Israel as God's people for the salvation and blessing of the world. This Christian aspiration – to be an elect people of God and therefore also in some sense 'children of Abraham' – has (in effect if not by intent) often functioned to erase Jewish peoplehood in the context of asserting the senses in which Christians are also God's people. Yoder's understanding of the problem of Christian supersessionism links this structure of thought with the social framework of Constantinianism. Accordingly, a non-Constantinian practice of Christian discipleship would presumably be non-supersessionist as well because 'Jews' and 'Christians' would now be free to exercise their common vocation as 'children of Abraham' in the world. In Cartwright's usage, however, this problem extends not only to the three varieties of 'punitive', 'economic', and 'structural' supersessionism (that have been identified by contemporary Christian theologians), but also to a complex *pluriform* structure of thought and practice that can be discerned at various levels of belief and practice, which can be said to have shaped Christian ecclesiology and the 'Christian imagination' in a variety of ways in past and present.

Talmud (Hebrew, 'study' or 'learning') Rabbinic Judaism produced *two* Talmuds: the one known as Babylonian is the most famous of the western world, and was completed around the fifth century CE; the other, known as the 'Palestinian' or 'Jerusalem' Talmud, was edited perhaps in the early fourth century CE. Both have as their common core the *Mishnah*, a collection of early rabbinic law, to which the amoraim (teachers) of respective locales added commentary and discussion (*gemara*). *Gemara* has also become a colloquial, generic term for the Talmud and its study, popularly applied to the Jewish Talmud as a whole, to discussions by rabbinic teachers on *Mishnah*, and to the decisions reached in these discussions.

Tanakh (Hebrew, also spelled **Tanach**) A modern acronym for *torah, neviim, et khetuvim*, the 'Torah, Prophets and Writings' that comprise the canonical Hebrew Bible.

Torah (Hebrew, literally '[the]Teaching') This term refers in the Tanakh to God's revealed Word to the people Israel, both in the example of the *aseret hadibberot*, or 'Ten Words' (alias Ten Commandments) of Exodus 20 and of all the words of the

Five Books of Moses (Pentateuch). The term also refers in the Bible to any teaching of God or of the prophets. In rabbinic literature, it also refers more broadly to all learning and teaching that interprets and enacts the Words of God and the prophets. The *Septuagint* or Greek translation of *Tanakh* mis-translates Torah as *nomos* or, in English, Law (for which the proper Hebrew term would be *halakhah* or *mishpat*).

Unitas Fratrum The name adopted by an historic 'Protestant' group associated with Peter Chelchitsky. Formed in 1467, this group lay claim to being the first Protestant Church. This Czechoslavakian precursor of the Reformation is one of Yoder's choice examples to refer to *non-Constantinian* forms of Christian peoplehood that have existed at various times throughout the history of Christianity. The Moravian Church, a denomination that is Pietist in its heritage, is one of the contemporary communions that trace their origins to this movement that Yoder says arose 'from below' in central Europe in the late fifteenth century.

Yavneh (also referred to as **Jabneh, Jamnia**) Hebrew name of the city of ancient Israel, near present day Tel Aviv, that became the seat of Judaism's first rabbinic school, founded by Yohanah ben Zakkai after the destruction of the Second Temple.

YHWH – (also spelled **JHWH**) The 'tetragrammaton' – Greek for 'four letters' – as it is sometimes referred to by Jewish and Christian writers alike, is regarded by Jews as the sacred name of God. In traditional Judaism, the name is not pronounced, but the Hebrew word *adonai* or something similar is substituted. In most English versions of the Bible, the Tetragrammaton is represented by 'LORD'.

Zionism The Jewish movement that arose in the late nineteenth century to re-establish a homeland for Jews and that informed the founding of the State of Israel in 1948. Not to be confused with the 'Christian Zionism' associated with dispensationalist pre-millennialism, this ideological movement was founded in Europe by Theodore Hertzl and other secular Jewish leaders concerned about the dangers of antisemitism for this 'people without a land'. Although Yoder makes very few direct references to this modern Jewish ideological movement, where he does refer to the historical movement that resulted in the establishment of the State of Israel in 1948, it is used as negative example – the outcome of the 'Christianization' of Judaism that transpired as part of the Constantinian establishment. As such it stands over against the form of Judaism in *galut* that Yoder regards as the proper vocation of God's people.

Ztz'l [as in the dedication of Yoder's collection of essays to Steven S. Schwarzschild] This is the acronym for *zichrono tzaddik leberakha* 'May the Righteous (or Pious) be Remembered for a Blessing', a sign of respect for the deceased who are great scholars. A simpler, more general acronym is z'l, *zichrono(a) leberakha*, 'May He(She) Be Remembered for a Blessing,' the honorific term for our term 'rest in peace'.

Scripture Index

NEW TESTAMENT

Subject Index

Name Index